Learning from the Past

Learning from the Past

Essays on Reception, Catholicity and Dialogue in Honour of Anthony N. S. Lane

Edited by
Jon Balserak and Richard Snoddy

Bloomsbury T&T Clark
An imprint of Bloomsbury Publishing Plc

B L O O M S B U R Y
LONDON · NEW DELHI · NEW YORK · SYDNEY

Bloomsbury T&T Clark

An imprint of Bloomsbury Publishing Plc

Imprint previously known as T&T Clark

50 Bedford Square	1385 Broadway
London	New York
WC1B 3DP	NY 10018
UK	USA

www.bloomsbury.com

**BLOOMSBURY, T&T CLARK and the Diana logo are trademarks
of Bloomsbury Publishing Plc**

First published 2015

British Library Cataloguing-in-Publication Data
A catalogue record for this book is available from the British Library.

ISBN: HB: 978-0-567-66090-9
ePDF: 978-0-567-66091-6
ePub: 978-0-567-66089-3

Library of Congress Cataloging-in-Publication Data
A catalogue record for this book is available from the Library of Congress.

Typeset by Deanta Global Publishing Services, Chennai, India
Printed and bound in Great Britain

CONTENTS

ABBREVIATIONS

ARG	*Archiv für Reformationsgeschichte*
CH	*Church History*
CO	John Calvin, *Ioannis Calvini opera quae supersunt omnia* (eds Guilielmus Baum, Eduardus Cunitz and Eduardus Reuss; 59 vols; Brunswick: Schwetschke, 1863–1900)
EvQ	*Evangelical Quarterly*
ExpTim	*Expository Times*
JEH	*Journal of Ecclesiastical History*
JPT	*Journal of Pentecostal Theology*
PG	J.-P Migne (ed.), *Patrologia cursus completus … Series graeca* (166 vols; Paris: Petit-Montrouge, 1857–83)
PL	J.-P Migne (ed.), *Patrologia cursus completes … Series latina* (221 vols; Paris: J.-P. Migne, 1844–65)
RelS	*Religious Studies*
TDNT	Gerhard Kittel and Gerhard Friedrich (eds), *Theological Dictionary of the New Testament* (trans. Geoffrey W. Bromiley; 10 vols; Grand Rapids: Eerdmans, 1964–76)
TWNT	Gerhard Kittel and Gerhard Friedrich (eds), *Theologisches Wörterbuch zum Neuen Testament* (11 vols; Stuttgart: Kohlhammer, 1932–79)
TynBul	*Tyndale Bulletin*
WA	Martin Luther, *D. Martin Luthers Werke: Kritische Gesamtausgabe* (73 vols; Weimar: Böhlau, 1883–2009)
WTJ	*Westminster Theological Journal*
WUNT	Wissenschaftliche Untersuchungen zum Neuen Testament

CONTRIBUTORS

Jon Balserak, Senior Lecturer in Early Modern Religion, University of Bristol, UK

Max Engammare, Director, Librairie Droz, Geneva, Switzerland

Paul Helm, formerly Professor of the History and Philosophy of Religion, King's College, London, UK

Matthew Knell, Lecturer in Historical Theology and Church History, London School of Theology, UK

Robert Letham, Director of Research, Wales Evangelical School of Theology, UK

Karin Maag, Director, H. Henry Meeter Center for Calvin Studies and Professor of History, Calvin College, USA

Richard A. Muller, P. J. Zondervan Professor of Historical Theology, Calvin Theological Seminary, USA

Herman J. Selderhuis, Professor of Church History and Church Polity, Theological University of Apeldoorn, Netherlands

Richard Snoddy, Associate Research Fellow and Visiting Lecturer, London School of Theology, UK

Dennis E. Tamburello, O.F.M., Professor of Religious Studies, Siena College, USA

Max Turner, Emeritus Professor of New Testament Studies, London School of Theology, UK

Jason Van Vliet, Professor of Dogmatics and Vice-Principal, Canadian Reformed Theological Seminary, Canada

J. Stephen Yuille, Pastor, Grace Community Church, Glen Rose, Texas, USA

Randall C. Zachman, Professor of Reformation Studies, University of Notre Dame, USA

PREFACE

This collection of essays is offered to our esteemed colleague Anthony N. S. Lane, Professor of Historical Theology at London School of Theology, in recognition of his contributions to the discipline over a long career of research and teaching.

Most of the essays here are oriented around two main foci, picking up themes that resonate with some of Tony Lane's most important work. The first broad theme is the reception of the thought of earlier generations of biblical interpreters and theologians, a field to which he has made significant contributions with his insightful studies of Calvin's relationship with the fathers and the medievals, especially *Calvin and Bernard of Clairvaux* and *John Calvin: Student of the Church Fathers*. The latter volume is a fine example of methodological rigour, and its judicious conclusions have challenged the received wisdom on the formative influences on Calvin. Speculative hypotheses about Calvin's indebtedness to a specific philosophical *schola* or theologian, popular throughout the twentieth century, could not stand against its careful, empirical approach. Tony Lane's work has helped us better understand how and why Calvin read the fathers. It lends further support to the recent revisionist historiography, which sees a greater continuity between the Reformation and the patristic and medieval Christian tradition, as opposed to the stark discontinuity assumed by many earlier scholars. Tony Lane's enthusiastic research in the field of reception history continues. It is, therefore, fitting that a number of the essays presented here explore the dynamics of textual transmission and consider the usage of the past across a broader period of the history of the church.

The second broad theme is dialogue. In *Justification by Faith in Catholic-Protestant Dialogue: An Evangelical Assessment,* Tony Lane analyses twentieth-century attempts at rapprochement, from Hans Küng's imagined dialogue between Karl Barth and the Council of Trent to the *Joint Declaration on the Doctrine of Justification* (1999), the result of discussions between Lutherans and Roman Catholics. He examines the documents against the backdrop of the Reformation controversies about justification, weighing the outstanding differences between the two traditions and identifying the deeper concerns and fears of the participants. His even-handed analysis of the doctrinal issues is coupled with reflection on the linguistic challenges hindering further agreement. While not uncritical of the agreed formulae, he expresses a cautious optimism about the convergence he discerns. An earlier moment of convergence was the Regensburg Colloquy of 1541. Tony Lane has published a series of articles on the agreement reached on justification at Regensburg, and his research continues with a monograph in preparation. Some of the essays offered here deal with the stance of opponents towards each other across confessional boundaries, though usually in less irenic contexts, and also with the contested site of 'catholicity'.

Tony Lane's interests range far beyond those already mentioned. His output includes a volume on Bernard of Clairvaux's doctrine of the cross, a series of studies on early modern patristic anthologies and work on Calvin beyond his reception of the fathers. He has edited Calvin's *Defensio sanae et orthodoxae de servitute et liberatione humani arbitrii* in both translation and in a critical edition. *A Concise History of Christian Thought* and, more recently, *Exploring Christian Doctrine* are the fruits of four decades in the lecture hall. He has taught at the London School of Theology, formerly London Bible College, since 1973 and thousands of students there have benefitted from his engaging lectures and passion for his subject. His standing in the academy was recognized by the award of a personal chair – Professor of Historical Theology – by Brunel University in 2000, and the degree of Doctor of Divinity by the University of Oxford in 2004. Always in demand, he has presented papers in many forums, from the Edinburgh Dogmatics Conference to the International Congress on Calvin Research, and from 2008 to 2010, he was President of the Society for Reformation Studies.

These essays are presented to Tony Lane by colleagues past and present, peers within the discipline and former students. It is hoped that these essays will shed light on the past and stimulate contemporary theological reflection, aims with which their honorand would, no doubt, heartily agree.

Jon Balserak
Richard Snoddy

Chapter 1

BERNARD OF CLAIRVAUX: FORERUNNER TO ST FRANCIS?

Dennis E. Tamburello, O.F.M.

It is a great privilege to contribute this chapter in honour of Anthony N. S. Lane, to celebrate his long career of stellar scholarship on Calvin, and more generally on church history and historical theology. It was inevitable that Tony and I would cross paths, as we are (to my knowledge) the only two people in the world who have written dissertations on John Calvin and Bernard of Clairvaux. I consider this a blessed happenstance.

What I have always admired most about Tony's work is its meticulously careful historical scholarship, and, in particular, his ability to make connections between theologians of different time periods, while respecting the integrity of each author in his or her own context. This aspect of Tony's scholarship has always been a model for my own modest efforts to contribute to the field.

And so, in honour of Tony, I would like to offer some reflections on the connections that exist between a religious figure whom we both admire, Bernard of Clairvaux, and the founder of my religious community, Francis of Assisi.

Consider this description of a Franciscan community in the thirteenth century:

> [The brothers] did not think selfishly of their own poverty and lack of even the necessities of life, and it is through the hardships and efforts faced by them that there is now enough to supply the [community] with all that is needed without dulling the realization that a [friar's] life is one of voluntary poverty for Christ's sake.[1]

---

1. *St. Bernard of Clairvaux: The Story of his Life as Recorded in the Vita Prima Bernardi by Certain of his Contemporaries, William of St. Thierry, Arnold of Bonnevaux, and Philip of Clairvaux, and Odo of Deuil* (trans. Geoffrey Webb and Adrian Walker; Westminster, MD: Newman Press, 1960), 14, p. 59. The words 'monastery' and 'monk's' were replaced by 'community' and 'friar's'.

The preceding quote is, to be honest, fraudulent. It is actually taken from the *Vita Prima Bernardi* written by William of St Thierry in 1147. I replaced the word 'monastery' with 'community' and the word 'monk' with 'friar'. In reading this description of what William calls the 'golden age of Clairvaux', I was struck by how much it sounded like a Franciscan text.

On the face of it, there seems to be much that the Cistercian and Franciscan traditions have in common. If we argue simply on the basis of parallels, of common ideas, it is not hard to find several, for example, the two orders' emphasis on poverty and simplicity of life, and their founders' passionate devotion to the humanity of Christ. I believe that on the basis of such parallels alone, Bernard is legitimately referred to as a forerunner to St Francis. In fact, in my introduction to the Crossroad Spiritual Legacy volume on Bernard, I refer to him affectionately as an 'honorary uncle' to St Francis.[2]

But the more interesting question is this: To what extent did the biographers and commentators of Francis's own age make this connection? The answer is that they clearly thought of Bernard as a forerunner to Francis. Francis's early biographers, especially Thomas of Celano and Bonaventure, often referred consciously to Bernard's *life* as a pattern or model for Francis. The early Franciscan writings also sometimes made connections to Bernard's *ideas* as foreshadowing those of Francis. Finally, there is evidence that the Franciscan sources often follow Bernard's *style of hagiography*.

It is perhaps worth noting that the only thing that Francis himself is ever reported to have said about Bernard is negative. This story shows up in the Assisi Compilation as well as several other later works (*Sayings of the Companions, The Mirror, The Book of Chronicles* and *The Kinship of St. Francis*). According to the introduction in volume 2 of *Francis of Assisi: Early Documents*, the Assisi Compilation 'presents anecdotes about Francis that could only have come from a day-to-day association with him'.[3] Thus we can safely take the following account as authentic.

When Francis is asked to consider adopting an existing monastic rule for his community, he responds as follows: 'My brothers! My brothers! God has called me by the way of simplicity and showed me the way of simplicity. I do not want you to mention to me any Rule, whether of St. Augustine, or of Saint Bernard, or of Saint Benedict.'[4]

Perhaps this explains why Francis does not refer explicitly to Bernard in any of his authenticated writings. There is one passage, however, that seems to show the influence of Bernard. In Francis's Letter to the Entire Order, he exhorts priests to

---

2. Dennis E. Tamburello, O.F.M., *Bernard of Clairvaux: Essential Writings* (Spiritual Legacy Series; New York: Crossroad Publishing Company, 2000), p. 14.

3. *Francis of Assisi: Early Documents* (eds Regis Armstrong, Wayne Hellman, and William Short; 4 vols; New York: New City Press, 1999–2002), vol. 2, p. 113.

4. Assisi Compilation 18, in ibid., pp. 132–3.

live up to their dignity. He says that just as the Blessed Virgin Mary is honoured as the bearer of Christ, and just as his tomb is held in veneration,

> how holy, just, and fitting must be he who touches with his hands, receives in his heart and mouth, and offers to others to be received the One Who is not about to die but Who is to conquer and be glorified, upon whom the angels longed to gaze.[5]

This passage echoes a statement in Bernard's first Sermon on the Epiphany of the Lord, in which Bernard speaks of John the Baptist trembling at the thought of touching the head of Christ at his baptism, for he is the divine Lord who was borne by the Virgin Mary, and whom the angels adore.[6]

Thomas of Celano

I Use of Bernard's Hagiographical Style

There is much evidence that Thomas of Celano, Francis's first biographer, drew consciously both from Bernard's life of St Malachy and from the early lives of Bernard himself in constructing his *Vita Prima* and *Vita Secunda* of St Francis.[7] Let us look at specific examples.

In Chapter 4 of the *First Life*, Celano relates that Francis, after having sold all of his belongings, asked to stay with the priest at San Damiano. Celano states that Francis 'pleaded, begging the priest with all his heart to allow him to stay with him for the sake of the Lord'.[8] In *The Life and Death of St. Malachy the Irishman*, Bernard describes how St Malachy sought out a holy man in the town where he was raised, and how he later sought out the bishop to be instructed by him.[9]

In the following chapter, Celano refers to Francis as 'the new athlete of Christ'. The context of this statement is that Francis's father Pietro had called together his friends and neighbours to try to find Francis and bring him to his senses. Celano recounts that Pietro's initial goal of 'freeing' his son turned eventually to a desire to 'destroy' him.[10] Similarly, Bernard recounts how St Malachy was sent to be bishop

---

5. *Early Documents*, vol. 1, p. 118.

6. Bernard of Clairvaux, *Sancti Bernardi Opera* (eds Jean Leclercq, C. H. Talbot, and Henri Rochais; 8 vols; Rome: Editiones Cistercienses, 1957–77), First Sermon on the Epiphany of the Lord 6, vol. 4, p. 298. The editors of *Francis of Assisi: Early Documents*, speak of influence here, but they do not explain how Francis would have come upon this sermon.

7. *Early Documents*, vol. 1, p. 14.

8. Celano, First Book 4.9, in ibid., pp. 189–90.

9. Bernard of Clairvaux, *The Life and Death of St. Malachy the Irishman* (trans. Robert T. Meyer; Cistercian Fathers Series, 10; Kalamazoo: Cistercian Publications, 1978), 2.4 and 4.8, pp. 19, 24.

10. Celano, First Book 5.10–12, in *Early Documents*, vol. 1, pp. 190–2.

to a hostile city and that Malachy quickly realized that he had been sent not to human beings, 'but to beasts'. Bernard asks, 'What could the athlete of the Lord do?'[11]

Chapter 5 of 1 Celano goes on to speak of how Francis goes forth into the city, 'carrying the shield of faith for the Lord'.[12] This echoes Bernard's account of Malachy going out to meet a prince who was threatening his life. Bernard speaks of him as 'fortified by the buckler of faith'. The prince and his army were unable to raise a hand against Malachy and his 'army' of three disciples.[13] Celano's later recounting of the story of Francis's rebuilding of San Damiano is reminiscent of Bernard's account of Malachy rebuilding the run-down monastery of Bangor.[14]

In Chapter 10 of 1 Celano, we hear the famous passage about Francis's way of greeting people:

> In all of his preaching, before he presented the word of God to the assembly, he prayed for peace saying 'May the Lord give you peace.' He always proclaimed this to men and women, to those he met and to those who met him. Accordingly, many who hated peace along with salvation, with the Lord's help wholeheartedly embraced peace.[15]

Bernard, in his life of Malachy, recounts how Malachy went out to the countryside and preached to the ungrateful:

> With those who hated peace he was a peacemaker at all times, both in and out of season. When cursed he prayed, when wrongfully accused he defended himself with the shield of patience and overcame evil with good. ... [S]o much have all things changed for the better that today one could apply to that people what God says through his prophet: Those who were not my people hitherto, are now my people.[16]

Though it may be disappointing to us Franciscans that many qualities and statements that we think of as uniquely Francis's were not actually so, it is important to understand that Celano was following the typical pattern of the medieval hagiographer.

Another example of this pattern is saints' ability to read hearts. Celano says of Francis that 'he opened up the hidden recesses of [the brothers'] hearts, and

---

11. Bernard, *St. Malachy*, 8.16, pp. 33–4. See footnote 61 on p. 135 for where Bernard got this term: possibly from Ignatius of Antioch, if not Augustine or Cassian.

12. Celano, First Book 5.11, in *Early Documents*, vol. 1, p. 191.

13. Bernard, *St. Malachy*, 12.26, pp. 43–4.

14. Celano, First Book 8.18, in *Early Documents*, vol. 1, p. 197; Bernard, *St. Malachy*, 6.12, p. 30.

15. Celano, First Book 10.23, in *Early Documents*, vol. 1, p. 203.

16. Bernard, *St. Malachy*, 8.17, pp. 34–5.

examined their consciences'.[17] Bernard similarly speaks of a priest in York who recognized St Malachy and exclaimed, 'This is the man of whom I have said, that from Ireland there shall come a bishop who knows the thoughts of men.'[18]

In these and other passages, Thomas of Celano emulates the hagiographical style of St Bernard's own writing.

II Use of Bernard's Life as a Model for Francis

Thomas also, however, often uses Bernard's own life as a model, following the hagiographical traditions of his own biographers (William of St Thierry et al.). For example, 1 Celano 11 speaks of Francis sharing a vision with the brothers: 'I saw a great multitude of people coming to us, wishing to live with us in the habit of a holy way of life and in the rule of blessed religion.'[19] William of St Thierry makes a similar statement about what happened to St Bernard when he was put in charge of the new foundation at Clairvaux:

> Longing for his work to bear rich fruit filled his heart, and as he stood still and closed his eyes for a moment in prayer, he saw coming down from the mountains round about and down into the valley below such a great company of men of every type and standing that the valley could not hold them all.[20]

It is not always clear that Celano is borrowing hagiographical themes directly from the lives of Bernard, but the parallels are often quite strong. Celano's description of Francis's mortification of the flesh appears to be indebted to the *Vita Prima* of Bernard. Thomas states:

> Unbending in his discipline, [Francis] was watchful of his guard at every hour. For if, as happens, any temptation of the flesh struck him, he would immerse himself in a ditch filled in winter with ice, remaining in it until every seduction of the flesh went away. The others avidly followed his example of mortifying the flesh.[21]

Now listen to William's account of what happened when Bernard allowed himself to get distracted by a woman:

> As soon as he realized what he was doing, he would be thoroughly ashamed of himself, and he would determine to punish himself most severely for what he had done. And so he would leap into a pool of cold water and stay up to his neck

17. Celano, First Book 18.48, in *Early Documents*, vol. 1, p. 225.
18. Bernard, *St. Malachy*, 15.35, p. 50.
19. Celano, First Book 11.27, in *Early Documents*, vol. 1, p. 206.
20. *Vita Prima Bernardi*, 9, p. 45.
21. Celano, First Book 16.42, in *Early Documents*, vol. 1, p. 221.

in it until the blood had almost frozen in his veins and his lust had been cooled by means of grace.[22]

Oddly enough, even Thomas of Celano's physical description of Francis may be indebted to William of St Thierry's description of Bernard in the *Vita Prima*. Thomas describes Francis as 'very eloquent, with a cheerful appearance and a kind face ... his voice was powerful, but pleasing, clear, and musical'.[23] William says of Bernard: 'his body was well proportioned, his face pleasing, his manner gentle and courteous, his mind keen, and his speech persuasive and appealing'.[24] It seems to me a pretty good wager that Thomas is using the First Life of Bernard as a source in these passages.

III Use of Bernard's Ideas

Finally, let us look at a few examples of how Celano uses *ideas* that were prominent in Bernard and the Cistercian tradition. In his description of the Poor Clares in Chapter 8 of the First Life, Celano speaks of the 'gem of humility'.[25] The monastic tradition often presents humility as the foundation of all virtues. Think, for example, of all the attention that Benedict gave to the steps of humility in the seventh chapter of his rule. Is it any accident that Bernard of Clairvaux's first published work was *The Steps of Humility and Pride*, a reflection on this very chapter in Benedict? In calling Pope Eugenius, who had been one of his monks, to humility in his *Five Books on Consideration* (*De consideratione*), Bernard says: 'No gem is more splendid' than humility.[26]

There are three instances where Thomas of Celano uses the Latin word *mellifluus*, 'flowing with honey'. One of these is a reference to Francis's own preaching at Greccio: 'Then he preaches to the people standing around him and pours forth sweet honey about the birth of the poor king and the poor city of Bethlehem'.[27] This term occurs frequently in the Cistercian tradition. Bernard himself came to be known as the 'Mellifluous Doctor'.

As one last example, we turn to *The Book of Remembrance of a Desire of a Soul*, also known as 2 Celano. Speaking of St Francis's dedication to prayer, Celano notes that Francis 'turned all his time into a holy leisure'.[28] The notion of *otium sanctum*

---

22. *Vita Prima Bernardi*, 3, p. 20.

23. Celano, First Book 29.83, in *Early Documents*, vol. 1, p. 253.

24. *Vita Prima Bernardi*, 3, p. 20.

25. Celano, First Book 8.19, in *Early Documents*, vol. 1, p. 198.

26. Bernard of Clairvaux, *Five Books on Consideration: Advice to a Pope* (trans. John D. Anderson and Elizabeth T. Kennan; Cistercian Fathers Series, 37; Kalamazoo: Cistercian Publications, 1976), 2.6.13, p. 63.

27. Celano, First Book 30.86, in *Early Documents*, vol. 1, p. 256. The other passages are 1 Celano, First Book 10.25 (p. 204) and 1 Celano, Third Book 125 (p. 295). See p. 204, footnoted.

28. Celano, Second Book 61.94, in *Early Documents*, vol. 2, p. 308.

was prominent in monastic literature, including works of Bernard such as the Sermons on the Song of Songs.[29] 2 Celano contains some other important parallels to the Sermons on the Song, such as its reference to discernment as the 'charioteer' of all the virtues.[30]

St Bonaventure: Focus on Bernard's Ideas

While Thomas of Celano refers most characteristically to the hagiographical narratives by and about Bernard, St Bonaventure tends to refer more often, sometimes explicitly, to the theological and spiritual writings of Bernard. Let us turn first to the *Legenda Maior*, his major life of St Francis. Bonaventure speaks in Chapter One of Francis meeting a knight of noble birth, who was nevertheless 'poor and badly clothed. Moved by a pious impulse [Latin *pio affectu*] of care for his poverty, he took off his own garments and clothed the man on the spot'.[31]

In his use of this phrase, Bonaventure is influenced by Bernard's usage in his treatise *De diligendo Deo* (*On Loving God*). There Bernard speaks of love as one of the 'four natural passions [*affectio naturalis*]'.[32] Love in the best sense is never motivated by fear or the desire for gain. Rather, it is the charity that comes from being a child of God.[33] Thus, Francis's pious 'impulse' could also be translated as a divinely motivated affection or love.

Later, Bonaventure recounts a story about a brother whose fasting led to his being besieged by hunger. Bonaventure tells us that Francis put some bread before the brother, but he himself ate first in order to save him from embarrassment. Bonaventure goes on to explain that Francis taught the brothers 'to follow discernment as the charioteer of the virtues [*aurigam virtutum*]'.[34] This phrase borrows from Sermon 49 on the Song of Songs, where Bernard says: 'Discretion ... is not so much a virtue as a moderator and guide of the virtues, a director of the affections, a teacher of right living'.[35]

---

29. Bernard of Clairvaux, *On the Song of Songs III* (trans. Kilian Walsh and Irene Edmonds; Cistercian Fathers Series, 31; Kalamazoo: Cistercian Publications, 1979), Sermon 58:1, p. 108.

30. Celano, Second Book 113.154, in *Early Documents*, vol. 2, p. 346 (see Bernard's Sermon on the Song of Songs [hereafter SC] 49.5 on discernment as regulator of the virtues). Another example is in 2 Celano, Second Book 52:85, in *Early Documents*, vol. 2, p. 303 (SC 43:3–5 on 'a bundle of myrrh abided in Francis').

31. The Major Legend of St. Francis [hereafter LM] 1.2, in *Early Documents*, vol. 2, p. 532.

32. Bernard of Clairvaux, *On Loving God, with an Analytical Commentary by Emero Stiegman* (Cistercian Fathers Series, 13B; Kalamazoo: Cistercian Publications, 1973, 1995), 8.23, p. 25.

33. See Stiegman's commentary, ibid., pp. 88–98.

34. LM 5.7, in *Early Documents*, vol. 2, p. 565.

35. *On the Song of Songs III*, SC 49.5, p. 25.

Finally, Bonaventure states in Chapter 9 (the topic of which is Francis's desire for martyrdom) that 'Jesus Christ crucified always rested like a bundle of myrrh in the bosom of [Francis's] soul.'[36] In his sermon on the Song of Songs 1.12 ('My beloved is to me a bunch of myrrh that lies between my breasts'), Bernard comments that 'under the name of myrrh she includes all the bitter trials she is willing to undergo through love of her beloved.'[37] Bonaventure's language here, while it does not seem to be taken directly from the Sermons on the Song of Songs, is at least suggestive of Bernard's.

Bonaventure does refer to Bernard explicitly in several of his sermons. In these cases, he points to Bernard's writings as presenting ideals that come to fulfilment in Francis.

For example, in a sermon that he preached in Paris on 4 October 1255, Bonaventure speaks of the humility of Francis:

> [Francis] can say to us: Learn from me for I am humble of heart. Learn, that is, to have true, not counterfeit, humility as hypocrites cunningly humble themselves. … He is not encouraging us to that sort of humility, but to humility of heart on which Saint Bernard writes: 'The truly humble man wants to be considered despicable rather than to be proclaimed a humble man.'[38]

The reference is to Sermon 16 on the Song of Songs. Bonaventure appears to quote it rather loosely. Bernard's exact words are: 'The truly humble man prefers to pass unnoticed rather than have his humility extolled in public. He is happy to be overlooked; if he has any pride at all it consists in despising praise.'[39]

It is worth mentioning here that although Bonaventure quotes Bernard on the subject of humility, this was not exactly Bernard's strong suit. However, in fairness to Bernard, he himself recognized this flaw in his character. In his first published work, *The Steps of Humility and Pride*, Bernard acknowledges frankly that he knows the steps of pride better than the steps of humility. He states: 'I can teach only what I know myself. I could not very well describe the way up because I am more used to falling down than to climbing.'[40]

---

36. LM 9.2, in *Early Documents*, vol. 2, p. 597.

37. Bernard of Clairvaux, *On the Song of Songs II* (trans. Kilian Walsh, OCSO; Cistercian Fathers Series, 7; Kalamazoo: Cistercian Publications, 1983), SC 42.11, p. 219.

38. Bonaventure's Evening Sermon on St. Francis, 1255, in *Early Documents*, vol. 2, p. 519.

39. Bernard of Clairvaux, *On the Song of Songs I* (trans. Kilian Walsh, OSCO; Cistercian Fathers Series, 4; Kalamazoo: Cistercian Publications, 1981), SC 16.10, p. 121. Bonaventure also refers to this text in a later sermon of 1267. See Morning Sermon on St. Francis, 1267, in *Early Documents*, vol. 2, p. 752.

40. The Steps of Humility and Pride 22:57, in Bernard of Clairvaux, *Treatises II* (trans. M. Ambrose Conway and Robert Walton; Kalamazoo: Cistercian Publications, 1973), p. 82.

In another sermon, preached eleven years later, Bonaventure praises Francis's natural compassion, which he contrasts with hardness of heart. 'Sirach warns: A hard heart shall fear evil at the last; and St. Bernard advises: "If you want to know what a hard heart is, ask Pharaoh."'[41] This is paraphrased from Bernard's First Book on Consideration.[42]

Finally, Bonaventure connects Francis's seeking only God's glory and not human praise to one of Bernard's Sermons on the Song of Songs:

> St. Francis was pleasing to God because he was faithful to having renounced all earthly desires. ... A faithful servant is one who does not look for human praise, as we learn from the text of St. Paul: If I yet pleased men, I should not be the servant of Christ. On this St Bernard writes: 'You are indeed a faithful servant when nothing of the Lord's abundant glory remains clinging to your hands. That glory comes not from you, it is channeled through you.'[43]

This theme also appears in the treatise *On Loving God*, where Bernard quotes Paul in 1 Corinthians 4.7, 'What have you that you have not received? And if you have received it, how can you boast of it as if you had not received it?'[44]

We can summarize by suggesting that both in the *Legenda Maior* and in his sermons, Bonaventure seems mainly to be interested in drawing on Bernard's ideas and ideals, not so much on the example of Bernard's life as we have seen in Celano.

Conclusions

Where does this leave us? Was Bernard of Clairvaux a forerunner to St Francis? We can certainly say yes, inasmuch as Bernard represented many ideas and ideals that later became part of the Franciscan movement. We have focused here on the textual evidence from the Franciscan sources. These connections strongly suggest that the early Franciscans themselves saw a link between Francis and Bernard. Given what he said about Bernard's rule, I am not sure Francis would have approved. On the other hand, I suspect that Bernard would have been happy to have his name and his ideas associated with St Francis.

---

41. Sermon on St. Francis, 1266, in *Early Documents*, vol. 2, p. 736.

42. *On Consideration* 1.2.2, p. 28. Here Bernard states: 'A hard heart is precisely one which does not shudder at itself because it is insensitive. But why ask me? Ask Pharaoh.'

43. Sermon on St. Francis, 1266, in *Early Documents*, vol. 2, p. 733. See *On the Song of Songs I*, SC 13.3, p. 90.

44. *On Loving God*, 2.3, p. 6.

Bibliography

Bernard of Clairvaux, *Bernard of Clairvaux: Essential Writings* (ed. Dennis E. Tamburello, O.F.M.; Spiritual Legacy Series; New York: Crossroad Publishing Company, 2000).

Bernard of Clairvaux, *Five Books on Consideration: Advice to a Pope* (trans. John D. Anderson and Elizabeth T. Kennan; Cistercian Fathers Series, 37; Kalamazoo: Cistercian Publications, 1976).

Bernard of Clairvaux, *The Life and Death of St. Malachy the Irishman* (trans. Robert T. Meyer; Cistercian Fathers Series, 10; Kalamazoo: Cistercian Publications, 1978).

Bernard of Clairvaux, *On Loving God, with an analytical commentary by Emero Stiegman* (Cistercian Fathers Series, 13B; Kalamazoo: Cistercian Publications, 1973, 1995).

Bernard of Clairvaux, *On the Song of Songs I* (trans. Kilian Walsh, OSCO; Cistercian Fathers Series, 4; Kalamazoo: Cistercian Publications, 1981).

Bernard of Clairvaux, *On the Song of Songs II* (trans. Kilian Walsh, OCSO; Cistercian Fathers Series, 7; Kalamazoo: Cistercian Publications, 1983).

Bernard of Clairvaux, *On The Song of Songs III* (trans. Kilian Walsh and Irene Edmonds; Cistercian Fathers Series, 31; Kalamazoo: Cistercian Publications, 1979).

Bernard of Clairvaux, *Sancti Bernardi Opera* (eds Jean Leclercq, C. H. Talbot, and Henri Rochais; 8 vols; Rome: Editiones Cistercienses, 1957–77).

Bernard of Clairvaux, *St. Bernard of Clairvaux: The Story of his Life as Recorded in the Vita Prima Bernardi by Certain of his Contemporaries, William of St. Thierry, Arnold of Bonnevaux, and Philip of Clairvaux, and Odo of Deuil* (trans. Geoffrey Webb and Adrian Walker; Westminster, MD: Newman Press, 1960).

Bernard of Clairvaux, *Treatises II* (trans. M. Ambrose Conway and Robert Walton; Kalamazoo: Cistercian Publications, 1973).

Francis of Assisi, *Francis of Assisi: Early Documents* (eds Regis Armstrong, Wayne Hellman, and William Short; 4 vols; New York: New City Press, 1999–2002).

Chapter 2

TWO ANNOTATED BOOKS FROM THE LIBRARY OF WILLIAM FAREL

Max Engammare

As with the personal libraries of Pierre Viret or John Calvin, the library of William Farel has not come down to us, at least not in an identifiable manner. This is because Viret, Calvin and Farel, unlike Heinrich Glareanus[1] or Erasmus,[2] did not insert their own bookplate inside the initial flap or on the title page of their books, nor did they take the liberty of stamping a *perlegi* at the end of the book after the manner of Montaigne, which signals to us that the book has been read. Because of Aimé-Louis Herminjard[3] and Alexandre Ganoczy, we know of the collection that is the focus of this chapter, which I now present to Anthony Lane. It is mentioned in the Geneva Academy catalogue of 1572, now in the Library of Geneva (BGE), though it has never been studied.

It is a collection of two texts: (1) *DD. Ioannis Œcolampadii et Huldrichi Zvinglii Epistolarum libri quatuor, præcipua cum religionis a Christo nobis traditæ capita, tum Ecclesiasticæ administrationis officia, nostro maxime seculo, tot hactenus erroribus perturbato, convenientia, ad adamussim experimentes … Purgatio, per Theodorum Bibliandrum, sacrarum literarum Tigurinæ Ecclesiæ professorem, conscripta*, Basle, Thomas Platter and Balthasar Lasius, March 1536.[4] 2) The correspondence

---

1. See Iain Fenlon and Inga Mai Groote (eds), *Heinrich Glarean's Books. The Intellectual World of a Sixteenth-Century Musical Humanist* (Cambridge: Cambridge University Press, 2013).

2. See Alexandre Vanautgaerden, '*Ex bibliotheca Erasmi*. Un 34e ouvrage: l'exemplaire des *Epistolæ* de Léon Ier (Paris, Josse Bade, 1511) du Cultura Fonds (Dilbeek)', *Bibliothèque d'Humanisme et Renaissance* 74 (2012), pp. 547–62 (with bibliography in notes, especially p. 553, n. 8).

3. *Correspondance des Réformateurs dans les pays de langue française* (col. and pub. Aimé-Louis Herminjard; 9 vols; Geneva: H. Georg, 1866–97), vol. 1, nr. 111, p. 256, n. 8. (Henceforth *Correspondance des Réformateurs*) Herminjard indicates that the gift of the correspondence between Zwingli and Oecolampadius was given to Farel by Oporin and the location was the Bibliothèque publique et universitaire de Genève (hereafter *BGE*).

4. Geneva, *BGE*, Bf 847/2.

between Oecolampadius and Zwingli is preceded in the artificial collection by the aphorisms of Vadian, *Joachimi Vadiani cons. Sangallensis Aphorismorum libri sex de consideratione eucharistiæ*, Zurich, Christoph Froschauer, [1536] (Vadian's preface to Pellikan is dated 21 May 1536).[5]

The sixteenth-century binding is covered with a manuscript parchment taken from a fifteenth-century antiphonal with the text and music of the Twelfth Sunday of the Year: 'Dum transiret Dominus per medios fines Tyri surdos fecit audire et mutos loqui.' It would seem that the binding was made for Farel, since on the back of the title page of aphorisms, he wrote a small obituary for Vadianus: 'Vadianus. Interfuit disputationi Bernensis præsidentem [?] primus anno 1528 ... obiit 1551.' This indicates that Farel had these two bound volumes from this date, especially as one marginal note of the correspondence refers to these aphorisms.[6] Surely, he read these aphorisms as is evident from some notes in his hand (e.g. pp. 3, 115, 172 or 214), including one on the *sublimis sensus* of the Song of Songs,[7] and from their inclusion in the final errata.

Specifically, one also finds on the back of the book, the horizontal label, corresponding to the Library of the Academy of Calvin: 'De Eucharist[ia] Vadiani aphorismi/Œcolampadii et Zvynglii epistolæ.'[8]

It is the bookseller and printer Joannes Oporinus who offered the correspondence between Oecolampadius and Zwingli to Farel, as we read in the note accompanying the gift: 'Dn. [=Domino] Guilhelmo Farello amico et fratri chariss.[imo] suo Joan.[nes] Oporinus D.D. [=dedit]' (Figure 1). One might even speculate that the Reformer received it from the printer in Basle in June 1538, when Farel was, along with Calvin, driven out of Geneva and they stopped in the Rhineland city and stayed with Oporinus, or in July, when he accepted the call of the Church in Neuchatel and quickly left Basle.[9] Therefore, it would certainly not seem inappropriate to think that Oporinus financed all, or part,

5. Geneva, *BGE*, Bf 847/1.

6. See *infra*, notes 21 and 22.

7. In the initial index, the aphorism on the Song of Songs indicates: 'Cantici canticorum sublimis sensus', f° [a6]v. The context is the Eucharistic disputes, since the previous aphorism deals with the understanding of this 'Hoc est corpus meum', not only 'carnalem et literalem sensum', but also symbolically: 'In symbolis enim panis et vini Dominus non corpus suum carnale sed memoriam sui adeoque esum (corporis) spiritualem consecrare nobis voluit' (cf. *Joachimi Vadiani cons. Sangallensis Aphorismorum libri sex* (Zurich: Froschauer, 1536), p. 115). The word 'corporis' was forgotten; it is placed on the errata list, f° [Y5], and Farel adds *in suo loco*, before the lines, p. 115. The aphorism criticizes the Anabaptists. For the Song of Songs, Vadian wrote: 'Cantica Salomonis si literam intueris, quid sunt aliud quam carmen amatorium, Veneribus et illecebris confertum?'

8. See Alexandre Ganoczy, *La Bibliothèque de l'Académie de Calvin. Le catalogue de 1572 et ses enseignements* (Geneva: Droz, 1969), nr. 108, pp. 196–7.

9. Jules Pétremand, 'Les progrès de la Réformation et les débuts de l'Eglise nouvelle dans le comté de Neuchâtel du départ au retour de Farel (1531–1538)', in *Guillaume Farel 1489–1565, Biographie Nouvelle* (Neuchatel and Paris: Delachaux & Niestlé, 1930), p. 416.

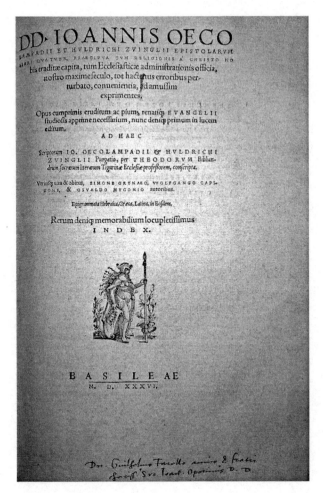

Figure 1 Farel's copy of *Epistolæ*, 1536.

of this edition prepared by the Zuricher (by adoption) Theodore Bibliander (Buchmann).[10] The first correction is, in fact, in the hand of Oporinus, the same by which the gift was given. On the first page of the long dedication of Theodore Bibliander to Philip Landgrave of Hesse, the word *violentiæ* is replaced in the margin by *innocentiæ* (f ° α2r °). Why was this done? Surely because, far from considering Philip of Hesse as *violentiæ apertum asylum*, which is not exactly a compliment, it is more appropriate to regard him as a 'free refuge of innocence'.

The correspondence of these Reformers is contained in two works, which Farel annotated conscientiously. We ought, first, to distinguish the insertion of errata in

---

10. Although Bibliander does not say anything in his long preface (almost seventy folio pages), he then cites printers Thomas Platter and Balthasar Lasius.

the text, from the summary sheet placed after the index.[11] This rare gesture, it seems to me, represents a desire to read the letters *in extenso*. The insertion performed, Farel starts by removing, with the stroke of a pen, in the dedication of Theodore Bibliander, the first line of the page δ ('[cor]pus, hoc est Ecclesiae homines. nam pios quidem percipere cum magno'), because this page repeats the last line of the page [γ6]v.[12] Since typographers, as we know, are not always very attentive, Farel's annotations are not limited to corrections of the edited text. When the letter of Oecolampadius to Zwingli from 3 January 1530 is reprinted a second time, it is after a fashion truly edited (folio 200r–v), Farel notes 'supra .170 fol. eadem'.[13] That is to say, his reading was particularly attentive.

There is also some underlining, as thus in a letter to Zwingli, '*Carnem ergo Christi edere, est credere ipsum pro nobis mortuum esse*', reflecting the memorial reading of the Supper: to eat the flesh of Christ is, in fact, to believe he died for us.[14]

Farel gives some biographical details, as he had done before for the aphorisms of Vadianus specifying the dates of the life and death of Johannes Oecolampadius at the beginning of 'De Obitu' by Simon Grynaeus: that the Basle Reformer 'Natus anno 1482 obiit 1531' (f° ζ v). He also adds at the beginning of the epitaph of Zwingli for Heinrich Wölfli (Lupulus) '1531. Octob. 11'.[15] (f° [θ_5]).

Farel again corrects phrases in portions of these introductions. Thus, in the fifth epitaph given by Heinrich Wölfi in memory of Zwingli, the Reformer has completed a verse: 'Quod Moses verpis olim, quod Paulus Achivis', highlighting *verpis* and

---

11. See *DD. Ioannis Œcolampadii et Huldrichi Zvinglii Epistolarum libri quatuor, præcipua cum religionis a Christo nobis traditæ capita, tum Ecclesiasticæ administrationis officia, nostro maxime seculo, tot hactenus erroribus perturbato, convenientia, ad adamussim experimentes ... Purgatio, per Theodorum Bibliandrum, sacrarum literarum Tigurinæ Ecclesiæ professorem, conscripta* (Basle: Thomas Platter and Balthasar Lasius, March 1536), f° [α5] (shortened hereafter to *Epistolæ*, 1536; of course, many of the references to *Epistolae* below are specifically to Farel's annotated copy). The gesture is not exhaustive (thus f° 117, line 30, *movet* to be corrected in *monet*), while the reader corrects other typos, such as the stray comma before *infantes* in the expression 'Quod apostoli baptizaverint infantes' (f° 111), or the sermon 33 and not 39 of Bernard de Clairvaux 'in Cantica' (f° 156 [wrongly numbered 151]), see folio 166 which was mangled on 269, etc.

12. It may also be noted that Nam is capitalized after the point. Further evidence of freedom or inattention of the typographers who composed the texts, even in Basle, with Platter and Lasius.

13. See *Briefe und Akten zum Leben Oekolampads, zum vierhundertjährigen Jubiläum der Basler Reformation* (ed. Ernst Staehelin; 2 vols; Leipzig: M. Heinsius Nachfolger, Eger & Sievers, 1927–34), vol. 2, pp. 405–7. Staehelin edited the letter on folio 170, providing variants of the version edited f° 200r–v.

14. *Epistolæ*, 1536, f° 115. Other underlining f° 118.

15. We note that Farel did not give the date of the death of Zwingli at the beginning of the first epitaph, which was written by Konrad Pellikan in Hebrew and placed on the verso of the previous page, another sign, perhaps, that Farel never mastered Hebrew.

transforming *quod* in *judaeis, et quod*, the adjective 'circumcised' demands here the substantive, the *verpis judaeis*: 'What Moses once was to circumcised Jews, and Paul to the Greeks, Zwingli was to the Zurichers' (f ° [θ5] v).[16]

The most interesting elements are the clarifications and additions written by Farel in the margins of the edition, because until the death of Zwingli and Oecolampadius, both in 1531, Farel was in contact with them. He was, in fact, a witness and a participant in the events that were discussed in their correspondences. In the third letter from Oecolampadius of 13 October 1530, 'in Christo Dilectis fratribus', Farel thus completes the title with the word, *valdensis*, since it was to Waldensians from Provence (Oecolampadius mentions further down in the letter persecution which they were the victims of), and identifies the first name of the initials G. M. mentioned near the beginning of the letter, *Georgio*, without giving the surname of a Waldensian minister whom he had previously met.[17] It was Georges Morel whom the Waldensians of Provence sent, along with Pierre Masson, to Oecolampadius and Bucer in 1530.[18] In a letter from Farel to Guerin Muete, dated 18 November 1532, written while he was at Morat, the Reformer expressed concern about George and some others who remained anonymous, not naming Morel by his first name, for security in case the letter fell into the hands of any inquisitor.[19]

In a series of testimonies of the Fathers, which Melanchthon sent to Myconius on the subject of the Supper,[20] supplemented by a series of other texts allegedly by Oecolampadius, Farel referred in an interesting manner to the Aphorisms of Vadianus, which he had also read. The passage concerns Origen, in his seventh homily on Leviticus, where there is absolutely no suggestion of eating flesh ('tunc carnalem manducationem ignoratam'): '[Origenes] dicit enim: Si quis secundum literam sequatur hoc quo is dictus est, nisi manduca veritis carnem filii hominis et biberitis sanguinem illius, litera occidit.' In the margin, Farel annotated 'in

16. The handwritten letters found above the first name Gerardus on the next page are only the mark from the annotation 'judaeis et quod', as the page was turned before the ink had dried.

17. 'Non sine magna in Christum voluptate, accepimus a G. M. fidelissimo vestræ salutis curatore, quæ vestræ religionis fides, quique ritus', *Epistolæ*, 1536, f° 2. Cf. *Correspondance des Réformateurs*, vol. 3, nr. 420 and p. 66, n. 13, with the extract of a letter from Georges Morel, who stopped in Neuchatel, Murten, Bern and Basle before pushing up to meet Oecolampadius in 1530. He was on his way when he met Farel.

18. Ernst Staehelin identified Morel in his edition, but without annotation (cf. *Briefe und Akten zum Leben Oekolampads*, vol. 2, nr. 788, p. 510).

19. 'Je vous prie, si avès aucunes novelles de George ne des autres, les communiqués, car mon cueur en est fort en soucy.' Cf. *Correspondance des Réformateurs*, vol. 2, nr. 395, p. 460 and n. 7.

20. The letter begins with the reminder of a promise: 'Mitto tibi locos veterum scriptorum de coena Domini, ut promissi, qui testantur illos idem sensisse, quod nos sentimus: videlicet, corpus et sanguinem Domini vere et adesse in coena Dominica.' Ibid., f° 135.

Aphoris[mos] Vadiani supra 89'.[21] The reference is accurate and rightly refers to p. 89 of the *Aphorisms* where the passage from Origen is found.[22] Further, there is a reference to Cyril of Alexandria (in a commentary on the verse 'Ego sum vitis vera, etc.'), which Farel supplements with a note to 'lib. 10, cap. 13'.[23]

In a letter from Oecolampadius to Farel, dated 2 August, Farel added 1524,[24] on what would have been the following day, 3 August 1524.[25] In another letter from 25 November, the year was changed to 1527;[26] 1526 for a letter from 9 March,[27] a fact which is of sufficient interest that I will return to it below; 1525 for a letter from 6 February;[28] 1525 for a letter from 1 July.[29] The adding of the year is a regular feature of Farel's annotating of the letters from the Basler to the Dauphinois, with the exception of a letter from 27 December 1526, the saints day of John the Evangelist ('in die Joannis Evangelistæ'), where 'Anno 1527' is printed,[30] as well as a letter from 25 July 1525.[31]

Farel may, however, be wrong in adding a date, and writing 1527 for 1528 in a letter from Oecolampadius to Farel from 22 March, as already mentioned in passing by Herminjard.[32]

There is also the supplying of the year in a letter from Oecolampadius to Martin Konrad and Konrad Sam from 8 November, to which Farel adds 1531,[33] as at the end of the last letter published by Bibliander in 1536, the letter of Oecolampadius to Leo Jud, dated 1 November, Farel writes in the margin 1531.[34]

---

21. *Epistolæ*, 1536, f° 142.

22. 'Videtur autem Origenem sequutus, qui Homilia in Leviticum septima, Agnoscite, inquit, quæ figuræ sint, quæ in divinis voluminibus scriptæ sunt, et ideo tanquam spirituales, et non tanquam carnales examinate et intelligite quæ dicuntur ...'

23. *Epistolæ*, 1536, f° 156v (wrongly numbered 151).

24. Ibid., f° 200. When Herminjard edited this letter, he simply put the year in parenthesis (cf. *Correspondance des Réformateurs*, vol. 1, nr. 110, pp. 253–4).

25. *Epistolæ*, 1536, f° 198.

26. *Epistolæ*, 1536, f° 201r°. Herminjard again put the year in parenthesis (Cf. *Correspondance des Réformateurs*, vol. 2, nr. 207, pp. 60–1).

27. *Epistolæ*, 1536, f° 201.

28. *Epistolæ*, 1536, f° 204.

29. *Epistolæ*, 1536, f° 205.

30. *Epistolæ*, 1536, f° 207. Without error, it was indeed 27 December 1526. Herminjard, when editing this letter, specified that the year had been written in German style, the year beginning on Christmas. (See *Correspondance des Réformateurs*, vol. 1, nr. 187, pp. 468–9).

31. *Epistolæ*, 1536, f° 208v.

32. *Epistolæ*, 1536, f° 185, and *Correspondance des Réformateurs*, vol. 2, nr. 226, pp. 118–19, n. 6. Notes 2 and 3 cite that the mother of Oecolampadius died in 1528 and the marriage of the latter with Wibrandis Rosenblatt (widow of master Ludwig Keller of Basle, she was the third wife of Capito, the fourth of Bucer).

33. *Epistolæ*, 1536, f° 212. Ernst Staehelin inserted '[1531]' in his edition (see *Briefe und Akten zum Leben Oekolampads*, vol. 2, pp. 707–8).

34. *Epistolæ*, 1536, f° 212v.

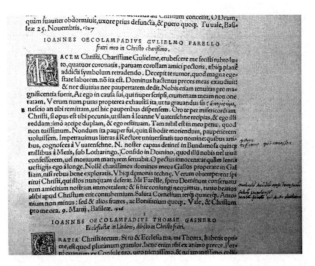

Figure 2 Farel's marginal annotations.

In a letter from Oecolampadius to an anonymous recipient (anonymous for Theodor Bibliander), Farel has not only added 1524 in the margin, but also written his name G. *Farello* to identify the 'N.' of the unknown recipient.[35]

Finally, the letter of 9 March 1526 is perhaps the most interesting, since Farel supplies the names of several individuals that Bibliander failed to identify in his edition (Figure 2).[36] Farel, then in Strasbourg, had sent some money to Oecolampadius, thinking of the needy, and the latter thanked him for it and mentioned Pierre Toussain to him, sending greetings at the end to a few friends there in Strasbourg. Toussain is not named, but is hidden behind an N., as he was imprisoned in Pont-à-Mousson, five miles from Metz.[37] Farel identified the man and the place adding in the margin 'Petrus Tossanus' and 'Pontamosson'. After having repeated to Farel how their friendship is precious to him, and hoping that God will keep it eternally, Oecolampadius salutes a certain Cornelius whom Farel identifies in the margin, 'Michaelem Arandium epis.[copum] Tricastorum'. This is Michel of Arande, the former Augustinian monk, who was responsive to evangelical ideas from the circle of Meaux, whom Marguerite of Navarre named in 1526, after his stay in Strasbourg, bishop of Saint-Paul-Trois-Châteaux, in the Dauphiné.[38]

---

35. *Epistolæ*, 1536, f° 206v, and *Correspondance des Réformateurs*, vol. 1, nr. 115, pp. 265–7. In the p. 265, n. 1, Herminjard wrote, 'The recipient's name, which is omitted in the printed letters of Oecolampadius, was openly restored by Farel himself in the copy that he had.'

36. *Epistolæ*, 1536, f° 201, and *Correspondance des Réformateurs*, vol. 1, nr. 170, pp. 417–19.

37. 'N. noster captus detinetur in Bundamosa quinque millibus a Metis, sub Lotharingo' (*Epistolæ*, 1536, f° 201).

38. See Nicolas Weiss, 'Quelques notes sur les origines de la Réforme et des guerres de religion en Dauphiné', *Bulletin de la Société de l'Histoire du Protestantisme Français* 56

Farel also identifies Antonius, stating 'Jacobum (Fabriti) Fabrum Stapulensem qui Anto.[nius] dicebatur'. Having misspelled *Fabri*, the other Latin name of Lefèvre, Farel writes *Fabrum Stapulensem* above the line. This is obviously Jacques Lefèvre d'Etaples, who in Strasbourg took the surname of Antonius Peregrinus, Antoine the Pilgrim.[39]

It might seem surprising that Farel does not recognize the last figure from the greetings, Bonifacius ('ac Bonifacium quoque'). It is certainly Boniface Wolfhard, vicar in St Martin's in Basle where Oecolampadius preached,[40] but as his identity was not hidden, it was not necessary to identify him more precisely and so Farel did not do so in his copy.

In conclusion, if Herminjard had spotted and used this copy, he overlooked much, as many like him at the time; there was no need to describe precisely and to learn lessons both curious and captivating. The study of annotated books has taken off in the last thirty years with the work of Roger Chartier, Anthony Grafton, Ann Blair and their students, the special issue of la *Revue de la Bibliothèque nationale, Scientia in margine* edited by Danielle Jacquart and Charles Burnett, the recent book by William Sherman,[41] as well as a few scattered articles.[42] We have noted in the aphorisms of Vadianus and more in the published correspondences of Zwingli and Oecolampadius, a careful reader, scrupulous annotator, hunter of misspellings who read these two books from the first line to the last, with pen in hand. We especially discovered Farel as a reader of his own life, rereading the letters that Oecolampadius sent to him, identifying the names of friends, paying attention to the years of his life just when he had been expelled from Geneva, from where he would finally find a haven on the shores of Lake Neuchatel. If annotators transform a printed book, often a bible, as a 'livre de raison', noting births, deaths and family weddings, Farel did this in a book full of the elements of his own life which had been published; this, I repeat, is a rare gesture that merits being repeated, and offered today to Tony Lane.

Translated from French by Jon Balserak.

(1907), pp. 316–61, 'Michel d'Arande', pp. 324–7. Michel d'Arande was received into his bishopric on 7 June 1526, the letter of Oecolampadius being dated 9 March of that year.

39. See Guy Bedouelle, *Lefèvre d'Etaples et l'intelligence des Ecritures* (Travaux d'Humanisme et Renaissance, vol. 152; Geneva: Droz, 1976), p. 107.

40. See *Correspondance des Réformateurs*, vol. 1, nr. 95, p. 202, and nr. 170, p. 419.

41. William H. Sherman, *Used Books. Marking Readers in Renaissance England* (Philadelphia: University of Pennsylvania Press, 2007).

42. I have also contributed some articles on the *Novum Testamentun* of Jan Laski (Joannes a Lasco), the *Biblia* of Jerome Bolsec, the *Ephemerides* of Pierre de Ronsard, the annotated editions of John Calvin, etc.

Bibliography

Bedouelle, Guy, *Lefèvre d'Etaples et l'intelligence des Ecritures* (Travaux d'Humanisme et Renaissance, vol. 152; Geneva: Droz, 1976).

Fenlon, Iain and Inga Mai Groote (eds), *Heinrich Glarean's Books. The Intellectual World of a Sixteenth-Century Musical Humanist* (Cambridge: Cambridge University Press, 2013).

Ganoczy, Alexandre, *La Bibliothèque de l'Académie de Calvin. Le catalogue de 1572 et ses enseignements* (Geneva: Droz, 1969).

Herminjard, Aimé-Louis *Correspondance des Réformateurs dans les pays de langue française* (collected and published Aimé-Louis Herminjard; 9 vols; Geneva: H. Georg, 1866–97).

Oecolampadius, Johannes, *Briefe und Akten zum Leben Oekolampads, zum vierhundertjährigen Jubiläum der Basler Reformation* (ed. Ernst Staehelin; 2 vols; Leipzig: M. Heinsius Nachfolger, Eger & Sievers, 1927–34).

Oecolampadius, Johannes, *DD. Ioannis Œcolampadii et Huldrichi Zvinglii Epistolarum libri quatuor, præcipua cum religionis a Christo nobis traditæ capita, tum Ecclesiasticæ administrationis officia, nostro maxime seculo, tot hactenus erroribus perturbato, convenientia, ad adamussim experimentes … Purgatio, per Theodorum Bibliandrum, sacrarum literarum Tigurinæ Ecclesiæ professorem, conscripta* (Basle: Thomas Platter and Balthasar Lasius, March 1536).

Pétremand, Jules, 'Les progrès de la Réformation et les débuts de l'Eglise nouvelle dans le comté de Neuchâtel du départ au retour de Farel (1531–1538)', in *Guillaume Farel 1489–1565, Biographie Nouvelle* (Neuchatel and Paris: Delachaux & Niestlé, 1930).

Sherman, William H., *Used Books. Marking Readers in Renaissance England* (Philadelphia: University of Pennsylvania Press, 2007).

Vadianus, Joachim, *Joachimi Vadiani Cons. Sangallensis Aphorismorum Libri Sex* (Zurich: Froschauer, 1536).

Vanautgaerden, Alexandre, 'Ex bibliotheca Erasmi. Un 34ᵉ ouvrage: l'exemplaire des *Epistolæ* de Léon Iᵉʳ (Paris, Josse Bade, 1511) du Cultura Fonds (Dilbeek)', *Bibliothèque d'Humanisme et Renaissance* 74 (2012), pp. 547–62.

Weiss, Nicolas, 'Quelques notes sur les origines de la Réforme et des guerres de religion en Dauphiné', *Bulletin de la Société de l'Histoire du Protestantisme français* 56 (1907), pp. 316–61.

Chapter 3

THE FREED WILL: CAN AUGUSTINE TEACH
US TO SEE CALVIN IN A NEW LIGHT?

Jason Van Vliet

Back in the fourth century, Evodius[1] had a question, to which his friend Augustine had an answer. This was his question:

> I am troubled exceedingly by the question how God can have foreknowledge of all future events, and yet how there can be no necessity for us to sin. … Since God had foreknowledge that [man] would sin, it must have happened of necessity, because God foreknew it would happen. How, then, is the will free, when the necessity seems so inescapable?[2]

Good question.

Apparently, Evodius has not been the only person to ask it. Throughout the ages, those with a philosophical bent have puzzled over similar conundrums, the determinists emphasizing causal necessity, the libertarians stressing the freedom of the will and the compatibilists searching for some happy medium between the two. Perhaps you yourself have tried to wrestle this riddle to the ground. If you are anything like me, perhaps you have not been completely victorious yet.

Certainly, the Reformers of the sixteenth century debated this question with representatives of the Roman Catholic Church. In June of 1519, Johann von Eck and Andreas Karlstadt took up the matter at a public disputation in Leipzig.[3] Eck affirmed the free choice of fallen human beings; Karlstadt denied it. Then, from

---

1. A brief biographical overview can be found in A. Di Berardino (ed.), *The Encyclopedia of the Early Church* (trans. Adrian Walford; Cambridge: James Clarke & Co., 1992), s.v. 'Evodius'.

2. Augustine, *The Problem of Free Choice* (trans. D. M. Pontifex; Ancient Christian Writers, 22; New York: Newman Press, 1955), 3.2.4.

3. Ronald J. Sider, *Andreas Bodenstein von Karlstadt: The Development of His Thought* (Leiden: E. J. Brill, 1974), pp. 71–81.

1524 to 1527, Desiderius Erasmus and Martin Luther engaged in a spirited, literary duel over this doctrine.[4] This time Erasmus was the one who argued in favour of free choice, while Luther refuted it. Finally, to cite but one more instance, during the 1540s, John Calvin and Albert Pighius exchanged books on this matter, each categorically disagreeing with the other.[5]

Inevitably, this question reaches out from the cerebral realm of theory, and it grabs hold of the nitty-gritty of daily life. For example, if I speak in a sharp, angry and inconsiderate way to one of my children, and if God knew about my outburst long before it occurred but did nothing to prevent it, then who is ultimately guilty for the sin committed against my child: God or me? That is a practical question with very real consequences for how my child and I will reconcile once again.

Since Evodius's question is so common, so historic and so practical, it behoves us to press on to the answer that Augustine gives to his friend's query. And, to be sure, that is the task at hand. However, we undertake this task with a larger goal in mind. We want to explore whether Augustine's answer to Evodius's query can help shed light on some misunderstandings surrounding John Calvin and his view on the human will. Calvin has the reputation of being a diehard determinist. After all, he is the theologian who stressed so strongly the sovereignty of God who, by his eternal decree, has decided all things, in detail, before the creation of the world. Where can anyone possibly find room for the free will of human beings in a theology such as that? And yet, here are a couple of quotable quotes from the man himself:

> If anyone, then, can use this word [free will] without understanding it in a bad sense, I shall not trouble him on this account.[6]
>
> If freedom is opposed to coercion, I both acknowledge and consistently maintain that choice is free, and I hold anyone who thinks otherwise to be a heretic.[7]

---

4. In 1524 Erasmus wrote his *Diatribe seu collatio de libero arbitrio*. Luther responded a year later with his *De servo arbitrio*. Gordon Rupp has provided an English translation of both in *Luther and Erasmus: Free Will and Salvation* (London: SCM Press, 1969). Next, in 1526 and 1527 Erasmus answered Luther with two more lengthy volumes, the *Hyperaspistes*. Luther did not reply to the *Hyperaspistes*.

5. Pighius began the debate with his *De libero hominis arbitrio et divina gratia, Libri decem* (Cologne: Melchior Novesianus, 1542). This work has not been translated. Calvin responded in his *Defensio sanae et orthodoxae doctrinae de servitute & liberatione humani arbitrii, adversus calumnias Alberti Pighii Campensis* (Geneva: Jean Girard, 1543). English translation: John Calvin, *The Bondage and Liberation of the Will: A Defence of the Orthodox Doctrine of Human Choice Against Pighius* (ed. A. N. S. Lane; trans. G. I. Davies; Grand Rapids: Baker Books, 1996).

6. John Calvin, *Institutes of the Christian Religion* (ed. John T. McNeill; trans. Ford Lewis Battles; Grand Rapids: Eerdmans, 1975), 2.2.8.

7. Calvin, *Bondage and Liberation*, p. 68.

Statements such as these have led at least one scholar, Vincent Brümmer, to conclude, 'Although we cannot deny that [Calvin] sometimes defends an uncompromisingly deterministic doctrine of divine predestination, at other times he seems to adopt a less negative attitude toward the role of human choice than this doctrine would lead one to expect.'[8]

Yet, how can uncompromising determinism and free human choice coexist in one coherent system of thought, or is John Calvin simply contradicting himself? The latter is certainly possible – after all, Calvin is but a fallible mortal as well – but when Calvin is viewed through the ancient lens of Augustine, we discover that there is much more coherence in his thought than we might first anticipate. In order to work this all out, we need to briefly explore the connection between Augustine and Calvin. Following that, we will be ready to analyse Augustine's view of the freedom of the will against the background of his opponents, which should, in turn, shed light on Calvin's view of the will within his polemical context.

The Connection between Augustine and Calvin

John Calvin was a keen 'student of the Church Fathers', to use the epithet given to him by the scholar we are honouring with this volume.[9] The statistics bear this out. Using his self-declared minimalist approach of only counting explicit quotations as valid citations,[10] Tony Lane tallied up no fewer than 1084 direct quotations from the Church Fathers in Calvin's 1559 edition of the *Institutes*.[11] That number alone should qualify Calvin as an ardent fan of the Church Fathers.

Yet, among all the Fathers that Calvin quoted, Augustine of Hippo was clearly his favourite. Once again, the numbers make the truth evident. Out of over 1,000 patristic citations in the *Institutes*, no less than 478 of them are from Augustine. Forty-four per cent of the time that Calvin turns to the Fathers, he reaches for his preferred *pater*, Augustine. Once the reformer of Geneva even quipped, 'If I wanted to weave a whole volume from Augustine, I could readily show my readers that I need no other language than his.'[12]

Narrowing our focus still more, it is especially on the topic of free choice that Calvin finds Augustine so uniquely helpful. As much as he appreciates the Church Fathers in general on all kinds of theological topics, concerning this particular matter of the human will, he says that they 'so differ, waver, or speak confusedly on this subject, that almost nothing certain can be derived from their writings.'[13]

---

8. Vincent Brümmer, 'Calvin, Bernard and the Freedom of the Will', *RelS* 30 (1994), pp. 437–55 (437).

9. On this topic see the worthwhile study by A. N. S. Lane, *John Calvin: Student of the Church Fathers* (Grand Rapids: Baker Books, 1999).

10. Lane, *John Calvin*, pp. xi–xiii.

11. Lane, *John Calvin*, pp. 55–61.

12. Calvin, *Institutes*, 3.22.8.

13. Ibid., 2.2.4.

There is, however, one shining exception: Augustine. 'Perhaps I may seem to have brought a great prejudice upon myself when I confess that all ecclesiastical writers, *except Augustine*, have spoken so ambiguously or variously on this matter that nothing certain can be gained from their writings.'[14]

Considering all of the above, it is neither illegitimate nor unnatural to view Calvin's understanding of the human will through the lens of Augustine's teaching on the topic. On the contrary, it is more than probable that Calvin would have been honoured by the comparison.

Augustine between Mani and Pelagius

Let us return to Evodius's question, as it is found in the dialogical treatise entitled *The Problem of Free Choice*. Augustine begins to answer by ensuring that he understands the question:

> This is no doubt what puzzles and troubles you, the apparent contradiction between saying that God has foreknowledge of all future events, and that we sin freely and not of necessity. ... You fear that the conclusion of this reasoning will be either blasphemous denial of God's foreknowledge, or, if this is impossible, admission that we sin of necessity and not freely. Is there any other point which troubles you?[15]

After which Evodius immediately confirms, 'Nothing else at present.'[16] To which Augustine, in part, answers:

> There is nothing so fully in our power as the will itself. ... We can truly say, we grow old of necessity and not of our own will; or, we are ill of necessity and not of our own will; or, we die of necessity and not of our own will; and so in other matters of the sort; but no one would be so mad as to venture to say, we do not will of our own will. Therefore, though God foreknows what we shall will in the future, this does not imply that we do not make use of our will.[17]

And a little later he adds:

> Our will would not be a will, if it were not in our power. Moreover, since it is in our power, it is free. What is not in our power, or may not be in our power, is not free to us.[18]

---

14. Ibid., 2.2.9; emphasis mine.
15. Augustine, *Free Choice*, 3.3.6.
16. Ibid., 3.3.6.
17. Ibid., 3.3.7.
18. Ibid., 3.3.8.

Two things are immediately clear. First, for Augustine the adjective 'free' in the phrase 'free will' means 'in our power'. That is to say, when our will is engaged and we really *want* something, then that desire arises, voluntarily, from within us. It is not foisted upon us by some external, coercive necessity such as the inevitable advance of the ageing process. Second, foreknowledge does not nullify, *ipso facto*, the voluntary exercise of a will. As a father I may know ahead of time that our son will eat Cheerios for breakfast tomorrow morning. After all, he loves that breakfast cereal and reaches for the same box every morning. However, my foreknowledge of my son's action will not forcibly coerce him to eat Cheerios tomorrow. He will freely and enthusiastically reach for that cereal box tomorrow, just like he did yesterday. To borrow some words from Augustine, the choice for Cheerios is 'in his power'.

Still, the conundrum is not nearly solved. Unlike an earthly father who knows something about his son's preferences at breakfast, the God described by Augustine knows everything (omniscience) and also rules over everything (omnipotence). Moreover, for my son to be truly free in his choice to eat Cheerios, does he not need to have the ability to surprise me one morning and ask for porridge rather than Cheerios? Furthermore, it is one thing if he can surprise me, but could he also surprise an omniscient, omnipotent God? And, to press the matter even further, could my son also surprise this omniscient and omnipotent God in his choice to either trust this God wholeheartedly or reject him resolutely? Obviously, that choice is of far greater significance than the menu options on our breakfast table. And so we seem to be back to square one. Rephrasing Augustine's earlier words, we stand at the uncomfortable crossroad where God's sovereignty over all future events must be impiously denied, or, if that cannot be denied, then human action, whether evil or good, is committed by necessity, not voluntarily.

Can Augustine give clear and consistent direction on where to proceed from here? The Bishop of Hippo is capable of giving sound guidance on this matter, but some scholars have questioned whether his instruction on the free will remained consistent throughout the years. For instance, in his classic biography Peter Brown opined that the early Augustine was so optimistic about the human will that 'indeed, Augustine was, on paper, more Pelagian that Pelagius'.[19] However, once Augustine actually met Pelagius, he changed his mind, according to Brown, and became much more pessimistic about what the human will could accomplish on its own.[20] Thus, the later, anti-Pelagian Augustine attributed everything to divine grace and nothing to human choice. At least, this is the way the situation is often portrayed.[21]

19. As quoted in Simon Harrison, *Augustine's Way into the Will: The Theological and Philosophical Significance of 'De libero arbitrio'* (Oxford: Oxford University Press, 2006), p. 23.

20. As quoted in Harrison, *Augustine's Way*, p. 23.

21. However, there are those who refute the thesis that Augustine changed his mind in a significant way and uphold the Church Father's own self-evaluation. See, for example, Marianne Djuth, 'The Hermeneutics of "De Libero Arbitrio" III: Are There Two Augustines?', in *Studia Patristica 27* (ed. William S. Babcock; Louvain: Peeters, 1993), pp. 281–9 (289).

Augustine himself, I am quite sure, would have protested against such an analysis. This opinion is corroborated by no one less than Augustine himself. Essentially, the charge of inconsistency regarding the human will was already levelled at him by Pelagius. Augustine also answers that charge in his *Retractions*. It takes a courageous, yet humble, person to write a book towards the end of his earthly sojourn and correct, retract or otherwise amend his previously published documents, yet that is precisely what Augustine does in his *Retractions*. Yet, when it comes to his treatise, *The Problem of Free Choice*, he does not retract anything he had written. In fact, he defends it vigorously against his Pelagian opponents who were attempting to point out that whereas Augustine now refutes them, earlier he had agreed with them that the will is free. Augustine does not back down. Instead he writes, 'It is one thing to inquire into the source of evil and another to inquire how one can return to his original good or reach one that is greater.'[22]

Indeed, throughout this section of his *Retractions,* Augustine is at pains to point out two key things.[23] In the first place, in his earlier work, *The Problem of Free Choice*, he refuted the deterministic dualism of the Manichaeans, while in his later works on the same doctrine, such as *On Nature and Grace*[24] and *Grace and Free Will*,[25] he repudiated Pelagian teachings. The former answered the question, 'From where does evil come?' The latter dealt with the topic, 'From where does salvation come?' Second, in this same section, he is equally adamant that we cannot simply speak about the human will in general. Rather, we must consistently distinguish between the human will *as it was created* and *as it fell under God's punishment* after the sin of Adam.[26] Thus, according to Augustine, the disparities noted by the Pelagians of old and the analysts of today are not changes in his own teaching but rather differences in the topics being addressed and the opponents being refuted.[27]

A more positive way of saying this is that documents come to life best within their own literary and historical context. For instance, in *The Problem of Free Choice*, Evodius and Augustine are discussing the freedom of the will against the background of the Manichaean religion.[28] Much like the Gnostics, the Persian prophet, Mani (216–76/77), taught a dualism of Light and Darkness, good and evil. According to him, both of these principles are independently eternal.[29] To make a long myth short, Darkness attacks the Light and, through a fierce battle,

22. Augustine, *The Retractions* (trans. Mary Bogon; The Fathers of the Church, 60; Washington: Catholic University of America Press, 1968), 1.8.2.

23. Ibid., 1.8.

24. Augustine, *On Nature and Grace* (trans. John Mourant and William Collinge; The Fathers of the Church, 86; Washington: Catholic University of America Press, 1992).

25. Augustine, *Grace and Free Will* (trans. Robert P. Russell; The Fathers of the Church, 59; Washington: Catholic University of America Press, 1968).

26. Augustine, *Retractions*, 1.8.5.

27. Djuth, 'Hermeneutics of "De Libero Arbitrio"', p. 289.

28. Augustine, *Retractions*, 1.8. Mani is mentioned numerous times.

29. Walter A. Elwell (ed.), *Evangelical Dictionary of Theology* (Grand Rapids: Baker Academic, 2nd edn, 2001), s.v. 'Manichaeism'.

manages to trap the primal man in its evil existence, although there remains a hopeful flicker of Light within him. The goal of the Manichaean religion is to help people overcome evil and release their inner Light by means of prophetic instruction and strict asceticism.[30] So, if the question is, 'From where does evil come?' then Mani answers, 'From the eternal principle of Darkness'. Moreover, since human beings are, from the very outset and by nature, trapped by Darkness, their wicked deeds are ultimately to be attributed, not to themselves, but to an external, eternal and evil force. They sin not because it is in their own power to do so, but because Darkness compels them to do so.

Precisely at this point, Augustine objects and states that 'we sin voluntarily and under no compulsion from anything superior, inferior or equal to us'.[31] He also adds, 'Our wills remain free and within our power'.[32] So, when Manichaeism is being refuted, Augustine speaks of a free will in the sense of freedom from external coercion, not freedom to do otherwise. As the bishop of Hippo once explained to Evodius, the human soul is not a stone.[33] It is not pulled down, inevitably, by the gravity of iniquity. If a soul sins, it is because it *wants* to sin.

Some years later, in his anti-Pelagian writings, Augustine is on to a different topic which also pertains to a different era in redemptive history. Whereas the Manichaean debate was about how human beings were originally created, the Pelagian polemics concern how fallen people can now be restored. Once again, some historical context is helpful. Pelagius (354–418), a British-born theologian, was also a monk who promoted asceticism.[34] However, in contrast to Mani and his version of asceticism, Pelagius strongly promoted the freedom of the will. For him, even the fallen human being is capable of following God's injunctions on his own, unassisted by any divine grace. However, he is able to follow divine commands more easily and swiftly if he accepts assistance from above.[35] Obviously, the key concept for Pelagius is *if he accepts*. In other words, for Pelagius, exercising the freedom of the will precedes the reception of any divine grace and always includes the choice to do otherwise.

Once again, Augustine steps in to correct. He advises his reader not to become proud, 'as if a man could be healed by the very same power by which he became corrupted'.[36] Even in the physical realm the process by which an infection invades the body is not necessarily the same as the means by which the body is healed

---

30. Erwin Fahlbusch and Geoffrey William Bromiley (eds), *The Encyclopedia of Christianity* (5 vols; Leiden: Brill, 1999–2003), s.v. 'Manichaeanism'.

31. Augustine, *Free Choice*, 3.4.9.

32. Ibid., 3.3.8.

33. Ibid., 3.1.2–3.1.3.

34. F. L. Cross and Elizabeth A. Livingstone (eds), *The Oxford Dictionary of the Christian Church* (New York: Oxford University Press, 3rd rev. edn, 2005), s.v. 'Pelagianism'.

35. Dom Mark Pontifex, 'Introduction', in *The Problem of Free Choice* (New York: Newman Press, 1955), p. 10.

36. Augustine, *On Nature and Grace*, 30.34.

from its infirmity. This applies also, and all the more so, to the salvation of both body and soul. Free choice was enough to bring the human race into a state of sinful corruption, but it is not sufficient to deliver it from that same corruption. To accomplish that, divine grace is needed. Augustine says it best when he writes:

> Free will is always present in us, but it is not always good. For it is either free of justice, while serving sin, and then it is evil; or it is free of sin, while serving justice, and then it is good. But the grace of God is always good and brings about a good will in a man who before was possessed of an evil will. It is by this grace, too, that this same good will, once it begins to exist, is expanded and made so strong that it is able to fulfill whatever of God's commandments it wishes, whenever it does so with a strong and perfect will.[37]

To summarize then, *contra* Mani, Augustine holds that with respect to external coercion, the will is always free, both at creation and at the present time. However, *contra* Pelagius, Augustine teaches that with respect to eternal salvation, the fallen will is not free, in and of itself, to choose which way it will go, for it is enslaved to sin. Therefore, the fallen will is a will that needs to be freed. And God's grace is the power that can liberate it. Yet, how can God's grace efficaciously liberate the human will without effectively coercing it into a new-found freedom? That is a question which Calvin answers in more detail than Augustine.

Calvin between Pocquet and Pighius

Since Calvin appreciated Augustine so much, particularly on the topic of the human will, it is not surprising that some of his comments on this topic are remarkably similar to those of his theological mentor. Consider the following quote: 'To will is in us all: but to will good is gain; to will evil, loss. Therefore simply to will is of man; to will ill, of a corrupt nature; to will well, of grace.'[38] If this statement of Calvin is compared with the above quotation from Augustine's *Grace and Free Will*, it is clear that although some words differ, the content is essentially the same. For both it is inconceivable that human beings would be, or ever become, will-less robots. Rather, the *soundness* of the will, whether it is evil or good, is the issue that needs urgent attention.

However, before looking more closely at the soundness of the will, it is good to take a moment to underline Calvin's strong affirmation that human beings really do have a genuine, active and accountable will. After all, his reputation as a will-denying determinist will not die easily.[39] Fortuitously, such confirmation is readily at hand in Calvin's polemic against the Libertines. In 1545 Calvin wrote a short treatise entitled *Against the Libertines*. These Libertines should not be

---

37. Augustine, *Grace and Free Will*, 15.31.

38. Calvin, *Institutes*, 2.3.5

39. Dewey J. Hoitenga Jr, *John Calvin and the Will: A Critique and Corrective* (Grand Rapids: Baker Books, 1997), p. 70.

confused with a political group which lobbied for influence in Geneva's city council and which went by the same name.[40] Instead, these particular Libertines were a group of charismatic, somewhat itinerant, preachers with names such as Coppin of Lille, Quintin of Hainaut, Claude Perceval and Anthony Pocquet.[41] Neither should these Libertines be thought of as libertarian in their view of the human will. In this respect, their title is rather misleading because there is a determinism in their theology that even Calvin could not stomach. The following anecdote makes the point:

> This notorious swine Quintin once found himself in a street where a man had just been killed. By chance a faithful believer was also there who said, 'Alas! Who has committed this wicked deed?' Immediately he replied in a jesting way, 'Since you want to know, it was I.' The other being completely surprised said, 'How can you be so flippant?' To which he replied, 'It isn't I, but God.' 'Why,' asked the other, 'must you attribute to God evils that He has commanded should be punished?' At which this swine disgorged even more forcefully his venom, saying, 'Yes, it's you, it's I, it's God! For whatever you or I do is God's doing! And whatever God does, we do; for God is in us!'[42]

It is astonishing how Quintin connects, or rather conflates, the will of God and the will of human beings. For Quintin, whatever God does, we do; and whatever we do, God does!

This view of the human will is shared by another Libertine, Anthony Pocquet, who wrote a document that is simply called 'Letter to My Disciples'.[43] In that letter, Pocquet makes the startling statement, 'Everything that is outside of God is nothing.' Moreover, everything that is outside of God is evil. Yet how can everything that is evil be nothing at the same time? It seems to be contradictory, if not entirely absurd. Yet Pocquet explains this by referring to his teaching of *cuider*, which is an old French word that means *to presume that something is so*. In other words, whereas traditional dualism, such as that of Mani, placed Good against Evil,

---

40. The political Libertines were also called Perrinists. It appears that Donald Smeeton does confuse the two groups in his article, 'Calvin's Conflict with the Anabaptists', *EvQ* 54 (1982), pp. 46–52.

41. The main historical and biographical details concerning the Libertines can be found in John Calvin, *Treatises Against the Anabaptists and Against the Libertines* (trans. B. W. Farley; Grand Rapids: Baker, 1982), pp. 200–6. Some additional information can be gleaned from George H. Williams, *The Radical Reformation* (Philadelphia: Westminster Press, 1962), pp. 598–602; Allen Verhey, 'Calvin's Treatise "Against the Libertines"', *Calvin Theological Journal* 15 (1980), pp. 190–219 (192–3); and B. W. Farley, 'Editor's Introduction', in *Against the Libertines*, pp. 162–4.

42. Calvin, *Against the Libertines*, pp. 238–9.

43. The only extant record of Pocquet's letter is found in chapter 23 of Calvin's *Against the Libertines*. There Calvin inserts it, section by section, interspersed with his own commentary on the letter.

Pocquet's modified dualism sets up Good versus presumed Evil, or God versus nothing. All the same, the net result is some form of pan(en)theism in which God is, or at least pervades, everything. And if Pocquet's theology is embraced, then, indeed, whatever God does we do and whatever we do, God does.

Calvin's response to the Libertines is terse yet enlightening. He says, 'In making this claim the Libertines attribute nothing to the will of man, no more than if he were a stone.'[44] The most remarkable aspect of this statement is not *what* is said, but *who* said it. Given Calvin's sustained emphasis on the sovereignty of God, someone might conclude that his theology squeezes the human will out into some tiny, dark, dusty and largely irrelevant corner of existence. In fact, this is clearly not the case. Rather, when someone like Anthony Pocquet does precisely that, Calvin forcefully rejects it, just as his predecessor, Augustine, did in discarding the unacceptable determinism of Mani. Thus, for both Augustine and Calvin, the human will is always free in the sense that it is self-determined and free from external coercion.[45]

Yet, how does all of this apply to soteriology, the doctrine of salvation, which was at the heart of so many debates during the Reformation? Narrowing the question still further, in the transition from unbelief to faith, does the self-determined, yet sinful, will take the lead and decide in its own power which course it wishes to pursue? This is precisely the question that Albert Pighius (1490–1542) pressed upon Calvin. A leading scholar in both philosophy and astronomy, Pighius turned to more ecclesiastical pursuits when in 1522 Pope Adrian VI summoned him to serve in Rome as a papal secretary. Some years later, though, he returned to his homeland, the Netherlands, where, among other things, he engaged in colloquia with Protestant Reformers, including John Calvin.[46] Eventually, the debates in person spilled over into volumes of ink-covered pages. Pighius's *Ten Books on Human Free Choice and Divine Grace* is a lengthy, and somewhat unwieldy, challenge to Calvin's teaching on the will.

For Pighius there are only two options. Either the will is equally free to aspire to evil or good, to faith or unbelief, or the will is coerced by God's sovereignty into doing whatever it does, again either towards good or evil, faith or unbelief. In this respect, Pighius was thinking along the same lines as Pelagius. However, Calvin responds by pointing out that Pighius has hung himself on the horns of a false dilemma. There are more options available to the human will than simply unfettered, libertarian freedom or external, forceful coercion. Calvin puts it this way:

> It is appropriate to note how the following four [claims] differ from one another: namely that the will is free, bound, self-determined, or coerced. People generally understand a free will to be one which has it in its power to choose good or

44. Calvin, *Against the Libertines*, p. 238.

45. Calvin, *Bondage and Liberation*, p. 69.

46. For more information on the Colloquia of Worms and Regensburg, see C. Augustijn, *De Godsdeinstgesprekken tussen Rooms-Katholieken en Protestanten van 1538 tot 1541* (Haarlem: Erven F. Bohn, 1967).

evil, and Pighius also defines it in this way. There can be no such thing as a coerced will, since the two ideas are contradictory. But our responsibility as teachers requires that we say what it means, so that it may be understood what coercion is. Therefore we describe [as coerced] the will which does not incline this way or that of its own accord or by an internal movement of decision, but is forcibly driven by an external impulse. We say that it is self-determined when of itself it directs itself in the direction in which it is led, when it is not taken by force or dragged unwillingly. A bound will, finally, is one which because of its corruptness is held captive under the authority of evil desires, so that it can choose nothing but evil, even if it does so of its own accord and gladly, without being driven by any external impulse.[47]

Thus, the bound will can be freed, not by its own power, but by the salvific strength of God's sovereign grace. Lest someone fear that this will now entail salvation by coercion, Calvin has an answer for that as well. While redeeming a person, God does not override, let alone nullify, the human will but rather renews and restores it. In his own words, 'our will is made new, and ... *we*, created anew in heart and mind, at length *will* what we ought to will.'[48] Elsewhere, Geneva's reformer also adds that when God works with His creatures, 'He guides all creatures *according to the condition and propriety which He had given each when He made them*'.[49] In other words, when God redeems a human being, He does not act as though He were saving a stone. God recognizes that in converting human beings He is dealing with people who have wills; after all, that is how He created them in the beginning. Through the entire process of salvation, then, God always respects the presence of that will and graciously works to restore the soundness of the sinful will. This also means that when someone embraces God in faith, she does it because her graciously renewed will really *wants* to do that.

Thus, *contra* the Libertines, Calvin affirms the real and abiding presence of the human will. However, *contra* Pelagius, he teaches that it is not the free will that leads to grace, but grace that frees the will.

Conclusion

Evodius had a good question. Not only he, but many others have asked it. Viewed through the lens of Augustine and his opponents, Calvin's perspective on the human will comes into sharper focus. It also addresses, at least in part, Evodius's question. God's omniscience and omnipotence do not eradicate the human will, but His sovereign grace can certainly liberate it to do what it was originally created

---

47. Calvin, *Bondage and Liberation*, p. 69.

48. Calvin, *Bondage and Liberation*, p. 174; emphasis mine. See also Calvin, *Against the Libertines*, p. 248.

49. Calvin, *Against the Libertines*, pp. 242–3; emphasis mine.

to do. The human will, free from external coercion yet bound by besetting sin, is freed by God to do what it was originally created to do: glorify its Creator.

Bibliography

Augustijn, C., *De Godsdeinstgesprekken tussen Rooms-Katholieken en Protestanten van 1538 tot 1541* (Haarlem: Erven F. Bohn, 1967).

Augustine, *Grace and Free Will* (trans. Robert P. Russell; The Fathers of the Church, 59; Washington: Catholic University of America Press, 1968).

Augustine, *On Nature and Grace* (trans. John Mourant and William Collinge; The Fathers of the Church, 86; Washington: Catholic University of America Press, 1992).

Augustine, *The Problem of Free Choice* (trans. D. M. Pontifex; Ancient Christian Writers, 22; New York: Newman Press, 1955).

Augustine, *The Retractions* (trans. Mary Bogon; The Fathers of the Church, 60; Washington: Catholic University of America Press, 1968).

Brümmer, Vincent, 'Calvin, Bernard and the Freedom of the Will', *RelS* 30 (1994), pp. 437–55.

Calvin, John, *Against the Libertines* (trans. B. W. Farley; Grand Rapids: Baker, 1982).

Calvin, John, *The Bondage and Liberation of the Will: A Defence of the Orthodox Doctrine of Human Choice Against Pighius* (ed. A. N. S. Lane; trans. G. I. Davies; Grand Rapids: Baker Books, 1996).

Calvin, John, *Institutes of the Christian Religion* (ed. John T. McNeill; trans. Ford Lewis Battles; Grand Rapids: Eerdmans, 1975).

Cross, F. L. and Elizabeth A. Livingstone (eds), *The Oxford Dictionary of the Christian Church* (New York: Oxford University Press, 3rd rev edn, 2005).

Di Berardino, A. (ed.), *The Encyclopedia of the Early Church* (trans. Adrian Walford; Cambridge: James Clarke & Co., 1992).

Djuth, Marianne, 'The Hermeneutics of "De Libero Arbitrio" III: Are There Two Augustines?', in *Studia Patristica 27* (ed. William S. Babcock; Louvain: Peeters, 1993), pp. 281–9.

Elwell, Walter A. (ed.), *Evangelical Dictionary of Theology* (Grand Rapids: Baker Academic, 2nd edn, 2001).

Fahlbusch, Erwin and Geoffrey William Bromiley (eds), *The Encyclopedia of Christianity* (5 vols; Leiden: Brill, 1999–2003).

Farley, B. W. (ed.), 'Editor's Introduction', in *Treatises Against the Anabaptists and Against the Libertines* (Grand Rapids: Baker, 1982), pp. 13–35.

Harrison, Simon, *Augustine's Way into the Will: The Theological and Philosophical Significance of 'De libero arbitrio'* (Oxford: Oxford University Press, 2006).

Hoitenga, Dewey J., Jr, *John Calvin and the Will: A Critique and Corrective* (Grand Rapids: Baker Books, 1997).

Lane, A. N. S., *John Calvin: Student of the Church Fathers* (Grand Rapids: Baker Books, 1999).

Pontifex, Dom Mark, 'Introduction', in *The Problem of Free Choice* (eds Johannes Quasten and Joseph C. Plumpe; New York: Newman Press, 1955), pp. 3–34.

Sider, Ronald J., *Andreas Bodenstein von Karlstadt: The Development of His Thought* (Leiden: Brill, 1974).

Smeeton, Donald, 'Calvin's Conflict with the Anabaptists', *EvQ* 54 (1982), pp. 46–52.

Verhey, Allen, 'Calvin's Treatise "Against the Libertines"', *Calvin Theological Journal* 15 (1980), pp. 190–219.

Williams, George H., *The Radical Reformation* (Philadelphia: Westminster Press, 1962).

Chapter 4

FACING POLAND: CALVIN'S POLISH CORRESPONDENCE AND THE GEOGRAPHY OF REFORMATION EUROPE[1]

Richard A. Muller

Calvin, Poland, and the Map of Europe

Calvin is typically depicted as facing to the west and north, as, in other words, exerting a profound influence on the religious life of France, England, the Low Countries and the Rhineland. This picture has merit, as long as it is modified by reflection on the other important proponents of the Reformed branch of Protestantism who exerted an influence equivalent to Calvin's on the Reformation in many of the same places – and as long as it is qualified by the recognition that Geneva was not the centre from which all things Reformed radiated and that the cultural map of early modern Europe, as illustrated by Calvin's own correspondence, offers a far broader perspective on the Reformation. Examination of Calvin's correspondence radically alters one's sense of the geographical and cultural map of the Northern Renaissance/Reformation as encountered and understood by a Renaissance humanist and religious reformer like Calvin. This is particularly the case when one looks not only at the letters to Calvin from various Polish churchmen and nobles and Calvin's responses, but also to the larger epistolary context in which Calvin and the Polish reformers appear not as the only correspondents but as epistolary partners with numerous others in a much larger 'republic of letters'.

First References: Poland in Calvin's Early Correspondence, 1538–48

Neither the Kingdom of Poland nor the Polish Reformation registered prominently on Calvin's horizon in the earlier part of his work in Geneva or, indeed, during his short stay in Strasbourg, although, as various early letters make clear, he was certainly aware, from the beginning, of the importance of Poland to Europe and

1. This chapter was initially presented as a lecture at the Biblijne Seminarium Teolog, in cooperation with the University of Wroclaw, Wroclaw, Poland, 28 May 2003.

European Christianity.[2] The Kingdom or Commonwealth of Poland-Lithuania was, at the time, one of the largest realms in Europe, rivalled in size only by the Kingdom of Sweden. Calvin's earliest letters, from 1528 to 1538 document the relatively narrow horizons of a young Calvin, who had not yet envisioned either the scope of the Reformation or the breadth of his own future task. As with other aspects of Calvin's work, his stay in Strasbourg marked an epoch. While in Strasbourg, Calvin began to participate in international reformist discussions like the colloquies at Frankfurt (February 1539), Hagenau (June 1540) and Regensburg (March 1541), set his gaze on the broader European reform and identified his return to Geneva as a ground for engagement in this larger task. In a letter written to Farel in January of 1539, several months after Calvin's arrival in Strasbourg, he wrote about political unrest in Germany providing an incentive to 'the Turk' to invade: The Turks, he comments, had already taken over Upper and Lower Wallachia and had threatened Poland with war if not permitted to pass through Polish lands.[3] There are, moreover, letters written from Frankfurt and Hagenau that document Calvin's growing sense of the importance of connection and dialogue with reformers throughout Europe.[4] In March 1541, while at the Diet of Regensburg, Calvin commented in a letter to

2. The most exhaustive listing of Calvin's Polish correspondence is found in Wieslaw Mincer, *Jan Kalwin w Polsce: Bibliografia/John Calvin in Poland: Bibliography* (Toruń: Wydawnictwo Uniwersytetu Mikołaja Kopernika, 2000), divided into Calvin's letters to Poles, #22–74 (pp. 18–27) and letters of Poles to Calvin, #74–134 (pp. 27–40). See the discussions of Calvin and the Polish Reformation in Émile Doumergue, *Jean Calvin, les hommes et les choses de son temps* (7 vols; Lausanne: G. Bridel, 1899–1927), vol. 7, pp. 479–507; Doumergue notes his reliance on Valérian Krasinski, *Histoire religieuse des peuples slaves* (1853), previously published in English as *Sketch of the Religious History of the Slavonic Nations* (Edinburgh: Johnstone and Hunter, 2nd edn, revised and enlarged, 1851). Krasinski also wrote *Historical Sketch of the Rise, Progress, and Decline of the Reformation in Poland: and the Influence which the Scriptural Doctrines have Exercised on that Country in Literary, Moral, and Political Respects* (2 vols; London: Murray, 1838–40). Also note Nancy Conradt, 'John Calvin, Theodore Beza and the Reformation in Poland' (unpublished doctoral dissertation, University of Wisconsin, 1974); and for further bibliography, also see Janusz Małłek, 'The Reformation in Poland and Prussia in the sixteenth century: similarities and differences', in Karin Maag (ed.), *The Reformation in Eastern and Central Europe* (Aldershot: Scolar Press, 1997), pp. 182–91.

3. Calvin to Farel (January 1539), in *CO*, vol. 10, col. 315; also in *Selected Works of John Calvin: Tracts and Letters* (eds Henry Beveridge and Jules Bonnet; 7 vols; Grand Rapids: Baker Book House, 1983), vol. 4, p. 105. The Latin texts of Calvin's works, including his letters, have been cited from *CO*; for the earlier letters, I have also examined A.-L. Herminjard, *Correspondance des Réformateurs dans les pays de langue française* (9 vols; Geneva and Paris, 1866–97).

4. Cf. the letters in Herminjard, *Correspondance*, vol. 5, pp. 247–60 (to Farel, 16 March 1539); vol. 6, pp. 234–41 (to Farel, 21 June 1540), 256–61 (to Guillaume de Tallis, 25 July 1540).

Farel that, if only Sigismund I of Poland were not so preoccupied with defence against the Tartars, he might be inclined to send military aid to Wallachia to fend off the Turk.[5] Calvin was, in other words, very aware of the political significance of Poland to Europe – but he was not yet thinking about his own relationship to the Reformation of the church in Poland-Lithuania.

The situation changed rapidly, however, in the next several years. There is evidence that, by 1545, his writings had been noticed by reformist nobles and churchmen in Poland, particularly in Crakow.[6] Late in 1548, moreover, Calvin began his correspondence with the Polish-born reformer, Jan Laski. By that time, Laski was an established humanist-reformer, some ten years Calvin's senior, who had spent a decade working for church reform in Poland and some six years forging the foundation of a Reformed communion in Emden. Laski, then in England, addressed a letter to Calvin from Windsor, hoping for the progress of the church of Christ, and commending himself to Calvin's prayers.[7] From this point on, Calvin engaged in a fairly extensive correspondence with four categories of individuals, all having an interest in the Polish Reformation: the Polish nobility, Reformist churchmen in Poland, Polish reformers in other lands, and non-Polish-born reformers involved in various ways with the reform of the church in Poland.

For convenience, I will distinguish primarily between letters to the nobility and letters to Reformers and offer two groupings of the latter, namely from 1548 to 1556 and from 1556 to 1563. The periodization of the letters to Reformers identifies an initial period of engagement about Poland prior to Laski's return to his homeland in 1556. Calvin's initial set of letters to reformers and churchmen tend to raise theological issues in brief. The greater substantive portions of the letters are devoted to relations between the reformers, specifically to introductions, recommendations, plans for cooperative efforts and colloquies and words of advice and counsel in the work of reform. After 1556 there is a shift in emphasis – first, because of the new role played by Laski in the Polish Reformation and, eventually, because of the rise of anti-trinitarian theology in Poland.

Calvin, Laski, and the Scope of Reformation, 1548–56

Calvin's correspondence concerning the Polish Reformation does not consist only of letters to Polish reformers: there are numerous references to reformers in or from Poland, namely Francesco Lismanino, Jan Laski and Johannes Utenhoven,

---

5. Calvin to Farel (28 March 1541), in *CO*, vol. 11, col. 178 (*Selected Works*, vol. 4, p. 243).

6. Williston Walker, *John Calvin: The Organizer of Reformed Protestantism, 1509–1564* (1906; repr., New York: Schocken Books, 1969), p. 394.

7. Laski to Calvin, 14 December 1548, in *Joannis a Lasco Opera tam edita quam inedita* (ed. Abraham Kuyper; 2 vols; Amsterdam: F. Muller; Den Haag: M. Nijhoff, 1866), vol. 2, p. 620.

that can be found throughout Calvin's correspondence with others, most notably the reformers of Zürich. As a group, these letters demonstrate the international breadth and the extensive cooperation within the reform movement. As noted above, Laski first wrote to Calvin in December of 1548.[8] There is a second letter from April of 1551.[9] A survey of Calvin's broader correspondence reveals, among others, a letter of November 1550 to Farel[10] that mentions Utenhoven's and Laski's work in London, and a letter of January 1551 to Viret that sends greetings from Laski to Viret.[11] Nor was Calvin Laski's sole major correspondent among the Reformers – there is extant a letter to Melanchthon from as early as 1543 and another from 1548[12] – and some eighteen letters to Bullinger and Hardenburg from 1544 through 1548, all prior to the initial contact with Calvin.[13] The scope of this broader correspondence places the work of Polish reformers in the centre of the larger European reform movement. In September 1552, Calvin wrote to the French congregation in London, exhorting them to harmony and indicating that he has heard from Laski, then a minister in that congregation, concerning their troubles.[14]

On 28 March 1554, Calvin wrote to Bullinger, commenting on the fate of Protestants exiled from England on the death of Edward VI, complaining about Castellio's book against the repression of heresy and indicating the difficulties that Laski had experienced in Denmark.[15] The same issue is raised in a letter of 24 May to Farel: Calvin laments the treatment of Laski at the hands of the Lutherans.[16] At about that time, Calvin also wrote to Laski, responding to Laski's letter of 13 March and voicing sympathy for the enormous difficulties that Laski and his congregation had experienced – both at the hands of Queen Mary of England, who had first dispersed the congregation and then had allowed Laski and his flock to leave England, and at the hands of Danish and, subsequently, German Lutherans, who had refused the congregation sanctuary and forced them to sail away, in incredibly difficult weather, from sanctuary first from Elsinore and then

---

8. Laski to Calvin, 3 December 1548, in *CO*, vol. 13, col. 111.

9. Laski to Calvin, 24 April 1551, in *Opera*, ed. Kuyper, vol. 2, p. 650; also in *CO*, vol. 14, cols 107–8.

10. Calvin to Farel, 10 November 1550, in *CO*, vol. 13, cols 654–9 (*Selected Works*, vol. 5, pp. 282–5).

11. Calvin to Viret, 24 January 1551, in *CO*, vol. 14, cols 27–8 (*Selected Works*, vol. 5, pp. 298–9).

12. In *Opera*, ed. Kuyper, vol. 2, #14, 49.

13. In *Opera*, ed. Kuyper, vol. 2, #14, 16, 19, 21, 23, 25, 28, 29, 30, 37, 39, 40, 41, 43, 44, 45, 47, 48.

14. Calvin to the French Congregation in London, 27 September 1552, in *Selected Works*, vol. 5, pp. 360–3.

15. Calvin to Bullinger, 28 March 1554, in *CO*, vol. 15, col. 95 (*Selected Works*, vol. 6, pp. 32–3).

16. Calvin to Farel, 25 May 1554, in *CO*, vol. 15, col. 141 (*Selected Works*, vol. 6, p. 39).

from Lübeck, Hamburg and Rostock. The congregation finally reached safety in Friesland and Laski eventually went on to Frankfurt.[17]

Writing to Vermigli in January 1555, Calvin indicates that he has received a letter from Laski and expresses some annoyance over differences with Laski over 'the gratuitous predestination of God' and over the doctrine of the Lord's Supper.[18] The comments on predestination are so brief as to allow no interpretation. The argument over the Lord's Supper, however, is more specific, involving the question of how Christ's body offers spiritual nourishment in the sacrament: Laski, in Calvin's view, teaches a doctrine amenable to his own and to that of Vermigli, given Laski's resistance to 'any fiction of a substance, or transfusion, or commingling of parts' – yet Laski is, in Calvin's view, too fond of his own terminology to stand in clear, overt agreement with the Genevan and Strasbourg definitions.[19] By the time of this interchange, Laski had written a major treatise on the sacraments and two catechisms, one for the exiled congregation in London and one for the church in Emden – and he had established his own emphasis on the sacrament as the communion of the body and blood of Christ. In his terms, believers participate in the body of Christ, becoming flesh of His flesh and bone of His bone, He the head, they the members – the linguistic stress is on 'communion' and 'participation'.[20]

A letter of Laski to Calvin, probably from September 1555, writes of

disturbances ... in the French Church [of Frankfurt am Main] from some aversion conceived, I know not why, against Valeran Poulain, for things distinct from his personal merits. For though I confess that many things are to be desired in him which he does not possess, just as in all of us, for we are all men yet, more than his personal character, namely, the fidelity of his ministry and his good name were attacked, and that not without danger to the whole church.[21]

In the same letter, Laski also writes:

In respect to the vicissitudes of my life, these indeed are not so vexatious as to prevent me from reaping great consolation from them, especially when I see that

---

17. Calvin to Laski, May 1554, in *CO*, vol. 15, col. 142 (*Selected Works*, vol. 6, pp. 40–3).

18. It is hard to believe that this is a reference to Laski's letter of 18 December 1555 (in *Opera*, ed. Kuyper, vol. 2, pp. 714–16), given that it raises neither of these issues: however, Laski to Calvin, 24 April 1551, in *Opera*, ed. Kuyper, vol. 2, p. 650 (*CO*, vol. 14, cols 107–8) does raise the eucharistic issue in precisely this way, and the more proximate letter of Laski to Calvin, 13 March 1554 (*CO*, vol. 15, cols 81–4) approaches the eucharistic debate by way of reference to Westphal's polemics against the Reformed.

19. Calvin to Vermigli (18 January 1555), in *CO*, vol. 15, col. 388 (*Selected Works*, vol. 6, p. 124).

20. Cf. Laski, *Catechismus ecclesiae Emdanae*, Q. & R. 67, in *Opera*, ed. Kuyper, vol. 2, p. 530, with idem, *Catechismus ecclesiae Londini*, Q. 240, in ibid., vol. 2, p. 468.

21. Laski to Calvin, 19 September 1555, in *CO*, vol. 15, cols 772–4 (Mincer #80).

by the divine blessing they have not been unfruitful. The inconveniences of my
health I reckon among my advantages, even should the flesh protest, as indeed I
see that I am not far from the haven after which we all sigh.[22]

This letter was followed fairly closely by two more from Laski to Calvin discussing
the internal difficulties of the church in Frankfurt.[23]

It is also at this juncture – late December 1555 – that Calvin's major
correspondence with various Polish dignitaries and reformers began, with the aid
of Francesco Lismanino: an initial grouping of some nine letters, sent together
with missives to Polish leaders by Vermigli, Musculus, Bullinger, Sturm, Zanchi
and Farel, most of them placed together in a packet to be carried to Poland by
Lismanino on his return.[24]

In April or May of 1556 Calvin wrote to Laski to discuss the latter's efforts to
draw together a conference with the Lutherans to be held at Spires. Given that
Laski had not written to Calvin concerning the actual plans, Calvin worries that
there was, perhaps, nothing to report! The situation, Calvin continues, is not
promising, inasmuch as the German princes tend to listen to the opponents of
Calvin and Laski and inasmuch as the opponents, in Calvin's view, are perverse and
unreasonable. Calvin also voiced his distrust of the reformist Catholic, Vergerio.[25]
Laski's own work at the time is clear from his letters – one of 6 May to the elector of
the Palatinate making reference to the importance of bringing an end to doctrinal
controversy in the church,[26] and one of 12 May to the senate of the city of Frankfurt,
protesting that it is not Laski and the Reformed, but the Lutheran clergy of the area
who are out of accord with the Augsburg Confession – which, in the 1540 version
(the *Variata*), as cited in Laski's letter, indicates that 'with the bread and wine the
body and blood of Christ are truly exhibited' in the Lord's Supper.[27]

Further developments are recorded in a letter from Laski to Calvin from early
April 1556, in which Laski notes further debate with the Lutherans and plans for
a colloquy,[28] and in Calvin's correspondence with Bullinger from later in the same
month. To Bullinger, Calvin writes with thanks for Bullinger's refutation of the
Lutheran, Westphal, and with less hopefulness of Laski's efforts to bring together

---

22. Laski to Calvin, 19 September 1555, in *CO*, vol. 15, cols 772–4 (Mincer #80).

23. Laski to Calvin, 14 October 1555, in *CO*, vol. 15, cols 818–20 (Mincer #81); and
Laski to Calvin, 18 December 1555, in *CO*, vol. 15, cols 890–2 and *Opera*, ed. Kuyper, vol. 2,
pp. 714–16 (Mincer #82).

24. Cf. Doumergue, *Jean Calvin*, vol. 7, pp. 486–7.

25. Calvin to Laski, April/May 1556, in *Selected Works*, vol. 6, pp. 265–7 (*CO*, vol. 16,
cols 170–2; Mincer #45).

26. Laski to the Elector of the Palatinate, 2 May 1556, in *Opera*, ed. Kuyper, vol. 2,
pp. 716–19.

27. Laski to the Senate of Frankfurt, 12 May 1556, in *Opera*, ed. Kuyper, vol. 2,
pp. 719–20.

28. Laski to Calvin, 2 April 1556, in *CO*, vol. 16, cols 92–5 (Mincer #90).

a colloquy with the Lutherans – and, as he had done in the slightly earlier letter to Laski, voices concern to Bullinger over the role of the converted Roman Catholic priest, Vergerio.[29]

In May, Laski went to Stuttgart and, initially by correspondence, subsequently by personal colloquy, attempted to generate a Protestant accord on the Lord's Supper with the Lutheran Reformer of Wurttemberg, Johannes Brenz, using the Augsburg Confession and the Colloquy of Regensburg as his primary points of reference.[30] Vergerio, whose potential role had troubled Calvin and Bullinger, played no role in the conference – the failure to reach an agreement appears to rest solely on Brenz's intransigent insistence on the ubiquity of the resurrected body of Christ and his refusal to allow any legitimacy to Laski's subscription to the Augsburg Confession.

In June 1556, writing to the church in Frankfurt, Calvin mentions Laski as respected for his doctrine and to be trusted in his adverse judgement on the doctrine of a dissident in Frankfurt, one Gisberg or Gueldrois, from Gelderland.[31] Still, Calvin was not entirely pleased with Laski's efforts in Germany – still, perhaps, worried over Laski's teaching on the Lord's supper as noted a year earlier to Vermigli,[32] and most certainly, as Calvin reported to Bullinger in July 1556, troubled by mixed reports of the debate between Laski and Brenz.[33] Again, one has a sensibility of an international cooperative effort, linked by correspondence between multiple authors: a letter from Vermigli had informed Calvin of Laski's debate with Brenz – and Calvin laments not having received a report directly from Laski.

Calvin and the Polish-Lithuanian Nobility

Calvin's major contacts with the political powers in Poland – the king, Sigismund August, and various members of the Polish-Lithuanian nobility – occurred *via* two distinct genres of letter: the dedicatory epistle and a more general correspondence. Calvin's dedicatory epistles, like those of his contemporaries, tend to be lengthy and filled with significant reflections often based on, but also looking well beyond, the scope and content of the volume itself. In his efforts to engage the leaders of

29. Calvin to Bullinger, 22 April 1556, in *CO*, vol. 16, cols 116–17 (*Selected Works*, vol. 6, pp. 268–9).

30. Laski to Brenz, 23 May 1556; Laski to Brenz, 25 May 1556; and Laski's report of the colloquies, n.d. (May 1556), in *Opera*, ed. Kuyper, vol. 2, pp. 720–3, 723–4, 724–30. The letters are sent from Stuttgart, where Laski had gone to confer with Brenz; Kuyper notes, but does not reproduce, a response from Brenz, dated 24 May to Laski's initial letter.

31. Calvin to the French Congregation in Frankfurt, 24 June 1556, in *CO*, vol. 16, col. 211 (*Selected Works*, vol. 6, p. 276).

32. See notes 18 and 19.

33. Calvin to Bullinger, 1 July 1556, in *CO*, vol. 16, col. 219 (*Selected Works*, vol. 6, pp. 284–6).

Poland-Lithuania, in addition to some fifty letters to various nobles, reformers and church bodies in Poland, Calvin wrote two substantial dedicatory epistles, each affixed to a major work – the letter to Sigismund August, King of Poland, affixed to Calvin's *Commentary on the Epistle of Paul to the Hebrews* (1549) and the letter to Nicholas Radziwil, high chancellor of Lithuania, prefaced to the *Commentary upon the Acts of the Apostles* (1560).

Calvin's overt connection with Poland began in 1549 when he dedicated his *Commentary on Hebrews* to King Sigismund August, 'by the grace of God, the king of Poland, grand duke of Lithuania, Russia, Prussia, and lord and heir of Muscovy'.[34] Sigismund August had, in 1548, succeeded his father, Sigismund I, to the throne – and Calvin took his accession as an opportunity to influence the reform of religion. Precisely what generated the letter is unclear – Calvin may have had word of the reformist influence of Francesco Lismanino, confessor to the Queen of Poland and a religious confidant of the king. Lismanino had gone to Poland as confessor to the Italian-born queen[35] and had, early on, been attracted to the theology of Calvin's *Institutes* – he is even said to have read from it, weekly, to King Sigismund August.[36]

In his dedicatory letter dated 23 May 1549, Calvin offers clear recognition of the importance of Poland both to the safety of Europe and to the reform of the church. He begins with the rhetorically and politically requisite acknowledgement of his relative station: all too often, he comments, inferior persons dedicate trifling works to rulers in order to gain a 'borrowed splendor' – he notes that he is 'an unknown and obscure man' in comparison to the king. It is the fame of Sigismund August's piety, Calvin continues, that leads him to offer a gift that 'piety will not permit [the king] to reject'.[37] Calvin drew a connection between the subject of the epistle, Christ's eternal priesthood, and the religious duties of the king, who is 'already engaged in the work of restoring the kingdom of Christ', both in his own rule and in the work of many of his servants and subjects. Such a king certainly also desires that 'the Son of God should reign alone and be glorified'.[38]

---

34. Cf. Oscar Bartel, 'Calvin und Polen', *Revue d'histoire et de philosophie religieuses* 45 (1965), pp. 93–108.

35. I.e., Bona Sforza, wife of Sigismund I, Queen Mother in the reign of Sigismund August.

36. Doumergue, *Jean Calvin*, vol. 7, p. 482; cf. the account in Wulfert De Greef, *The Writings of John Calvin: An Introductory Guide* (trans. Lyle D. Bierma; Grand Rapids: Baker, 1993), pp. 212–14.

37. John Calvin, *Commentaries on Hebrews*, Epistle Dedicatory, in *CTS Hebrews*, p. xix (*CO*, vol. 13, col. 281). I have cited Calvin's commentaries from *Commentaries of John Calvin* (46 vols; Edinburgh: Calvin Translation Society, 1844–55; repr. Grand Rapids: Baker Book House, 1979). The set is abbreviated as *CTS*, followed by the biblical book, and, when applicable, the volume number of the commentary on that particular book.

38. Calvin, *Commentaries on Hebrews*, Epistle Dedicatory, in *CTS Hebrews*, p. xx (*CO*, vol. 13, col. 282).

The king's father, he noted, had once received the dedication of Johann Eck's treatise on the mass – Sigismund August, Calvin hopes, will see the contradiction between Eck's views on the sacrifice of the mass and the biblical teaching concerning Christ's sacrifice once, for all time; this truth, Calvin continues, should inspire the king to promote the Reformation in Poland. Much of the remainder of Calvin's letter is devoted to an attack on Johann Eck and on Eck's theology as emblematic of the problems and abuses of the Roman Church. Calvin reflects briefly on the rejection, by Sigismund August's father, of the baneful influence that Eck hoped to have on religion in Poland: the Polish crown had refused to engage in religious persecution. (The elder Sigismund had refused to follow the example, cited by Eck, of Henry VIII of England, and had reportedly responded that, whereas King Henry set himself against Luther, he, Sigismund would be the king 'both of the sheep and of the goats'.[39]) Calvin proposes that Sigismund August go beyond the policy of his father and become a monarch like Hezekiah or Josiah, engaged actively in the reform of religion – inspired, he hopes, by the message of the Epistle to the Hebrews concerning the divinity, governance and sole priesthood of Christ. The connection between Calvin's interpretation of Hebrews and reform is made specifically in the epistle's identification of Christ as priest eternally and once for all time – a point explicitly contrary to Eck's work on the sacrifice of the mass, where Christ's sacrifice is said to be renewed daily.[40] What is more, Calvin here expresses in a more contextual and applied form the basic political theory that he was developing in the *Institutes* – the Christian prince opposes persecution and supports the free exercise of true religion.

Although he had also begun a correspondence with Laski (then in London) that continued throughout the years 1550 through 1554, and although he was quite aware of the religious situation in Poland, Calvin did not immediately follow up his initial letter to King Sigismund August. In March 1552, Calvin had heard in a letter from Ambrosius Moibanus of the positive reception of his writings in Hungary and Poland.[41] He also knew, sometime after the fact, of a Diet held at Petricov in 1551, writing to Farel in January of 1554 that 'various barons in Poland, having set aside papism, have embraced the Reform: the king is not ignorant of this, but he does not prevent it'.[42] The timing of Calvin's second letter is significant: it coincides with the beginnings of Calvin's relationship with Francesco Lismanino. In 1553, Lismanino was able to travel to Geneva to meet Calvin. There he renounced his vows to the priesthood and married. He also, presumably, informed Calvin in some detail of the progress of the Polish Reformation.

---

39. Cited in Fernand de Schickler, 'La Congrégation évangélique de Cracovie', in *Bulletin de la Société de l'Historie du Protestantisme Français* (15 December 1880), pp. 529–46 (532).

40. Calvin, *Commentaries on Hebrews*, Epistle Dedicatory, in *CTS Hebrews*, pp. xxii–xxiv (*CO*, vol. 13, cols 283, 285).

41. Ambrosius Moibanus to Calvin, 24 March 1552, in *CO*, vol. 14, p. 307.

42. Calvin to Farel, 20 January 1554, in *CO*, vol. 15, col. 13, n. 7; cf. Doumergue, *Jean Calvin*, vol. 7, p. 483.

Late in 1554, Lismanino appears to have encouraged Calvin to write to Sigismund August – this is, at least, a reasonable hypothesis given Calvin's comments, at the beginning of the letter, that he had been 'encouraged' to write by a 'revered brother' loyal to the king and 'perfectly acquainted with [the king's] views' – a description that fits well with Lismanino.[43] The timing of the letter to Sigismund August also agrees with Calvin's solidification of his position in Geneva after the Bolsec Controversy and in the final phases of his conflict with the Perrinists. Calvin's letter is lengthy and, whereas the first letter to Sigismund August can be viewed as a position-paper calling the king to assume the reformist role of a sixteenth-century Hezekiah, this second letter is virtually a treatise on the abuse of religion by the papacy, the consequent papal forfeiture of any right to ecclesial headship, the absence of any Petrine succession in the church and the religious duties of the monarch in such a situation.[44]

Calvin's sense of the importance of the moment and the probability of the identity of the 'revered brother' loyal to the king and to the cause of reform are also indicated by the letters that he sent, shortly after his writing to Sigismund August – both dated 26 December, one to Johann Wolf, the other to Heinrich Bullinger, in Zürich. The letters indicate that Lismanino had gone to Zürich seeking advice there as well as in Geneva concerning the reform in Poland. Calvin commends him to Wolf and Bullinger, indicating the importance of his work.[45] Calvin also notes that he has received a letter from Jan Laski indicating that another colleague was about to return to Poland with messages to the king and the nobles, and he comments that Lismanino was the bearer of a copy of the preface of Calvin's most recent refutation of the Lutheran, Westphal.[46] These latter pieces of information indicate, albeit obliquely, Calvin's recognition that the Polish reformers had an interest in his refutations of various Lutherans and that he was probably aware of the difficulties being caused for the Reformation in Poland by continuing tensions between the Reformed and the stricter Lutherans – Westphal, Andreae and Brenz – over the Lord's supper. These letters, taken as a group, indicate that Calvin's letters to the Polish nobility were part of a larger effort of several Protestant leaders to influence the political powers in Poland to adopt a broadly Reformed Protestantism, not, indeed, to adopt a specifically Calvinian approach.

43. Calvin to Sigismund August, 5 December 1554, in *CO*, vol. 15, col. 329, cf. n. 2, where the editors concur that the 'reverend brother' must be Lismanino (*Selected Works*, vol. 6, p. 99).

44. Calvin to Sigismund August, 5 December 1554, in *CO*, vol. 15, cols 329–35 (*Selected Works*, vol. 6, pp. 101–9).

45. Calvin to Wolf, 26 December 1554; and Calvin to Bullinger, 26 December 1554, in *CO*, vol. 15, cols 357, 358 (*Selected Works*, vol. 6, pp. 109–10, 110–12).

46. Calvin to Bullinger, 26 December 1554, in *Selected Works*, vol. 6, pp. 110–11, referring probably to the letter, Laski to Calvin, 13 March 1554, sent from Emden, in *CO*, vol. 15, cols 81–4 (not in Laski, *Opera*, ed. Kuyper).

In the context of these plans and interactions, Calvin indicates to Sigismund August that his appeal is humble, even though he presumes to offer advice to a king. Calvin's approach is based on the assumption that the king is a servant of Christ who recognizes the need of all such servants, from the highest to the lowest, to submit willingly – not to Calvin! – but to the 'heavenly teaching' of Christ. David himself taught that earthly rulers ought to 'kiss the Prince and chief of all kingdoms' and to 'listen to him speaking by the mouth of those whom he has appointed to teach'.[47]

Given his sense of Sigismund August's approach to religion, Calvin states that he will not dwell on all of the 'clouds of ignorance', the 'abuses and corruptions' and the 'foul errors' in which 'nearly the whole world is immersed'. His intention is not to engage the king in a 'superfluous discussion' of things already known. The first and foremost royal duty, given the beginnings of reform in Poland, is the use of royal power to recall the Polish people to obedience to Christ and away from 'popery'. This would make the king a partner in the great battle of the ages, fought against Satan for 'the glory of God in the kingdom of Christ, for the purity of religious worship', indeed, 'for the salvation of the human race'.[48] The universal extent of the problem is matched, Calvin adds, by the international scope of the enemy: this is no mere domestic problem for Poland – nor should the king be induced to hesitate in his work, abashed by those enemies who claim to be 'the high priests of religion' and 'the keepers of holy things'. It is the usual tactic of 'the papists', Calvin argues, to press the issue of the hierarchy of church. These claims are false – and they rest on two false premises: first that, because supremacy was given to the Apostle Peter, 'the whole Papal priesthood descends even to the present times in uninterrupted succession from the Apostles themselves'; and second that, therefore, 'the right and authority of spiritual government belongs to them exclusively'.[49]

Calvin next devotes space to refuting these two premises – noting that he has argued the problem of papal supremacy at greater length elsewhere. Here he notes rhetorically how strange it is that the Apostle Paul taught that there was one God, one faith, one spirit, one Lord and one body of the church and then omitted what some claim is the greatest proof of such unity (Eph. 4.5), namely that there is a 'single sovereign pontiff' who preserves the unity of the church! One ought not to presume that the Apostle was so forgetful. And, of course, Paul explains himself in another text, Galatians 2.7 – he indicates that he had the 'same apostleship among the Gentiles' as had been 'given to Peter among the Jews'. The text not only indicates

47. Calvin to Sigismund August, 5 December 1554, in *CO*, vol. 15, col. 330 (*Selected Works*, vol. 6, p. 100).

48. Calvin to Sigismund August, 5 December 1554, in *CO*, vol. 15, cols 330–1 (*Selected Works*, vol. 6, pp. 100–1).

49. Calvin to Sigismund August, 5 December 1554, in *CO*, vol. 15, col. 331 (*Selected Works*, vol. 6, p. 102).

'equality between the two' but also a division of labour, with the result that it is the apostleship of Paul that applies to Christians, not that of Peter![50]

This argument brings Calvin to the major topical link between his first letter to the king and this second one: the references to the Epistle to the Hebrews and Christ's eternal priesthood – this time, however, interpreted not in its limited sense as a refutation of the Roman mass, but in a broader sense as excluding all other claims to headship; if Christ is the sole high priest forever, Calvin argues, there can be no earthly high priest – if such dignity belongs to Christ alone, it cannot belong to the pope or to the bishops.[51] Calvin does not, however, extend his argument to the annihilation of episcopacy. He counsels the king that it is certainly proper for a single 'archbishop' to have 'a certain preeminence in the illustrious kingdom of Poland', not for the sake of establishing his sole lordship, but for the sake of assuming synodical or conciliar leadership and thereby maintaining order and unity in the Polish church.[52] The point reveals a Calvin who recognized the necessity of varying church polity from country to country at the same time that he assumed a necessary and positive connection between the secular and the spiritual governance of a realm. He did not expect Poland to adopt a polity like that of Geneva, nor did he connect a particular pattern of church governance with reform. It may also evidence a connection between Calvin's thought and late medieval conciliar theory.

These potentially positive statements about the Polish episcopacy lead back to polemics. Calvin draws together the two lines of argument – Christ's sole headship and the limited function of bishops – to argue that the papacy has, by misconduct, superstition, false doctrine and pride, abdicated any claim to supremacy and, more than that, sacrificed any influence to the good. Calvin clearly knows that Sigismund August had intended to attempt reform with the aid of Rome. This, Calvin contends, is an illusion: 'your majesty is greatly deceived', he writes, if 'you wait until the authority of that sect [namely, the papacy] intervenes' in the cause of reform. In Calvin's view, Rome oppresses the church and breeds confusion – and it is the duty of 'the pious and Christian prince' to intervene and restore order.[53] What Calvin pleads for, in his conclusion, is a limited reform of the church instituted by the king in his assembly of nobles, to be accomplished in two stages – an initial appointing of godly teachers and pastors to present the truth of the gospel without entirely setting aside the order of the church, followed by a new ordinance for ordaining a reformed clergy under the supervision of the monarch and the diet of

50. Calvin to Sigismund August, 5 December 1554, in *CO*, vol. 15, cols 331–2 (*Selected Works*, vol. 6, pp. 102–3).

51. Calvin to Sigismund August, 5 December 1554, in *CO*, vol. 15, col. 332 (*Selected Works*, vol. 6, pp. 103–4).

52. Calvin to Sigismund August, 5 December 1554, in *CO*, vol. 15, col. 333 (*Selected Works*, vol. 6, p. 104).

53. Calvin to Sigismund August, 5 December 1554, in *CO*, vol. 15, col. 333 (*Selected Works*, vol. 6, p. 105).

the realm.[54] As in Calvin's letters of support and advice to Polish reformers, there is no rigid pattern identified as correct or necessary and there is a willingness to support the reform of the Polish church while allowing for a fairly broad range of confessional, doctrinal and political models. Calvin does not pretend to overrule the Polish reformers themselves. (This attitude would shift, of course, as tensions arose in Poland between trinitarian and anti-trinitarian Protestantism.)

Calvin's letter of December 1554 to Sigismund August was, as the letter itself and other correspondence of the time well indicate, the opening salvo of a major effort to influence reform in Poland. It was, in fact, a theological-political tractate designed to set a tone and undergird an agenda for church reform – and it was followed by a series of letters to various Polish dignitaries and churchmen. We have, moreover, a clear sense of their identity given that, towards the end of 1555, after Lismanino had returned to Poland, he reinforced his request by sending Calvin the names of various Polish nobles with whom Calvin might correspond in the interest of church reform. The king is first on the list, followed by the name of 'the most illustrious' Nicholas Radziwil, 'the illustrious count palatine of Sendomir' (Spytka Jordana), and 'the illustrious' Jan, 'count Tarnowski, governor of Crakow'.[55] With this incentive began an extensive Polish correspondence, with letters to Radziwil, Jordana, Tarnowski, Jan Laski and more than half a dozen other Polish notables and reformers.

Calvin would write to Radziwil on four separate occasions: in three letters dated between 1555 and 1558,[56] and in the dedicatory epistle of his commentary on Acts, dated 1560.[57] Calvin was aware not only of his political importance in Poland-Lithuania but also of Radziwil's promotion of Reformation, his call, as of 1553, for evangelical preachers to come to Poland and perhaps of his ultimately successful effort to have the Bible translated into Polish (1563). The first of these letters, written on 13 February 1555,[58] encourages Radziwil to continue his efforts and bring the Reformation in Poland-Lithuania to completion. Only a few days earlier Calvin had strongly recommended Lismanino in a letter to Bullinger. There, Calvin had also noted his last letter to Sigismund August, commenting that he had been quite circumspect and had only written to the king in answer to the king's own questions – Lismanino, he added, had a copy and could show it to Bullinger if Bullinger so desired.[59] Shortly afterward Calvin wrote again to

---

54. Calvin to Sigismund August, 5 December 1554, in *CO*, vol. 15, cols 335–6 (*Selected Works*, vol. 6, pp. 108–9).

55. Lismanino to Calvin, 15 November 1555, in *CO*, vol. 15, cols 868–71.

56. Calvin to Nicholas Radziwil, in *CO*, vol. 15, cols 428–9 (13 February 1555), 906–8 (December 1555); vol. 17, cols 181–2 (24 May 1558).

57. Calvin, *Commentary upon the Acts*, Epistle Dedicatory, in *CTS Acts*, vol. 1, pp. xv–xxiv (*CO*, vol. 18, cols 155–61).

58. Calvin to Nicholas Radziwil (13 February 1555), in *Selected Works*, vol. 6, pp. 133–5 (*CO*, vol. 15, cols 428–9; Mincer #36).

59. Calvin to Bullinger, 9 February 1555, in *CO*, vol. 15, col. 425 (*Selected Works*, vol. 6, pp. 132–3).

Bullinger, commending Lismanino.[60] To Radziwil, Calvin speaks rather vaguely of his hopes for church reform and his continuing deep concern for Poland: the letter is primarily an exhortation, recognizing the great difficulty of the reform, noting without specification the 'obstacles of Satan' – in short, there is little political or theological content.[61]

Certainly to the dismay of Calvin and, indeed, of Laski, Sigismund August had not rejected the papacy and differed with various Polish nobles, including Radziwil, concerning the course of church reform.[62] These concerns are apparent in December 1555, when Calvin again wrote to the King of Poland, pressing him to expedite the Reformation and, again, comparing Sigismund August to David, Hezekiah and Josiah.[63] Presumably Calvin had taken the news of the Diet of Petricov (28 July 1555) as an incentive for his communication with Sigismund August. Calvin had heard, by way of his colleague Viret, that the Diet had called for a general council of the church in Poland, with the king presiding; that at the council the Bible should be the standard by which issues of religion ought to be decided; that the names of Laski, Melanchthon, Calvin and Beza had been favourably noted as potential advisors; and that the Diet hoped for a new confession of faith, worship in the vernacular, communion in both kinds, the marriage of clergy and the repudiation of various church abuses.[64]

Calvin's letter to Sigismund August reflects his concerns over the king's hesitation. Where, with Radziwil, Calvin had spoken more or less gently, particularly with reference to Radziwil's own role in reform and even with regard to the problems faced by Poland, he becomes quite pointed and polemical with the king, even impatient. He calls on Sigismund August to cast off the 'darkness' and 'corruptions of Popery', and a 'polluted and perverted worship of God' that has 'gone astray after human devices'.[65] He speaks of a 'dawn' of 'true religion' and warns the king not to be slothful in view of the duty set by God on monarchs in the cause of true religion. The king knows too well of the importance of the maintenance of true religion for Calvin to need to remind him! The example of David, all by itself, renders 'sluggishness … altogether inexcusable'. David, Calvin reminds Sigismund August, strove to rebuild the temple, even after he had learned that this task would

60. Calvin to Bullinger, 24 February 1555, in *CO*, vol. 15, col. 450 (*Selected Works*, vol. 6, pp. 151–2).

61. Calvin to Nicholas Radziwil (13 February 1555), in *CO*, vol. 15, cols 428–9 (*Selected Works*, vol. 6, pp. 133–5).

62. Laski to Calvin, 19 September 1555, in *CO*, vol. 15, col. 773; cf. *Selected Works*, vol. 6, p. 244, n. 1.

63. Calvin to Sigismund August, King of Poland, 24 December 1555, in *CO*, vol. 15, cols 892–4 (*Selected Works*, vol. 6, pp. 244–7).

64. Viret to Calvin, in *CO*, vol. 15, col. 700; cf. Doumergue, *Jean Calvin*, vol. 7, pp. 483–4.

65. Calvin to Sigismund August, 24 December 1555, in *CO*, vol. 15, cols 893–4 (*Selected Works*, vol. 6, p. 245).

only be completed by his son, Solomon. 'Wherefore', Calvin continues, 'it becomes a Christian king so much more courageously to bring together all his means for the reconstruction of God's temple, and strive with all his might, that the worship of God lie no longer defaced and unseemly ruins'. In Calvin's view, Sigismund August has no excuse – for his nobility are far less troublesome than the ancient Jewish people were to David, Hezekiah and Josiah. Indeed, says Calvin, perhaps reflecting on his contacts with Radziwil, certainly reflecting the concerns voiced by Laski, the 'Polish nobility shows a prompt and cheerful disposition to embrace the faith of Christ'. The 'wise prince' ought to rouse himself and 'put his hand' to work – indeed, Calvin concludes, 'if the opportunity offered by God is neglected, you may afterwards stand in vain before a door that is closed'.[66]

If Sigismund August was, afterwards, less than pleased with Calvin, one need look no further than the tone of this letter. Yet Calvin, from his perspective, certainly felt he was doing no less than expressing the meaning of Scripture and exercising his office. Given this, it is of interest that, at the time that Calvin wrote this letter, he was deeply immersed in the study of the Psalter: he had begun expounding the Psalms in 1552 and would produce the first edition of his commentary in 1557.[67] What is more, his appeal to David, so prominent in the letter, reflects his interpretation of the Psalms in a highly literal, historical manner – the interpretative patterns of the commentary, in other words, are reflected in his advice to Sigismund August.

There is also a letter of December 1555 addressed to Count Tarnowski, who was fourth among the nobles on Lismanino's list.[68] The letter introduces Calvin to Tarnowski and attempts to convince him to go beyond the mere removal of abuses in the church to full Reformation by supporting those who are already at work reviving the gospel in Poland. The tone is vastly different from that of the somewhat angry letter to the king. Calvin approaches Tarnowski as one who might become energized to sponsor reform. He implores Tarnowski to be a strong supporter of the cause. God has opened a door, Calvin comments, and the gospel calls out to the king and all the nobles to respond.[69] The metaphor is significant, inasmuch as Calvin had, earlier in the month, warned Sigismund August that the door might close if he did not act.

On the same day in November 1558 that he wrote to Bullinger of his concerns for Poland and of a request from Jan Utenhoven that he become more involved in the Polish Reformation, Calvin also wrote again to Tarnowski – this letter

---

66. Calvin to Sigismund August, 24 December 1555, in *CO*, vol. 15, col. 894 (*Selected Works*, vol. 6, p. 246).

67. Cf. the details of his work in De Greef, *Writings of Calvin*, p. 105.

68. Calvin to Count Tarnowski, 29 December 1555, in *CO*, vol. 15, cols 908–10 (*Selected Works*, vol. 7, pp. 423–7); also, Calvin to Count Tarnowski, 15 November 1559, in *CO*, vol. 17, cols 673–6; and Calvin to Count Tarnowski, 5 June 1560, in *CO*, vol. 18, cols 102–3.

69. Calvin to Count Tarnowski, 29 December 1555, in *CO*, vol. 15, cols 908–10 (*Selected Works*, vol. 7, pp. 424–5).

was a response to one from Tarnowski,[70] from 1556, two and a half years before. Calvin responds, now, appreciative of Tarnowski's honesty and also with some appreciation of the nobleman's fear of unrest. Calvin, however, presses the point of the need for reform above all else with citations from Xenophon and Psalm 46: Xenophon indicates the great civic importance of religion – the psalm teaches of the power of God as our 'refuge and strength' in times of trouble. Tarnowski, Calvin insists, ought to rely on God and worry less about human unrest![71] The correspondence continued into 1559 and 1560, with Tarnowski's response and two further letters from Calvin.[72] As was the case with Sigismund August, Tarnowski remained reluctant to broaden the reform or to take sides with a particular party – Calvin both cajoled and accused: on the one hand he could argue that Tarnowski ought to realize that true religion was never a source of discord and that his refusal to abolish false religion on political grounds might be taken as a claim that Tarnowski was wiser than God; on the other hand, he could praise Tarnowski's good intentions and press him on towards further reform. In any case, the appeal was unsuccessful and we have no further response form Tarnowski.

In 1559 Calvin also began a correspondence with various officials and ministers in Poland-Lithuania over the influence there of the anti-trinitarian, Giorgio Blandrata.[73] To one of these clergymen, Jan Lusen, Calvin expressed worries over the heresy and then – quite remarkably – indicated that he refrained from attacking various Polish supporters of the anti-trinitarian Franciscus Stancarus because he was not well acquainted with them and because he felt that, if they were not attacked, they might be brought back into communion more easily.[74] Still, Calvin did engage the issue, writing in the same year his *Answer to the Polish Brethren respecting the manner in which Christ is mediator, in order to refute the error of Stancarus* (1560). He also sought the aid of the Waldensians, exhorting them to be in direct contact with Polish Christians and to support an orthodox Protestantism in Poland against the inroads of Stancarus and Blandrata – although he cautions against sending the Waldensian Confession to the Poles, given the vagueness of its eucharistic language and the possibility of causing theological confusion.

The second edition of Calvin's commentary on Acts, dated 1 August 1560, dedicated to Nicholas Radziwil, demonstrates Calvin's continued awareness of the

---

70. Tarnowski to Calvin, 26 June 1556, in *CO*, vol. 16, cols 214–15 (Mincer #102).

71. Calvin to Tarnowski, 19 November 1558, in *CO*, vol. 17, cols 382–3 (Mincer #47, dated 13 December).

72. Tarnowski to Calvin, 12 May 1559, in *CO*, vol. 17, cols 517–20 (Mincer #103); Calvin to Tarnowski, 15 November 1559, in *CO*, vol. 17, cols 673–6 (Mincer #48); Calvin to Tarnowski, 9 June 1560, in *CO*, vol. 18, cols 102–3 (Mincer #57).

73. Cf. the summary in De Greef, *Writings of Calvin*, pp. 179–81.

74. Calvin to Lusen, 8 June 1560, in *CO*, vol. 18, cols 102–3 (*Selected Works*, vol. 7, pp. 112–14 dated 9 June).

various religious and political forces at work in Poland-Lithuania.[75] Calvin indicates that the purpose of his letter is exhortation to one who had already responded to the 'pure doctrine of the Gospel'. Calvin praises Radziwil for continuing to press for reform against increasing opposition.[76] The alteration of issues between Calvin's last letter to the king and this correspondence with Radziwil is also significant: whereas to the king Calvin has emphasized the international dimensions of the reform and the problem of the papacy, Calvin now indicates that although there are no foreign troubles for Poland, there are major internal problems – false accusations and all manner of deceit are directed against the reformers in Poland. These troubles, moreover, are exacerbated by the presence of the false teachers Franciscus Stancarus and Giorgio Blandrata, both in Calvin's estimation, followers of the 'ungodliness of Servetus'. He worries that Christians in Poland have let these heretical foxes sneak into their churches.[77] There then follows a long diatribe against the 'Antichrist of Rome', the 'Popish synagogue', and the Council of Trent – which the Pope and his supporters are not 'ashamed' to claim is a 'holy, general, and lawful Council', even though, in Calvin's view it hardly represents the true church.[78]

Letters to Reformers and Clergy in Poland, 1556–63

From the time of Laski's return to Poland in 1556 to the year before Calvin's death, there is a correspondence of considerable proportions that documents another dimension of Calvin's relationship to the Reformation in Poland – here he appears as the valued colleague and supporter of the efforts of Laski, Utenhoven and Lismanino, and as an advisor who had himself, in his own context, encountered and debated some of the internal problems of Protestantism that had recently surfaced in Poland, for instance, the anti-trinitarian problem.

The synod that met at Pinczow in early May 1556 hoped to build on the momentum generated by the Diet of Petricov the year before. It sent two synodical letters, one from the gathered ministers and nobles to Calvin, inviting him to come to Poland,[79] and the other from the ministers to the Council in Geneva

---

75. Calvin, *Commentary upon the Acts*, Epistle Dedicatory, in *CTS Acts*, vol. 1, pp. xv–xxiv (*CO*, vol. 18, cols 155–61). N.B., the first edition of the commentary was published in two volumes, 1552–54. The first of these, on Acts 1–13, had been dedicated to Christian III of Denmark, the second, covering Acts 14–28, to the crown prince Frederick of Denmark, who had been made co-regent by his father.

76. Calvin, *Commentary upon the Acts*, Epistle Dedicatory, in *CTS Acts*, vol. 1, p. xvi (*CO*, vol. 18, col. 156).

77. Calvin, *Commentary upon the Acts*, Epistle Dedicatory, in *CTS Acts*, vol. 1, pp. xx–xxi (*CO*, vol. 18, col. 158).

78. Calvin, *Commentary upon the Acts*, Epistle Dedicatory, in *CTS Acts*, vol. 1, pp. xxi–xxiv (*CO*, vol. 18, cols 160–1).

79. *CO*, vol. 16, col. 129.

requesting that Calvin be given leave from his work to spend several months in Poland.[80] Calvin waited until March 1557 to reply. He then wrote a general epistle to the ministers and nobles of Poland, apologizing for his inability to accept their invitation to visit Poland in the cause of reform, noting both his inability to set aside his duties in Geneva and the presence of Jan Laski in Poland. Calvin indicated that he did not doubt that he could work well with Laski and that, indeed, it would be 'a source of great pleasure' to work cooperatively with him – but Laski's skills, he concluded, rendered his presence unnecessary.[81] Laski, at the time was involved in an attempt to gather Polish Protestants into a united church, Doumergue suggests, similar to the Church of England.[82] At about the same time, Calvin wrote to Utenhoven, thanking the latter for his information concerning the state of reform in Poland, commenting on the abilities of Laski and then offering a series of remarks that also serve to define and clarify Calvin's reluctance to intervene, at that time, in more than very limited and specific ways in the Polish Reformation. Calvin expresses, among other things, a worry that he stands in disfavour with Sigismund August, and a conviction that his energy is best used in correspondence with Radziwil.[83]

On 19 February 1557, Utenhoven wrote to Calvin from Crakow about his and Laski's efforts in Poland – he noted in particular that the king had not yielded to complaints of the papal nuncio and others antagonistic to the reformers. Laski had been favourably received.[84] Laski himself added a few lines to Utenhoven's letter: 'I am at present so overwhelmed with cares and business, my dear Calvin, that I can write nothing. On the one hand the enemies, on the other false brethren assail us, so that we have no rest. But we have many pious men, thanks be to God, who are both an aid and a consolation to us … farewell.'[85] Calvin's response, written in March of 1557, praises both Utenhoven and Laski, expresses relief that an order to exile Lismanino has been lifted and looks towards the progress of reform – but it also expresses worries: Calvin indicates that he refrains from writing another letter to the king, given that he has had no reply to a letter sent from Geneva by way of Lismanino, and that he has the impression that the monarch might hold him in disfavour at the moment. He also notes that, a war having been concluded, the king's interests ought to return to the reform of the church. He nonetheless indicates his intention to support Laski by writing to 'the prince palatine of Vilna',

---

80. *CO*, vol. 16, cols 131–2.

81. Calvin to the Ministers and Nobles of Poland, 8 March 1557, in *CO*, vol. 16, cols 420–1; in *Selected Works*, vol. 6, pp. 317–19, dated 17 March.

82. Doumergue, *Jean Calvin*, vol. 7, pp. 488–9.

83. Calvin to Utenhoven, 1557, in *CO*, vol. 16, cols 672–4 (*Selected Works*, vol. 6, pp. 323–5): the letter is undated and assigned to October 1557 in *CO*, to March 1557 in *Selected Works*.

84. Laski to Calvin, 19 February 1557, in *Opera*, ed. Kuyper, vol. 2, p. 746 (not listed in Mincer).

85. Laski to Utenhoven, 21 February 1557, in *Opera*, ed. Kuyper, vol. 2, pp. 746–8.

namely Radziwil. Calvin had also received reports that various persons in Poland had spoken of strife between him and Laski. This he denies and indicates that he rebutted the claim with the statement, 'The piety of M. Laski is so perfectly known to me, that I am fully convinced he will labor faithfully and strenuously in extending the kingdom of Christ.'[86]

From the same time, March 1557, there is a brief but significant mention of Laski in a letter to Bullinger. Calvin speaks of a projected meeting with Bullinger, noting that he was waiting until then to discuss some of Bullinger's concerns regarding Laski.[87] A letter to Bullinger from May 1557 comments to the effect that Laski is an 'excellent man' but a bit 'too austere' – that he ought not to be overly critical of the Waldensians, whose articles of faith ought to be considered among the Reformed Protestant confessions.[88] Laski, apparently, had continued his efforts to unify the various parties in Poland and had expressed reservations concerning Waldensians living in Poland. Calvin not only cautioned an irenic approach in this matter, but he also suggested that the Augsburg Confession, as interpreted by Melanchthon (namely the 1541 *Variata*) be used as one of the unifying documents. Laski, in the meantime, presided over a synod in which the Reformed delegates, representing both Bohemian and Genevan Protestants, invited the Lutherans to contemplate union.[89] Writing again to Bullinger in July, Calvin mentions Laski's ecumenical efforts, in particular, a private debate with Brenz – and, given Calvin's feelings concerning Brenz, is quite sceptical of a good result. In Calvin's view, Laski had evidenced 'greater courage than prudence' in engaging the 'snappish' Brenz – who, unlike Melanchthon was a confirmed opponent of the Reformed.[90] In August of the same year, Calvin writes to Bullinger still expressing disappointment over the outcome of a debate between Laski and the Lutheran, Brenz, but indicating that further discussions with the Lutherans might be fruitful, if only Melanchthon would state his true opinions against the 'immensity of Christ's body and its adoration'.[91] Bullinger responded in October, in a letter to Lismanino, indicating that he was not altogether pleased with either the Waldensian Confession or the Augsburg Confession.[92]

86. Calvin to Utenhoven, 1557, in *CO*, vol. 16, col. 673 (*Selected Works*, vol. 6, p. 325).

87. Calvin to Bullinger, 17 March 1557, in *CO*, vol. 16, cols 426–7 (*Selected Works*, vol. 6, pp. 322–3).

88. Calvin to Bullinger, 30 May 1557, in *CO*, vol. 15, col. 502 (*Selected Works*, vol. 6, pp. 332–4).

89. Doumergue, *Jean Calvin*, vol. 7, pp. 488–9.

90. Calvin to Bullinger, 31 August 1557, in *CO*, vol. 16, col. 595 (*Selected Works*, vol. 6, pp. 350–2).

91. Calvin to Bullinger, 31 August 1557, in *CO*, vol. 16, col. 598 (*Selected Works*, vol. 6, pp. 350–2).

92. Bullinger to Lismanino, 25 October 1557, in *CO*, vol. 16, col. 680; cf. Doumergue, *Jean Calvin*, vol. 7, p. 489.

A letter from Calvin to Bullinger, written in February 1558 mentions Laski in connection with an almost conspiratorial problem – Calvin indicates that he has heard from Beza that Bullinger had entrusted a letter to a certain 'Englishman', hoping that the letter would be carried to Calvin in Geneva. The Englishman had never arrived. Calvin notes the improbability that the Englishman had died between Zürich and Geneva and raises the possibility of a 'deception' – the evidence for which is augmented by the fact that the Englishman claimed, untruthfully, to be the bearer of letters from Laski – this in the midst of distress over the failure of the colloquy in Worms between the Reformed and the Lutherans.[93] A letter then arrived from Utenhoven in Crakow, who told of the success of the spread of the Reformation, noting, however, some dissent among Poles more favourable to the Bohemian Brethren and the Lutherans than to the Reformed.[94]

Writing to Bullinger in November 1558, Calvin indicates that he had been hampered by an illness from writing as many letters to Poland as had been requested by Utenhoven – but that he 'was by no means inattentive to the welfare of Poland'.[95] At about this time, Calvin resumed his correspondence with Count Tarnowski in a packet of five letters.[96] This is also the point at which Calvin's attentions shifted from the general reform of the Polish church that he had emphasized in his letters to the king, Nicholas Radziwil, and Count Tarnowski and others, to the anti-trinitarian issue. In May of 1558, troubles in the Italian refugee congregation in Geneva came to a head in the confrontation between Calvin and Giorgio Blandrata – Blandrata had fled, first to Bern, and then to Poland. He was followed, shortly afterwards, by other Italian anti-trinitarians – Lelius Socinus, Valentine Gentile and Franciscus Stancarus. Given the hostility between Calvin and these refugees, several Polish clergymen and educators attempted to bring about a reconciliation. The first of these, Petrus Statorius, the rector of the gymnasium in Pinczow, received an abrupt reprimand from Calvin – who informed him that he ought not to intervene in matters of which he was ignorant.[97] Statorius sent a conciliatory message to Calvin and Calvin responded in kind.[98] Lismanino also had become sympathetic to the views of Blandrata and, together with ministers of Vilnius, had attempted a similar reconciliation with Calvin – with an equally pointed result.[99]

93. Calvin to Bullinger, 23 February 1558, in *CO*, vol. 17, col. 61 (*Selected Works*, vol. 6, pp. 410–12).

94. Utenhoven to Calvin, 30 July 1558, in *CO*, vol. 17, cols 266–7; cf. Doumergue, *Jean Calvin*, vol. 7, p. 490.

95. Calvin to Bullinger, 19 November 1558, in *CO*, vol. 17, col. 387 (*Selected Works*, vol. 6, pp. 479–81).

96. Surveyed in Doumergue, *Jean Calvin*, vol. 7, pp. 490–1.

97. Statorius to Calvin, 8 August 1559, in *CO*, vol. 17, cols 600–3 (Mincer #101); Calvin to Statorius, 15 November 1559, in *CO*, vol. 17, cols 676–7 (Mincer #52).

98. Calvin to Statorius, 5 June 1559, in *CO*, vol. 18, cols 101–2 (Mincer #61).

99. Calvin to Lismanino, 7 October 1561, in *CO*, vol. 19, cols 41–3 (Mincer #64); Calvin to [Lismanino and] the Ministers of Vilnius, 9 October 1561, in *CO*, vol. 19, cols 38–40

Calvin also addressed several other Polish dignitaries and clergy – Jan Tarnowski, Jan Lusen, Stanislas Stadnitzki and Jakob Sylvius – warning about the rise of anti-trinitarianism, in particular noting the heresies of Stancarus.[100] Given that Laski died in 1560 and that Lismanino had expressed sympathy for the heretics, Calvin saw the need for a larger intervention – the crisis elicited from him no less than four treatises, two specifically against Stancarus, written in 1560 and 1561,[101] and two more, from 1563, on the trinitarian definitions themselves.[102] Calvin wrote to Bullinger in May – he was deeply troubled over the spread of anti-trinitarianism in Crakow – commenting that the Italians had caused enormous trouble and that various Polish pastors, 'through ignorance more than malice' had followed them: perhaps Bullinger also would write to Poland in defence of the Trinity.[103] Calvin's final letter to Poland, the formal epistle of admonition of 1563, warned against the 'pernicious' errors of Stancarus, Blandrata, Gentile and Alciati, who had reverted to identifying Christ as mediator in his human nature only and who spoke of God the Father alone as divine.[104]

Some Conclusions

Calvin's Polish correspondence indicates a significant movement towards a national Reformation in Poland in the second half of the sixteenth century, a

---

(Mincer #70). On Blandrata's relationship to Calvin and for a translation of Calvin's *Responsio ad quaestiones Georgii Blandratae*, see Joseph N. Tylenda, 'The Warning that Went Unheeded: John Calvin on Giorgio Blandrata', in *Calvin Theological Journal* 12 (1977), pp. 24–62.

100. Calvin to Tarnowski, 5 June 1560, in *CO*, vol. 18, cols 102–3 (Mincer #57); Calvin to Lusenius, 8 June 1560, in *CO*, vol. 18, cols 100–1 (Mincer #56); Calvin to Stadnitzki, 4 March 1561, in *CO*, vol. 18, cols 378–80 (Mincer #62); Sylvius to Calvin, 20 October 1562, in *CO*, vol. 19, cols 558–61 (Mincer #130); Calvin to Sylvius, April 1563, in *CO*, vol. 19, cols 729–30 (Mincer #66).

101. *Responsio ad fratres Polonos, quomodo mediator sit Christus, as refutandum Stancaro errorem*, in *CO*, vol. 9, cols 333–42; *Ministrorum ecclesiae Genevensis responsio as nobiles Polonos et Franciscum Stancarum Mantuanum de controversia mediatoris*, in *CO*, vol. 9, cols 345–58. Cf. the translation and analysis by Joseph N. Tylenda, 'Christ the Mediator: Calvin versus Stancaro', *Calvin Theological Journal* 8 (1973), pp. 5–16; and idem, 'The Controversy on Christ the Mediator: Calvin's Second Reply to Stancaro', *Calvin Theological Journal* 8 (1973), pp. 131–57.

102. *Brevis admonitio Ioannis Calvini ad fratres Polonos, ne triplicem in Deo essentiam pro tribus personis imaginando, tres sibi deos fabricent*, in *CO*, vol. 9, cols 629–38; *Epistola Ioannis Calvini qua fidem admonitionis ab eo nuper editae apud Polonos confirmat*, in *CO*, vol. 9, cols 641–50.

103. Calvin to Bullinger, 1 May 1563, in *CO*, vol. 20, cols 2–3.

104. Calvin, *Epistola … apud Polonos*, in *CO*, vol. 9, cols 645–6.

movement supported by major European reformers, by important members of
the clergy and by a notable coalition among the Polish nobility. The density of
the correspondence when all of the various writers have been drawn into focus, is
remarkable. It documents a large-scale reformist endeavour and an international
effort to win the Polish-Lithuanian kingdom for the Reformation, an effort in
which, moreover, it is rather difficult to identify an absolutely chief figure. This
latter point is of particular importance with respect to our understanding of
Calvin. When he wrote in an advisory manner to other reformers about their
own work in other localities, he typically evidenced respect, deference to their
approaches and context. He acknowledged Laski's importance and, in conjunction
with other reformers, sought to reinforce rather than supervise Laski's work. On
Laski's return to Poland in 1556, with Utenhoven, Calvin appears to have been
quite certain that the Polish reform had found its leaders. Only after Laski's death
in 1560, with the defection of Lismanino to the side of the anti-trinitarians, did
Calvin intervene with substantial theological advice.

As for Calvin's vision of Poland itself, what is clear from the size and scope of the
correspondence is that Calvin had a significant interest in the Polish Reformation
and an accurate assessment of the views of the Polish nobility concerning the
church, its reform and its relationship to the state. One can speculate that Calvin
and the other reformers involved in the correspondence had a vision of a broadly
European Reformed faith, one with national rootage in England, in various free
cities, most notably Strasbourg and Emden, potentially portions of the Low
Countries, in the Swiss cantons, Hungary and Poland. The vision, of course,
did not materialize – nor, however, did the Reformed faith and its international
connections immediately disappear: the Consensus of Sendomir (1570) marked
a momentary stabilization of Polish Protestantism and a truce between the
Lutherans and the Reformed. Some two thousand Protestant churches could
be counted in Poland-Lithuania in the early seventeenth century,[105] and the late
sixteenth- and seventeenth-century records of eastern European students and
scholars in Swiss and Dutch academies and universities attest to the continuing
intellectual commerce with the more western branches of the Reformed
community. From the perspective of history, however, these events – as illustrated
by Calvin's correspondence – offer evidence of the significant place of Poland in
the sixteenth-century movement towards church reform and indicate that the
geography of the European Reformation, as conceived by the humanistically
trained Reformers and united by the Latinity of the Northern Renaissance, was
broadly centred on the continent of Europe, from England and France in the west
to the Polish-Lithuanian commonwealth in the east.

---

105. Cf. Doumergue, *Jean Calvin*, vol. 7, p. 504, citing Krasinski, *Histoire*, pp. 154, 159.

Bibliography

Bartel, Oscar, 'Calvin und Polen', *Revue d'histoire et de philosophie religieuses* 45 (1965), pp. 93–108.

Calvin, John, *Commentaries of John Calvin* (46 vols; Edinburgh: Calvin Translation Society, 1844–55; repr. Grand Rapids: Baker Book House, 1979).

Calvin, John, *Ioannis Calvini opera quae supersunt omnia* (eds Guilielmus Baum, Eduardus Cunitz and Eduardus Reuss; 59 vols; Brunswick: Schwetschke, 1863–1900).

Calvin, John, *Selected Works of John Calvin: Tracts and Letters* (eds Henry Beveridge and Jules Bonnet; 7 vols; Grand Rapids: Baker Book House, 1983).

Conradt, Nancy, 'John Calvin, Theodore Beza and the Reformation in Poland' (unpublished doctoral dissertation, University of Wisconsin, 1974).

De Greef, Wulfert, *The Writings of John Calvin: An Introductory Guide* (trans. Lyle D. Bierma; Grand Rapids: Baker, 1993).

De Schickler, Fernand, 'La Congrégation évangélique de Cracovie', in *Bulletin de la Société de l'Historie du Protestantisme Français* (15 December 1880), pp. 529–46.

Doumergue, Émile, *Jean Calvin, les hommes et les choses de son temps* (7 vols; Lausanne: G. Bridel, 1899–1927).

Herminjard, A.-L., *Correspondance des Réformateurs dans les pays de langue française* (9 vols; Geneva and Paris, 1866–97).

Krasinski, Valérian, *Historical Sketch of the Rise, Progress, and Decline of the Reformation in Poland: And the Influence which the Scriptural Doctrines have Exercised on that Country in Literary, Moral, and Political Respects* (2 vols; London: Murray, 1838–40).

Krasinski, Valérian, *Sketch of the Religious History of the Slavonic Nations* (Edinburgh: Johnstone and Hunter, 2nd edn, revised and enlarged, 1851).

Lasco, Joannis à, *Opera tam edita quam inedita* (ed. Abraham Kuyper; 2 vols; Amsterdam: F. Muller; Den Haag: M. Nijhoff, 1866).

Małłek, Janusz, 'The Reformation in Poland and Prussia in the Sixteenth Century: Similarities and Differences', in Karin Maag (ed.), *The Reformation in Eastern and Central Europe* (Aldershot: Scolar Press, 1997), pp. 182–91.

Mincer, Wieslaw, *Jan Kalwin w Polsce: Bibliografia/John Calvin in Poland: Bibliography* (Toruń: Wydawnictwo Uniwersytetu Mikołaja Kopernika, 2000).

Tylenda, Joseph N., 'Christ the Mediator: Calvin versus Stancaro', *Calvin Theological Journal* 8 (1973), pp. 5–16.

Tylenda, Joseph N., 'The Controversy on Christ the Mediator: Calvin's Second Reply to Stancaro', *Calvin Theological Journal* 8 (1973), pp. 131–57.

Tylenda, Joseph N., 'The Warning that Went Unheeded: John Calvin on Giorgio Blandrata', *Calvin Theological Journal* 12 (1977), pp. 24–62.

Walker, Williston, *John Calvin: The Organizer of Reformed Protestantism, 1509–1564* (1906; repr., New York: Schocken Books, 1969).

Chapter 5

RE-VISITING JOHN CALVIN'S HOSTILITY TOWARDS FRENCH NICODEMISM*

Jon Balserak

Yet we fight not only with the papists but also with those good-for-nothings who arrogantly boast that they are Nicodemites.[1]

Introduction

These words do not come from one of Calvin's anti-Nicodemite treatises of the late 1530s or early 1540s but from a 1556 lecture on Hosea 4.15. In this year, Calvin and the Venerable Company of Pastors had begun training and sending ministers into France to serve Reformed congregations there. This lecture on Hosea constituted part of their theological instruction for which Calvin lectured through all the Minor Prophets, Daniel, Jeremiah, Lamentations and Ezekiel, stopping on 2 February 1564 at Ezekiel 20.44 when he became too ill to continue.[2] Much could be said about this quote, but I will consider one aspect, namely, its harshness.

* Very helpful comments were made on the first version of this chapter by Paul Helm and by Kenneth Woo. A subsequent version was presented as a paper at a seminar at the University of Bristol in September 2014. My colleague Gavin D'Costa gave me very useful feedback on that occasion. A revised version was then read at the Sixteenth Century Studies Conference in New Orleans on 17 October 2014. I am grateful to Carlos Eire, who was the responder for our session, for his penetrating thoughts on my paper and on our session. Ray Mentzer also gave very useful reflections on the paper and session, for which I thank him. Many of those who attended the session raised insightful questions, in particular, Esther Chung-Kim, Ward Holder, Peter Opitz and John Thompson. All errors remaining in the chapter are, of course, my own.

1. '*sed cum nebulonibus istis, qui iactant se Nicodemitas*' (*CO*, vol. 42, col. 290).

2. This work was begun following the tumultuous events of the summer of 1555, which witnessed the removal of the Perrinists from Geneva; see, Robert Kingdon, *Geneva and the Coming of the Wars of Religion in France, 1555–1563* (Geneva: Droz, 1956), p. 2. Some of *Les enfants de Genève*, as the Perrinists were called, were put to death and some fled to

This has been addressed by others, with the motivating influence of Calvin's theology of worship receiving expert treatment from the likes of Carlos Eire and David F. Wright.[3] A number of scholars have contemplated the possibility that Calvin's severity towards Nicodemism originates from 'self-revulsion' due to his own dissimulation at some point after his conversion.[4] A particularly provocative reading of the issue was produced in the 1970s by Eugénie Droz who contended that it was inspired not by theological concerns but by the desire to draw refugees to Geneva.[5] To my mind, the issue becomes even more intriguing when we reflect on the idea that his antipathy towards Nicodemism seems to have grown *more* intense over time, so that by the 1550s and into the 1560s, Calvin could lump

Bernese territory. The significance of these events is brilliantly reflected in Calvin's letters from the summer of 1555 (e.g. *CO*, vol. 15, cols 640–2, 676–85). For more on the politics of Calvin's Geneva, see Amédée Roget, *Histoire du peuple de Genève depuis la Réforme jusqu'à l'Escalade* (7 vols; Geneva: Jullien, 1870–83) and William Naphy, *Calvin and the Consolidation of the Genevan Reformation* (Manchester: University of Manchester Press, 1994). On the nature of Calvin's audience for these lectures – which was mostly French – see, Peter Wilcox, 'The lectures of John Calvin and the nature of his audience', in *ARG* 87 (1996), pp. 136–48. Wilcox corrects Parker, *Calvin's Old Testament Commentaries* (Edinburgh: T&T Clark, 1986), pp. 13–29. Training continued in the Genevan Academy, established in 1559, prior to which time lectures were held in the Auditoire; see Karin Maag, *Seminary or University? The Genevan Academy and Reformed Higher Education, 1560–1620* (Aldershot: Ashgate, 1995). For more on Calvin's purpose in sending ministers into France, see Jon Balserak, *Establishing the Remnant Church in France; Calvin's Lectures on the Minor Prophets, 1556–1559* (Leiden: Brill, 2011).

3. See Carlos Eire, *War Against the Idols. The Reformation of Worship from Erasmus to Calvin* (Cambridge: Cambridge University Press, 1986); David F. Wright, 'Why was Calvin so severe a critic of Nicodemism?', in David F. Wright, A. N. S. Lane and Jon Balserak (eds), *Calvinus Evangelii Propugnator: Calvin Champion of the Gospel; Papers Presented at the International Congress on Calvin Research, Seoul, 1998* (Grand Rapids: CRC Product Services, 2006), pp. 66–90. Much has been written on Nicodemism: see *inter alia*, Carlo Ginzburg, *Il Nicodemismo, Simulazione e dissimulazione religiosa nell' Europa del '500* (Turin: Guilio Einaudi, 1970); Francis Higman, 'The Question of Nicodemism', in Wilhelm Niesel (ed.), *Calvinus Ecclesiae Genevensis Custos; Die Referate des Congrès International des Recherches Calviniennes … Vom 6. bis 9. September 1982 in Genf* (Frankfurt am Main: Peter Lang, 1984), pp. 165–70; Perez Zagorin, *Ways of Lying; Dissimulation, Persecution, and Conformity in Early Modern Europe* (Cambridge, MA: Harvard University Press, 1990), pp. 63–82; Olivier Millet, *Calvin et la dynamique de la parole: Etude de rhétorique réformée* (Genève: Editions Slatkine, 1992), pp. 480–504, *et passim*, as well as works cited below.

4. Wright, 'Why was Calvin so severe a critic of Nicodemism?', p. 87. The scholars who briefly contemplate this possibility include Eugénie Droz, whose work will be mentioned in a moment, and Paul Sprenger, *Das Rätsel um die Bekehrung Calvins* (Neukirchen: Kreis Moers, 1960), p. 33, as cited in Eire, *War Against the Idols*, p. 237, n. 13.

5. Eugénie Droz, *Chemins de l'hérésie. Textes et documents* (4 vols; Geneva: Slatkine Reprints, 1970–76), vol. 1, pp. 173–271.

Nicodemites together with 'papists', identifying the two groups as one common enemy against whom 'we fight'.[6] Why would this be?

Calvin on the Nicodemites: A New Perspective

One thing scholars have overlooked in addressing the reasons for Calvin's severity towards Nicodemism is the possible significance of the looming French civil wars, the first of which began in the spring of 1562. It is on this that this chapter will focus.

Let me, therefore, state that I think Calvin, from the mid-1550s onwards, wanted war in France. This assertion builds on the findings of my 2014 monograph, *John Calvin as Sixteenth-Century Prophet*,[7] and will be probed in the analysis that follows. This chapter, then, will be asking: How would Calvin have viewed the Nicodemites if it were his desire to actively support a military uprising in the country?[8] To be more precise about what I mean, I contend that Calvin sought to encourage the use of military force against the French monarch and those in authority around him initiated by a French noble as *one* of a number of possible options available to the Huguenots for reforming the French church (other options would have included the evangelization of the French population

6. This is my own assessment of Calvin's feelings. I will, though, note that it is intimated by George Tavard, 'Calvin and the Nicodemites', in Randall C. Zachman (ed.), *John Calvin and Roman Catholicism; Critique and Engagement, Then and Now* (Grand Rapids: Baker, 2008), pp. 59–78, (59–60). I am aware of the fact that Tavard may well have misread Calvin's *Excuse*, but it still can be shown that he discusses four kinds of Nicodemites, whereas by the 1550s, he seems both harsher towards Nicodemites and unwilling to make such distinctions. For a discussion of the positions of Bucer, Melanchthon, Capito and others who were more accepting of Nicodemism than was Calvin, see Eire, *War Against the Idols*, pp. 245–50, *et passim*; Peter Matheson, 'Martyrdom or Mission? A Protestant Debate', *ARG* 80 (1989), pp. 154–72; Francis Higman, 'Bucer et les nicodémites', in Christian Krieger and Marc Lienhard (eds), *Martin Bucer and Sixteenth Century Europe. Actes du colloque de Strasbourg (28–31 août 1991)* (2 vols; Leiden: E. J. Brill, 1993), vol. 2, pp. 645–58; Jean Rott and Olivier Millet, 'Miettes historiques Strasbourgeoises', in Pierre Barthel, Rémy Scheurer, and Richard Stauffer (eds), *Actes du Colloque Guillaume Farel, Neuchâtel 29 septembre – 1er octobre 1980* (2 vols; Neuchâtel: Revue de théologie et de philosophie, 1983), vol. 1, pp. 253–77 (268–75); and Wright, 'Why was Calvin so severe a critic of Nicodemism?', pp. 77–88.

7. Jon Balserak, *John Calvin as Sixteenth-Century Prophet* (Oxford: Oxford University Press, 2014).

8. This essay addresses Calvin's political thought, which is complex and has been extensively treated. See the (generally) conservative readings of Calvin set out in these works: Émile Doumergue, *Jean Calvin, les hommes et les choses de son temps* (7 vols; Lausanne: G. Bridel & Cie., 1899–1927), vol. 5; Marc-Edouard Chenevière, *La Pensée Politique de Calvin* (Paris: Editions Je Sers, 1937); Josef Bohatec, *Calvins Lehre von Staat und Kirche* (Breslau: M & H Marcus, 1937). More recently: Quentin Skinner, *The Foundations of Modern Political Thought*

and the deliberate targeting of nobles for conversion – nobles who, sitting in parliament, would have been able to contribute to more favourable conditions for the Reformed religion). This would have been something Calvin considered more seriously as more peaceful options began to appear ineffectual or impossible. But one thing he plainly would not countenance was capitulation. Thus, as the situation in France became more intractably hostile towards the Reformed religion, the use of force became an increasingly appealing option to him. This would have, I believe, been particularly true after the death of King Henry II in the summer of 1559 when the staunchly Roman Catholic House of Guise obtained greater influence over the French throne through their connections to Catherine de Médici, Henry II's widow.

To make its argument, this chapter will, first, make a case for this new perspective and, second, demonstrate how considering things from this vantage point might illumine our understanding of Calvin's harsh attitude towards Nicodemism.

Reform and Revolt

Calvin's plans to reform France included seeking to instigate the use of armed force by a noble, or nobles, against the King. Now consider the following five points. Given that an important part of this chapter's argument rests on timing, I will try to be as clear as I can regarding the dates for the events about which I am writing.

(2 vols; Cambridge: Cambridge University Press, 1978); Harro Höpfl, *The Christian Polity of John Calvin* (Cambridge: Cambridge University Press, 1982); John R. Witte, *The Reformation of Rights* (Cambridge: University of Cambridge Press, 2007); Paul-Alexis Mellet, *Les Traités monarchomaques. Confusion des temps, résistance armée et monarchie parfaite (1560–1600)* (Geneva: Droz, 2007). For scholarship that does a good job of highlighting some of the more radical (if you will) qualities of Calvin's political thought, see Michael Walzer, *The Revolution of the Saints: A Study in the Origins of Radical Politics* (Cambridge, MA: Harvard University Press, 1965); Louis Arénilla, 'Le Calvinisme et le droit de résistance à l'Etat', *Annales: Economies, Societes, Civilizations* 22 (1967), pp. 350–69; Jean Boisset, 'La Non-violence et la tradition réformée', *Bulletin de la Société d'Histoire du Protestantisme Français* 113 (1967), pp. 202–19; Carlos Eire, *War Against the Idols*, pp. 271–5, 282–9; Ralph Hancock, *Calvin and the Foundations of Modern Politics* (Ithaca and London: Cornell University Press, 1989); Max Engammare, 'Calvin monarchomaque? Du soupçon à l'argument', *ARG* 89 (1998), pp. 207–26; Philip Benedict, 'The Dynamics of Protestant Militancy: France, 1555–1563', in Philip Benedict, Guido Marnef, Henk van Nierop, and Marc Venard (eds), *Reformation, Revolt and Civil War in France and the Netherlands 1555–1585* (Amsterdam: Royal Netherlands Academy of Arts and Sciences, 1999), pp. 35–50; Denis Crouzet, 'Calvinism and the Uses of the Political and the Religious (France, ca. 1560–ca. 1572)', in *Reformation, Revolt and Civil War*, pp. 99–114; David Whitford, 'Robbing Paul to Pay Peter; The Reception of Paul in Sixteenth-Century Political Theology', in R. Ward Holder (ed.), *A Companion to Paul in the Reformation* (Leiden: Brill, 2009), pp. 573–606 (603–4).

(1) By the early 1550s, Calvin came to believe that France was in the grip of tyrannical kings who were imposing idolatry on the country.

One can find clear assertions from Calvin concerning the tyranny of kings as early as the early 1550s. We need look no further for this than Max Engammare's research on Calvin's sermons.[9] But the same can be found with, if anything, greater regularity in his lectures on the prophets and also in some of his letters. Of these letters, one of the best examples is the dedicatory letter Calvin wrote for his lectures on the prophet, Daniel, which he addressed 'to all the pious worshippers of God who desire the kingdom of Christ to be rightly established in France'. In this letter, one finds Calvin identifying the French king not only as a tyrant but as one who sought to replace gospel worship with wicked idolatry and used violent means to remove the gospel from his territory. As this point seems uncontroversial and given the brevity that constrains chapters such as this, I will assume it and move on.[10]

(2) Calvin came, by the early 1550s, to believe that French kings had, by imposing idolatry, forfeited their right to hold power.[11]

Calvin embraced, I contend, a nascent form of the idea that the monarch rules under a contract or covenant, the terms of which he must obey.[12] Exactly when he came to adopt this view is a difficult question to answer with precision, but it would appear to have been relatively late in his life. He does not mention anything related to a contract in his 1540 handling of Romans 13, the locus classicus for the notion of the inviolability of the ruler.[13] He also does not mention it in early editions of the *Institutio Christianae Religionis*. In fact, I have yet to find him intimating anything

9. Max Engammare, 'Calvin monarchomaque? Du soupçon à l'argument', pp. 207–26.

10. See Calvin, *Praelectiones ioannis calvini in librum prophetiarum danielis*, … (s.l.: apud Bartholomaeum Vincentium, 1571), fols *iiiv–*ivr (the dedicatory epistle is not included in the *Calvini Opera* edition of the Daniel lectures, but it can be found in *CO*, vol. 18, cols 614–24. I have accessed it via an older printing of these *praelectiones*).

11. This point – and really this whole chapter – assumes a connection between Calvin's political and religious thought, which is acknowledged by others and which this chapter will explore. The late Robert Kingdon, for instance, speaks in one of his papers of 'Calvin's views on idolatry and their implications for political resistance' (Robert Kingdon, 'Calvin and Calvinists on Resistance to Government', in David F. Wright, A. N. S. Lane, and Jon Balserak (eds), *Calvinus Evangelii Propugnator*, pp. 54–65 (57)). Sheldon Wolin speaks of 'Calvin's thought … revealing … the interpenetration of political and religious modes of thought' (Sheldon Wolin, 'Calvin and the Reformation: The Political Education of Protestantism', *The American Political Science Review* 51/2 (1957), pp. 428–53 (429)). By citing these scholars here, I am not suggesting that they supported the position for which I am arguing in this chapter.

12. There is a considerable amount of scholarship on the rise of the idea of covenant in medieval and Early Modern Europe, but still extremely valuable is William J. Courtenay, *Covenant and Causality in Medieval Thought: Studies in Philosophy, Theology, and Economic Practice* (London: Variorum, 1984). See also, Peter Lillback, *The Binding of God: Calvin's Role in the Development of Covenant Theology* (Grand Rapids: Baker and Paternoster, 2001).

13. *CO*, vol. 49, cols 252–3.

on the matter until the early 1550s. So, for instance, in remarks from his 1552 Acts commentary, one finds him asserting: 'If a king, or ruler, or magistrate, becomes so lofty that he diminishes the honor and authority of God, he is but a man.'[14] The first requirement of this covenant, according to Calvin, would appear to be ensuring the flourishing of the true religion within the monarch's realm.[15] Hence the implementation and support of idolatrous worship by a king is the cardinal sin. So Calvin declares in a sermon on Genesis from 1560: 'If kings wish to force their subjects to follow their superstitions and idolatries, they are no longer kings.'[16]

The lateness of his articulating of these views has presented something of a problem for scholars, I would suggest. Until recently, scholars relied heavily on the *Institutio* for their assessments of Calvin's political views. What this meant was that they tended to read his 1559 *Institutio* and to find in it remarkably strong assertions on the need for believers to submit to civil authority, even if it was wicked. Accordingly, their thinking was guided by the strength and preponderance of such assertions and by the authority of the *Institutio*, and they concluded that Calvin was conservative or, at least, they failed to see that he adapted his views on a king's ruling via contract late in his life. A case in point is the (otherwise excellent) article by Harro Höpfl and Martyn P. Thompson.[17] They and other scholars have

14. *CO*, vol. 48, col. 109 (Commentary on Acts 5.29). I owe this quotation to Hugues Daussy, 'Les huguenots entre l'obéissance au roi et l'obéissance à Dieu', *Nouvelle Revue du XVIe Siècle* 22 (2004), pp. 49–69 (53).

15. Calvin's insistence that the magistrate see to the flourishing of the true religion may be found in numerous places in his corpus such as, for instance, *CO*, vol. 37, col. 210 (commentary on Isaiah 49.23); also in Calvin's dedicatory letter to his commentary on Paul's epistles to Timothy written to the Duke of Somerset, *CO*, vol. 13, cols 16–18, or in a later articulation from his sermons on 1 Samuel (*CO*, vol. 51, col. 797) – I owe this last reference to W. Fred Graham, *The Constructive Revolutionary; John Calvin and his Socio-economic Impact* (Lancing: University of Michigan Press, 1987), p. 159. There are numerous other places one could look, including (especially) Calvin's Psalms commentary.

16. See, Jean Calvin, *La servante chassée: sermon inédit sur l'histoirè d'Agar (23 mars 1560)* (ed. Max Engammare; Geneva: Minizoé, 1995), pp. 28–9, as cited by Kingdon, 'Calvin and Calvinists on Resistance to Government', pp. 54–65 (57).

17. Höpfl and Thompson state: 'Calvin had gone out of his way to insist that the duty to obey rulers was not conditional on either the title or the good conduct of rulers.' (Harro Höpfl and Martyn P. Thompson, 'The History of Contract as a Motif in Political Thought', *The American Historical Review* 84/4 (1979), pp. 919–44 (929).) They also point us to Chenevière, *La Pensée Politique de Calvin*, pp. 124–8; and J. Bohatec, *Calvins Lehre von Staat und Kirche*, pp. 62–9. Höpfl repeats his views later, see *Luther and Calvin on Secular Authority* (ed. Harro Höpfl; Cambridge: Cambridge University Press, 1991), p. 84, n.110. But for broad support of the position for which I am arguing under point two, see Winthrop Hudson, 'Democratic freedom and religious faith in the reformed tradition', *CH* 15 (1946), pp. 181–4 (though Hudson identifies the principles of natural law as the rule according to which magistrates must govern, and does so in a manner that I find too speculative. Furthermore, of course, Hudson does not identify the notion of contract in quite the same manner as I do).

overlooked the significance of the fact that in 1559 Calvin added in *Institutio* 4.20.32 a new portion of text related to Daniel's disobeying of King Darius's requirement to worship idols (Dan. 6.22), which comports precisely with the sentiments cited by me in the previous paragraph regarding the idea of a contract.

> For this reason, Daniel denies he had sinned in any way against the king when he refused to obey the king's impious edict, since the king had exceeded his limits; nor had he merely been unjust towards humankind but, by raising up his horn against God, had abrogated his own power (*potestatem sibi ipse abrogaverat*).[18]

Thus, while the *Institutio* undoubtedly contains extremely strong statements on the need to obey even a wicked king, Calvin added to it in 1559 material on rule by contract, which radically alters his position on the nature of civil authority. It alters his position because in the new material one finds – in addition to ideas about the individual's need to obey authority, which were in the *Institutio* from 1536 – Calvin discussing a new requirement placed on the civil authority himself – a requirement that can be broken and will have consequences if it is broken. We will look at the nature of those consequences momentarily, but *that* they are added is, in my judgement, indisputable.

So then, turning to the France of the 1550s and 1560s, it would appear that Calvin believed that French kings had forfeited their right to hold office. One of the places this is most clearly expressed is in his lectures. 'Kings', Calvin declares in one of many examples to which I could point, 'and those who occupy the seats of judgment wish to be sacrosanct', but that means they would like to be able to sin freely. 'In short', he says in a 1557 lecture on Amos, kings do not consider themselves to belong to the common class of human beings and 'would like to rule without equity, because power is, for them, nothing except unrestrained license'.[19] Kings 'want to be adored in the place of God'.[20] Kings are of the belief that 'their tyranny cannot stand unless the gospel is abolished'.[21] Darius will condemn those kings who profess themselves to be 'catholic or Christian kings or defenders of the faith (*protectores fidei*)', mocking the French kings' profession,[22] since Darius

---

18. *CO*, vol. 2, col. 1117.

19. *CO*, vol. 43, cols 79–80 (Lecture on Amos 5.10).

20. *CO*, vol. 41, col. 7 (Lecture on Dan. 6.6–7).

21. *CO*, vol. 43, col. 127 (Lecture on Amos 7.10–13).

22. See Marc Bloch, *Les rois thaumaturges: Etude sur le Caractere Surnaturel Attribue a la Puissance Royale Particulierement en France et en Angleterre* (Oxford: Oxford University Press, 1924), pp. 51–157, 460–77; Percy Schramm, *Der König von Frankreich: das Wesen der Monarchie vom 9. zum 16. Jahrhundert, ein Kapitel aus der Geschichte des abendländischen Staates* (Weimar: H. Böhlaus Nachfolger, 1939); Joseph R. Strayer, 'France: The Holy Land, the Chosen People, and the Most Christian King', in Theodore Rabb and Jerrold Seigel (eds), *Action and Conviction in Early Modern Europe; Essays in Memory of E. H. Harbison* (Princeton: Princeton University Press, 1969), pp. 3–16; Nancy Lyman Roelker, *One King, One Faith; The Parlement of Paris and the Religious Reformations of the Sixteenth Century* (Berkeley: University of California Press, 1996). A standard in the field that focuses on

renounced idolatry (Dan. 6.25–27), but those today who profess to be the faith's defenders seek not only to bury true piety but also to 'willingly extinguish [God's] name from the world'.[23] Thus, rather than merely being 'but a man' (as he stated in the 1552 Acts commentary), by 1561 'kings are gross and stupid (*fatui … ac bruti*), such that they are like horses and brute beasts'.[24] Therefore, it would appear, they are no longer kings.

(3) From as early as 1536 – but especially by the late 1550s – Calvin believed there existed individuals within the government who had the duty to protect the people from a tyrannical king – in the case of France, these were the 'Princes of the Blood'.

Calvin did, as is well known, write about a particular class who served in the role of protector or guardian of citizens against a tyrannical king, referring to them as popular (or lesser or inferior) magistrates[25] – a notion strongly associated with the Lutheran Magdeburg Confession of 1550[26] – and arguing that they not only existed within some ancient governments but also that the estates or parliaments of modern kingdoms may perform the same function in his own day.[27]

England but produces results useful for understanding Europe more broadly is found in Ernst Kantorowicz, *The King's Two Bodies: A Study in Medieval Political Theology* (Princeton, NJ: Princeton University Press, 1957).

23. *CO*, vol. 41, col. 30 (Lecture on Dan. 6.25–27). Calvin uses precisely the same language in his dedicatory letter to these Daniel lectures. See, among many other examples, *CO*, vol. 40, col. 108 (Lecture on Ezek. 4.4–8) and *CO*, vol. 44, col. 349 (Lecture on Zechariah 13.4).

24. *CO*, vol. 41, col. 3 (Lecture on Dan. 6.3–5).

25. Höpfl notes that the French editions of the *Institutes* omit the word 'popular'. See *Luther and Calvin on Secular Authority*, p. 82, n. 104.

26. It is also associated with later writings by men some of whom were associates of Calvin, such as François Hotman's *Francogallia* (1573), Théodore de Bèze's *De Jure Magistratum* (1574) and also the *Vindiciae Contra Tyrannos* (1579), which is pseudonymous but thought to have been authored by Philippe de Mornay – men sometimes identified as Monarchomachs.

27. See *CO*, vol. 1, col. 248 (1536 *Institutio*). There is much written on the development of theories of resistance. In relation specifically to Calvinists' thinking, see, *inter alia*, Henri Strohl, 'Le Droit a la resistance d'apres les conceptions protestantes', *Revue d'histoire et de philosophie religieuses* (1930), pp. 126–39 (132–3); Hans Baron, 'Calvinist republicanism and its historical roots', *CH* 8 (1939), pp. 30–42 (38–41); Hudson, 'Democratic freedom and religious faith in the reformed tradition', pp. 187–78; J. T. McNeill, 'The Democratic Element in Calvin's thought', *CH* 18 (1949), pp. 153–71 (160–3); Skinner, *Foundations*, vol. 2, pp. 192–3; H. A. Lloyd, 'Calvin and the Duty of Guardians to Resist', *JEH* 32 (1981), pp. 65–7; Peter Stein, 'Calvin and the Duty of Guardians to Resist: a Comment', *JEH* 32 (1981), pp. 69–70; Walter Ullmann, 'Calvin and the Duty of the Guardians to Resist: A Further Comment', *JEH* 32 (1981), pp. 499–501; Carlos Eire, *War Against the Idols*, pp. 282–9; also numerous pieces by Robert Kingdon, such as, 'Calvin and Calvinists on Resistance to Government', pp. 54–65; Hancock, *Calvin and the Foundations of Modern Politics*, pp. 70–81.

The fact that Calvin speaks about this in his 1536 *Institutio*, while simultaneously making some of his strongest assertions on the need to obey even a wicked magistrate leads us to conclude that he apparently saw these two ideas as compatible. Yet, this has not stopped many, including G. P. Gooch (1898), Michael Walzer (1965) and Quentin Skinner (1978) from accusing Calvin of equivocation.[28] Another complaint one hears is that Calvin is simply unclear on the duties of the popular magistrate. This is, I think, more justified. As many have rightly asserted, Calvin's treatment of this in the *Institutio* is frustratingly sketchy. 'Calvin never defined the role of "inferior magistrates"' and said essentially nothing on what they are required, or permitted, to do.[29] This lack of clarity has contributed to scholars concluding that he is conservative in his thinking on the question of resistance. This verdict garners strong support from Calvin's numerous assertions about the need to obey the magistrate.[30] Thus, the consensus position among scholars is that Calvin merely 'open[ed] the *possibility* of more active resistance' but never contemplated or authorized it.[31]

I dissent from this reading of Calvin on the popular magistrate and on active resistance for three reasons. The first is that Calvin, so far from merely contemplating a possibility of more active forms of resistance, grappled in later life (specifically, the 1560s) with the idea that even ordinary individuals might be permitted, in special circumstances, to rise up against a tyrant. Though he seems ultimately to have moved away from embracing such a position, the fact that he wrestled with the issue is a significant indicator of his mindset in the late 1550s and

28. See, for instance, Gooch, *English Democratic Ideas in the Seventeenth Century* (Cambridge: Cambridge University Press, 1898), p. 6, as cited in Hudson, 'Democratic freedom and religious faith in the reformed tradition', p. 186, n. 16.

29. Eire, *War Against the Idols*, p. 289; also, Walzer, *The Revolution of the Saints*, p. 23; Skinner, *Foundations*, vol. 2, p. 192.

30. A brilliant example reads: 'It is impossible to resist the magistrate without, at the same time, resisting God himself' (*Institutio* 4.20.23, as cited in Eire, *War Against the Idols*, p. 289).

31. This possibility, it is argued, was taken up and expanded upon by later Calvinists, such as the Monarchomachs, but not by Calvin himself. The full citation from Kingdon reads: 'In normal circumstances, Calvin did not contemplate or authorize resistance more active than this [referring to facing martyrdom for disobeying the command of a government]. He did, however, lay open the possibility of more active resistance, even armed resistance, in a celebrated passage towards the end of his *Institutes*, in 4.20.31' (Robert Kingdon, 'Calvin's Socio-Political Legacy: Collective Government, Resistance to Tyranny, Discipline', in David Foxgrover (ed.), *The Legacy of John Calvin; Papers Presented at the 12th Colloquium of the Calvin Studies Society, April 22–24, 1999* (Grand Rapids: CRC Product Services, 2000), pp. 112–23 (119; italics in the quote in the body of the page is mine)). See also Hudson, 'Democratic freedom and religious faith in the reformed tradition', p. 184; Skinner, *Foundations*, vol. 2, p. 192; Eire, *War Against the Idols*, pp. 288–9 (289), where Eire declares that it remained for Calvin's followers to 'create a forceful theory of resistance'. On Monarchomachs, Paul-Alexis Mellet, *Les Traités monarchomaques*.

early 1560s and suggests that he may well have done more than merely open up the possibility of aggressive responses to tyranny.[32]

The second is that it seems undeniable to me that Calvin's previously noted 1559 addition to *Institutio* 4.20.32 adds an important element to his understanding of the role of the popular magistrate, particularly in relation to the duty that Calvin insists belongs to the popular magistrate, namely the duty to defend the populace of a country from their king when the latter is attempting to impose idolatry on the former. It adds the significant notion that the lesser magistrate may conclude that, through such an attempt to impose idolatry on his subjects, that king has abrogated his authority and holds office illegitimately. In this regard, some scholars have argued that Calvin had access to the 1550 Magdeburg Confession, which had been written to defend the attempt by Magdeburg to reject the emperor Charles V's efforts to impose the 1548 Augsburg Interim on the city[33] – and I think the evidence of Calvin's corpus shows those scholars are right.

The third reason, which is probably the most powerful, is because I find Calvin asserting more on the popular magistrate's duties, and, by extension, on the question of resistance, elsewhere (i.e. outside of the *Institutio*) – and this, incidentally, with particular reference to France. So, in a letter from 16 April 1561 to Admiral de Coligny, Calvin writes, among other things, about the ill-fated Conspiracy of Amboise but also about a man who had come to him with a plot to topple the king of France: 'I admitted [to this man] that it was true that if the Princes of the Blood wished to be maintained in their rights for the common good and if the Parliament joined them in their fight, then it would be lawful for all good subjects to support their efforts (*prêter main forte*, which given the context likely means something like "give them armed support").'[34] I concede that Calvin's stance in this letter still rings a conservative note. Nonetheless, his comments here hint strongly at the idea that, whatever Calvin may have had in mind when he initially wrote in 1536, by 1561 he seems to have believed

---

32. See Willem Nijenhuis (ed.), 'The limits of civil disobedience in Calvin's last-known sermons: development of his ideas on the right of civil resistance', in *Ecclesia Reformata: v. 2: Studies on the Reformation* (Leiden: Brill, 1994), pp. 73–94. I am aware that some of the citations mentioned by Nijenhuis to support his position seem to offer tenuous support, at best. Nonetheless, I still think his discussion is a valuable one and that he demonstrates Calvin's willingness to contemplate the notion of an individual rising up against civil authority. Here I disagree with David Whitford, who, in his fine chapter in the Brill volume on Paul in Reformation thought, argues that Calvin's additions to the last chapter of the 1559 *Institutio* represent a defense of the rights of individuals to rise up against civil authority; see, Whitford, 'Robbing Paul to Pay Peter', pp. 603–4.

33. See, *inter alia*, Whitford, 'Robbing Paul to Pay Peter', pp. 603–4.

34. *CO*, vol. 18, col. 426. Indeed, the translation found in Calvin's letters is 'to lend them armed assistance'. See *Letters of John Calvin* (trans. Marcus Gilchrist; ed. Jules Bonnet; 4 vols; Philadelphia: Presbyterian Board of Publications, 1858), vol. 4, p. 176.

that 'curb[ing] the tyranny of kings' (*Institutio* 4.20.31)[35] includes within it
the notion of armed resistance. In fact, I cannot interpret the assertion in any
other way. We know, as well, that Calvin's harsh criticism of the Conspiracy
of Amboise did not keep him from acknowledging that it would have been a
fundamentally different undertaking if it had been led by a Prince of the Blood.
So he would seem to make this point in a letter to John Sturm, dated 23 March
1560, in which it seems pretty obvious that he was not yet aware of the fate
of the major players in the Amboise plot of 15 March. Even in criticizing it,
Calvin says to Sturm that the latter is exactly right to say that 'all depends
on their gaining Antoine of Navarre to their plans'.[36] On the same matter,
we know that Calvin remarks that he would have supported the scheme if it
had been led by the man 'who ought to be chief of the Council of the King
according to the laws of France', or in other words, Antoine of Navarre or his
brother Louis of Condé.[37]

What we can see, then, is that by at least 1560 (and I think it could have been
earlier[38]) Calvin seems to have come to the conclusion that armed resistance
against the monarch, led by popular magistrates and participated in by the
common people, was legitimate. In some ways, this assertion is not a wholly new
one. Walzer argued that in *Institutio* 4.20.30–31, Calvin 'merely readmitted ...
tyrannicide under the cover of divinity'.[39] Likewise, Denis Crouzet interpreted
Calvin as approving of tyrannicide in relation to the Amboise Conspiracy in his
letter dated 23 March to Sturm, cited just a moment ago.[40] So my conclusions up
to this point, though not commonplace, are not new. But in what remains, I will
break what so far as I have been able to determine *is* new ground. Below, I will
argue that Calvin, on the basis of the three beliefs set down heretofore, acted to
prompt and encourage the use of military force against the French monarch by a
Prince of the Blood. He did this, I contend, in two significant ways, commencing
in the mid-1550s.

(4) He sought to encourage the Princes of the Blood to rise up against the
French government through any means, including the use of military force.

---

35. *CO*, vol. 1, col. 248 (from 1536 *Institutio*). This appears in 4.20.31 in the 1559
Institutio.

36. *CO*, vol. 18, col. 39.

37. Henri Naef, *La Conjuration d'Amboise et Genève* (Geneva: Jullien, 1922), pp. 462–3,
as cited by Kingdon, *Geneva and the Coming of the Wars*, p. 69. See also, Kingdon, 'Calvin
and Calvinists on Resistance to Government', pp. 54–65. I am very aware that Calvin
expressed his disapproval of the conspiracy with some vehemence; see, for instance, his
letter to Bullinger in May 1560, *CO*, vol. 18, cols 83–5.

38. See, Balserak, *John Calvin as Sixteenth-Century Prophet*, pp. 114–26.

39. Walzer, *The Revolution of the Saints*, p. 63.

40. Denis Crouzet, 'Calvinism and the Uses of the Political and the Religious (France, ca.
1560–ca. 1572)', pp. 99–113 (103).

Calvin's letters make clear that he was in touch with French nobles, specifically Antoine of Navarre and Louis of Condé, throughout the second half of the 1550s and into the 1560s. His contact, particularly with Antoine, exhibits the appropriate courtesies expected during this era when addressing nobility, but also manifests remarkable intensity and purposefulness.[41]

At this point, it is worth recalling that Calvin was not opposed to doing something illegal to advance the gospel. He was involved in a number of subversive activities in his endeavours to reform France. He actively encouraged the Huguenot churches to meet in secret against the will of the French government.[42] He engaged in an illegal book trade focused on France.[43] He also orchestrated the sending of Reformed ministers into France, as I have already mentioned. In relation to this, he kept it secret not only from the French government but also from the Little Council for the first year. He apparently then helped to hide it from the new king of France, Charles IX, in 1561.[44] So Calvin was more than willing to engage in subversive activities for the sake of the French church.

It will perhaps come as no surprise, then, to find that in September of 1560 Calvin was involved with Theodore Beza in a plot to give troops and money to Antoine of Navarre to use 'to aggressively assert his right to lead a regency government and

---

41. See, for instance, Calvin's earnest pleas to Antoine of Navarre in December 1557 (*CO*, vol. 16, cols 730–4) and in June 1558 (*CO*, vol. 17, cols 196–8). Calvin writes in a letter to Sulzer dated 1 October 1560 that the King of Navarre remains silent, but the churches of Gascony 'enjoy a certain degree of peace', adding: 'Our Beza is with him (*apud eum est*)' (*CO*, vol. 18, cols 202–4 (204)). A letter of Calvin to Sturm, written in November 1560, alludes to the fact that François Hotman had gone to visit the King of Navarre to urge him to do more for the gospel in France (*CO*, vol. 18, cols 231–2). Likewise, Calvin complains to Bullinger about the lack of progress in a letter dated 7 December 1560, see, *CO*, vol. 18, cols 254–6. Other examples abound.

42. Oddly, Höpfl goes so far as to say that Calvin instructed churches to refrain from preaching when it was forbidden by the local authorities (Höpfl, *The Christian Polity of John Calvin*, p. 210). He cites letters 3185 and 3188 to support his point, neither of which seems to the present author to carry us towards the conclusion Höpfl asserts in the body of his text, namely, 'Calvin counselled submission'. Meanwhile, he overlooks letters in which Calvin mentions churches having 'secret meetings (*secreti conventus*)' (*CO*, vol. 17, cols 311–12). On the general matter of Calvin's interactions with the French churches, see Philip Benedict, 'The Dynamics of Protestant Militancy: France, 1555–1563', pp. 35–50; Denis Crouzet, 'Calvinism and the Uses of the Political and the Religious (France, ca. 1560–ca. 1572)', pp. 99–113. For thoughts on Calvin's willingness to break the law for the gospel, see Jon Balserak, 'Examining the Myth of Calvin as a Lover of Order', in Peter Opitz (ed.), *The Myth of the Reformation* (Göttingen: Vandenhoeck & Ruprecht, 2013), pp. 160–75.

43. See Jeannine Olson, *Calvin and Social Welfare: Deacons and the Bourse française* (London and Toronto: Associated University Presses; Selinsgrove: Susquehanna University Press, 1989), pp. 51–69.

44. Kingdon, *Geneva and the Coming of the Wars*, p. 35.

then promote Reformed rights of worship'.[45] That this happened in 1560 comes as no surprise either, as the death of King Henry II in July 1559 had ushered in what was for Calvin a profoundly frustrating situation. Following these events, Calvin had urged Antoine to do his utmost to assert himself and even insisted in one letter that the regency had been effectively stolen from the King of Navarre by the Guises.[46] Thus, the plot appears to some degree to have been an act of desperation. Following the death of Francis II on 5 December 1560, this desperation was turned to joy. Calvin writes to John Sturm that it appeared 'there was no remedy from the extreme evils being experienced, when all of a sudden God appeared from heaven and he who had previously pierced the eye of the father has now struck the ear of the son'.[47] He seems, in many ways, to have felt a corner had been turned, though he does caution against too great an exuberance at the news of the king's death. Yet, his enthusiasm is short-lived, and soon Calvin is beginning again to ply Antoine of Navarre to do all he can to support the Reformed cause.[48]

I do not think, given what we have seen up to this point, that it is stretching our reading of the data to say that this September 1560 plot was not an isolated foray into such aggressive political manoeuvering. Precisely when such plotting would have begun is hard to say with certainty, but the material covered in the next point would seem to suggest the mid-1550s as its point of commencement.

(5) He sought to prepare the ground in France so that when he found a noble willing to instigate a military uprising, that noble would find a ready army within the country.

Even if he could find a willing noble, he still needed troops. Through the ministerial-training lectures, Calvin sought to prepare the Reformed congregations in France to take up arms when the call came, by inculcating into their ministers several crucial points.

45. Philip Benedict, 'Prophets in Arms? Ministers in War, Ministers on War: France 1562–74', *Past and Present* 214: Issue suppl. 7 (2012), p. 171, n. 21. See Calvin's letter to Beza dated 10 September 1560 (*CO*, vol. 18, cols 177–80). As Alain Dufour comments, this plot 'had Calvin's approval (since the first prince of the blood was directing it). Calvin took charge even of collecting funds borrowed left and right, up to 50,000 pounds' (Alain Dufour, *Théodore de Bèze: poète et théologien* (Geneva: Droz, 2009), p. 74). See also, idem, 'L'affaire de Maligny (Lyon, 4–5 September 1560) vue à travers la correspondance de Calvin et de Bèze', *Cahiers d'Histoire* 8 (1963), pp. 269–80; *Correspondance de Théodore de Bèze, Tome III: 1559–1561* (eds H. Meylan and A. Dufour; Travaux d'humanisme et Renaissance, 61; Geneva: Droz, 1663), pp. 63–70.

46. See Calvin's letter to Hotman and Sturm, 4 June 1560, *CO*, vol. 18, cols 97–100 (98).

47. *CO*, vol. 18, col. 270. Calvin complained almost constantly in letters about the Guises and plainly believed they were utterly wicked.

48. Any idea that things had really changed was fairly quickly quashed. By January 1561, Calvin was writing both to Antoine of Navarre and to his wife, the Queen of Navarre, urging greater work to bring about the progress of the gospel in France and expressing intense frustration at the situation as it stood. See, *inter alia*, *CO*, vol. 18, cols 311–12, 312–14.

First, Calvin spoke of Romanist priests and kings as 'covenant breakers' and 'reprobate'. He identified them as 'mad' and 'addicted' to idolatry. In this regard, I have already mentioned the contempt and intense vitriol Calvin hurls at the French kings. They are the 'enemy', who hate, harass, assault and seek to kill the pious remnant (who are 'us', in Calvin's language).[49] Second, he contended that the Reformed community were at 'war' with the papists and (as we have seen) with the Nicodemites too – a war that was both spiritual and this-worldly.[50] Third, he prayed for and about the war, declaring that God is 'on our side' and urging God to defend God's people as He had done of old (*olim*) in defending Israel from pagan nations such as the Philistines. Calvin eagerly asserted that God stands with us to defend our cause and to protect our safety.[51] These references to war cannot be interpreted as merely spiritualized warfare, as one finds in, say, Ephesians 6. This assertion applies particularly to Calvin's prayers. He begins praying about the war in 1556, that is, six years before the first of the civil wars began. It appears that all his prayers are about the same war which, at some point, while continuing to be a spiritual conflict, takes on a this-worldly, military aspect.

> Grant, almighty God, as of old you testified your favor towards your Church by not sparing the greatest Kings, that we today also might know you to be the same (*eundem*) towards all your faithful people who call upon you. And because the power and cruelty of our enemies are so great, raise up your hand against them, and show that you are the perpetual defender of your Church, so that we may have reason to give glory to your goodness through Christ Jesus our Lord, Amen.[52]

This is a prayer following his lecture on Jeremiah 51.32 and was prayed (I am quite sure) following the initiation of war – but it is not markedly different from earlier prayers, which shadow the Old Testament prayers for God's aid in battle.

49. The locus classicus for Calvin on priests, is Micah 2.6–7 (see *CO*, vol. 44, cols 435–8); see also, *CO*, vol. 37, col. 472 (Lecture on Jer. 1.1–3). On kings, see, for instance, *CO*, vol. 43, col. 516 (Lecture on Habakkuk 1.16); *CO*, vol. 38, col. 385 (Lecture on Jer. 22.15); and *CO*, vol. 40, col. 540 (Lecture on Dan. 1.5). On the psychology of idolatry, see Eire, *War Against the Idols*, pp. 216–20. For more on all of this, see Balserak, *John Calvin as Sixteenth-Century Prophet*, pp. 102–78.

50. *CO*, vol. 42, col. 323 (Lecture on Hos. 6.3); *CO*, vol. 43, col. 377 (Lecture on Micah 5.9); *CO*, vol. 43, col. 435 (Lecture on Nahum 1.1). For more, see my *John Calvin as Sixteenth-Century Prophet*, pp. 102–78.

51. On God being on the Huguenots' side, see *CO*, vol. 42, cols 407–8 (Lecture on Hos. 9.17). Calvin, *Praelectiones in duodecim Prophetas minores ...* (Geneva: Jean Crespin, 1567), p. 554. The prayers with which Calvin ended these lectures are not recorded in the *Calvini Opera* edition of Calvin's works. Therefore, I accessed them via older printed versions of his lectures. For more, see my *John Calvin as Sixteenth-Century Prophet*, pp. 102–78.

52. Calvin, *Praelectiones in Librum prophetiarum Ieremiae, et Lamentationes ...* (Geneva: apud I. Crispinum, 1563), fol. 387r.

This was the message he sent into France through the mouths of his ministers. There is not a hint of peacemaking in these training lectures. Nor could Calvin have been ignorant of the tensions building in France.[53] He also could not possibly have been ignorant of the fact that the Huguenots had standing militias from 1558 onwards. Despite this, one finds remarkable belligerence throughout these lectures. 'We, therefore', he declared in a 1558 lecture on Malachi 2.4, 'are able boldly to overthrow the whole of the papacy.'[54] (And we know, of course, that Calvin vigorously supported Louis of Condè's armed uprising in response to the Massacre of Vassy in the spring of 1562.) Through this message carried by his ministers, then, Calvin sought to build gradually a collective who believed in war and were ready for it, and were in effect merely waiting for a leader to call them to rise up to participate in this war.

What Does All This Have to Do with Nicodemism?

In summary, from ca. 1555 onwards Calvin's plans to reform France included seeking to instigate the use of armed force. I am aware of Calvin's early conservatism but feel it has been overemphasized. I am also aware that some try to use Calvin's quelling of riots, iconoclasm and vandalism[55] as an argument against what I am saying. Here I concur with Kingdon, who sees such behaviour as a sign not of his conservatism but merely of his pragmatism.[56]

---

53. He had written to Bullinger on 5 October 1559 of his fear that there would 'be no end to the bloodshed' (*CO*, vol. 17, col. 656, as cited in *John Calvin* (eds G. R. Potter and M. Greengrass; New York: St. Martin's Press, 1983) p. 163). He also wrote to Bullinger on 1 November 1560 lamenting that 'civil war in France is inevitable (*Ergo intestinum bellum in Gallia*)' (*CO*, vol. 18, col. 230).

54. *CO*, vol. 44, col. 433.

55. He states this in a letter, dated 26 February 1561, to the church of Paris, see *CO*, vol. 18, cols 376–8 (378).

56. Calvin's disapprobation of such practices, Kingdon argues, is founded on the fact that they 'may inflame public opinion without profitable result'. Kingdon, furthermore, contends that 'here we see again, … that Calvin's scruples had a practical base'. Kingdon, *Geneva and the Coming of the Wars*, pp. 111–12. Additionally, a few comments I have found from some of Calvin's trainees help support my case as they seem to suggest quite strongly that what these ministers imbibed from Calvin's lectures was, in fact, the idea of war. Kingdon records that ministers associated with Geneva, such as Jacques Ruffy, Augustin Marlorat and Martin Tachard, were linked with some of the violence that arose within France in the late 1550s and early 1560s. Marlorat, for instance, 'was accused of preaching war', a charge to which he replied by declaring 'that if [I] preached war, it was as [I] learned it in the word of God' (Kingdon, *Geneva and the Coming of the Wars*, p. 111. The report that records his answer is in the third person. I replaced 'he' with 'I' because it reads better). About these men, Kingdon writes: 'While these shreds of evidence are not conclusive and while there is nothing to tie these inciting activities

How does this help us understand Calvin's attitude towards the Nicodemites? It helps because it provides us with a crucial perspective from which to assess that attitude. It allows us to consider that, for Calvin, the Nicodemites may have been viewed as opponents not only spiritually but also politically and militarily.

Here the idea of Calvin's attitude towards Nicodemism hardening in later life resurfaces. For the considerations in this chapter help us to make sense of *why* his antipathy would have grown more intense over time. It would have, because Calvin, as time continued, would have begun thinking more seriously about the prospect of war and, thus, would surely have wondered on which side the Nicodemites would fight. Supporting this assertion further, I will say that it is wrong to think that the early flurry of writings from the late 1530s culminating in the anti-Nicodemite treatises of 1543 and 1544 represented the peak of Calvin's anti-Nicodemite sentiment or that his continued aggression towards them appeared only in his lectures on the prophets. Rather, Calvin's post-1544 aggression towards the Nicodemites appears in many places. We find, for instance, that in 1549 his *De vitandis superstitionibus* was published, which was a translation into Latin of his *Petit traicté* and *Excuse*. Calvin also, again in 1549, preached against the Nicodemite position in sermons on Psalm 16.4, Hebrews 13.13, and Psalms 27.4 and 27.8; these would be revised and published as *Quatre Sermons* in 1552. The year 1550 saw a reprint of *De vitandis superstitionibus* with the position of the Zurich ministers (Bullinger among them) included. Calvin's sermons on Acts, preached between late 1549 and early 1551, included references to the Nicodemites. He added material to his Romans commentary in 1551 censuring Nicodemite practices, and likewise, to his commentary on the gospel of John, which appeared in 1553 (see esp. on Jn 7.50[57]), and on Acts 21.26, which appeared in 1554.[58]

Thus, this chapter has sought to demonstrate that Calvin, from the mid-1550s onwards, wanted war in France in order to establish the gospel in the country and that his antipathy towards Nicodemism grew over time as more peaceful options for establishing the gospel in the country became less and less possible. He, in many places, reiterates his intense anger towards Nicodemism. And what we see is that this anger grew, arguably due to the fact that he came increasingly to view the Nicodemites as 'enemies', not only spiritually but also politically and militarily.

---

directly to Geneva, it is clear that in some areas Calvin's envoys were responsible for stimulating war fervor.' Despite conceding that it is impossible conclusively to tie this violence to Geneva, Kingdon reiterates the fact that all three of these men 'had been carefully trained and were highly regarded by Geneva' (Kingdon, *Geneva and the Coming of the Wars*, p. 111).

57. Commentary on John 7.50, *CO*, vol. 47, col. 187.

58. Wright, 'Why was Calvin so severe a critic of Nicodemism?', p. 74.

Bibliography

Arénilla, Louis, 'Le Calvinisme et le droit de résistance à l'Etat', *Annales: Economies, Societes, Civilizations* 22 (1967), pp. 350–69.

Balserak, Jon, *Establishing the Remnant Church in France; Calvin's Lectures on the Minor Prophets, 1556–1559* (Leiden: Brill, 2011).

Balserak, Jon, 'Examining the Myth of Calvin as a Lover of Order', in Peter Opitz (ed.), *The Myth of the Reformation* (Göttingen: Vandenhoeck & Ruprecht, 2013), pp. 160–75.

Balserak, Jon, *John Calvin as Sixteenth-Century Prophet* (Oxford: Oxford University Press, 2014).

Baron, Hans, 'Calvinist republicanism and its historical roots', *CH* 8 (1939), pp. 30–42.

Benedict, Philip, 'The Dynamics of Protestant Militancy: France, 1555–1563', in Philip Benedict, Guido Marnef, Henk van Nierop, and Marc Venard (eds), *Reformation, Revolt and Civil War in France and the Netherlands 1555–1585* (Amsterdam: Royal Netherlands Academy of Arts and Sciences, 1999), pp. 35–50.

Benedict, Philip, 'Prophets in Arms? Ministers in War, Ministers on War: France 1562–74', *Past and Present* 214: Issue suppl. 7 (2012), pp. 163–96.

Beza, Theodore, *Correspondance de Théodore de Bèze, Tome III: 1559–1561* (eds H. Meylan and A. Dufour; Travaux d'humanisme et Renaissance, 61; Geneva: Droz, 1663).

Bloch, Marc, *Les rois thaumaturges: Etude sur le Caractere Surnaturel Attribue a la Puissance Royale Particulierement en France et en Angleterre* (Oxford: Oxford University Press, 1924).

Bohatec, Josef, *Calvins Lehre von Staat und Kirche* (Breslau: M & H Marcus, 1937).

Boisset, Jean, 'La Non-violence et la tradition réformée', *Bulletin de la Société d'Histoire du Protestantisme Français* 113 (1967), pp. 202–19.

Calvin, John, *Ioannis Calvini opera quae supersunt omnia* (eds Guilielmus Baum, Eduardus Cunitz, and Eduardus Reuss; 59 vols; Brunswick: Schwetschke, 1863–1900).

Calvin, John, *John Calvin* (eds G. R. Potter and M. Greengrass; New York: St. Martin's Press, 1983).

Calvin, John, *La servante chassée: sermon inédit sur l'histoirè d'Agar (23 mars 1560)* (ed. Max Engammare; Geneva: Minizoé, 1995).

Calvin, John, *Letters of John Calvin* (ed. Jules Bonnet; trans. Marcus Gilchrist; 4 vols; Philadelphia: Presbyterian Board of Publications, 1858).

Calvin, John, *Luther and Calvin on Secular Authority* (ed. Harro Höpfl; Cambridge: Cambridge University Press, 1991).

Calvin, John, *Praelectiones in duodecim Prophetas minores* (Geneva: Jean Crespin, 1567).

Calvin, John, *Praelectiones in Librum prophetiarum Ieremiae, et Lamentationes* (Geneva: apud I. Crispinum, 1563).

Calvin, John, *Praelectiones ioannis calvini in librum prophetiarum danielis,* (s.l.: apud Bartholomaeum Vincentium, 1571).

Chenevière, Marc-Edouard, *La Pensée Politique de Calvin* (Paris: Editions Je Sers, 1937).

Courtenay, William J., *Covenant and Causality in Medieval Thought: Studies in Philosophy, Theology, and Economic Practice* (London: Variorum, 1984).

Crouzet, Denis, 'Calvinism and the Uses of the Political and the Religious (France, ca. 1560–ca. 1572)', in Philip Benedict, Guido Marnef, Henk van Nierop, and Marc Venard (eds), *Reformation, Revolt and Civil War in France and the Netherlands 1555–1585* (Amsterdam: Royal Netherlands Academy of Arts and Sciences, 1999), pp. 99–113.

Daussy, Hugues, 'Les huguenots entre l'obéissance au roi et l'obéissance à Dieu', *Nouvelle Revue du XVIe Siècle* 22 (2004), pp. 49–69.

Doumergue, Émile, *Jean Calvin, les hommes et les choses de son temps* (7 vols; Lausanne: G. Bridel & Cie., 1899–1927).

Droz, Eugénie, *Chemins de l'hérésie. Textes et documents* (4 vols; Geneva: Slatkine Reprints, 1970–76).

Dufour, Alain, 'L'affaire de Maligny (Lyon, 4–5 septembre 1560) vue à travers la correspondance de Calvin et de Bèze', *Cahiers d'Histoire* 8 (1963), pp. 269–80.

Eire, Carlos, *War Against the Idols. The Reformation of Worship from Erasmus to Calvin* (Cambridge: Cambridge University Press, 1986).

Engammare, Max, 'Calvin monarchomaque? Du soupçon à l'argument', *ARG* 89 (1998), pp. 207–26.

Ginzburg, Carlo, *Il Nicodemismo, Simulazione e dissimulazione religiosa nell' Europa del '500* (Turin: Guilio Einaudi, 1970).

Gooch, G. P., *English Democratic Ideas in the Seventeenth Century* (Cambridge: Cambridge University Press, 1898).

Graham, W. Fred, *The Constructive Revolutionary; John Calvin and his Socio-economic Impact* (Lancing: University of Michigan Press, 1987).

Hancock, Ralph, *Calvin and the Foundations of Modern Politics* (Ithaca and London: Cornell University Press, 1989).

Higman, Francis, 'Bucer et les nicodémites', in Christian Krieger and Marc Lienhard (eds), *Martin Bucer and Sixteenth Century Europe. Actes du colloque de Strasbourg (28–31 août 1991)* (2 vols; Leiden: E. J. Brill, 1993), vol. 2, pp. 645–58.

Higman, Francis, 'The Question of Nicodemism', in Wilhelm Niesel (ed.), *Calvinus Ecclesiae Genevensis Custos; Die Referate des Congrès International des Recherches Calviniennes ... Vom 6. bis 9. September 1982 in Genf* (Frankfurt am Main: Peter Lang, 1984), pp. 165–70.

Höpfl, Harro, *The Christian Polity of John Calvin* (Cambridge: Cambridge University Press, 1982).

Höpfl, Harro and Martyn P. Thompson, 'The History of Contract as a Motif in Political Thought', *The American Historical Review* 84/4 (1979), pp. 919–44.

Hudson, Winthrop, 'Democratic freedom and religious faith in the reformed tradition', *CH* 15 (1946), pp. 177–94.

Kantorowicz, Ernst, *The King's Two Bodies: A Study in Medieval Political Theology* (Princeton, NJ: Princeton University Press, 1957).

Kingdon, Robert, 'Calvin and Calvinists on Resistance to Government', in David F. Wright, A. N. S. Lane, and Jon Balserak (eds), *Calvinus Evangelii Propugnator: Calvin Champion of the Gospel; Papers Presented at the International Congress on Calvin Research, Seoul, 1998* (Grand Rapids: CRC Product Services, 2006), pp. 54–65.

Kingdon, Robert, 'Calvin's Socio-Political Legacy: Collective Government, Resistance to Tyranny, Discipline', in David Foxgrover (ed.), *The Legacy of John Calvin; Papers Presented at the 12th Colloquium of the Calvin Studies Society, April 22–24, 1999* (Grand Rapids: CRC Product Services, 2000), pp. 112–23.

Kingdon, Robert, *Geneva and the Coming of the Wars of Religion in France, 1555–1563* (Geneva: Droz, 1956).

Lillback, Peter, *The Binding of God: Calvin's Role in the Development of Covenant Theology* (Grand Rapids: Baker and Paternoster, 2001).

Lloyd, H. A., 'Calvin and the Duty of Guardians to Resist', *JEH* 32 (1981), pp. 65–7.

Maag, Karin, *Seminary or University? The Genevan Academy and Reformed Higher Education, 1560–1620* (Aldershot: Ashgate, 1995).

Matheson, Peter, 'Martyrdom or Mission? A Protestant Debate', *ARG* 80 (1989), pp. 154–72.

McNeill, John T., 'The Democratic Element in Calvin's Thought', *CH* 18 (1949), pp. 153–71.

Mellet, Paul-Alexis, *Les Traités monarchomaques. Confusion des temps, résistance armée et monarchie parfaite (1560–1600)* (Geneva: Droz, 2007).

Millet, Olivier, *Calvin et la dynamique de la parole: Etude de rhétorique réformée* (Genève: Editions Slatkine, 1992).

Naef, Henri, *La Conjuration d'Amboise et Genève* (Geneva: Jullien, 1922).

Naphy, William, *Calvin and the Consolidation of the Genevan Reformation* (Manchester: University of Manchester Press, 1994).

Nijenhuis, Willem (ed.), 'The limits of civil disobedience in Calvin's last-known sermons: development of his ideas on the right of civil resistance', in *Ecclesia Reformata: v. 2: Studies on the Reformation* (Leiden: Brill, 1994), pp. 73–94.

Olson, Jeannine, *Calvin and Social Welfare: Deacons and the Bourse française* (London and Toronto: Associated University Presses; Selinsgrove: Susquehanna University Press, 1989).

Parker, T. H. L., *Calvin's Old Testament Commentaries* (Edinburgh: T&T Clark, 1986).

Roelker, Nancy Lyman, *One King, One Faith; The Parlement of Paris and the Religious Reformations of the Sixteenth Century* (Berkeley: University of California Press, 1996).

Roget, Amédée, *Histoire du peuple de Genève depuis la Réforme jusqu'à l'Escalade* (7 vols; Geneva: Jullien, 1870–83).

Rott, Jean and Olivier Millet, 'Miettes historiques Strasbourgeoises', in Pierre Barthel, Rémy Scheurer, and Richard Stauffer (eds), *Actes du Colloque Guillaume Farel, Neuchâtel 29 septembre—1er octobre 1980* (2 vols; Neuchâtel: Revue de théologie et de philosophie, 1983), vol. 1, pp. 253–77.

Schramm, Percy, *Der König von Frankreich: das Wesen der Monarchie vom 9. zum 16. Jahrhundert, ein Kapitel aus der Geschichte des abendländischen Staates* (Weimar: H. Böhlaus Nachfolger, 1939).

Skinner, Quentin, *The Foundations of Modern Political Thought* (2 vols; Cambridge: Cambridge University Press, 1978).

Sprenger, Paul, *Das Rätsel um die Bekehrung Calvins* (Neukirchen: Kreis Moers, 1960).

Stein, Peter, 'Calvin and the Duty of Guardians to Resist: A Comment', *JEH* 32 (1981), pp. 69–70.

Strayer, Joseph R., 'France: The Holy Land, the Chosen People, and the Most Christian King', in Theodore Rabb and Jerrold Seigel (eds), *Action and Conviction in Early Modern Europe; Essays in Memory of E. H. Harbison* (Princeton: Princeton University Press, 1969), pp. 3–16.

Strohl, Henri, 'Le Droit a la resistance d'apres les conceptions protestantes', *Revue d'histoire et de philosophie religieuses* (1930), pp. 126–39.

Tavard, George, 'Calvin and the Nicodemites', in Randall C. Zachman (ed.), *John Calvin and Roman Catholicism; Critique and Engagement, Then and Now* (Grand Rapids: Baker, 2008), pp. 59–78.

Ullmann, Walter, 'Calvin and the Duty of the Guardians to Resist: A Further Comment', *JEH* 32 (1981), pp. 499–501.

Walzer, Michael, *The Revolution of the Saints: A Study in the Origins of Radical Politics* (Cambridge, MA: Harvard University Press, 1965).

Whitford, David, 'Robbing Paul to Pay Peter; The Reception of Paul in Sixteenth Century Political Theology', in R. Ward Holder (ed.), *A Companion to Paul in the Reformation* (Leiden: Brill, 2009), pp. 573–606.

Wilcox, Peter, 'The lectures of John Calvin and the nature of his audience', in *ARG* 87 (1996), pp. 136–48.

Witte, John R., *The Reformation of Rights* (Cambridge: University of Cambridge Press, 2007).

Wolin, Sheldon, 'Calvin and the Reformation: The Political Education of Protestantism', *The American Political Science Review* 51/2 (1957), pp. 428–53.

Wright, David F., 'Why was Calvin so severe a critic of Nicodemism?', in David F. Wright, A. N. S. Lane, and Jon Balserak (eds), *Calvinus Evangelii Propugnator: Calvin Champion of the Gospel; Papers Presented at the International Congress on Calvin Research, Seoul, 1998* (Grand Rapids: CRC Product Services, 2006), pp. 66–90.

Zagorin, Perez, *Ways of Lying; Dissimulation, Persecution, and Conformity in Early Modern Europe* (Cambridge, MA: Harvard University Press, 1990).

Chapter 6

THE PROTESTANT IMAGE OF THE COUNCIL OF TRENT*

Herman J. Selderhuis

The topic of this chapter is expansive, comprehensive and poorly understood. It is expansive because it presupposes that there is an 'image' of Trent – that is, that Protestants have some conception of the Council of Trent; comprehensive because it presupposes that there is only one understanding of Trent and that something like 'Protestants' exist as a monolith; and poorly understood precisely because, so far, substantive discussions have been carried out primarily by German Lutheran theologians. I will, despite the diversity within Protestantism, try to regard it as a denominational unit, and will mainly direct my attention to the early modern period, although I will say something about the newer developments in Protestants' understanding of Trent at the end.

1 Challenge and Beginning: Scepticism and Rejection

The Protestant view of Trent has for centuries largely been characterized by the reactions of the leading Reformers to the convocation of the council and its first decisions.[1] Thus, the negative image of Trent among Protestants was already established even before there was a council at all. The text of the convocation and the unfavourable political situation for Protestants made them feel certain that nothing good was to be expected from this council. That a council should be called had long

* A German version of this chapter was presented at the conference 'Das Konzil von Trient und die katholische Konfessionskultur (1563-2013)' organized by the Gesellschaft zur Herausgabe des *Corpus Catholicorum* e.V., Freiburg, 18–21 September 2013. I want to thank Jim West for his translation.

1. Erwin Iserloh, 'Luther und das Konzil von Trient', in *Kirche-Ereignis und Institution. Aufsätze und Vorträge* (2 vols; Münster: Aschendorff, 1985), vol. 2, pp. 181–93; Ernst Koch, 'Die Deutschen Protestanten und das Konzil von Trient', in Wolfgang Reinhard and Heinz Schilling (eds), *Die katholische Konfessionalisierung* (Schriften des Vereins für Reformationsgeschichte, 198; Gütersloh: Gütersloher Verlagshaus, 1995), pp. 88–103; Robert Stupperich, 'Die Reformatoren und das Tridentinum', *ARG* 47 (1956), pp. 20–63.

been a desire on the part of the Reformers,[2] as well as reform-minded Catholics as, for example, was shown in the years 1518–63 when in German language areas alone, a total of 562 publications are known that deal with the topic of a council.[3] Luther had repeatedly called for a council and such a council should be, in his opinion, a free, general, Christian and German one. What he meant by 'free' was that it was not to be led by the Pope or by the Curia but by the Holy Scriptures and be an open discussion held with an open Bible. 'German' referred to the belief that the ecclesiastical and, consequently, societal conflicts were being played out in the empire. When in June 1536 news came of the appointment of the council, to begin on 23 May 1537 in Mantua, the Reformers were very doubtful whether these two requirements – that it be free and German – would be met, and whether it was even to be hoped that anything positive would come from the council. Luther and Melanchthon could offer advice, but they were rejected as participants. Melanchthon had somewhat higher hopes than Luther. Luther saw the council as very similar to that which was held in Constance from 1414 to 1418 and therefore republished three letters of John Hus in 1536.[4] Luther feared that the council would only confirm the course of Rome and reinforce the power of the Pope. In his *On Councils and Churches*,[5] he wrote that if the Pope stood above the council, this was not a Christian congregation but a dictatorship. Thus the image of Trent was widely preconceived. Luther's warning triumphed over Melanchthon's optimism and the Schmalkaldic League refused to participate in the Council in 1537.

This position had not changed in 1542 as a new council tender was granted on 22 May. Over the full width of the Protestant spectrum there was scepticism – which became apparent in a variety of portrayals of events[6] – resulting essentially in the rejection of such a council. This scepticism was strengthened by the fact that the sessions, even before Luther's view of the proceedings had been made public, had been a disappointment. Even those Reformers such as Martin Bucer and Philipp Melanchthon who over the years had shown a willingness to talk, and had assumed an attitude that was described by Luther (in relation to Melanchthon) as pussyfooting about, expressed their critical disappointment. Perhaps they had already given up hope after working so hard to bring about a reconciliation through discussions of religion. The invitations to the council – the Protestants were invited to attend all three sessions – were rejected by the Protestant princes.[7]

2. Eike Wolgast, 'Das Konzil in den Erörterungen der kursächsischen Theologen und Politiker 1533–1537', *ARG* 73 (1982), pp. 122–52.

3. Thomas Brockmann, *Die Konzilsfrage in den Flug- und Streitschriften des deutschen Sprachraums 1518–1563* (Göttingen: Vandenhoeck and Ruprecht, 1998), p. 399.

4. *WA*, vol. 50, pp. 23–4.

5. Ibid., pp. 509–653.

6. Hugo Holstein, *Die Reformation im Spiegelbilde der dramatischen Literatur des sechzehnten Jahrhunderts* (Halle: Verein für Reformationsgeschichte,1886), pp. 227–8.

7. Hubert Jedin, *Geschichte des Konzils von Trient* (4 vols; Freiburg, Herder, 1949–75), vol. 1, pp. 256–8.

The theologians had to follow the princes' example and so they did. Luther had already set the tone in his *Against the Papacy at Rome, An Institution of the Devil* and made therein quite clear what he thought of the council.[8] His death on 18 February 1546 ensured that this remained his position. On 11 February 1545, after they had heard that the council had already begun its work, Johannes Bugenhagen, Caspar Cruciger and Philipp Melanchthon drafted a report in which they hinted that 'we would request of the Emperor and the Emperor has assured us that you shall hear us, and that our basic teachings will be displayed to the council',[9] but after learning of the first decrees, the picture was clear for the Protestants. Melanchthon said the council erred, and its decisions, especially about justification, were contrary to the gospel. His greatest difficulty was the Tridentine condemnation of the assurance of salvation. Trent brings the believer to the point of despair.[10] He expressed his opinion of the council in such a way that it was clear to everyone what he thought of it: 'We are not alone but others agree that in this council of Trent we are not heard, nor are other learned and free worshippers of God allowed to defend sufficiently the truth.'[11] His attitude was the same as that of the states at the Diet of Worms in 1545. Martin Bucer informed Philip of Hesse of his view of Trent.[12] The Strassburger knew, like no other, the various positions because he had actively participated in religious discussions and was the most 'ecumenical' Reformer. He complained that this was not the council that they had been promised. He clarified himself in an open letter to the council participants, accusing them of having done nothing against false doctrine and the corrupt behaviour of the church hierarchy.[13] It was clear to him 'that the Council of Trent mocks loudly'.[14] The Protestants stayed away: physically as well as ecclesiastically and theologically, and this distance and the perception of this distance was characteristic of the image of Trent for the Protestants at that time and has remained so ever since.

The many writings of the Protestant side rejected, for the same reasons mentioned above, any participation in such a council and unanimously made comparison to the Council of Constance where the condemnation of Hus was clear from the very

8. *WA*, vol. 54, pp. 195, 206–99.

9. Melanchthon, *Philippi Melanthonis opera quae supersunt omnia* (eds C. G. Bretschneider and H. E. Bindseil; 28 vols; Halle: C. A. Schwetschke, 1834–60), vol. 6, col. 45.

10. Melanchthon, *Melanchthons Werke in Auswahl* (eds Robert Stupperich et al.; 7 vols; Gütersloh: Gerd Mohn, 1951–75), vol. 6, p. 319.

11. Melanchthon, *Melanchthons Werke in Auswahl*, vol. 1, p. 446, lin. 10–13.

12. Martin Bucer, *Martin Bucers Deutsche Schriften* (eds R. Stupperich, Marijn de Kroon, Hartmut Rudolph, Stephen E. Buckwalter, Cornelis Augustijn Hans Schulz, Christoph Strohm, and Thomas Wilhelmi; 17 vols; Gütersloh: Gerd Mohn/Gütersloher Verlagshaus, 1960–2004), vol. 13, pp. 203–25.

13. Bucer, *Ad patres in synodo Tridentina, qui Deum timent, de causis, quae pios homines ab ea synodo absterrent* (Neuburgi Danubij: Kilian, 1546), vol. 16, col. 8930.

14. Quotation in Robert Stupperich, 'Die Reformatoren und das Tridentinum', p. 43. See also Martin Bucer's 'Zwei Decret des Trientischen Concili', in *Deutsche Schriften*, vol 15, cols 245–69.

outset. There was no safe conduct for the Bohemian. There would be none now and any participation by the Protestants would be dangerous. This comparison with the events of the Council of Constance in 1415 and the opponents of Hus was drawn by Luther, as already mentioned concerning his editions of the letters of Hus, and it had a significant effect among the Protestants in justifying the rejection of the decisions of Trent. One can rightly say that the image of Trent has largely remained determined. The theological content was crucial in the Protestants' rejection of the council's decisions when the determinations in the 'Proposita a Legatis' of 30 June 1546 were adopted by the Decree of 13 January 1547. These decisions were seen as significant because of their rejection of the Lutheran doctrine of justification and the Calvinist doctrine of election.[15] Although the information that they had from the council was not always complete, it was enough to know the intentions of the council and to reject its position.

John Calvin followed the course of events and carefully studied the promulgations of the council as is made clear by his publications.[16] The complaint sent by the Pope to Emperor Charles V, the 'Admonitio paterna', after the emperor had promised a national or even general council at the Diet of Speyer, was published by Calvin with sharply ironic annotations.[17] Calvin's criticism of the Council of Trent was sharp. He called it a trap, which the Germans would be stupid to fall into as by doing so they would be going directly into the mouth of the wolves. In any case, the council is useless because what would be discussed there, namely, the teachings of the Reformation, had long been condemned. Calvin's suspicions were then confirmed by the declarations of the council itself. On 3 March 1547 the Council concluded its work and was adjourned until 1551. In December 1547 the detailed reaction of Calvin appeared in his *Antidotum*,[18] the content of which was based on a thorough examination of the decrees. No later than August 1547 he had the texts of the first session of the council, as well as details of the discussions.[19] In this work Calvin provides the full text of the resolutions along with critical comments on each. In this he was chiefly interested in the doctrine of justification as described by Trent, which he carefully analysed and rejected. Along with Melanchthon, he says that

15. H. Rückert, *Die Rechtfertigungslehre auf dem tridentinischen Konzil* (Bonn: de Gruyter, 1925).

16. See also Maarten Stolk, 'Calvin und Katholizismus', in Herman J. Selderhuis (ed.), *Calvin Handbuch* (Tübingen: Mohr Siebeck, 2008), pp. 104–12.

17. John Calvin, 'Admonitio paterna Pauli III. Ad Carolum V, cum scholiis', in *CO*, vol. 7, cols 249–88.

18. John Calvin, 'Acta Synodi Tridentinae cum Antidoto', in *CO*, vol. 7, cols 341–64. See also W. F. Dankbaar, 'Calvijns oordeel over het concilie van Trente, inzonderheid inzake het rechtvaardigingsdecreet', in *Hervormers en Humanisten. Een bundel opstellen* (Amsterdam: Ton Bolland, 1978), pp. 67–99.

19. Possible explanations why Calvin was informed at such an early stage are given by Eberhard Busch, *Calvin Studienausgabe, vol. 3: Reformatorische Kontroversen* (Neukirchen-Vluyn: Neukirchener Verlag, 1999), p. 110, n. 13.

from the Reformation point of view, the Tridentine notion of justification does away with the assurance of salvation, and the fear of God and death returns. Unlike Melanchthon, who ranked the decrees as 'cloaca diaboli' and described the council fathers as 'vera diaboli membra', Calvin sought a dialogue. The Genevan Reformer, in his rejection of the primacy of the Pope, looked more closely at the council's ideas.[20] It was not a mere rejection of the council and its decrees but a substantive discussion that occupies his *Acta Synodi Tridentinae, Cum Antidoto*[21] and he, consequently, only calls it a 'Censura'. The work of Calvin, which soon appeared in a French translation edited by Calvin himself,[22] was seen as a threat, as shown by the traditionalists' response to him, for example, that of John Cochlaeus.[23] Calvin expressed himself with ridicule and mockery concerning the actions and objectives of the council. Many of the participants he classified as uneducated and some even as stupid. In addition, some have a morally dubious reputation. But more importantly, the council is, in his opinion, nothing more than an instrument of the Pope which seeks, not to reform but to counter, the Reformation. However, Calvin's view of Trent was not wholly negative, because he agreed with some of the anathemas pronounced, openly and explicitly. Thus the condemnation of Pelagianism and antinomianism gets his full affirmation, and he expresses differences on other issues and is more critical than the formulations in some of the decrees. On the Calvinist side, the reaction of Innocent Gentillet is also noteworthy. He worked as a lawyer and politician in the 1570s and 1580s in southeastern France, and in his writing, the political aspect of Trent is also discussed.[24] *Le bureau du Concile de Trente* was published in 1586 and appeared soon after in Latin, Dutch[25] and German editions. Gentillet saw Trent as a threat to the political situation in France because of the excommunication of the king of Navarre by Pope Sixtus V and because the French clergy had asked King Henry III whether the decisions of Trent could not be part of French law. This reference to the political significance of Trent is also found in the Dutch literature, as will become apparent below.

20. T. W. Casteel, 'Calvin and Trent: Calvin's Reaction to the Council of Trent in the Context of his Conciliar Thought', *HTR* 63 (1970), pp. 91–117 (100–14).

21. *CO*, vol. 7, cols 442–73.

22. The title was 'Les Actes du Concile de Trente: avec le remede contre la poison', and it was published in 1548.

23. John Calvin, *Ioannis Calvini in Acta Synodi Tridentinae Censura et eiusdem Brevis Confutatio circa duas praecipue calumnias, per Ioannem Cochlaeum* (Behem, 1548).

24. Robert M. Kingdon, 'Some French Reactions to the Council of Trent', *CH* 33 (1964), pp. 149–56.

25. *Examen ende proeve des conciliums van Trenten: Daer by even als in een waechschaele ghesien ende beproeft werdt, dat dit concilium in veele poincten ende articulen reghelrecht contrarie is ende strijdet soo wel teghens d'oude concilien ende canones, als teghens d'authoriteyt vande con.ke ma.t van Vranckrijcke/Eerst in Fransois beschreven door Innocent Gentillet ..., ende nu onlancx in Nederduytsche taele overgheset* (Delf: Bruyn Harmansz. Schinckel, 1589).

The image of Trent held by the Swiss Protestants was largely determined by three reports by Heinrich Bullinger to the Zurich authorities on behalf of the Zurich clergy.[26] In the first report, dated 1 August 1546,[27] Bullinger, who, like Calvin, was informed accurately about the events of the council, stated why Zurich could not attend the proceedings at Trent. Although they were willing to discuss the issues, they could still not attend because they feared that the council would do to them what had been done to Hus in Constance. If the council is only there to deny heresies, and the Zurichers are branded as heretics from the outset, it is just too dangerous to go there. According to Bullinger, the council simply wants to condemn Protestant doctrine as heresy, which will be easy because the plaintiffs and the judges are the same people. In addition, for the people of Zurich, the position of the Pope is problematic. You can, first, only recognize Christ as Lord; and second, one is bound to obey on earth only the Zurich authorities. In the second report, dated 5 July 1551,[28] the papal invitation to the second session is discussed again in detail but Bullinger could come to no other conclusion than to reject it. The decisions already made at the first meeting make participation impossible, and reaffirm his belief that the council has not been held in the old apostolic tradition. It is not surprising that his third report, which appeared on 13 May 1562,[29] was decidedly negative. Because nothing has changed in the council, Bullinger has come to the conclusion that Zurich cannot respond differently than it has in its first two reactions.

The picture was clear among all Protestants: Trent takes place in the wrong place, with the wrong people, under the wrong conditions, thus leading to incorrect results. Trent changes nothing, but only confirms the Catholic condemnation of Protestants and their teachings.

2 Continuation and Conclusion: Disappointment and Rejection

Even the relocation of the Council in March 1547 to Bologna was interpreted in Protestant publications as a fraud. Although the outbreak of typhoid in Trent had been given by officials as the reason, Protestant authors saw it as a papal trick.[30] This

26. Rudolf Pfister, 'Zu Bullingers Beurteilung des Konzils von Trient', in Ulrich Gäbler and Erland Herkenrath (eds), *Heinrich Bullinger 1504–1575; Gesammelte Aufsätze* (2 vols; Zürich: Zürcher Beiträge zur Reformationsgeschichte, 1975), vol. 1, pp. 123–40.

27. 'Antwort der Predigeren zu Zürich/uff des Papst Laden in das Concilium zu Trient/1546. Concipiert von Hrn. Heinrich Bulling', in *Heinrich Bullinger Bibliographie* (eds Joachim Staedtke and Erland Herkenrath; 3 vols; Zurich: TVZ, 1972–2004), vol. 1, nr. 733 (henceforth *HBBibl I*).

28. *HBBibl I*, p. 229, nr. 27.

29. 'Antwort der Kirchendieneren zu Zürich/auf des Pabst drittes Einladen auf das Concilum zu Trient/An. 1562. Authore Hrn. Heinrich Bullinger', in *HBBibl I*, p. 716, nr. 27.

30. Thomas Brockmann, *Die Konzilsfrage in den Flug- und Streitschriften des deutschen Sprachraums 1518–1563*, pp. 404–5, n. 3.

criticism and scepticism are the reasons that during the second meeting, only a few Protestant jurists and theologians attended, and only because they were forced to do so by the Emperor.[31] The theologians who were delegated from Saxony – Philipp Melanchthon, Erasmus Sarcerius and Valentin Pacaeus – were stuck in Nuremberg in February 1552, probably because Maurice of Saxony had developed a scheme that attendance at the council seemed to make redundant.[32] The jurists and theologians who were present – and they were not among the leaders – then insisted on a free council, and the resumption of talks on the measures taken in the first period of doctrinal decisions. The council fathers, by contrast, were determined to continue from where they had concluded in 1546. Accordingly, it quickly became clear that the Protestant presence would change nothing. Their opinion of Trent, therefore, also did not change at all. The Council of Trent in 1546, the Schmalkaldic war in 1547 and the Augsburg Interim of 1548 were all united in one design; they were all directed against the Reformation of Luther. The emperor was very successful and basically had the final say over the Protestant princes, and even if the developments of the council were not completely according to the views of Charles V, the Protestants expected very little from him in any event.

The third session of the council was seen by Lutherans as crucial. If reunification were still possible, it would be now or never. But soon after its opening, the sense grew that there would be a lasting rupture leading to a decisive and final separation. On the one hand, the council was seen as a turning point in that it was seen as a break with tradition and with the views and decisions of the early church, and on the other, it was seen as a continuation of both an unbiblical theology and an unbiblical practice. Very significant and formative for the image of Trent was the criticism of Gnesio-Lutheran theologians like Matthias Flacius Illyricus, who was working at the time in Regensburg, and Nicolaus Gallus, superintendent in Regensburg who had carefully followed the course of the council over the years.[33] They published several journals and in 1563 presented a declaration that was signed by 34 Gnesio-Lutheran theologians and which accused the council of wanting to destroy true religion and the true church.[34] In other publications during the years 1562 and 1563, Flacius and Gallus made it clear that this council was not free and had not taken the Scriptures as the norm. Their criticism was that many of the delegates were not even able to read the Bible in the original languages, and regarding this criticism even Luther's foe Erasmus would have agreed. For a general public

31. Helmut Meyer, 'Die deutschen Protestanten an der zweiten Tagungsperiode des Konzils von Trient 1551/52', *ARG* 55 (1964), pp. 166–209.

32. Koch, *Die Deutschen Protestanten*, p. 93, n. 1.

33. Robert Kolb, 'The German Lutheran Reaction to the Third Period of the Council of Trent', *Luther Jahrbuch* 51 (1984), pp. 63–95.

34. Mathias Flacius Illyricus and Nicolaus Gallus, *Protestatio concionatorum aliquot Augustanae Confessionis, adversus conventum Tridentinum, perniciem verae religioni & Ecclesiae molientem … Accessit Norma simul et praxis constituendae religionis ac Ecclesiae, dirimendarumque controversiarum, jam pontifice & synodo recepta ac usitata* (s.l., 1563).

that was, apparently, not well acquainted with Reformation doctrine, a booklet was published by Flacius entitled *A True Warning*[35] which sought to warn it of the seductive dimension of the decrees. The power of the pope and the powers of the bishops were seen by Flacius as a threat to Protestant territories and, thus, by so stating his opinion of Trent, he showed that the political dimension clearly played a significant role. He was not concerned with political independence but with the politics of the government as displayed in the introduction and implementation of the Reformation. Also striking in the polemics of Flacius and Gallus is the fact that the position of the Pope is described in much greater detail than, for example, the Mass or the doctrine of justification. This theme is dealt with by Martin Chemnitz in the much more influential work *Examen Concilii Tridentini*, published in 23 editions between 1564 and 1574.[36] Unlike Flacius and Gallus, Chemnitz was provided the opportunity to systematically and thoroughly engage the official texts of the Council of Trent.

One feature of the early modern view of Trent among Protestants is the relatively great importance placed on the historical component and the conspicuous absence of the recognition of the reforming endeavours of the council. As for the historical component, although content and theology are, indeed, discussed by the Protestant side, the council is, nonetheless, severely criticized as a deviation from the way early church councils were organized. This break with tradition can only be rejected and will have negative consequences: such is their final verdict. Regarding the reforming aspect of the council, nothing is said. Trent is not perceived in the early modern literature as an initiative to eliminate church abuses and to revive the church again.

Politics

One aspect that has been mentioned only briefly is the political dimension of the council and the resulting image of Trent as a political threat or, as Leopold von Ranke put it, 'a conquering power.'[37] The decisions of the council evoked the impression of a strong church, which was once more closing ranks and which had set out to regain lost ground, by force if necessary, and to strengthen its position over secular rulers as well. Although it was also true of certain Catholic

---

35. Mathias Flacius Illyricus and Nicolaus Gallus, *Trewe Warnung für dem hochschedlichen betrug des Bapsts vnnd seines Concilij, damit sie vndter einem schein des nachgebens etlicher geringer Artickel, die einfeltigen Christen zu allen jren greweln zwingen, vnd auffs höchste verbinden wöllen* (Regensburg: Geißler, 1563).

36. Reinhard Mumm, *Die Polemik des Martin Chemnitz gegen das Konzil von Trient* (Leipzig: Erster Teil, 1905).

37. 'Nach dem tridentinischen Concilium, ward Rom noch einmal eine erobernde Macht; es machte Entwürfe, es fing Unternehmungen an, wie sie von diesem sieben Hügeln in der alten Zeit, in den mittlern Jahrhunderten ausgegangen waren' (Leopold von Ranke, *Die römischen Päpste in den letzten vier Jahrhunderten* (Hamburg: Neuausgabe, 2013), p. 317).

princes, Trent was seen by most Protestant authorities as a threat to their recently recovered independence. The connection of Trent with Spain was understood in this regard as massively threatening. This is particularly evident in the history of the Dutch revolution. William of Orange, even as a Catholic, made it clear that he would accept the decrees of the council only in so far as they did not restrict freedom of religion.[38] On 31 December 1564, he publicly declared in a meeting of the 'Raad van State': 'Je suis à rester décidé Catholique, mais je ne puis approuver que les princes veuillent commander aux consciences humaines et la liberté de foi supprimer et de religion.'[39] This political reserve was further underpinned by the transition to Calvinist theology. After the start of the revolt against Spain in 1566, Trent and Spain were seen as a unity. The General Acts declared in 1598 that the reason that Spain went to war against the Netherlands was because Spain's claim to the papal Roman religion was foundational, and her desire to dominate Europe through this religion was divinely appointed.[40] To be against Spanish domination was understood to be, at the same time, opposed to the decrees of Trent, and vice-versa. Thus Trent was seen as a symbol of oppression and resistance to Dutch independence, and the Pope and his power were also pictorially represented as the enemies of freedom.

3 Description and Image: Separation and Rejection

Only a few remarks can be made in this chapter concerning the image of Trent in Protestant historiography, in part because there is little research on this topic. What is clear is that from the outset, in denominational church histories like the *Magdeburg Centuries* was laid a foundation of belief that centuries of decay culminated in the grand finale of the council. Popular with Protestants was the work of Fra Paolo Sarpi (1552–1623), the Catholic Venetian who, in 1619, anonymously published his *Istoria del Concilio Tridentino*. This strongly critical history of the Council was published in London after research in the archives of Rome and Venice.[41] Sarpi's main concern was the freedom of Venice to defend itself against the council and to reject, on historical grounds, the absolutism of the Pope, but his account contained so much criticism of the council that Sarpi was often used by the Protestant side as a source of arguments against Trent. It appeared in German, English, French and Latin translations initiated in almost all cases by Protestant

---

38. See F. Willocx, *L'Introduction des décrets du Concile de Trente dans les Pays-Bas et dans la Principauté de Liége* (Louvain: Librairie Universitaire, 1929), pp. 124–36.

39. Quotation from L. J. Rogier, *Geschiedenis van het katholicisme in Noord-Nederland in de 16ᵉ en 17ᵉ eeuw* (3 vols; Amsterdam: Urbi et Orbi, 1947), vol. 1, p. 270.

40. A. T. van Deursen, *Honni soit qui mal y pense? De Republiek tussen de mogendheden (1610–1612)* (Amsterdam: Noord-Hollandsche Uitgevers Maatschappij, 1965), p. 28.

41. David Wootton, *Paolo Sarpi: Between Renaissance and Enlightenment* (Cambridge: Cambridge University Press, 1983).

theologians. The English Protestant scholar and poet of *Paradise Lost* John Milton called Sarpi 'the great unmasker'.[42] One of the works of Sarpi was reissued in French by Pierre Jurieu (1637–1713), one of the leading theologians of the Huguenots in the seventeenth century and, from 1682 until his death, professor and pastor in Rotterdam.[43] In 1682, shortly after he began working in Rotterdam, he published a short version of Sarpi's conciliar history in Geneva, and it included an extensive introduction preceded by a listing of the arguments of the Protestant side against the council.[44] The aim of this discourse was made clear in the subtitle, namely 'pour prouver que les Protestants ne sont pas obligez à se soumettre à ce dernier Concile'. From a French perspective, in particular, Jurieu analysed the decrees of Trent, with his final judgement being that, other than calling for a council, Protestants do not need to abide by its decisions. The arguments are the same as those seen in the Reformers of the sixteenth century, namely that the council is not free and is not universal, etc. Instead, there is an emphasis on the rights of the Catholic bishops who are in serious danger from the council and the claims to power by the Pope. In the opinion of Jurieu, this interest is also the reason that the decrees were not well accepted in France by the Catholic clergy.[45] From the political perspective there were also problems with Trent because by virtue of the decrees the clergy in the land were deemed to be independent princes, and the French princes could not accept that.[46] Jurieu used his Protestant opinion of Trent in order to call for French Catholicism to be accepting of the Huguenots at a time when the Revocation of the Edict of Nantes (1685) was already in the offing. Are not even the Huguenots French and is that not how it has been in France forever? But which understanding of Trent should you then follow? Jurieu's image of Trent is that the council is essentially hostile to both the French Protestants and the French Catholics.

Mention can here be made of a representative of the tradition of Scottish Calvinism, the theologian William Cunningham (1805–61), and his two volume *Historical Theology*, which reached a wide readership because his book served as teaching material for the study of theology.[47] He devotes twelve pages to

42. Peter Burke, 'The great unmasker: Paolo Sarpi, 1551–1613', *History Today* 15 (1965), pp. 426–32 (430).

43. F. R. J. Knetsch, *Pierre Jurieu. Theoloog en politikus der refuge* (Kampen: Kok, 1967); Hartmut Kretzer, *Calvinismus und französische Monarchie im 17. Jahrhundert. Die politische Lehre der Akademien Sedan und Saumur, mit besonderer Berücksichtigung von Pierre du Moulin, Moyse Amyraut und Pierre Jurieu* (Berlin: Duncker & Humblot, 1975).

44. Pierre Jurieu, *Abbrege de l'Histoire du concile de Trente avec un discours contenant les Reflexions Historiques sur les Conciles & particulierement sur la conduite de celuy de Trente,* … (Geneva: J. Herman Widerhold, 1682).

45. Jurieu, *Abbrege*, p. 52, n. 44.

46. See, '… petits Souverains independans des Princes', Jurieu, *Abbrege*, p. 80.

47. William Cunningham, *Historical Theology. A Review of the Principal Doctrinal Discussions in the Christian Church since the Apostolic Age* (2 vols; Edinburgh: T&T Clark, 1862).

the Council of Trent – which he suggests is a mini-history of the Church of Rome[48] – because this council has become so decisive for Catholic doctrine and its relation to the Reformation. Cunningham can only see the council as an act of Rome against the newly resurrected truth of God. The council was completely dominated by the Roman Curia, which succeeded in implementing its decrees with cunning and deceit. Most participants were 'just the creatures and hired agents of the Pope'.[49] The large majority of the council's participants were Italians and so it never was a universal council. Some of them were even made bishops overnight so that they could participate at all. Cunningham confirmed that the views of Luther were portrayed very inaccurately and had been compiled only from select individual publications and statements of the Reformer, and yet Trent was still responsible for the condemnation of the gospel of grace as this message had been rediscovered by Luther. Cunningham is positive that there is not as much Pelagianism in the decrees of Trent as in the writings of Luther's first Roman opponents, but still enough 'to charge the Church of Rome with perverting the gospel of the grace of God, and subverting the scriptural method of salvation'.[50] This picture of Trent as a council that purposefully opposed the revealed will of God,[51] coming to a head in the idea that the pope is the Antichrist, has been part of the tradition of Puritanism and much of Orthodox Calvinism to the present day.

For example – and an important one at that – is the eighty-page presentation of the council by Reinhold Seeberg, a German Protestant, in the last part of his well-known and widely used textbook *The History of Dogma*.[52] Seeberg called the clear rejection of Protestantism the main goal of the council and this is the same judgement Seeberg makes on the efforts to reform the church.[53] This goal also meant that the council's decrees 'have raised medieval theology to the level of dogma', which then led to an 'abrasion or concealment of doctrinal contradictions'.[54]

For Seeberg, Trent is the birth of the essence of Catholicism, which he summarizes in relation to God and to the relationship of church and state under the term 'legalism'. For Luther, he then used the term 'Pneumatismus' because 'the idea of grace in early Christianity has been restored and the religion of salvation

---

48. 'In short, the history of the Council of Trent is just an epitome or miniature of the history of the Church of Rome.' Cunningham, *Historical Theology*, vol. 1, p. 488.

49. Ibid., vol. 1, p. 487.

50. Ibid., vol. 1, p. 494.

51. 'determined opposition to God's revealed will, …', Cunningham, *Historical Theology*, vol. 1, p. 488.

52. Reinhold Seeberg, *Lehrbuch der Dogmengeschichte* (4 vols; Leipzig: W. Scholl, 1895–1920), vol. 4, pp. 753–834.

53. 'aber auch die praktischen Reformen … verfolgten schließlich die Absicht, die Kirche zu kräftigen, um den Protestantismus allseitig überwinden zu können' (Seeberg, *Dogmengeschichte*, vol. 4, p. 754, n. 52).

54. Seeberg, *Dogmengeschichte*, vol. 4, pp. 755–6.

has been freed from legalism'.[55] It is typical of the image of Trent held by Protestants that the council and its decrees are always compared with the theology of Luther and the other Reformers; consequently, a negative portrait is always offered, and encouraged. The image of Trent can be summarized thusly: it is the council that exalts tradition above Scripture, the Pope above the council, and works above grace.

4 Development and Discussion: Understanding and Opening

A preliminary look at some recent essays relating to church history gives the impression that their representation of Trent is geared more towards understanding and conversation and therefore is less negative and dismissive. This means that the image of Trent among Protestants seems to have changed. Noticeably, there is frequent emphasis that the reforming efforts and reforming measures of the council,[56] as well as the interest of the council fathers in the Reformers' concerns, have not been well understood and that the contra-decisions were not basically directed against the Reformation itself.[57] Also, the fact that the decree 'De iustificatione', with its thirty-three canons, did not name the Reformers, and condemned no one, is considered positive and seen as an opportunity for dialogue, even though the discussions about the Joint Declaration on the Doctrine of Justification (1999) also show that this positive representation is not all that convincing.

In more recent overviews of the history of the Reformation, there is no uniform portrayal of Trent. Thomas Kaufmann called the council 'a turning point in church history'[58] because here the demarcation against Reformation theologians is finally completely set. Hubert Kirchner, in his contribution to the *Kirchengeschichte in Einzeldarstellungen*, wrote that the council was 'too much of a reform of the form, the discipline, the right form'.[59] Because there was insufficient theological reflection, the council had not done what the Reformation actually intended to do. These evaluations show that here the council is once again being viewed from the perspective of the Reformation. But, the difference with the early modern assessment is that the council is always more harshly judged mainly by its own aims and content, and according to its structure and composition. In addition, the council is seen in retrospect as the final missed opportunity to prevent a definitive

---

55. Seeberg, *Dogmengeschichte*, vol. 4, p. 833.

56. 'das Reformanliegen wie ein gewisser roter Faden durch alle Sitzungen hindurchzieht'. Hubert Kirchner, *Reformationsgeschichte von 1532–1555/1566* (Berlin: Evangelische Verlagsanstalt, 1987), p. 161.

57. H. G. Pöhlmann, *Das Konkupiszenzverständnis der Confessio Augustana, der Confutatio und des Konzils von Trient* (Münster: Aschendorff, 1981), pp. 389–95.

58. Thomas Kaufmann, *Geschichte der Reformation* (Frankfurt am Main/Leipzig: Verlag der Weltreligionen, 2009), p. 670.

59. Kirchner, *Reformationsgeschichte*, p. 170, n. 56.

schism. A confessional judgement in the sense of whether or not the council was biblical or unbiblical can only be found in certain circles of Puritan Calvinism, but the criticism there is widely held.

On the other hand, there are also Protestant portrayals of Trent which, probably attempting to give the impression of ecumenical sentiments, act as if the Council of Trent never took place, and try to demythologize its decisions. An example is a joint statement by senior American Evangelicals and Catholics that fails to mention the Declarations of Trent and which puts the emphasis on the shared responsibility of both denominations to proclaim the Gospel of Christ in this world. Reactions from other Evangelicals seem to suggest that you should probably forget what Trent told you to believe. They also warn the Catholics that they will actually be anathematized by their own church if they sign this declaration because it is claimed in this statement that people receive salvation from grace through faith.[60] But, fortunately, more recently the orthodox Protestant side has presented reputable evidence about Trent and seen it more in context and understood the decisions less from the perspective of the former Protestant polemics.[61]

Conclusion

The image of Trent for Protestants was negative even before the council began. After the promulgation of the Tridentine decrees, Protestants were confirmed in their views precisely because the decrees were judged in the light of this negative presumption. Protestant historiography has consequently seen Trent, for centuries, from the perspective of the 'anathemas', and never from the perspective of the reforms. Despite a long list of 'in house' disagreements, Protestant splits, and disputes, the image of Trent was, for centuries, a unifying force in that the council had rejected the message of the Reformation and had destroyed the unity of the church.

One can speculate on the question of whether the image of Trent would have been different if the Protestants had attended and participated actively. Such speculations bring historical research and the church absolutely nothing. But if historians are trying to explore the image of Trent, explain it, and put it in historical perspective, then the modern church can and will benefit from it. The year 2013 was noteworthy because both the conclusion of the Council of Trent and the publication of the Heidelberg Catechism (on its 450th anniversary) were celebrated, and that confluence was indeed fitting.

---

60. Mary Jo Anderson, 'Catholics vs. Evangelicals', *Crisis* 13/9 (October 1995), pp. 25–8.

61. An example is the essay by Craig Carpenter on Calvin's 'Antidotum' as the starting point, but the results of recent Calvin research in this debate have turned in a new direction. Craig B. Carpenter, 'A Question of Union with Christ? Calvin and Trent on Justification', *Westminster Theological Journal* 64 (2002), pp. 363–86.

Bibliography

Anderson, Mary Jo, 'Catholics vs. Evangelicals', *Crisis* 13/9 (October 1995), pp. 25–8.

Brockmann, Thomas, *Die Konzilsfrage in den Flug- und Streitschriften des deutschen Sprachraums 1518–1563* (Göttingen: Vandenhoeck and Ruprecht, 1998).

Bucer, Martin, *Martin Bucers Deutsche Schriften* (eds R. Stupperich, Marijn de Kroon, Hartmut Rudolph, Stephen E. Buckwalter, Cornelis Augustijn Hans Schulz, Christoph Strohm, and Thomas Wilhelmi; 17 vols; Gütersloh: Gerd Mohn/Gütersloher Verlagshaus, 1960).

Bullinger, Heinrich, *Heinrich Bullinger Bibliographie* (ed. Joachim Staedtke and Erland Herkenrath; 3 vols; Zurich: TVZ, 1972–2004).

Burke, Peter, 'The great unmasker: Paolo Sarpi, 1551–1613', *History Today* 15 (1965), pp. 426–32.

Busch, Eberhard, *Calvin Studienausgabe, vol. 3: Reformatorische Kontroversen* (Neukirchen-Vluyn: Neukirchener Verlag, 1999).

Calvin, John, *Ioannis Calvini opera quae supersunt omnia* (eds Guilielmus Baum, Eduardus Cunitz, and Eduardus Reuss; 59 vols; Brunswick: Schwetschke, 1863–1900).

Carpenter, Craig B., 'A Question of Union with Christ? Calvin and Trent on Justification', *Westminster Theological Journal* 64 (2002), pp 363–86.

Casteel, T. W., 'Calvin and Trent: Calvin's Reaction to the Council of Trent in the Context of his Conciliar Thought', *HTR* 63 (1970), pp. 91–117.

Cunningham, William, *Historical Theology. A Review of the Principal Doctrinal Discussions in the Christian Church since the Apostolic Age* (2 vols; Edinburgh: T&T Clark, 1862).

Dankbaar, W. F., 'Calvijns oordeel over het concilie van Trente, inzonderheid inzake het rechtvaardigingsdecreet', in W. F. Dankbaar (ed.), *Hervormers en Humanisten. Een bundel opstellen* (Amsterdam: Ton Bolland, 1978), pp. 67–99.

Flacius Illyricus, Mathias and Nicolaus Gallus, *Protestatio concionatorum aliquot Augustanae Confessionis, adversus conventum Tridentinum, perniciem verae religioni & Ecclesiae molientem. … Accessit Norma simul et praxis constituendae religionis ac Ecclesiae, dirimendarumque controversiarum, jam pontifice & synodo recepta ac usitata* (s.l., 1563).

Flacius Illyricus, Mathias and Nicolaus Gallus, *Trewe Warnung für dem hochschedlichen betrug des Bapsts vnnd seines Concilij, damit sie vndter einem schein des nachgebens etlicher geringer Artickel, die einfeltigen Christen zu allen jren greweln zwingen, vnd auffs höchste verbinden wöllen* (Regensburg: Geißler, 1563).

Gentillet, Innocent, *Examen ende proeve des conciliums van Trenten: Daer by even als in een waech-schaele ghesien ende beproeft werdt, dat dit concilium in veele poincten ende articulen reghel-recht contrarie is ende strijdet soo wel teghens d'oude concilien ende canones, als teghens d'authoriteyt vande con.ke ma.t van Vranckrijcke/Eerst in Fransois beschreven door Innocent Gentillet …, ende nu onlancx in Nederduytsche taele overgheset* (Delf: Bruyn Harmansz. Schinckel, 1589).

Holstein, Hugo, *Die Reformation im Spiegelbilde der dramatischen Literatur des sechzehnten Jahrhunderts* (Halle: Verein für Reformationsgeschichte,1886).

Iserloh, Erwin, 'Luther und das Konzil von Trient', in *Kirche-Ereignis und Institution. Aufsätze und Vorträge* (2 vols; Münster: Aschendorff, 1985), vol. 2, pp. 181–93.

Jedin, Hubert, *Geschichte des Konzils von Trient* (4 vols; Freiburg, Herder, 1949–75).

Jurieu, Pierre, *Abbrege de l'Histoire du concile de Trente avec un discours contenant les Reflexions Historiques sur les Conciles & particulierement sur la conduite de celuy de Trente, …* (Geneva: J. Herman Widerhold, 1682).

Kaufmann, Thomas, *Geschichte der Reformation* (Frankfurt am Main/Leipzig: Verlag der Weltreligionen, 2009).

Kingdon, Robert M., 'Some French Reactions to the Council of Trent', *CH* 33 (1964), pp. 149–56.

Kirchner, Hubert, *Reformationsgeschichte von 1532–1555/1566* (Berlin: Evangelische Verlagsanstalt, 1987).

Knetsch, F. R. J., *Pierre Jurieu. Theoloog en politikus der refuge* (Kampen: Kok, 1967).

Koch, Ernst, 'Die Deutschen Protestanten und das Konzil von Trient', in Wolfgang Reinhard and Heinz Schilling (eds), *Die katholische Konfessionalisierung* (Schriften des Vereins für Reformationsgeschichte, 198; Gütersloh: Gütersloher Verlagshaus, 1995), pp. 88–103.

Kolb, Robert, 'The German Lutheran Reaction to the Third Period of the Council of Trent', *Luther Jahrbuch* 51 (1984), pp. 63–95.

Kretzer, Hartmut, *Calvinismus und französische Monarchie im 17. Jahrhundert. Die politische Lehre der Akademien Sedan und Saumur, mit besonderer Berücksichtigung von Pierre du Moulin, Moyse Amyraut und Pierre Jurieu* (Berlin: Duncker & Humblot, 1975).

Luther, Martin, *D. Martin Luthers Werke: Kritische Gesamtausgabe* (73 vols; Weimar: Böhlau, 1883–2009).

Melanchthon, Philipp, *Melanchthons Werke in Auswahl* (ed. Robert Stupperich; 7 vols; Gutersloh: Gerd Mohn, 1951–75).

Melanchthon, Philipp, *Philippi Melanthonis opera quae supersunt omnia* (eds C. G. Bretschneider and H. E. Bindseil; 28 vols; Halle: C. A. Schwetschke, 1834–60).

Meyer, Helmut, 'Die deutschen Protestanten an der zweiten Tagungsperiode des Konzils von Trient 1551/52', *ARG* 55 (1964), pp. 166–209.

Mumm, Reinhard, *Die Polemik des Martin Chemnitz gegen das Konzil von Trient* (Leipzig: Erster Teil, 1905).

Pfister, Rudolf, 'Zu Bullingers Beurteilung des Konzils von Trient', in Ulrich Gäbler and Erland Herkenrath (eds), *Heinrich Bullinger 1504–1575; Gesammelte Aufsätze* (2 vols; Zürich: Zürcher Beiträge zur Reformationsgeschichte, 1975).

Pöhlmann, H. G., *Das Konkupiszenzverständnis der Confessio Augustana, der Confutatio und des Konzils von Trient* (Münster: Aschendorff, 1981).

Ranke, Leopold von, *Die römischen Päpste in den letzten vier Jahrhunderten* (Hamburg: Neuausgabe, 2013).

Rogier, L. J., *Geschiedenis van het katholicisme in Noord-Nederland in de 16ᵉ en 17ᵉ eeuw* (3 vols; Amsterdam: Urbi et Orbi, 1947).

Rückert, H., *Die Rechtfertigungslehre auf dem tridentinischen Konzil* (Bonn: de Gruyter, 1925).

Seeberg, Reinhold, *Lehrbuch der Dogmengeschichte* (4 vols; Leipzig: W. Scholl, 1895–1920).

Stolk, Maarten, 'Calvin und Katholizismus', in Herman J. Selderhuis (ed.), *Calvin Handbuch* (Tübingen: Mohr Siebeck, 2008), pp. 104–12.

Stupperich, Robert, 'Die Reformatoren und das Tridentinum', *ARG* 47 (1956), pp. 20–63.

van Deursen, A. T., *Honni soit qui mal y pense? De Republiek tussen de mogendheden (1610–1612)* (Amsterdam: Noord-Hollandsche Uitgevers Maatschappij, 1965).

Willocx, F., *L'Introduction des décrets du Concile de Trente dans les Pays-Bas et dans la Principauté de Liége* (Louvain: Librairie Universitaire, 1929).

Wolgast, Eike, 'Das Konzil in den Erörterungen der kursächsischen Theologen und Politiker 1533–1537', *ARG* 73 (1982), pp. 122–52.

Wootton, David, *Paolo Sarpi: Between Renaissance and Enlightenment* (Cambridge: Cambridge University Press, 1983).

Chapter 7

SEVENTEENTH-CENTURY FRENCH CONVERSION NARRATIVES: MAKING SENSE OF SHIFTING CONFESSIONAL ALLEGIANCES

Karin Maag

On 25 July 1593, the French king, Henri IV, officially converted from the Reformed faith to Roman Catholicism. Although Henri IV had acceded to the French throne in 1589 following the death of Henri III (the last of the Valois monarchs), the new king seemed unlikely to be able to restore peace to France after nearly thirty years of civil war unless he adopted the Catholic faith of the majority. Yet his conversion, though welcomed by moderate French Catholics and by the Pope, caused consternation among his Huguenot subjects and suspicion among ultra-Catholics, who struggled to accept that his conversion was genuine.[1] Indeed, part of the challenge facing the king was the different audiences who interpreted his decision either favourably or negatively, based as much on their own perceptions of the king's motivations and credibility as on the monarch's actual change of beliefs and worship practices. Therefore, Henri IV's effort to win over Catholics in France, in particular, included an extensive publicity campaign to explain the reasons behind his conversion.[2]

Following on from Henri IV's example, this chapter seeks to examine the justifications provided for other French conversions, whether from the Reformed faith to Catholicism or vice versa. In many cases, the new converts published an account of the reasons that led to their change of confessional allegiance. This

---

1. For more on Henri IV's conversion and its impact, see Michael Wolfe, *The Conversion of Henri IV* (Cambridge, MA: Harvard University Press, 1993); idem, 'The Conversion of Henri IV and the Origins of Bourbon Absolutism', *Historical Reflections* 14 (1987), pp. 287–309.

2. For some of the works defending the king's conversion published in 1593 and in the following years, see the 'Actes et mémoires de la conversion et absolution de Henri IIII, Roy de France et de Navarre', Collection Dupuy 119, fols 1–110, held in the Bibliothèque Nationale in Paris. Other works from the king and his circle defending his conversion are listed in Ronald Love, *Blood and Religion: The Conscience of Henri IV, 1553–1593* (Montreal and Kingston: McGill-Queen's University Press, 2001), p. 408.

chapter examines a sampling of these writings, concentrating on the rationales the converts gave for their dramatic religious reversal. By analysing key aspects of these accounts, such as intended audience, stated aims and similarities of arguments and reference points (even when the converts were moving in opposite directions), this chapter allows for further reflections on French conversion narratives in the late sixteenth and seventeenth centuries as both polemical texts and didactic tools in the ongoing controversy between Protestants and Catholics in early modern France.

The sample of five French conversion narratives discussed in this chapter includes two from men going from Catholicism to the Reformed faith (the former Jesuit Pierre Jarrige in 1648 and the former Carmelite François de La Motte in 1675) and three from those moving in the opposite direction, from the Reformed faith to Catholicism (the former French pastors Jacques Vidouse in 1608, Claude de La Parre in 1669, and Alexandre Vigne in 1685).[3] The first and most striking common feature of these five accounts is that all five were penned by members of the clergy. Indeed, the surviving published conversion narratives from early modern France stem disproportionately from clergy, rather than from lay writers, largely because a conversion account was a document that such 'high-value' clerical converts were expected to produce.

Because these accounts had a dual audience of former and new co-religionists, and thus were multipurpose texts, the conversion narratives in this sample did not solely focus on laying out each writer's individual reasons for making the confessional change. Instead, the authors took the opportunity to present briefly or at greater length the differences in doctrine, faith and practice between the two confessional groups, with the aim of convincing their readership that the church the converts had recently joined was, in fact, the true church. In many ways, these polemical sections of the conversion narratives hold the fewest surprises: the authors on each side reiterated long-held doctrinal and ecclesiological claims and rarely ventured into any new or unusual topics.

---

3. Pierre Jarrige, *Declaration du Sieur Pierre Jarrige, Cy devant Jesuite Profès du quatriesme voeu & predicateur. Prononcée dans le Temple de l'Eglize Françoise de Leide le 25. De Mars 1648* (Leiden: Jean du Pré, 1648); François de La Motte, *Les Motifs de la Conversion à la Religion Réformée du Sieur François De La Motte, Cy-Devant Predicateur de l'Ordre des Carmes, prononcez en partie par luy-meme dans l'Eglise de la Savoye le jour de son Abjuration* (London: Pitt, 1675); Jacques Vidouse, *La Conversion de Jacques Vidouze, ministrdla[sic] la religion prétendue réformée, rengé sous l'Eglise Catholique, Apostolique & Romaine. Avec les causes & raisons evidentes qui l'ont esmeu à ce faire. Sous l'adveu de Monseigneur le Cardinal de Surdy, Archevesque de Bourdeaux, & Primat d'Aquitaine* (Lyon: Leon Savine, 1608); Claude de La Parre, *Les Motifs de la conversion du Sieur La Parre cy-devant Ministre à Montpellier* (Paris: Claude Desprez, 1669); Alexandre Vigne, *Lettre de Monsieur Vigne, cy devant ministre de Grenoble, A Messieurs de La Religion Pretendüe Reformee. Il propose les principaux motifs de sa conversion, prouve aux Protestants par leurs propres Principes, qu'il n y a rien dans la Croyance, dans le Culte, & dans le Gouvernement de l'Eglise Catholique qui leur donne un juste sujet de separation* (Grenoble: Fremon, 1685).

On the Catholic side, the chief accusations against the Reformed church included its fragmentary doctrine and sacraments and its recent emergence, compared to the full and complete doctrine, sacraments and unity of the Catholic church since the days of the early church onwards.[4] The Reformed emphasis on the reading and interpretation of Scripture opened the door to Catholic converts' critiques of too much individual interpretation and diversity of doctrine among Protestants, compared to the unifying power and weight of tradition in shaping the teachings of the Catholic church.[5] Using unity, truth and holiness as his benchmarks, for instance, Claude de La Parre argued at length that the Huguenot church could in no way measure up to the Catholic church according to these criteria.[6] His approach left no room for Reformed doctrinal perspectives: from La Parre's point of view, the Huguenots simply had to concede that they were wrong and that the Catholic church had always been the locus of the true, unified and holy faith.

Yet La Parre's hard-line stance was not the only possible approach a Catholic convert could take. Of the three proponents of the Catholic faith and doctrine in this sample group, Alexandre Vigne made the most effort to address Protestant critiques of Catholic beliefs and practices, perhaps because of his intended audience of former co-religionists. For instance, although he defended the use of images in worship, he noted that 'the key is not to imagine that there is something divine in these images, and to avoid giving them any part of worship that is only owed to God'.[7] Acknowledging that it was possible to misunderstand the purpose of images and give them misplaced worship brought Vigne closer to the Reformed critique of such practices, although he did highlight Protestant inconsistencies in this domain by noting both the Lutheran and Anglican use of images in their places of worship. Vigne's defence of the Catholic cult of relics was both short and unconvincing – his strongest argument in favour of the practice was to ask his readership rhetorically whether they would refuse to venerate the hand of Paul, given that 'this hand has written such excellent letters'.[8] In the end, Vigne's defence of the Catholic church was honest enough to admit that there had been problems in Catholic practice in the past, but according to him, these issues had since been satisfactorily resolved: 'These shadows that had spread into the Lord's house due to the dissoluteness of the past century, have now melted away, and now we can see clearly.'[9]

Vigne's willingness to acknowledge that there had been serious shortcomings in the Catholic church can be taken as an indicator that he was, in fact, serious in his intent to address a Protestant readership and convince them that their preconceptions about the Catholic church's corruption could safely be laid to rest. His awareness of the issues that caused Protestants to question the legitimacy of the

---

4. Vidouse, *La Conversion*, pp. 10–13.

5. See Vigne, *Lettre*, p. 72.

6. La Parre, *Motifs de la conversion*, pp. 22–162.

7. Vigne, *Lettre*, p. 49 (here and in all subsequent instances of quotations from primary and secondary French sources, the translations are the author's own).

8. Vigne, *Lettre*, p. 55.

9. Vigne, *Lettre*, p. 66.

Catholic church, such as the use of images and relics, made him more moderate in his defence of these practices. In that sense, his approach was closer to that of Jean Gesse-Loumelongue, a lay Protestant from Mauvezin, in the south-west of France, who converted to Catholicism in 1665. Élisabeth Labrousse analysed Gesse-Loumelongue's conversion account, which has been preserved both in manuscript and in printed form. Along the same lines as Alexandre Vigne, Gesse-Loumelongue articulated a carefully limited support for the cult of saints and the use of images in worship, so long as these did not rival the worship that was owed to God alone.[10] Labrousse also noted Gesse-Loumelongue's moderate tone and unwillingness to condemn his former co-religionists harshly, at least in his manuscript account.[11] The more open approach adopted by both Vigne and Gesse-Loumelongue offers an alternative to the more rigid stance adopted by La Parre and Vidouse.

For their part, those converting to the Reformed faith were equally keen to lay out the reasons why their confessional choice was the correct one, although their rationales focused more on a condemnation of the Catholic church's teaching, for which they found no scriptural justification. Pierre Jarrige, for instance, condemned the Catholic doctrines and practices of transubstantiation, purgatory, indulgences, the invocation of the saints and the sacrifice of the Mass, asserting in each case that there was no scriptural basis for any of these.[12] Similarly, François de La Motte objected strongly to a wide range of Catholic teachings, but also critiqued what he saw as the corruption of the Catholic church, especially among its leaders. Among the practices that La Motte saw as particularly open to corruption, he listed auricular confession and clerical celibacy.[13] La Motte also offered a pointed critique of the Catholic cult of saints, highlighting specific examples of abusive practices he had witnessed.[14] In contrast to these failings of the Catholic church, La Motte highlighted the Reformed church's faithfulness to Scripture and to the practices of the early church, and the central authority of Christ in the Reformed confession.

10. Élisabeth Labrousse, 'La Conversion d'un Huguenot au Catholicisme en 1665', *Revue d'histoire de l'église de France* 64 (1978), pp. 55–68 (65).

11. Labrousse, 'La Conversion', pp. 67–8. Labrousse's subsequent analysis of the published version of Gesse-Loumelongue's conversion narrative shows that it was redacted, likely by the Catholic priest of Mauvezin, to make it harsher and less open to Protestant perspectives. See Labrousse, 'Note complémentaire', *Revue d'histoire de l'église de France* 64 (1978), pp. 251–2.

12. Jarrige, *Declaration*, pp. 7–50.

13. La Motte, *Les Motifs*, pp. 83–100, 103–7.

14. La Motte, *Les Motifs*, pp. 54–77. Among his most effective passages is his description of a set of relics held in a Carmelite convent in Vennes in Brittany. According to the nuns, the relics came from some of the eleven thousand virgins who were supposedly massacred by the Huns in the first centuries after Christ. Yet the nuns admitted that the medical experts sent by the bishop to verify the authenticity of the relics had concluded that many of the bones were actually from horses – see pp. 73–4.

As this overview of the doctrinal themes and polemical issues in these texts shows, there was little that was new or surprising in these parts of the conversion narratives. Of greater interest are the elements of the texts that dealt more directly with the conversion and its motivations. Whether they were moving from Catholicism or from Protestantism to the rival church, these men's leadership role as preachers and teachers in their orders and churches prior to their conversion had given them access to the pulpit; now, as new converts, they were expected to use the same skill set to testify to their new perspective and attempt to draw others of their former co-religionists to follow suit.[15] As Didier Boisson notes when discussing the Catholic clergy's conversion to the Reformed faith, such narratives were almost de rigueur, and were directed both to other Catholics, to urge them to take the same step, and to fellow Protestants, to convince them that the conversion in question was a genuine one.[16] The same approach seemingly held true for those converting to Catholicism: they too urged their former fellow believers to make the same transition and declared their unshakeable intention to uphold the Catholic faith. Indeed, Alexandre Vigne's justification for his conversion to Catholicism in 1685 (the crucial date of the revocation of the Edict of Nantes) was written in the form of an open letter to his former colleagues in the Reformed pastorate in Grenoble, urging them to join him in putting an end to their separation from the Catholic church.[17]

Yet we should not necessarily take the authors' own statements as to their intended audiences at face value. As Susan Rosa points out in her analysis of the 1670 conversion of the Prince de Tarente,

> The récit de conversion therefore requires a special kind of reading, one which both acknowledges its opacity and recognizes the kinds of insights it can provide. Such a reading focuses on both document and context, approaching the arguments of the text not as transparent and unproblematic evidence of the contents of the convert's mind.[18]

---

15. In his analysis of seventy different French conversion narratives, Thierry Wanegffelen indicates that accounts stemming from clergy were particularly prominent before 1610, whereas lay nobles' conversion texts became more numerous after that point. Yet, the clerical conversion narratives in my (admittedly small) sample group ranged from 1608 to 1685. See Thierry Wanegffelen, 'Récits de conversion des XVIe et XVIIe siècles: discours confessionel et experience individuelle', in Jean Christophe Attias (ed.), *De la conversion* (Paris: Cerf, 1998), pp. 183–202.

16. Didier Boisson, *Consciences en liberté? Itinéraires d'ecclesiastiques convertis au protestantisme, 1631–1760* (Paris: Champion, 2009), p. 252.

17. In fact, Vigne began by claiming that he had hoped to preach his conversion from his Reformed pulpit, but felt his co-religionists would not accept his message, just as the Jews had hardened their hearts against the apostle Stephen's preaching. Vigne, *Lettre*, p. 1.

18. Susan Rosa, 'The Conversion to Catholicism of the Prince de Tarente, 1670', *Historical Reflections* 21 (1995), pp. 57–75 (63).

In other words, these conversion narratives were often instances of a polemical genre rather than unique testimonies. As such, many of the themes that appeared in one account were replicated in another, even in cases when the converts were moving in opposite directions.

One of the most commonly reiterated themes in these conversion narratives was the strong rejection of any possible material advantage gained by the convert in making the transition from one confessional group to the other. In each instance of the texts in the sample, the authors firmly rebutted allegations or suggestions that the reasons for their change of heart could be traced to inducements offered to them by the leadership or membership of their new confession.[19] For instance, both Pierre Jarrige and François de La Motte were quick to point out that their move from Catholicism to the Reformed faith actually resulted in a loss of status and material security, since they had left the comfort of their respective orders to adopt Protestantism. For both these men, the loss of status was compounded by the challenges of exile: Pierre Jarrige sought refuge in the Netherlands following his 1647 conversion, whereas François de La Motte headed for England. As Jarrige noted,

> Therefore, the reasons for this change have nothing to do with the desire for material goods, since I left the Jesuits as naked as a newborn. ... Neither was it ambition or a craving for high regard that drove me, for what can I aspire to when I live among people who for the love of Jesus Christ are considered in France as trash and the scum of the earth? While the faithful are honored in these beautiful united provinces thanks to the mercy of God and the care of our lords of the States, I am unknown here, a foreigner, and unfamiliar with the language of this land.[20]

Indeed, Jarrige's difficulties in finding his place in Dutch society and in the Dutch Reformed context may help to explain why, in his case at least, his conversion did not last: by 1650, he had returned to the Catholic faith.[21] Echoing Jarrige's concerns about the challenges of finding one's place in a new country and a new confessional setting, François de La Motte noted in his conversion account that he had elected 'to come live and die in a land where I have no expectations or fortune to be made

19. In reality, as Keith Luria notes, there were definite practical inducements to convert, especially to adopt Catholicism in the later seventeenth century. See 'The Politics of Protestant Conversion to Catholicism in seventeenth-century France', in Peter van der Veer (ed.), *Conversion to Modernities: The Globalization of Christianity* (New York: Routledge, 1996), pp. 23–46 (32).

20. Jarrige, *Declaration*, pp. 51–2.

21. For more on Jarrige's career and his confessional jumps, see Didier Boisson, 'Conversion et reconversion au XVIIe siècle: les itinéraires confessionels de François Clouet et de Pierre Jarrige', *Bulletin de la société de l'histoire du protestantisme français* 155 (2009), pp. 447–67.

apart from what flows out of your charity alone.'[22] At the same time La Motte highlighted the attractiveness of Catholicism for French converts going the other way: 'They are pushed to it by self-interest and kept in [Catholicism] by it: self-interest makes them switch and keeps them from switching back.'[23] Thus from the perspective of these two converts to the Reformed faith, the advantages in terms of material goods and security were entirely on the Catholic side. In articulating this stance, the two men neatly highlighted the personal cost of their own new commitment and made a plea for support.

Yet, those making the change in the other direction, out of the Reformed faith and to Catholicism, were equally prone to reject any accusations that their choice was motivated by any material inducements. Writing to his former co-religionists in 1685, the ex-Huguenot pastor of Grenoble Jacques Vigne stated, 'I have not left you to go look elsewhere for more honors, more wealth, and more esteem. I was a pastor, but now I am a sheep, and after having been a leader, I am now the very last. I see no advantage in my current state compared to what I could have achieved among you.'[24] In the same vein, Claude de La Parre revisited the challenges that had given him pause as he contemplated moving from the Reformed faith to Catholicism: 'I had been an instructor and a professor, but now I had to become a novice and a schoolboy, and begin again, so to speak, with my ABCs. I had gained a reputation and friends: these would be lost to me if I changed religion.'[25] Although the pastors converting to the Catholic faith did not have to leave their homeland, their conversion did remove them from their leadership roles in their former faith communities and from their customary spheres of influence.

Having dealt with the charge of converting for material gain or other advantages, the writers were also all keen to point out that the reasons for their conversion had nothing to do with any moral failings or personal difficulties that they had been experiencing in their original church. They were quick to reject any attacks on their integrity, both so as to refute accusations that they had converted in order to escape any retribution for misbehaviour, and to highlight their admirable reputations both before and after their conversion. The aim here seems to have been to reassure the new community that the convert was not coming in with a trail of scandal behind him. These strong statements about the converts' moral conduct before and after their conversion made sense in the polemical context, as former co-religionists did tend to attack the convert's character and highlight his moral flaws in an attempt to discredit the value of the conversion. For example, Pierre Jarrige's conversion in 1647 led to a prolific sequence of works beginning in 1648, attacking and defending his adoption of the Reformed faith. As Didier Boisson notes, out of ninety-seven polemical works published in French in 1648, thirty-two, or nearly one-third of the total output, dealt with Jarrige's conversion.

22. La Motte, *Les Motifs*, p. 2.
23. La Motte, *Les Motifs*, p. 109.
24. Vigne, *Lettre*, p. 6.
25. La Parre, *Les Motifs de la Conversion*, p. 11.

On the Catholic side, he was condemned for departing the faith after supposedly having become frustrated at his lack of advancement in the Jesuit order.[26] In response, in his conversion narrative Jarrige highlighted his key responsibilities in the Jesuit order and the confidence his superiors had placed in him. He denied that he faced any bar to advancement. He even included a letter of testimonial about his character from the La Rochelle pastor Philippe Vincent who had served as Jarrige's point of contact at the moment of his conversion in 1647.[27] For his part, Claude de La Parre highlighted his clean personal and professional record among his Huguenot co-religionists prior to his conversion:

> Everyone knows that I have lived from childhood onwards without reproach and without any critique from the academies and synods that oversaw my conduct. In fact, I was met with great approval and was considered to be a man of integrity and a very zealous pastor. If necessary, I can produce properly drawn-up attestations about me from age fifteen onwards, but the most recent one, from the church of Montpellier, will suffice to show that I had no stain of any kind on my character when I left them.[28]

As for Jacques Vidouse, his conversion to Catholicism in 1608 led to a sharp response from his fellow pastors. Indeed, in the same year, they published a strong critique of his confessional change, in which they laid out (as the title of their work put it) 'the true causes that led him to return to his vomit, over against the false pretexts that he tried to use to cover up the infamy of his rebellion'.[29] Vidouse's own conversion narrative was a response to this text, in which he charged those writing these critiques of being motivated by hypocrisy and malice, and of falsely attacking his honour and personal reputation.[30]

After having dealt with charges that they had converted for personal gain or to escape the consequences of their personal failings, the writers of these conversion accounts stressed that their decision to change confessional allegiances was not taken lightly or without due reflection. Indeed, the common approach of the writers was to emphasize just how carefully they had considered the issues, so as to underscore the serious intent of their new commitment. Thus Alexandre Vigne

---

26. Boisson, 'Conversion et reconversion', p. 456. In his polemic against François Clouet (another convert to the Reformed faith), the noted Catholic polemicist François Véron went so far as to say that the main reason for the existence of the Huguenots was that they purged these rotten members from the Catholic church. See Boisson, 'Conversion et reconversion', pp. 453–4.

27. Jarrige, *Declaration*, pp. 53–4, 58–68.

28. La Parre, *Les Motifs de la conversion*, p. 5.

29. Louis Desgraves, 'Un Aspect des controverses entre catholiques et protestants, les récits de conversion (1598–1628)', in Roger Duchene (ed.), *La Conversion au XVIIe siècle* (Marseille: Centre méridional de rencontres sur le XVIIe siècle, 1983), pp. 89–110 (103).

30. Vidouse, *La Conversion*, pp. 6–7.

noted, 'My transformation did not take place all of a sudden, but after a lengthy process of reflection and prayer and reading that I let myself be convinced.'[31] Similarly, La Motte pointed out, 'My transformation is not a product of my unsettled mind. I undertook nothing lightly. For seven years I have been reasoning, wrestling, resisting, and becoming convinced in the depths of my being, without being able to take the step [until now].'[32] Pierre Jarrige asserted, 'I did nothing in haste, but proceeded with a careful and moderate spirit, which calmly sought the truth while following heavenly guidance.'[33] For his part, in perhaps the most moving account of how personal circumstances allowed for in-depth reflection on which church really taught the true faith, the former Huguenot pastor of Montpellier, Claude de La Parre testified that during his early years in the Reformed pastorate, he went through an extensive period of illness and weakness. Although he did eventually recover his strength after ten to twelve years, the illness left him with a permanently weakened voice, making it impossible for him to preach, and to take up the work of Reformed ministry that had been his career and his calling. La Parre testified that this lengthy period of ill-health and enforced inaction was God's way of giving him the time and space he needed to reflect on the differences between the two confessional groups. As he noted, '[These were] the means that God used to have me find the right path that led me to the true Church, outside of which there is no salvation.'[34]

Apart from underscoring that conversion was a process that took time, rather than a sudden event (which could have been construed by opponents as a sudden mental aberration or a sign of flightiness), the writers of these accounts also emphasized the role that reading played in their conversion process. For those converting to Protestantism, reading the Bible proved to be a key transformative experience.[35] In Pierre Jarrige's case for instance, he testified that he had originally been shaped intellectually more by Cicero than by the Scriptures, but that beginning sixteen years before his conversion, he had started to read works by Reformed theologians in order to help his senior colleague, the Jesuit Audibert, prepare for oral debates against the pastors of La Rochelle. From that point on, he

31. Vigne, *Lettre*, p. 6.
32. La Motte, *Les Motifs*, p. 1.
33. Jarrige, *Declaration*, fol. *4v.
34. La Parre, *Les Motifs de la conversion*, pp. 6–10.
35. For example, the former Franciscan Gaspar Martin testified that the assignment given to him by his superiors in 1607 and 1610 to read the Bible in French to refute Huguenot teachings led him to re-evaluate his beliefs and opened his eyes to the truths of the Reformed faith. See Françoise Moreil, 'Gaspar Martin, le capucin réformé, pasteur de la principauté d'Orange au XVIIe siècle', *Bulletin de la société de l'histoire du protestantisme français* 2010 (156), pp. 49–68 (53). One indicator of the popularity of these conversion narratives was the number of reprints of each text. In Martin's case, his conversion account was published by Reformed presses in four different locations (Die, Geneva, Montpellier and Orange) in the space of the same year (1615). See Desgraves, 'Un Aspect des controverses', p. 103.

began to be influenced by the Scriptures, and over a period of ten months, he read Reformed doctrinal works and Catholic responses. In the process, he reported that he had 'consulted the Scriptures in an impartial fashion. Finally, everything – reason, Scripture, the inspiration of the Holy Spirit – spoke to my heart in support of the faith that I am embracing.'[36] In highlighting the reasons that convinced him to adopt the Reformed faith, Jarrige echoed the approach taken by other converts, who also spoke of a process that was divinely inspired, matured over time and involved intense scrutiny of the texts and teachings of the two faiths.

Given their stated reliance on their readings in shaping their new religious convictions, it is not surprising that the writers of the texts in the sample group all made reference to a similar set of model converts and conversion experiences, either from Scripture or from church history. Thierry Wanegffelen suggests that those converting to Catholicism were more likely to use St Augustine of Hippo as a role model, whereas converts to the Reformed faith were more prone to draw parallels between their experiences and those of the Apostle Paul.[37] For his part, Didier Boisson finds extensive references to Paul's experience in Protestant conversion accounts, alongside some references to Augustine and to Abraham.[38] Yet, the evidence from the five texts in the selected sample provides both a greater range of models and less clear demarcations between preferred models for converts to Catholicism versus Protestantism. For instance, in his prayer of thanksgiving that described his move from the Catholic church to the Reformed faith, François de La Motte listed a profusion of biblical characters who had experienced similar radical changes, including Abraham, Lot, Jacob, Joseph and Daniel from the Old Testament, and the blind man healed by Jesus in the New Testament.[39] By the end of his conversion account preached to the congregation of the Savoy church in London, La Motte also brought up the example of St Augustine:

> Saint Augustine was known as the Son of Monica's Tears, because that good mother cried so much that God finally granted his conversion. Today, I dare to take on the same characteristics: I see myself in your midst as the result of your hopes, the child of your prayers and the son of your pious longings.[40]

Thus, La Motte saw no problems in blending together both biblical and non-scriptural examples to illustrate his conversion experience. For their part, those converting to Catholicism, including Jacques Vidouse and Claude de La Parre, were prone to refer to the apostle Paul, highlighting especially the hostility he encountered after he became a Christian. As La Parre stated, 'Together with the

36. Jarrige, *Declaration*, p. 6.

37. Wanegffelen, 'Récits de conversion', pp. 198–200.

38. Didier Boisson, *Consciences en liberté?*, pp. 252–76. See especially pp. 263–8 for a careful analysis of the biblical and historical figures used as models in these Reformed conversion narratives.

39. La Motte, *Les Motifs*, fol. B3r.

40. La Motte, *Les Motifs*, p. 116.

blessed saint Paul, I affirm that it makes little difference to me that I am condemned by you or by the opinion of men. God is my judge.'[41] Here the emphasis was not so much on Paul's own conversion experience but on the Jews' hostile response to his religious choice. Perhaps because those converting to Catholicism felt they were returning to the true faith, Paul's dramatic Damascus road conversion did not quite fit the authors' needs. However, their common perception that their former co-religionists were angry about their departure did lead these writers to build connections between the hostility Paul encountered and their own experience.

Having considered carefully the common elements that surface in each of the texts in the sample, it is also worth analysing the distinctive features of these accounts based on their confessional choice. Scholars who have focused on narratives of conversion to Catholicism have highlighted the importance converts ascribed to both political and religious motivations. As Keith Luria points out, 'Religious conversion may have entailed an internal movement of conscience, but to be acceptable, the change had to bring the conscience in line with external authority – the Church, and, in the French Catholic case, the monarchy.'[42] The three Huguenot pastors who converted to Catholicism each highlighted the central role of the Catholic church in their conversion, often personifying the church as their mother. Thus Jacques Vidouse, who had previously served as a Huguenot pastor in the Agenois, described the warmth of the welcome he received upon his conversion, in spite of his previous hostility: 'The church is so kind and so generous in overcoming hostility, that she calls to herself those who want to hurt her, that she revives those who, having dishonored her in the past, now finally give to her the honor that children owe to their mother.'[43] This image of the church as a loving mother, seeking out her children who had gone astray appears again in Alexandre Vigne's conversion account. Addressing his former co-religionists, Vigne asked, 'Why do you not therefore listen to this Mother's voice? Why do you flee from her, as if she were the enemy of Jesus Christ?'[44] This rhetorical question opened the door for Vigne to lay out the Catholic claim to unbroken tradition and uniformity of doctrine in the Catholic church from the time of the apostles onwards. In Claude de La Parre's conversion account, the authority of the church and of the monarchy came together in his preface, which was dedicated to Louis XIV. While it is clear that La Parre's preface was intended to flatter the king, the former Huguenot did equate Protestant refusal to accept the Catholic faith to resistance to the king, thus bringing together political and religious pressures on Huguenots to convert.[45] In La Parre's eyes, the Huguenot argument that they were faithful subjects of the king even though they did not share the royal faith was an

41. La Parre, *Les Motifs de la conversion*, p. 5. See also Vidouse, who highlighted the Jews' attacks on Paul 'through flogging, through exile, and through death'. Vidouse, *La Conversion*, p. 6.

42. Luria, 'The Politics of Protestant Conversion to Catholicism', p. 39.

43. Vidouse, *La Conversion de Jacques Vidouze*, p. 8.

44. Vigne, *Lettre*, p. 2.

45. La Parre, *Les Motifs de la conversion*, fol. a iii v.

unacceptable position. Similarly, Alexandre Vigne urged his former co-religionists to convert to Catholicism in order to put an end to the long-running schism and bring unity and peace to France 'under the reign of our wise Solomon'.[46] The reference to the kingship of Solomon, during which Israel's political and religious systems were tightly interwoven, was calculated to carry weight with a Huguenot readership.

For those converting to the Reformed faith, the source of authority that encouraged their change of allegiance was not so much the church personified as a mother or political leaders, but the direct action of God, turning them towards the truth. As Jarrige noted, 'My conversion is the result of God's eternal decree, and is the work of his outstretched arm.' In his letter of resignation from the Jesuits, which Jarrige included in his conversion narrative, the former Jesuit concluded that he was impelled by 'the knowledge I received from God, that the path I was on was not that of salvation, and that there are many grave errors and corruptions that hold sway in the Roman Church. In contrast, the faith of the Reformed churches, which I wish to join, conforms in all aspects to the truth of God'.[47] In Jarrige's account, God was the prime mover, and truth was the goal. The Reformed church taught the truth, but the church itself was not the reference point for the new convert, unlike in the Catholic conversion narratives. In the same vein, François de La Motte emphasized the importance of coming to a sure conviction of the truth as a key feature of his conversion experience. The Reformed church itself was not the draw, but rather its faithfulness to the teachings of God in Scripture. He concluded his justification of his confessional choice by stating, 'Thanks to God, I am not speaking as someone without knowledge in this area; I spent much too long weighing the reasons on one side and on the other. I know where I am coming from, I know what I am leaving, and I am certain about what I am taking up'.[48] This emphasis on an unshakeable inner conviction based on study, reflection, the Word of God and the direct action of God on the convert's life was a hallmark of these Protestant conversion narratives.

Taken together, these five texts represent only a small sample of the numerous conversion accounts that were available in print from 1593 onwards. Although much of the scholarship in the field has stated that these conversion narratives were formulaic and did not offer much in the way of individual motivations, a careful reading suggests otherwise. Although the converts did not necessarily go into detail about their inward faith, they did seek to provide a coherent and credible defence of their actions, and in so doing, revealed much about their personal circumstances and outlook, both before and after their conversion. A further and wider study of these texts will help build up a better picture of the cross-confessional currents that moved people from one church to the other, and sometimes back again, during the century following Henri IV's conversion.

46. Vigne, *Lettre*, p. 75.
47. Jarrige, *Declaration*, fol. *4v and pp. 69–70.
48. La Motte, *Les Motifs*, p. 115.

Bibliography

Bibliothèque Nationale, Paris. Collection Dupuy 119, 'Actes et mémoires de la conversion et absolution de Henri IIII, Roy de France et de Navarre'.

Boisson, Didier, *Consciences en liberté? Itinéraires d'ecclesiastiques convertis au protestantisme, 1631–1760* (Paris: Champion, 2009).

Boisson, Didier, 'Conversion et reconversion au XVIIe siècle: les itinéraires confessionels de François Clouet et de Pierre Jarrige', *Bulletin de la société de l'histoire du protestantisme français* 155 (2009), pp. 447–67.

Desgraves, Louis, 'Un Aspect des controverses entre catholiques et protestants, les récits de conversion (1598–1628)', in Roger Duchene (ed.), *La Conversion au XVIIe siècle* (Marseille: Centre méridional de rencontres sur le XVIIe siècle, 1983), pp. 89–110.

Jarrige, Pierre, *Declaration du Sieur Pierre Jarrige, Cy devant Jesuite Profès du quatriesme voeu & predicateur. Prononcée dans le Temple de l'Eglize Françoise de Leide le 25. De Mars 1648* (Leiden: Jean du Pré, 1648).

Labrousse, Élisabeth, 'La Conversion d'un Huguenot au Catholicisme en 1665', *Revue d'histoire de l'église de France* 64 (1978), pp. 55–68.

Labrousse, Élisabeth, 'Note complémentaire', *Revue d'histoire de l'église de France* 64 (1978), pp. 251–2.

La Motte, François de, *Les Motifs de la Conversion à la Religion Réformée du Sieur François De La Motte, Cy-Devant Predicateur de l'Ordre des Carmes, prononcez en partie par luy-meme dans l'Eglise de la Savoye le jour de son Abjuration* (London: Pitt, 1675).

La Parre, Claude de, *Les Motifs de la conversion du Sieur La Parre cy-devant Ministre à Montpellier* (Paris: Claude Desprez, 1669).

Love, Ronald, *Blood and Religion: The Conscience of Henri IV, 1553–1593* (Montreal and Kingston: McGill-Queen's University Press, 2001).

Luria, Keith, 'The Politics of Protestant Conversion to Catholicism in seventeenth-century France', in Peter van der Veer (ed.), *Conversion to Modernities: The Globalization of Christianity* (New York: Routledge, 1996), pp. 23–46.

Moreil, Françoise, 'Gaspar Martin, le capuchin réformé, pasteur de la principauté d'Orange au XVIIe siècle', *Bulletin de la société de l'histoire du protestantisme français* 156 (2010), pp. 49–68.

Rosa, Susan, 'The Conversion to Catholicism of the Prince de Tarente, 1670', *Historical Reflections* 21 (1995), pp. 57–75.

Vidouse, Jacques, *La Conversion de Jacques Vidouze, ministrdla[sic] la religion prétendue réformée, rengé sous l'Eglise Catholique, Apostolique & Romaine. Avec les causes & raisons evidentes qui l'ont esmeu à ce faire. Sous l'adveu de Monseigneur le Cardinal de Surdy, Archevesque de Bourdeaux, & Primat d'Aquitaine* (Lyon: Leon Savine, 1608).

Vigne, Alexandre, *Lettre de Monsieur Vigne, cy devant ministre de Grenoble, A Messieurs de La Religion Pretendüe Reformee. Il propose les principaux motifs de sa conversion, prouve aux Protestants par leurs propres Principes, qu'il n y a rien dans la Croyance, dans le Culte, & dans le Gouvernement de l'Eglise Catholique qui leur donne un juste sujet de separation* (Grenoble: Fremon, 1685).

Wanegffelen, Thierry, 'Récits de conversion des XVIe et XVIIe siècles: discours confessionel et experience individuelle', in Jean Christophe Attias (ed.), *De la conversion* (Paris: Cerf, 1998), pp. 183–202.

Chapter 8

THE SOURCES OF JAMES USSHER'S PATRISTIC CITATIONS ON THE INTENT AND SUFFICIENCY OF CHRIST'S SATISFACTION

Richard Snoddy

James Ussher is a theologian whose importance to modern scholars has only recently begun to reflect his stature among his contemporaries.[1] There has been considerable interest in his thought on the nature and sufficiency of Christ's satisfaction, a subject of intense debate in the early seventeenth century, and a greater appreciation of his indirect influence on the Synod of Dort and the Westminster Assembly.[2] Ussher rejected the teaching that Christ died for the elect alone, a doctrine now generally labelled as limited atonement, though particular redemption better reflects seventeenth-century expressions of this idea. He put forward a view that has come to be known as hypothetical universalism, the belief that Christ died for all humanity, making salvation possible upon the condition of faith. This was affirmed within a predestinarian framework, maintaining individual election and the necessity of God's special grace in the application of the redemption obtained at the cross.

---

1. The most important of recent studies is Alan Ford, *James Ussher: Theology, History, and Politics in Early-Modern Ireland and England* (Oxford: Oxford University Press, 2007).

2. Crawford Gribben, 'Rhetoric, Fiction and Theology: James Ussher and the Death of Jesus Christ', *Seventeenth Century* 20 (2005), pp. 53–76; Jonathan D. Moore, *English Hypothetical Universalism: John Preston and the Softening of Reformed Theology* (Grand Rapids, MI: Eerdmans, 2007), esp. pp. 173–86, 208–13; Garry J. Williams, 'The Definite Intent of Penal Substitutionary Atonement', in David Gibson and Jonathan Gibson (eds), *From Heaven He Came and Sought Her: Definite Atonement in Historical, Biblical, Theological, and Pastoral Perspective* (Wheaton, IL: Crossway, 2013), pp. 461–82 (462–8); Richard Snoddy, *The Soteriology of James Ussher: The Act and Object of Saving Faith* (New York: Oxford University Press, 2014), pp. 40–92. On the polemical context, see especially, G. Michael Thomas, *The Extent of the Atonement: A Dilemma for Reformed Theology from Calvin to the Consensus* (Bletchley: Paternoster, 1997); Richard A. Muller, *Calvin and the Reformed Tradition: On the Work of Christ and the Order of Salvation* (Grand Rapids, MI: Baker Academic, 2012), 70–160.

This chapter looks beyond Ussher's published writings on this controversy to a set of notes in which he gathered citations from patristic and medieval authorities under the heading *An Christus passus fuerit pro omnibus* (whether Christ suffered for all). It will give some insight into his pattern of work as he sought to buttress his position with patristic support and demonstrate the catholicity of his views. It will identify the key sources for his patristic citations, showing that much of this material came to him through mediating channels and that these mediators contributed to the shape of his argument as he presented his case to fellow clergy through the medium of the epistolary tract. Before exploring these notes however, it is necessary to outline the historical context and the broad contours of Ussher's hypothetical universalism.

On the eve of the Synod of Dort, the Essex nonconformist Ezekiel Culverwell circulated a manuscript tract on the preaching of the gospel. Culverwell took issue with the idea that on the cross Christ made satisfaction for the sins of the elect alone. While he acknowledged that God had ordained some to life and others to death, 'his reveiled will is hee would have many to beleive and to bee saved who by ther owne fault perish and that god loves thees, and offers his sonn to them, that they might therby bee moved to accept his mercye offered, and bee saved'.[3] In the preaching of the gospel, Christ was truly offered to all on the condition of faith, reprobate included, even if enjoyment of the benefits of that general offer were restricted to the elect.[4] Culverwell gave the manuscript to his brother-in-law Laurence Chaderton, master of Emmanuel College, who in turn passed it on to Ussher.[5]

Ussher sent his own thoughts to Culverwell on 3 March 1618 in a paper entitled *The True Intent and Extent of Christ's Death and Satisfaction*.[6] He recognized that this was a slippery subject (*lubricus locus*) that 'doth now much trouble the Church', the discourse dominated by 'two extremities of opinions'.[7] At one extreme, the benefits of Christ's death were extended too far as if God were actually reconciled

---

3. Bodleian Library, Oxford, MS Rawlinson C849, fols 282r–283r (282v).

4. Culverwell would further develop his pastoral concerns in print. Ezekiel Culverwell, *A Treatise of Faith* (London, 1623), pp. 25–6, 41–2.

5. The surviving copy of the manuscript is annotated in Ussher's hand, but it is important to note that the critical annotations that follow Culverwell's treatise are the objections of the supralapsarian particularist Chaderton copied onto the manuscript by Ussher, whose own views were much closer to Culverwell's. See Snoddy, *The Soteriology of James Ussher*, p. 52, n. 63.

6. This was published after Ussher's death in *The Judgement of the Late Arch-Bishop of Armagh, … Of the Extent of Christs death, and satisfaction, &c.* (ed. Nicholas Bernard; London, 1657), pp. 1–18; reproduced in *The Whole Works of the Most Rev. James Ussher, D.D., Lord Archbishop of Armagh, and Primate of All Ireland* (eds Charles R. Elrington and J. H. Todd; 17 vols; Dublin: Hodges and Smith, 1829–64; henceforth *WJU*), vol. 12, pp. 551–60.

7. *WJU*, vol. 12, p. 553.

to mankind, discharging every man from his sins, and only lack of faith preventing his enjoyment of those benefits. At the other extreme, those benefits were contracted 'into too narrow a room; as if none had any kind of interest therein, but such as were elected before the foundation of the world'.[8] Ussher offered a middle way by positing a disjunction between Christ's satisfaction and its application. Satisfaction renders 'the sins of mankind fit for pardon', whereas 'the particular application makes the sins of those to whom that mercy is vouchsafed to be actually pardoned'. 'God is made placable to our nature' by satisfaction, but not truly appeased until the sinner receives Christ and His benefits. In that sense, 'all men may be said to have interest in the merits of Christ', though not all will partake.[9] Ussher deployed the analogy of medicine prepared and medicine applied, safeguarding divine monergism with his insistence that 'when the remedy is prepared, we are never the nearer, except he be pleased of his free mercy to apply the same to us ... for the universality of the satisfaction derogates nothing from the necessity of special grace in the application'.[10] The former 'may well appertain to the common nature, which the son assumed', but the latter is 'a special privilege' of the elect.[11]

Ussher's paper, though probably intended for Culverwell alone, was soon passing from hand to hand among the Puritan clergy, 'many copies of it scattered abroad ... by some liked, and by some not'.[12] Nicholas Bernard, Ussher's chaplain and first biographer, later claimed that a member of the British delegation had carried a copy to the Synod of Dort, where a letter of objection to Ussher's position was composed.[13] Ussher was under pressure to defend his views. In his second letter, *An Answer of the Archbishop of Armagh, to Some Exceptions Taken Against his Aforesaid Letter*, he rejected the accusation of Arminianism.[14] His first letter had been written 'to ward off the blow given by the Arminians' and he pleaded that although 'I failed of mine intent, I ought to be accounted rather an oppugner than anywise an abettor of their fancies'.[15] He rejected the Arminian view that Christ's satisfaction 'hath impetrated reconciliation and remission of sins' for the world, and that as a consequence 'God offereth unto every man those means that are necessary to salvation, both sufficiently and effectually', with the acceptance or rejection of the means dependent on human volition. His disagreement with the Arminians was therefore not on the extent of the atonement but its efficacy.[16] He likewise rejected the 'extreme absurdity' of limited atonement. [17] If Christ died

8. Ibid., vol. 12, pp. 553–4.

9. Ibid., vol. 12, pp. 554–5.

10. Ibid., vol. 12, pp. 557–8.

11. Ibid., vol. 12, p. 559.

12. Jasper Heartwell to Ussher, 7 July 1618, in *WJU*, vol. 16, p. 356.

13. Bernard in *The Judgement*, sig. A3v.

14. Ussher, *An Answer*, in *WJU*, vol. 12, pp. 561–71 (563). This letter was first published by Bernard in *The Judgement* (1657), pp. 19–40.

15. *WJU*, vol. 12, p. 565.

16. Ibid., vol. 12, pp. 564–5.

17. Ibid., vol. 12, p. 565.

only for the elect and in no sense (*nullo modo*) for others, it is simply absurd to bind sinners to believe that Christ died for them, binding the conscience of the reprobate to believe an untruth.

Ussher persevered in his middle course. He reiterated his argument that Christ 'intended by giving satisfaction to God's justice to make the nature of man which he assumed, a fit subject for mercy'. This changes the nature of the relationship between God and all humanity, elect and reprobate. However, it is clear from Scripture that beyond this general intention, 'the principal end of the Lord's death' was the salvation of the elect for whom He died 'in a special manner'. Christ can be said in one respect to have died for all, and in another respect not to have died for all.[18] Ussher relates satisfaction and application to the two distinct aspects of Christ's priestly office, oblation and intercession, with a different scope assigned to each. The former 'prepares the way for God's mercy, by making the sins of all mankind pardonable ... and so puts the sons of men only in a possibility of being justified', the latter 'produceth this *potentia in actum*, that is, procureth an actual discharge from God's anger; and maketh justification, which before was a part of our possibility, to be a part of our present possession'.[19] The medicinal metaphor is foregrounded once again.

The position laid out in these epistolary tracts is one that Ussher held through the remainder of his career. Richard Baxter claimed that Ussher led John Davenant to subscribe to hypothetical universalism. [20] If this is true, then Ussher's influence on the debates of the following decades was considerable. Davenant played an important role at the Synod of Dort, agitating for hypothetical universalism and ensuring that Reformed theology would continue to tolerate a range of opinions on the sufficiency of Christ's satisfaction. The Synod backed away from a strict particularist formula that would have excluded from the Reformed camp those that held to hypothetical universalism.[21] Likewise, advocates for hypothetical universalism at the Westminster Assembly ensured that there was sufficient

18. Ibid., vol. 12, p. 567.

19. Ibid., vol. 12, p. 568–9. Ussher located impetration at the point of Christ's intercession rather than His satisfaction.

20. Richard Baxter, *Reliquiæ Baxterianæ: or, Mr Richard Baxter's Narrative of the Most Memorable Passages of his Life and Times* (London, 1696), lib. 1, p. 206; cf. Moore, *English Hypothetical Universalism*, pp. 173–4.

21. William Robert Godfrey, 'Tensions within International Calvinism: The Debate on the Atonement at the Synod of Dort, 1618–1619' (unpublished doctoral dissertation, Stanford University, 1974); Jonathan D. Moore, 'James Ussher's Influence on the Synod of Dordt', in Aza Goudriaan and Fred van Lieburg (eds), *Revisiting the Synod of Dordt (1618–1619)* (Leiden: Brill, 2011), pp. 163–80; idem, 'The Extent of the Atonement: English Hypothetical Universalism versus Particular Redemption', in Michael A. G. Haykin and Mark Jones (eds), *Drawn into Controversie: Reformed Theological Diversity and Debates Within Seventeenth-Century British Puritanism* (Göttingen: Vandenhoeck & Ruprecht, 2011), pp. 124–61 (144–8).

ambiguity in the confessional standards to prevent the exclusion of their views. During the debate, Edmund Calamy argued for an understanding of the matter 'in the sence of our devines in the sinod of Dort'. Christ paid the price for all, His intention 'absolute for the elect, conditionall for the reprobate, in case they doe beleive'.[22] Ussher therefore exerted indirect influence on two of the most important public codifications of Reformed theology.

Behind Ussher's two letters lie a set of notes on the intent of Christ's death. Amidst the vast quantity of Ussher's papers that survive, there are several pages of commonplace notes on the question headed *An Christus passus fuerit pro omnibus*. Unlike the disappointingly blank pages of *loci* such as *An Deus Auctor peccati*, this is a *locus* for which the notes appear to have taken on a life of their own, sprawling to take over pages headed *De poenit. peccati* and *De praedestinatione et reprobatione*.[23] Here, Ussher gathered together dozens of citations from patristic and medieval authorities. The uniformity of the hand and ink across the vast majority of the patristic material suggests a concentrated period of engagement with the question. The date cannot be ascertained with certainty but both citations from Chrysostom are supplied with reference to Sir Henry Savile's edition of Chrysostom, so it can be no earlier than 1612.[24] An interlinear note 'vid. Abbot', lying above the citation from Ambrose on Luke's Gospel and struck through, is almost certainly a reference to Robert Abbot's *De Gratia, et Perseverantia Sanctorum* (1618).[25] This could bring the notes forward to 1618, though as an interlinear remark it could have been

22. Chad van Dixhoorn (ed.), *The Minutes and Papers of the Westminster Assembly, 1643-1652* (5 vols; Oxford: Oxford University Press, 2012), vol. 3, pp. 692–702 (692); cf. Alex F. Mitchell and John Struthers (eds), *Minutes of the Sessions of the Westminster Assembly of Divines* (Edinburgh: William Blackwood, 1874), pp. 152–60 (152). See also, Lee Gatiss, '"Shades of Opinion within a Generic Calvinism". The Particular Redemption Debate at the Westminster Assembly', *Reformed Theological Review* 69 (2010), pp. 101–18; idem, 'A Deceptive Clarity? Particular Redemption in the Westminster Standards', *Reformed Theological Review* 69 (2010), pp. 180–96; Moore, 'The Extent of the Atonement', pp. 148–52; Robert Letham, *The Westminster Assembly: Reading Its Theology in Historical Context* (Phillipsburg, NJ: P & R Publishing, 2009), pp. 176–82.

23. Bodleian, MS Barlow 13, fols 185v–188r. This chapter focuses on the patristic material, leaving the medieval authorities to one side. On commonplaces and note-taking more generally in the early modern period, see Ann Blair, 'Reading Strategies for Coping with Information Overload ca.1550–1700', *Journal of the History of Ideas* 64 (2003), pp. 11–28; eadem, 'Note Taking as an Art of Transmission', *Critical Inquiry* 31 (2004), pp. 85–107; eadem, *Too Much to Know: Managing Scholarly Information before the Modern Age* (New Haven, CT: Yale University Press, 2010).

24. John Chrysostom, Τῶν εὑρισκομένων τόμος πρῶτος (-ὄγδοος) (ed. Sir Henry Savile; 8 vols; Eton, 1610–13). The citations are from the fourth volume, published in 1612.

25. Bodleian, MS Barlow 13, fol. 186r; cf. Robert Abbot, *De gratia, et perseverantia sanctorum. Exercitationes aliquot habitæ in Academiæ Oxoniensi* (London, 1618), p. 94, where he reflects on Ambrose's use of *specialiter*.

added later than the text it annotates. This chapter will proceed to argue that these notes leave subtle traces of influence in the letters of 1618, so this must be regarded as the latest possible date for the major part of these notes.

Many themes and motifs that are present in Ussher's writing on the intent and sufficiency of Christ's satisfaction are addressed in the patristic citations appended to this chapter. Incarnation is foundational. Christ shares the common nature of all humanity so that it is all humanity for whom Christ makes satisfaction, with His divine nature conferring infinite value on His sacrifice. God's universal salvific will is strongly affirmed, with a universal intent in Christ's death a seemingly logical corollary. Though Christ has taken the punishment for all, not all are saved. Those who do not believe cheat themselves of the benefits of Christ's death, and the doctrines of election and the necessity of special grace do not diminish the culpability of unbelief.

Ussher was one of the leading patristic scholars of his day. According to Bernard, Ussher realized as a young man the importance of the patristic past as a key polemical battleground. Between 1601 and 1619, he undertook the arduous exercise of reading the entire extant patristic corpus.[26] Although he was an expert in this field, there are signs that when he turned to the controversy on the nature and sufficiency of Christ's satisfaction, he made use of two controversial works of the previous generation as shortcuts to *loci classici* and other useful material. There is evidence in the notes that he made use of *De redemtione generis humani* by the moderate Heidelberg theologian, Jacobus Kimedoncius, and also *Controversiæ de mortis Christi efficacia* by Johann Paul Windeck, a Roman Catholic, Professor and Canon at Marchdorff at the time of writing.[27]

The most obvious evidence for Ussher's use of Kimedoncius and Windeck is the small number of direct references to their works.[28] Some of these references come in the simple form of author name and page number, but on occasion Ussher proceeds to brief interaction with these sources. For example, he disputes Windeck's representation of Faustus of Riez as a champion of orthodoxy against

---

26. Nicholas Bernard, *The Life & Death of the Most Reverend and Learned Father of Our Church Dr. James Usher, Late Arch-Bishop of Armagh, and Primate of All Ireland* (London, 1656), p. 29.

27. Jacobus Kimedoncius, *De redemtione generis humani. Libri tres: Quibus copiosè traditur controversia, de redemtionis et gratiæ per Christum universalitate, et morte ipsius pro omnibus. Accessit tractatio finitima de diuina prædestinatione* (Heidelberg, 1592); Johann Paul Windeck, *Controversiæ de mortis Christi efficacia, inter Catholicos et Calvinistas hoc tempore disputatæ* (Cologne, 1603).

28. There are two direct references to Kimedoncius, one with regard to Theophylact, the other to Prosper's *Epistola ad Augustinum*. The latter reference lies within a citation from Primasius and is struck through. There are three direct references to Windeck, one with regard to Prosper's *Responsiones ad objectionum Vincentianarum*, another to three appearances of Faustus of Riez and the final one to Windeck's inclusion of a passage from Innocent III.

the Pelagians. Faustus was himself a Semipelagian and the main polemical target of his *De gratia Dei et libero arbitrio* was the doctrine of Augustine. Ussher's choice of the word *fingit* (*'ut fingit P. Windeck'*) intimates a deliberate misrepresentation on Windeck's part.[29] Such direct references are clear evidence of Ussher's use of these works, but it is only when one begins to compare the text of citations that the true extent of the interaction becomes clearer.

Of particular significance is Ussher's handling of a citation from Ambrose's commentary on Luke. In the second occurrence of this citation in the notes, one finds Ussher deciding between variant readings to arrive at the form of words that would appear in his second letter of 1618. The majority textual tradition reads: *Et si Christus pro omnibus passus est, pro nobis tamen specialiter passus est; quia pro Ecclesia passus est* ('And if Christ suffered for all, yet he suffered particularly for us, because he suffered for the church'). Ussher, however, begins with the unusual *Etsi Christus pro omnibus mortuus sit*. Above this he then writes the majority *passus est* before striking through *passus* and *sit* to finally settle on *mortuus est*.[30] This final rendering matches that given by Kimedoncius, a well-recognized variant within the textual tradition and, indeed, the form typically found in early modern print, but the original *mortuus sit* is the reading found in Windeck.[31] The supposition that Windeck is Ussher's source here is strengthened by the bracketed *quoad efficaciam sc[ilicet]* following the citation, which echoes Windeck's bracketed editorial comment, *quoad efficaciam*.

The first occurrence of this Ambrose citation is found on the first page of the notes and takes the final *mortuus est* form without any sign of emendation. Here

29. Bodleian, MS Barlow 13, fol. 187r.

30. Bodleian, MS Barlow 13, fol. 186r; cf. Ambrose, *Expositio evangelii secundum Lucam*, 6.25; *PL*, vol. 15, col. 1675A.

31. Kimedoncius, *De redemtione*, p. 407; Windeck, *Controversiæ de mortis Christi efficacia*, p. 236. The *mortuus est* form is found in the early *Opera* of Johann Amerbach (Basel, 1492), its revision by Conradus Leontorius (Basel, 1506) and in the edition published by Adam Petri with Andreas Hartmann/Cratander (Basel, 1516; with an imprint in Nuremberg, 1516). It is found in the Erasmus editions of Basel (1527, 1538, 1555) and Paris (1529, 1539, 1549), in that of Jean Gillot/Gillotius Campanus (Paris, 1568) and in the edition begun by Felix de Montalto (later Pope Sixtus V) printed at Rome (1579–87) and Paris (1584–86), and later reprinted at Paris (1603, 1614) and Cologne (1616). The superior *passus est* reading was preferred by Johannes Coster who emended the Erasmus text from a wider selection of manuscripts (Basel, 1567) and was the form later chosen by the Benedictines of St. Maur (Paris, 1686–90), whose work would constitute the basis of subsequent editions. It is certain that Ussher consulted the first Parisian printing of the Montalto edition during the preparation of these notes (a solitary reference 'vid col.1331.edit.prioris Paris' is found after Ambrose [5] in his notes and this passage matches the text in col. 1131 [actually cols 1130–1] only in vol. 2 of that edition); his toying briefly with *passus est* here suggests that he also referred to Coster's edition. On the manuscript variants, see *Corpus Christianorum, Series Latina* (194 vols; Turnhout: Brepols, 1953–), vol. 14, p. 183.

it is not found amidst a list of quotes but in a paragraph that reads much more like Ussher constructing an argument in terms that would be found in the letters:

> I would have both parts of that proposition of S. Ambrose (lib. 6. in Luc. cap. 7.) to be maintayned: Etsi Christus pro omnibus mortuus est; pro nobis tamen specialiter passus est, quia pro Ecclesia passus est. Prosper I am sure in his oppositions against the Semipelagians (the great patrons of universal grace) laboureth to uphold bothe: whose moderation if some of our men would follow in their disputes against the Arminians (the right heyres of the Semipelagians;) they would not runne themselves upon those rockes of absurdityes, that a man should be bound in conscience to beleeve that which is untrue, and charged to take that which he hath nothing to do with.[32]

It would be a reasonable conjecture to regard this as being added at a later phase in Ussher's work on this subject. The asymmetry of the *mortuus est* variant appears to have given Ussher greater scope for nuance. He introduces this form of the Ambrose citation in the second letter to buttress his argument that in different respects Christ can be said to have died for all and not to have died for all. While Christ can be said to have died for all in the sense that all receive benefit from His death in some manner, He suffered specially for the elect. In consecrating Himself to the work of the cross 'he did specially sanctify himself' that the elect might also be sanctified through the truth (Jn 17.19).[33]

Another example comes alongside a more problematic citation from Ambrose: *Propterea enim descendit ut credas. Si non credis, non descendit tibi, non tibi passus est* ('For this reason [Christ] came down, that you may believe. If you do not believe, he did not descend for you, he has not suffered for you.') Ussher deflects this potential difficulty with a comment that if unbelievers do not share in the 'effect' of Christ's death, it does not necessarily follow that Christ could in no manner be said to have died for them: *At non sequit[u]r, si non participat infidelis effectu[m] mortis Chr[ist]i ergo pro eo plane nullo modo mortuu[m] esse.*[34] What is not immediately apparent is that Ussher's words are merely a paraphrase of Windeck's comment on the same point: *Non participat infidelis effectu[m] mortis Christi, quid tum postea? Num sequitur pro eo planè nullo modo mortuum esse?*[35] At first sight Ussher's objection appears to be his own editorial commentary, but a comparison of texts reveals that it is lifted from elsewhere. This point is then echoed in the second letter of 1618, where Ussher insists that although Christ can be said to have died for the elect in a special manner, 'to infer from hence, that in no manner of respect he died for any others, is but a very weak collection'.[36]

---

32. Bodleian, MS Barlow 13, fol. 185v.

33. Ussher, *An Answer*, in *WJU*, vol. 12, p. 567.

34. Bodleian, MS Barlow 13, fol. 186r; cf. Ambrose, *De fide ad Gratianum Augustum*, 4.2; *PL*, vol. 16, cols 621D–2A.

35. Windeck, *Controversiæ de mortis Christi efficacia*, p. 236.

36. Ussher, *An Answer*, in *WJU*, vol. 12, p. 567; cf. p. 565 for *nullo modo*.

There are also traces of interaction with Kimedoncius in the notes beyond the explicit references. For example, in a passage from Prosper's *Epistola ad Augustinum*, Ussher glosses the expression *divinae misericordiae sacramentum* with the words *promissio gratiae*. This interlinear comment is probably derived from Kimedoncius's bracketed *promissio nempe gratiae, vt hodie loquu[n]tur,* which occurs at the same place in his reproduction of this passage.[37]

A far more complex pattern of interaction is found in a citation from Prosper of Aquitaine's response to the Vincentian Articles.[38] Ussher begins with a discussion of the provenance of this work. Windeck attributes the work to Augustine and subjects Theodore Beza to a wholly undeserved lashing (*flagellat*) for daring to suggest otherwise.[39] Ussher points out that the scholarly consensus now holds that Prosper was the author of this work once falsely imposed on Augustine. This is made clear in the Basel edition of Augustine, and also in the edition issuing from Louvain.[40]

Ussher then proceeds to cite his text from the Douai edition of Prosper.[41] The paragraph bears a number of interlinear annotations. The first of these is the comment *in effectu sc[ilicet]*, which comes above the following clause with a line tying it to *proprietas*: *redemptionis proprietas haud dubie penes illos est, de quibus princeps hujus mundi missus est foras.* This annotation echoes Windeck's bracketed 'IN EFFECTV' inserted between *proprietas* and *haud* in his lower-case text.[42] Indeed, even though Ussher begins his citation from the Douai edition and includes a lengthy sentence that precedes the citation as found in Windeck, he appears to be copying his text from Windeck at this point. Between *proprietas* and *haud* Ussher has written *in* and subsequently struck through it, as if he had caught himself making a mistake, corrected it and demoted *in effectu* to the more appropriate status of an interlinear annotation. A further interlinear comment glosses Prosper's description of the beverage of immortality (*poculum immortalitatis*) prepared from human weakness and divine power with the words *Christi mortem intellige.* Again, these words are imported from elsewhere, this time not from Windeck, but from Kimedoncius, where they occur as a bracketed

37. Bodleian, MS Barlow 13, fol. 187r; Kimedoncius, *De redemtione*, p. 438.

38. Bodleian, MS Barlow 13, fol. 186v. The citation is from Prosper, *Responsiones ad objectionum Vincentianarum*, 1 and is too lengthy to reproduce in full here. See Prosper [7] in the appended citations.

39. Windeck, *Controversiæ de mortis Christi efficacia*, pp. 239–40.

40. Augustine, *Primus [–Decimus] Tomus Operum Divi Aurelii Augustini Hipponensis Episcopi* (ed. Desiderius Erasmus; 10 vols; Basel: Froben, 1556), vol. 7, col. 1352. For the Louvain edition see, for example *D. Aurelii Augustini Hipponensis Episcopi … Opera tomis decem comprehensa* (10 vols; Antwerp: Plantin, 1576–77), vol. 7, p. 577.

41. Ussher's reference is 'oper.fol.136.b.' Comparison with early modern editions of Prosper reveals that he was using *Divi Prosperi Aquitanici Episcopi Rhegiensis, Opera* (Douai: Bogardi, 1577), fol. 136v.

42. Windeck, *Controversiæ de mortis Christi efficacia*, p. 240.

comment in his citation.[43] Another probable trace of influence from Kimedoncius follows shortly afterwards at the end of the paragraph: *si non bibitur, non medetur (al. proficit)*. This is almost certainly a nod towards the variant reading found in Kimedoncius.[44]

It appears that Ussher was working with both the Douai edition of Prosper and Windeck's tome open before him as he copied out the passage, with the comment of Kimedoncius being added at that time or subsequently. This reflects deliberation over a passage that would prove important in Ussher's formulation of his atonement theology. The citation was brought forward in the final paragraph of Ussher's second letter of 1618 at the climax of his argument, but the medicinal analogy is present also at the end of the first letter.[45] Ussher was fond of Prosper's distinction between the properties of the gospel medicine and its application, and the metaphor recurs frequently in his later preaching. For example, he claimed that Christ's blood shed on the cross is 'not sufficient for thy redempc[i]on, for though it give contentment to Gods justice, yet it is but as a medicyne that is prepared, now the medicyne helpes not by being prepared but by being applyed'.[46] Ussher made good use of this illustration, but it hardly constitutes an argument for hypothetical universalism. Theodore Beza used precisely the same imagery to distinguish between redemption accomplished and applied.[47]

Sadly, Ussher's copy of Windeck's *Controversiæ de mortis Christi efficacia* sheds little additional light on his use of this work. Ussher was not always a great annotator of books. There are a few annotations, mostly simple vertical lines in the margin to highlight a passage. There is a correction of a chapter number in the reference to Ambrose on Luke, and the reassignment of a citation from Haymo to Primasius is certainly in Ussher's neat hand.[48]

A glance at Table 1 shows that the bulk of the citations could have come from Kimedoncius or Windeck. All but two of the citations in the major section are found in these two works. Apart from some small clusters, the order of the citations in these authors does not match that found in Ussher's notes, but Ussher could have been working from an intermediate set of notes, perhaps something akin to the *lemmata* described by Ann Blair, simple bibliographical references that he organized to suit his own purposes as he wrote out the texts.[49]

43. Kimedoncius, *De redemtione*, p. 410.

44. Ibid., pp. 67, 249, 410.

45. Ussher, *An Answer*, in *WJU*, vol. 12, pp. 570–1; Ussher, *The True Intent and Extent*, in *WJU*, vol. 12, p. 559.

46. Bodleian, MS Eng.th.e.25, fol. 74v (1626). Other occurrences of this analogy may be found in Balliol College, Oxford, MS 259, second pagination, fol. 227v (c. 1624); Bodleian, MS Eng.th.e.25, fols 38v, 54r, 55r, 91v, 112v (1626); *WJU*, vol. 13, pp. 160–1, 176, 270 (1640); Cambridge University Library, MS Mm.6.55, fols 53r, 60r–v (1648).

47. Theodore Beza, *Altera Brevis Fidei Confessio*, in *Confessio Christianæ Fidei* (Geneva: Vignon, 1577), p. 254.

48. Trinity College, Dublin, shelfmark E.gg.3. See esp. pp. 236, 251.

49. Blair, 'Note Taking', pp. 98–9.

For example, he brings together citations from Chrysostom, Theophylact and Primasius on Hebrews 2. The two additional citations could be easily explained. The first is from Ambrose's *De fide ad Gratianum Augustum* and there it lies in fairly close proximity to the citation that immediately follows in Ussher's notes (about one and a half columns in Migne). Encountering one text in Windeck and Kimedoncius could have recalled to mind the other, either from past direct encounter or mediated via another polemical work. Alternatively, being a less than helpful text, it may have driven Ussher *ad fontes* to read it in context and there discover another equally unhelpful passage. The second additional citation is from Primasius on Hebrews 9, and in Ussher's notes follows Chrysostom on the same chapter. One citation seems to have drawn forth the other through a process of association.

Ussher was not content merely to copy out text from Kimedoncius and Windeck. Again and again, even when there is a clear reference to Kimedoncius or Windeck, there are indications that he was checking the sources against standard editions. For example, in the material drawn from Faustus of Riez and the Council of Arles, there are page references to Windeck for the Faustus material at the beginning, but interspersed with the citations are references to both Marguerin de La Bigne's *Bibliotheca Patrum* and Heinrich Canisius's *Antiquæ Lectionis*.[50] Ussher's interest in textual matters extended to the handling of sources by the censors. Following a citation out of Antonius Melissa's *Sententiae*, probably from Basil, he discusses the treatment of the text as found in Latin in La Bigne's *Bibliotheca Patrum*. While the Spanish *Index Expurgatorius* simply stipulated the deletion of the text, its Roman counterpart would tolerate an explanatory gloss. The words *Deus non omnium Deus est, sed eorum qui per charitate in ipsius quasi familiam recepti, & ipsi coniuncti sunt* could perhaps be understood in this way: *non esse omnium Deum singulari illo, ac peculiari modo, quo electis, & praedestinatis, qui ipsis in bonum salutis aeternae efficaciter vertat.*[51]

All of this reflects a considerable amount of interaction with the texts and questions of provenance, transmission and reception. Care was required in citation as one's case would be seriously undermined by the exposure of any lapse in probity. The challenge was all the greater in view of the belief, widespread among Protestant theologians, that patristic texts had been corrupted or even wholly fabricated by their Roman opponents. One of Ussher's correspondents,

---

50. Correlation of page numbers shows that Ussher was using the second edition, Margarinum de La Bigne, *Sacræ Bibliothecæ Sanctorum Patrum seu scriptorum ecclesiasticorum probabilium* (9 vols; Paris: s.n., 1589); Henricus Canisius, *Antiquæ Lectionis, seu antiqua monumenta ad historiam mediae aetatis illustrandam* (6 vols; Ingolstadt: Angermarium, 1601–04).

51. Bodleian, MS Barlow 13, fol. 185v; *Index Librorum Expurgatorum, Illustrissimi ac Reuerendis[simi] D. D. Gasparis Quiroga* (Saumur: Portau, 1601, following the Madrid edition of 1584), p. 18; Richard Gibbings (ed.), *The Index Expurgatorius of Rome* (Dublin: Milliken and Son, 1837), p. 172.

Thomas James, Bodley's first librarian in Oxford, believed that such 'shameless forgeries' had made the world 'turn, or continue popish'. Proof positive for his conspiracy theory came in the form of the *Index Expurgatorius* by which new editions of the Fathers were being silently corrected to bring them into line with Tridentine dogma.[52] The Roman counterfeiters 'doe adde, and take away, alter and change the words, according to the pleasure of their Lord the Pope' in order to delude the world 'with a shew of Antiquitie'.[53] Like James, Ussher sought to liberate Protestant scholars from dependency on a corrupted textual tradition and the collation of manuscript witnesses was a lifelong endeavour. What could have been his *magnum opus* in this field, his *Bibliotheca Theologica*, still languishes in manuscript, several scholars either dying or being brought to despair in their attempts to edit it.[54]

That Ussher was using secondary sources as a means of access to patristic material is clear, but is there nothing in these notes that comes from his own unmediated reading of the Fathers? There are citations in these notes that are not found in Kimedoncius or Windeck. Almost all of these lie on the first page, straddling a block of material from Ambrose and Prosper. They are written in smaller script than the remainder of the notes, with finer nibs, and in different inks. This suggests that these citations were added on different occasions over a period of time, while the uniformity of the hand in the greater part of the notes indicates a concentrated effort. What is most striking is the brevity and relative obscurity of these excerpts. These are not *loci classici* of the debate about the nature and sufficiency of Christ's satisfaction. They would be considered off the beaten track in any discussion of the subject. For example, there are eight excerpts attributed to Sedulius.[55] For Ussher, however, Sedulius was not some rarely trodden byway. In 1622 Ussher would publish his research on the primitive Church in Britain and Ireland, a work in which Sedulius would play a starring role. It is a reasonable assumption that he would have carefully studied Sedulius in the previous decade and that these

52. For James's correspondence with Ussher, see *WJU*, vol. 15, pp. 206–7, 262–7.

53. Thomas James, *A Treatise of the Corruption of Scripture, Councels, and Fathers, by the Prelats, Pastors, and Pillars of the Church of Rome, for Maintenance of Popery and Irreligion* (London, 1612), sig. A4r.

54. Ussher's original may be found in British Library, Harleian MS 822. Copies survive in Bodleian, MSS e Mus. 46–47; Bodleian, MSS Add. D35–36; Trinity College Dublin, MS 795, 5 vols. On attempts to edit the work, see Hugh Trevor-Roper, 'James Ussher, Archbishop of Armagh', in *Catholics, Anglicans and Puritans: Seventeenth Century Essays* (London: Secker & Warburg, 1987), pp. 120–65 (161f). For a survey of approaches to the Fathers in early modern England, see Jean-Louis Quantin, *The Church of England and Christian Antiquity: The Construction of a Confessional Identity in the 17th Century* (Oxford: Oxford University Press, 2009).

55. Or six if one combines the two citations from *Carmen Paschale* with their supporting prose from the *Opus Paschale*.

citations come from his own reading.[56] The works of Antonius Melissa, Basil of Seleucia and Photius are all sources of multiple citations in Ussher's works from the early 1620s onwards.[57] Photius and Sedulius had already appeared in *De successione* in 1613.[58] These were patristic authorities with whom Ussher engaged repeatedly.

This sheds light on Ussher's pattern of work in the acquisition, storage and re-presentation of patristic material. Citations were added to the notes on an *ad hoc* basis as Ussher encountered them in his reading of the Fathers, but a period of intense study on the topic sees him using secondary polemical sources as a shortcut to the *loci classici*. These mediators leave fingerprints in Ussher's commonplace notes and ultimately shape the presentation of his case to his fellow clergy. The influence is subtle, but it can be discerned. Intertextual excavation reveals that Ussher's reading of Windeck is one stratum in the archaeology of his patristic knowledge, lying below the surface of his argument on the intent and sufficiency of Christ's satisfaction, and contributing to its contours. The debt is unacknowledged and perhaps one that Ussher would not have wanted to be widely known among his contemporaries.

The Fathers were not ornamental for Ussher. He drew on them for substance, not for mere display. There are no patristic citations in the first letter of 1618, but three

Table 1 Ussher's citations collated with Kimedoncius and Windeck

Author	Citation	Kimedoncius	Windeck
fol. 185v		Page no.	Page no.
Photius	*Bibliotheca*, 54		
Sedulius [1]	*In epist. ad Titum*, 2		
Ambrose [1]	*In Lucam*, 6.25	407	236
Prosper [1]	*De vocat. gent.*, 1.9	77, 244, 419	
Prosper [2]	Ibid., 1.25	117, 420f	

56. Ussher, *An epistle [...] concerning the religion anciently professed by the Irish and Scottish; Shewing it to be for substance the same with that which at this day is by publick authoritie established in the Church of England*, in Christopher Sibthorp, *A friendly advertisement to the pretended Catholickes of Ireland* (Dublin, 1622). See also, Ussher, *A Discourse of the Religion Anciently Professed by the Irish and British*, in *The Workes of the Most Reverend Father in God, Iames Vssher* (London, 1631). This is the version found in *WJU*, vol. 4, pp. 235–381. While Ussher makes no distinction in the notes under discussion, it is clear from the first edition of the *Discourse* that he was aware of the confusion of Coelius Sedulius with Sedulius Scottus, and doubted that the author of *Carmen Paschale* 'were the same with our Sedulius' (p. 33; cf. *WJU*, vol. 4, p. 283). For his more extensive discussion of the source material in *Britannicarum ecclesiarum antiquitates* (Dublin, 1639), see *WJU*, vol. 6, pp. 319–32.

57. These can easily be traced through the author index in *WJU*, vol. 17.

58. Ussher, *Gravissimæ quæstionis, de Christianarum Ecclesiarum [...] successione et statu* (1613); *WJU*, vol. 2, pp. 1–413 (from revised edition, 1687).

Author	Citation	Kimedoncius	Windeck
Prosper [3]	Ibid., 2.2	78, 244	
Prosper [4]	Ibid., 2.16		(68), 243
Sedulius [2]	*In epist. ad Rom.*, 8		
Pelagius [1]	*In epist. ad Rom.*, 8		
Sedulius [3]	*In epist. ad Rom.*, 15		
Sedulius [4]	*In epist. I ad Tim.*, 2		
Pelagius [2]	*In epist. I ad Tim.*, 2		
Sedulius [5]	*Carmen Paschale*, 5		
Sedulius [6]	*Opus Paschale*, 5		
Basil [?]	Antonius Melissa, *Sententiae*, 1.3		
Ennodius	*Benedictio Cerei*		
Basil of Seleucia	*Orationes*, 19		
Sedulius [7]	*Carmen Paschale*, 5		
Sedulius [8]	*Opus Paschale*, 5		
fol. 186r			
Ambrose [2]	*De fide ad Grat. Aug.*, 4.2		
Ambrose [3]	Ibid., 4.2	406	236
Ambrose [1]	*In Lucam*, 6.25	407	236
Ambrose [4]	*In Psalmum 118*, 8		(154), 236
Ambrose [5]	Ibid., 19	408f	
Chrysostom [1]	*In epist. ad Heb.*, 4		74
Theophylact	*In epist. ad Heb.*, 2	97	
Primasius [1]	*In epist. ad Heb.*, 2	420	251
Primasius [2]	*In epist. I ad Tim.*, 2		249
fol. 186v			
Prosper [5]	*Resp. Gall.*, 1.9	418f	(151), 243f
Prosper [6]	Ibid., 2.9		244, 32
Prosper [7]	*Resp. Vinc.*,1	66f, 249, 409f	239f
fol. 187r			
Prosper [8]	*Epist. ad Augustinum*	437f	
Faustus of Riez [1]	*De gratia Dei*, 1.16		247
Faustus of Riez [2]	Ibid, 1.16		248
Faustus of Riez [3]	*Epist. ad Lucidum*		264
Council of Arles			266
Chrysostom [2]	*In epist. ad Heb.*, 17	247, 416	237
Primasius [3]	*In epist. ad Heb.*, 9		
Leo I	*De passione Domini*, 13.3	(118), 127, 421	128

Page number in brackets denotes reference to passage rather than quotation.

key passages are adduced in the second letter.[59] Under the pressure of criticism, Ussher appealed to the Fathers in an effort to gain polemical traction but they had already contributed substantially to his thought on this controversial matter. The survival of his commonplace notes affords a glimpse behind his published writings to his habits of reading, his borrowing across confessional boundaries and the complexities of his reception of the Fathers.

59. To the first letter is appended a passage from Aquinas (*Summa Contra Gentiles*, 4.55) that supports Ussher's concluding argument that Christ's death 'may be counted a kind of universal cause of the restoring of our nature, as Adam was of the depraving of it'. Ussher,

Appendix

Ussher's Citations

The following citations appear as given by Ussher, grouped by author alphabetically. The actual order in which they occur in his notes can be seen in Table 1. These citations may be of interest to those studying early modern debates on Christ's satisfaction as being what Ussher felt worth recording in his notes. References to Migne are given in the footnotes for the reader's convenience, but Migne is no safe guide to the text as it would have stood in printed editions available for seventeenth-century readers.

Ambrose

1. Et si Christus pro omnibus mortuus est, pro nobis tamen specialiter passus est, quia pro Ecclesia passus est.[60]
2. Quis me admittet, nisi omnipotentem annunciem Christu[m]? Clausae sunt portae, non cuicunq[ue] aperiuntur, *non quicunq[ue] vult*, nisi qui fideliter credit, ingreditur. Custoditur aula imperialis.[61]
3. Propterea enim descendit ut credas. Si non credis, non descendit tibi, non tibi passus est.[62]
4. Mysticus sol ille justitiae omnibus ortus est, omnibus venit, omnibus passus est, et omnibus resurrexit. Ideo a[utem] passus est, ut tolleret peccatu[m] mundi. Si quis a[utem] non credit in Christum, generali beneficio ipse se fraudat. ut si quis clausis fenestris radios solis excludat, non ideo sol non ortus est omnibus, quia calore ejus se ipse fraudavit: sed quod solis est, praerogativam suam servat; quod imprudentis est, com[m]unis a se gratiam lucis excludit.[63]
5. Quamvis diffusa per omnes et in omnes et supra omnes potestates sit; qui omnibus ortus ex Virgine est, et bonis et malis; sicut et solem suu[m] oriri jubet super bonos et malos: illu[m] tamen fovet, qui appropinquat sibi. Sicut [e]n[im] a se fulgorem solis excludit, qui fenestras domus suae clauserit, locumq[ue] tenebrosum in quo diversetur, elegerit: ita qui se averterit a sole justitiae, non potest splendorem ejus aspicere. In tenebris ambulat, et in omniu[m] luce ipse sibi causa est caecitatis. Aperi igitur fenestras tuas, ut tota domus tua veri fulgore solis illuceat. Etc. [In Ambrose, the following is

---

The True Intent and Extent, in *WJU*, vol. 12, pp. 559–60. The patristic citations in the second letter are from Ambrose (*Expositio evangelii secundum Lucam*, 6.25) and Prosper (*De vocatione omnium gentium*, 1.9; *Responsiones ad objectionum Vincentianarum*, 1). The first and third of these are discussed above. Ussher, *An Answer*, in *WJU*, vol. 12, pp. 567, 570–1.

60. Ambrose, *Expositio evangelii secundum Lucam*, 6.25; *PL*, vol. 15, col. 1675A.

61. Ambrose, *De fide ad Gratianum Augustum*, 4.2; *PL*, vol. 16, col. 620B.

62. Ambrose, *De fide ad Gratianum Augustum*, 4.2; *PL*, vol. 16, cols 621D–2A.

63. Ambrose, *In Psalmum CXVIII*, 8; *PL*, vol. 15, col. 1318C.

found in the place of Ussher's *etc.*: aperi oculos tuos, ut videas orientem tibi solem justitiae. Sed cave ne eos ulla stipulae festuca perturbet. Si quid sordis in oculo fuerit mentis tuae, non poteris intueri: si quid aegritudinis, plus gravabit; confusam oculorum aciem lux ferit, majoremque dolorem excitat. Sit ergo simplex oculus tuus; ne incipiat totum corpus tuum esse tenebrosum, et vacillet in lumine, sicut sunt caecorum vestigia.] Numquid si quis ostia domus suae claudat, solis est culpa quod non illuminat domum ejus?[64]

Basil [?]

Οὐ πάντων Θεὸς ὁ Θεός, ἀλλὰ τῶν οἰκειωθέντων αὐτῷ διὰ τῆς ἀγάπης.[65]

Basil of Seleucia

Christus propter omnes venit.[66]

Chrysostom

1. Ὅπως χάριτι Θεοῦ ὑπὲρ παντὸς γεύσηται θανάτου· οὐχὶ τῶν πιστῶν μόνον, ἀλλὰ καὶ τῆς οἰκουμένης ἁπάσης· αὐτὸς μὲν γὰρ ὑπὲρ πάντων ἀπέθανε. Τί δὲ, εἰ μὴ πάντες ἐπίστευσαν; αὐτὸς τὸ ἑαυτοῦ πεπλήρωκε.[67]

   Mutianus: Ut gratia Dei pro omnibus gustaret mortem; non pro fidelibus tantum, sed et pro mundo universo. Nam *ipse quidem pro omnibus mortuus est. Quid autem si non omnes credunt? Ille* [(tamen)] *quod suum erat implevit.*[68]

2. Εἰς τὸ πολλῶν ἀνενεγκεῖν ἁμαρτίας. Διὰ τί δὲ πολλῶν εἶπε, καὶ μὴ πάντων; ἐπειδὴ μὴ πάντες ἐπίστευσαν· ὑπὲρ ἁπάντων μὲν γὰρ ἀπέθανενς [*sic*], εἰς τὸ σῶσαι πάντας, τὸ αὐτοῦ μέρος· ἀντίρροπος γὰρ ἦν ὁ θάνατος ἐκεῖνος τῆς πάντων ἀπωλείας· οὐ πάντων δὲ τὰς ἁμαρτίας ἀνήνεγκε, διὰ τὸ μὴ θελῆσαι αὐτούς.[69]

   Mutianus: Ad multorum auferenda peccata? Quare multorum et non omnium? Quia non omnes crediderunt. Pro omnibus quidem mortuus est, hoc est, quantum in ipso est. Sufficiebat mors illius ad medendum omnium mortialium perditioni: non autem omnium peccata abstulit, propterea quod noluerunt.[70]

---

64. Ambrose, *In Psalmum CXVIII*, 19; *PL*, vol. 15, col. 1481C–D.

65. Antonius Melissa, *Sententiae sive loci communes*, 1, sermo 3; *PG*, vol. 136, col. 784C.

66. Ussher's reference is 'in Homiliis. (p. 181.)'. This short text appears to be a paraphrase of a passage in *B. Basilii Seleuciæ Isavriæ Episcopi: Orationes XLIV* ([Heidelberg]: Dausqueius, 1604), p. 181 (Oratio XIX, in Centurionem). Expounding Matthew 8:7, Basil writes, '*Ego* inquit, *veniens curabo eum. Ego, qui hominum studio in hominem me indui, qui propter omnes veni, no[n] vnum despiciam, curabo eum.*' Cf. *PG*, vol. 85, cols 237C, 238C.

67. Chrysostom, *In Epistolam ad Hebraeos*, Hom. 4; *PG*, vol. 63, col. 39.

68. Mutianus, *Interpretatio*; *PG*, vol. 63, col. 264.

69. Chrysostom, *In Epistolam ad Hebraeos*, Hom. 17; *PG*, vol. 63, col. 129.

70. Mutianus, *Interpretatio*; *PG*, vol. 63, col. 347.

Also:

Quare multorum, et non omnium? quia non omnes credunt. Pro omnibus mortuus est, hoc est quantum in ipso. Ejus momenti est unius, cujus momenti est omniu[m] perditio. Non enim omniu[m] peccata abstulit; propter quod credere noluerunt.

Council of Arles

Juxta praedicandi recentia statuta Concilii damno vobiscu[m] sensu[m] illu[m], etc. qui dicit, quod Christus Dominus Salvator noster mortem non pro omniu[m] salute susceperit. Contra vero asserit: Christu[m] Dominu[m] et Salvatorem nostru[m], quantum pertinet ad diuitias bonitatis suae, pretiu[m] mortis pro omnibus obtulisse: et quia nullu[m] perire velit, qui est salvator omniu[m] hominu[m], maxime fideliu[m], diues in omnibus qui invocant illu[m].[71]

Ennodius Ticinensis

Sufficit ad reparationem aeternitatis perditae, quod non a nobis, sed pro nobis, agnus occisus est.[72]

Faustus of Riez

1. Dominu[m] nostru[m] Jesum Christu[m] aiunt humanam carnem non pro omnium salute sumpsisse, nec pro omnibus mortuum esse. Hoc omnimodis Catholica detestatur Ecclesia.[73]
2. Sicut omnes resurgemus, licet non omnes immutabimur: ita Dominu[m] redemptorem cu[m] generalis misericordiae beneficio venisse testamur, etsi illud infidelitas, quia noluit, non recepit. Nam Deum quolibet tempore qui quaesivit, invenit, et qui invenisse non visus est, non quaesivit.[74]
3. Anathema illi, qui dixerit quod Christus non pro omnibus mortuus sit, nec omnes homines salvos esse velit.[75]

Leo I

Effusio pro injustis sanguinis justi tam potens fuit ad privilegium, tam dives ad pretiu[m], ut si universitas captivoru[m] in redemptorem suu[m] crederet, nullu[m] tyrannica vincula retinerent.[76]

---

71. Council of Arles; *PL*, vol. 53, cols 683D–4B; vol. 125, cols 81C–2A.

72. Ennodius, *Benedictio cerei*; *PL*, vol. 63, col. 260A. Ussher gives his source as Johann Jacob Grynaeus, *Monumenta S. Patrum Orthodoxographa hoc est, Theologiae Sacrosanctæ ac Syncerioris Fidei Doctores* (2 vols; Basel, 1569), vol. 2, p. 283.

73. Faustus of Riez, *De gratia Dei et libero arbitrio*, 1.16; *PL*, vol. 58, col. 808C–D.

74. Faustus of Riez, *De gratia Dei et libero arbitrio*, 1.16; *PL*, vol. 58, col. 809A–B.

75. Faustus of Riez, *Epistola ad Lucidum*; *PL*, vol. 53, col. 682C; vol. 125, col. 80B–C.

76. Leo, *Sermo LXIV, De passione Domini XIII*, 3; *PL*, vol. 54, col. 359B.

Pelagius

1. Quod dicit, pro omnibus notandum quia non pro aliquantis.[77]
2. Si ipsi tamen vocanti Deo consentire voluerint.[78]

Photius [Cyril of Alexandria]

Nestoriam asserunt, quandoquidem nostrae Christus naturae sit particeps factus, et Deus omnes homines *similiter* salvos fieri velit, unumquemlibet, etiam per arbitrii sui libertatem, (διὰ τὴν τῆς φυσικῆς προαιρέσεως ἀξίαν) proprium peccatum corrigere, et Deo dignum se facere.[79]

Primasius

1. Quod a[utem] dicit, pro omnibus illu[m] gustasse mortem: quidam doctores ita absolute intelligunt, ut dicatur, pro omnibus pro quibus gustavit, id est, pro electis, ad vitam aeternam praedestinatis. At vero quidam ita generaliter accipiunt, ut dicatur [Ussher here brackets: 'pro omnibus fidelibus atque infidelibus mortem gustasse, dicentes: Ipse quidem', words which are absent or lacking (*desunt*) in Primasius but restored (*restituta*) by Haymo] pro omnibus mortuus est, licet omnes non salventur. *Et quid si omnes non credunt? ille tamen quod su[u]m erat, fecit.* Unde beatus Prosper hanc ponit similitudinem: Est quilibet medicoru[m] peritissimus, qui veniens in civitatem populosam, ubi multi infirmi habentur, temperat potionem contra omnia genera infirmitatum, et convocat omnes, dicens: Venite omnes populi, qui variis infirmitatibus laboratis, et bibite ex hac potione, quam causa salutis vestrae praeparavi: spondeo vobis cum obtestatione, quod si quis biberit ex ea, medelam statim *consequetur*. (ita Haymo. Primas. *consequi merebitur*.) Qui credunt verbis illius, accedunt, bibunt et sanantur: qui vero renuunt bibere, non sanantur, sed in sua infirmitate contabescunt: Quantum ergo ad medici devotionem pertinet, pro omnium illoru[m] salute potionem temperavit; licet non prosit, nisi his, qui ex ea biberunt. Ita et Christus, quantum in se fuit, pro omnibus mortuus est, quanquam non prosit ejus passio, nisi solummodo iis, qui in eum credere volunt.[80]
2. Qui dedit redemptionem semetipsu[m] pro omnibus. Pro omnibus quidem effusus est sanguis Christi; sed credentibus prodest, incredulis vero erit in

---

77. Pelagius, *In Romanos*, 8. All but the last three words are now considered an interpolation of Pseudo-Jerome. A. Souter, *Pelagius's Expositions of the Thirteen Epistles of St Paul* (3 vols; Cambridge: Cambridge University Press, 1922–31), vol. 2, p. 69; vol. 3, p. 17.

78. Pelagius, *In Epist. I ad Timotheum*, 2; Souter, *Pelagius's Expositions of the Thirteen Epistles of St Paul*, vol. 2, p. 480.

79. Photius, *Bibliotheca*, 54; *PG*, vol. 103, cols 95A, 96A. In a note Ussher questions the bracketed fragment: 'that I think is not in the Greek; but a gloss of [Andreas] Schottus the Jesuite'.

80. Primasius, *In epistolam ad Hebraeos*, 2; *PL*, vol. 68, col. 700C–D; cf. Haymo of Halberstadt in *PL*, vol. 117, cols 836D–7B.

condemnationem: sicut alibi ipse dicit; Aliis sumus odor vitae in vitam, aliis odor mortis in mortem.[81]

3. Notandum a[utem] ad multorum tollenda peccata illum esse oblatu[m], et non omnium: quia non omnes credituri sunt. Tale quid et ipse Dominus Apostolis: Hic est sanguis meus novi testamenti, qui pro vobis, et pro multis effundetur in remissionem peccatoru[m].[82]

Prosper

1. Habet ergo populus Dei plenitudinem suam: et quamvis magna pars hominu[m], salvantis gratiam aut repellat aut negligat, in electis tamen et praescitis, atq[ue] ab omnium generalitate discretis, specialis quaedam censetur universitas; ut de toto mundo totus mundus liberatus, et de omnibus hominibus omnes homines videantur assumpti.[83]

2. Sed quid illud sit, quod haec eadem natura in omnibus hominibus ante reconciliationem mala, (al. rea,) in omnibus misera, non in omnibus justificatur, et a pereuntibus quadam sui parte discernitur ab eo qui venit quaerere et salvare quod perierat, humano sensu prorsus non potest indagari.[84]

3. Apparuit ergo (ut Apostolus [Tit. 2] ait) gratia salutaris Dei omnibus hominibus, et tamen ministri gratiae odio erant omnibus hominibus. Et cum alii essent qui oderant, alii qui odiis persequentium premebantur: neutra tamen pars nuncupatione omniu[m] hominu[m] privabatur; habente quidem salutis suae damnu[m] rebelliu[m] portione, sed obtinente plenitudinis censum, fidelium dignitate. Dicit [e]n[im] Joannes [1.Jo.2.] Apostolus etc. non pro nostris a[utem] tantum, sed etiam pro totius mundi.[85]

4. Nulla igitur ratio dubitandi est, Jesu[m] Christu[m] Dominu[m] nostrum pro impiis et peccatoribus mortuu[m], a quoru[m] numero (si aliquis) liber inventus est, non est pro omnibus mortuus Christus. Sed prorsus pro omnibus mortuus est. Nemo ergo omniu[m] hominu[m] ante reconciliationem, quae per Christi sanguinem facta est, non aut peccator aut impius fuit.[86]

5. Nullus omnino est ex omnibus hominibus, cujus natura in Christo Domino nostro suscepta non fuerit; quamvis ille natus sit in similitudine carnis peccati, omnis a[utem] homo nascatur in carne peccati. Deus ergo Dei filius, mortalitatis humanae particeps factus absq[ue] peccato, hoc peccatoribus et mortalibus contulit, ut qui nativitatis ejus consortes fuissent, vinculum peccati et mortis evaderent. Sicut itaq[ue] non sufficit hominu[m] renovationi, natu[m] esse hominem Jesu[m] Christu[m], nisi in ipso eodem de quo ipse ortus est, spiritu renascantur: sic non sufficit hominum redemptioni, crucifixu[m] esse Dominu[m] Christu[m], nisi com[m]oriamur ei, et

---

81. Primasius, *In epistolam I ad Timotheum*, 2; *PL*, vol. 68, col. 663C.

82. Primasius, *In epistolam ad Hebraeos*, 9; *PL*, vol. 68, col. 746D.

83. Prosper, *De vocatione omnium gentium*, 1.9; *PL*, vol. 51, col. 661A.

84. Prosper, *De vocatione omnium gentium*, 1.25; *PL*, vol. 51, col. 686A.

85. Prosper, *De vocatione omnium gentium*, 2.2; *PL*, vol. 51, col. 688B–C.

86. Prosper, *De vocatione omnium gentium*, 2.16; *PL*, vol. 51, cols 702D–3A.

consepeliamur in baptismo [...] Cum itaq[ue] rectissime dicatur Salvator pro totius mundi redemptione crucifixus, *propter veram humanae naturae susceptionem, et propter communem in primo homine omniu[m] perditionem*: potest tamen dici pro his tantum crucifixus, quibus mors ipsius profuit. Dicit [e]n[im] Evangelista: quia Jesus moriturus erat pro gente, [nec] non tantum pro gente, sed etiam ut filios Dei dispersos congregaret in unum. In [Joh.1.] sua [e]n[im] venit, et sui eu[m] non receperunt. Quotquot a[utem] receperunt eu[m], etc. [Ussher's etc. = dedit eis potestatem filios Dei fieri: qui non ex sanguinibus, neque ex voluntate carnis, neque ex voluntate viri, sed ex Deo nati sunt.] Diversa ergo ab istis sors eoru[m] est, qui inter illos censentur, de quibus dicitur, Mundus eu[m] non cognovit. ut possit secundum hoc dici: Redemptor mundi dedit *pro mundo* sanguinem suum, et *mundus redimi noluit*; quia lucem tenebrae non receperunt. Et tenebrae receperunt; quibus dicit Apostolus: Fuistis [Ephes.5.] aliquando tenebrae, nunc a[utem] lux in Domino. Ipse vero Dominus Jesus, qui dixit se venisse quaerere et salvare, quod perierat: Non veni, [Luc.19.] inquit, nisi ad oves q[u]ae perierant domus Israël.[87]

6. Qui dicit quod non pro totius mundi redemptione Salvator sit crucifixus; non ad sacramenti virtutem, sed ad infideliu[m] respicit partem: cum sanguis domini nostri Jesu Christi pretium totius mundi sit. A quo pretio extranei sunt, qui aut delectati captivitate, redimi noluerunt: aut post redemptionem ad eamdem sunt servitutem reversi. Non a[utem] cecidit verbu[m] Domini, neq[ue] evacuata est mundi redemptio. Quia etsi non cognovit mundus Deu[m] in vasis irae; cognovit tamen mundus Deu[m] in vasis misericordiae, quae Deus nullis eoru[m] bonis meritis praecedentibus, eruit de potestate tenebraru[m], et transtulit in regnu[m] filii dilectionis suae.[88]

7. Contra vulnus originalis peccati, quo in Adam omniu[m] hominu[m] corrupta et mortificata natura est, et unde omniu[m] concupiscentiarum morbus inolevit, veru[m] et potens ac singulare remediu[m] est mors filii Dei Domini nostri Jesu Christi: qui liber a mortis debito, et solus absq[ue] peccato, pro peccatoribus et debitoribus mortuus est. Quod ergo ad magnitudinem et potentiam pretii, et quod ad *unam pertinet causam generis humani*, sanguis Christi redemptio est totius mundi. Sed qui hoc saeculu[m] sine fide Christi et sine regenerationis sacramento pertranseunt, redemptionis alieni sunt. Cum itaq[ue] *propter unam omniu[m] naturam, et unam omniu[m] causam a Domino nostro in veritate susceptam*, recte omnes dicantur redempti, et tamen non omnes a captivitate sint eruti; redemptionis proprietas [in effectu sc.] haud dubie penes illos est, de quibus princeps hujus mundi missus est foras, et jam non vasa Diaboli, sed membra sunt Christi. Cujus mors non ita impensa est humano generi, ut ad redemptionem ejus, etiam qui regenerandi non erant pertinerent: sed ita, ut quod per unicu[m] exemplu[m] gestum est pro universis, per singulare sacramentu[m] celebraretur in singulis. Poculu[m]

---

87. Prosper, *Responsiones ad capitula calumniantium Gallorum*, 1.9; *PL*, vol. 45, col. 1838.

88. Prosper, *Responsiones ad capitula calumniantium Gallorum*, 2.9; *PL*, vol. 45, col. 1842.

quippe immortalitatis, quod confectum est de infirmitate nostra et virtute divina ^{Christi mortem intellige}, habet quidem in se ut omnibus prosit; sed si non bibitur, non medetur (al. proficit.).⁸⁹

8. Pro universo a[utem] humano genere mortu[um] esse dominu[m] nostru[m] Jesu[m] Christu[m], et neminem prorsus a redemptione sanguinis ejus exceptu[m], etiamsi omnem hanc vitam alienissima ab eo mente pertranseat: quia ad omnes homines pertineat divinae misericordiae ^{promissio gratiae} sacramentu[m]: quo ideo plurimi non renoventur, quia quod nec renovari utile habeant praenoscantur. Itaq[ue] quantum ad Deu[m] pertinet, omnibus paratam vitam aeternam: quantum a[utem] ad arbitrii libertatem, ab his eam apprehendi, qui Deo sponte crediderint, et auxiliu[m] gratiae merito credulitatis acceperint.⁹⁰

Sedulius

1. Illuxit gratia Dei. Ideo omnes indifferenter doce. Omnibus hominib[us]. Nullam conditionem excipiens.⁹¹
2. Pro omnibus tradidit eu[m], non solum pro sanctis: non solum pro magnis, sed pro minimis omnino qui sunt in Ecclesia.⁹²
3. Christus sua morte omnes salvavit a morte.⁹³
4. Qui omnes homines vult salvos fieri. Si ipsi jam vocanti Deo consentire voluerint: aut omnes homines, scil[icet] praedestinatos. Sive, omnes homines h[oc] e[st] omnem sexu[m], gentem, conditionem, etc.⁹⁴
5. Credite jam Christu[m], pro cunctis credite passum.⁹⁵
6. Cuncti, qui hactenus manetis in fide, Christum pro mundi salute passum fuisse jam credite.⁹⁶
7. Huic reus est mundus, salvatus sanguine justo.⁹⁷
8. Huic ipse reus est mundus, cujus sanguine liberatus est a peccato.⁹⁸

Theophylact

Gustavit mortem non pro fidelibus solum, sed pro universo terraru[m] orbe. Nam etsi haudquicquam omnes sunt salvi effecti, ipse tamen peregit quod sua intererat.⁹⁹

89. Prosper, *Responsiones ad objectionum Vincentianarum*, 1; *PL*, vol. 45, col. 1844.

90. Prosper, *Epistola ad Augustinum*, 6; *PL*, vol. 44, col. 951.

91. Sedulius Scotus, *In epistolam ad Titum*, 2; *PL*, vol. 103, col. 247D.

92. Sedulius Scotus, *In epistolam ad Romanos*, 8; *PL*, vol. 103, col. 80D.

93. Sedulius Scotus, *In epistolam ad Romanos*, 15; *PL*, vol. 103, col. 121C.

94. Sedulius Scotus, *In epistolam I ad Timotheum*, 2; *PL*, vol. 103, col. 232A.

95. Coelius Sedulius, *Carmen paschale*, 5; *PL*, vol. 19, col. 720A.

96. Coelius Sedulius, *Opus paschale*, 5; *PL*, vol. 19, col. 720B.

97. Coelius Sedulius, *Carmen paschale*, 5; *PL*, vol. 19, col. 727A.

98. Coelius Sedulius, *Opus paschale*, 5; *PL*, vol. 19, col. 728A.

99. Theophylact, *In epistolam ad Hebraeos*, 2; *PG*, vol. 125, col. 210B. Rendered in Latin as found in Kimedoncius, *De redemtione*, p. 97.

Bibliography

Balliol College, Oxford	MS 259
Bodleian Library, Oxford	MS Barlow 13
	MS Eng.th.e.25
	MS Rawlinson C849
British Library, London	Harleian MS 822
Cambridge University Library	MS Mm.6.55

Abbot, Robert, *De gratia, et perseverantia sanctorum. Exercitationes aliquot habitæ in Academiæ Oxoniensi* (London, 1618).

Baxter, Richard, *Reliquiæ Baxterianæ: or, Mr Richard Baxter's Narrative of the Most Memorable Passages of his Life and Times* (London, 1696).

Bernard, Nicholas, *The Life & Death of the Most Reverend and Learned Father of Our Church Dr. James Usher, Late Arch-Bishop of Armagh, and Primate of All Ireland* (London, 1656).

Beza, Theodore, *Altera Brevis Fidei Confessio*, in *Confessio Christianæ Fidei* (Geneva: Vignon, 1577).

Blair, Ann, 'Note Taking as an Art of Transmission', *Critical Inquiry* 31 (2004), pp. 85–107.

Blair, Ann, 'Reading Strategies for Coping with Information Overload ca.1550–1700', *Journal of the History of Ideas* 64 (2003), pp. 11–28.

Blair, Ann, *Too Much to Know: Managing Scholarly Information before the Modern Age* (New Haven, CT: Yale University Press, 2010).

Corpus Christianorum, Series Latina (194 vols; Turnhout: Brepols, 1953–).

Culverwell, Ezekiel, *A Treatise of Faith* (London, 1623).

Ford, Alan, *James Ussher: Theology, History, and Politics in Early-Modern Ireland and England* (Oxford: Oxford University Press, 2007).

Gatiss, Lee, 'A Deceptive Clarity? Particular Redemption in the Westminster Standards', *Reformed Theological Review* 69 (2010), pp. 180–96.

Gatiss, Lee, '"Shades of Opinion within a Generic Calvinism". The Particular Redemption Debate at the Westminster Assembly', *Reformed Theological Review* 69 (2010), pp. 101–18.

Godfrey, William Robert, 'Tensions within International Calvinism: The Debate on the Atonement at the Synod of Dort, 1618–1619' (unpublished doctoral dissertation, Stanford University, 1974).

Gibbings, Richard (ed.), *The Index Expurgatorius of Rome* (Dublin: Milliken and Son, 1837).

Gribben, Crawford, 'Rhetoric, Fiction and Theology: James Ussher and the Death of Jesus Christ', *Seventeenth Century* 20 (2005), pp. 53–76.

Index Librorum Expurgatorum, Illustrissimi ac Reuerendis[simi] D. D. Gasparis Quiroga (Saumur: Portau, 1601, following the Madrid edition of 1584).

James, Thomas. *A Treatise of the Corruption of Scripture, Councels, and Fathers, by the Prelats, Pastors, and Pillars of the Church of Rome, for Maintenance of Popery and Irreligion* (London, 1612).

Kimedoncius, Jacobus, *De redemtione generis humani. Libri tres: Quibus copiosè traditur controversia, de redemtionis et gratiæ per Christum universalitate, et morte ipsius pro omnibus. Accessit tractatio finitima de diuina prædestinatione* (Heidelberg, 1592).

Letham, Robert, *The Westminster Assembly: Reading Its Theology in Historical Context* (Phillipsburg, NJ: P & R Publishing, 2009), pp. 176–82.

Migne, J.-P. (ed.), *Patrologia Graeca* (166 vols; Paris, 1857–83).

Migne, J.-P. (ed.), *Patrologia Latina* (221 vols; Paris, 1844–65).

Mitchell, Alex F., and John Struthers (eds), *Minutes of the Sessions of the Westminster Assembly of Divines* (Edinburgh: William Blackwood, 1874).

Moore, Jonathan D., *English Hypothetical Universalism: John Preston and the Softening of Reformed Theology* (Grand Rapids, MI: Eerdmans, 2007).

Moore, Jonathan D., 'The Extent of the Atonement: English Hypothetical Universalism versus Particular Redemption', in Michael A. G. Haykin and Mark Jones (eds), *Drawn into Controversie: Reformed Theological Diversity and Debates Within Seventeenth-Century British Puritanism* (Göttingen: Vandenhoeck & Ruprecht, 2011), pp. 124–61.

Moore, Jonathan D., 'James Ussher's Influence on the Synod of Dordt', in Aza Goudriaan and Fred van Lieburg (eds), *Revisiting the Synod of Dordt (1618-1619)* (Leiden: Brill, 2011), pp. 163–80.

Muller, Richard A., *Calvin and the Reformed Tradition: On the Work of Christ and the Order of Salvation* (Grand Rapids, MI: Baker Academic, 2012).

Quantin, Jean-Louis, *The Church of England and Christian Antiquity: The Construction of a Confessional Identity in the 17th Century* (Oxford: Oxford University Press, 2009).

Snoddy, Richard, *The Soteriology of James Ussher: The Act and Object of Saving Faith* (New York: Oxford University Press, 2014).

Thomas, G. Michael, *The Extent of the Atonement: A Dilemma for Reformed Theology from Calvin to the Consensus* (Bletchley: Paternoster, 1997).

Trevor-Roper, Hugh, 'James Ussher, Archbishop of Armagh', in *Catholics, Anglicans and Puritans: Seventeenth Century Essays* (London: Secker & Warburg, 1987), pp. 120–65.

Ussher, James, *An epistle ... concerning the religion anciently professed by the Irish and Scottish; Shewing it to be for substance the same with that which at this day is by publick authoritie established in the Church of England*, in Christopher Sibthorp, *A friendly advertisement to the pretended Catholickes of Ireland* (Dublin, 1622).

Ussher, James, *The Judgement of the Late Arch-Bishop of Armagh, ... Of the Extent of Christs death, and satisfaction, &c.* (ed. Nicholas Bernard; London, 1657).

Ussher, James, *The Whole Works of the Most Rev. James Ussher, D.D., Lord Archbishop of Armagh, and Primate of All Ireland* (eds Charles R. Elrington and J. H. Todd; 17 vols; Dublin: Hodges and Smith, 1829–64).

Van Dixhoorn, Chad (ed.), *The Minutes and Papers of the Westminster Assembly, 1643-1652* (5 vols; Oxford: Oxford University Press, 2012).

Williams, Garry J., 'The Definite Intent of Penal Substitutionary Atonement', in David Gibson and Jonathan Gibson (eds), *From Heaven He Came and Sought Her: Definite Atonement in Historical, Biblical, Theological, and Pastoral Perspective* (Wheaton, IL: Crossway, 2013), pp. 461–82.

Windeck, Johann Paul, *Controversiæ de mortis Christi efficacia, inter Catholicos et Calvinistas hoc tempore disputatæ* (Cologne, 1603).

Chapter 9

THE WESTMINSTER ASSEMBLY AND THE COMMUNION OF SAINTS

Robert Letham

The Westminster Assembly, and English Puritanism in general, has received bad press over the years. It has been widely considered to be marked by dour, joyless, legal rigidity, opposed in every way to anything remotely resembling enjoyment of God's creation and the gospel of redemption, liberation and creative renewal. In part, this is due to its opponents' eventual triumph; with the Restoration of the monarchy, history was written by the winners and the defeated Puritans demonized.

Virtually all – of whatever persuasion – have accepted the spin given by Restoration historians, the eventual winners of the turmoil from 1640 to 1660. According to this standard belief, the Westminster divines were not representative of the Church of England. This thinking painted the Presbyterians as extremists, destabilizing both church and nation. So effective was this campaign that the conclusions of Restoration historians, until recently, have been accepted virtually without question. Winston Churchill confidently predicted during the Second World War that history would paint him in a favourable light since he would be writing it himself.[1] So, too, the winners in 1660 wrote the received tradition. With the general acceptance of this paradigm came, particularly in Presbyterian minds, caricatures of Anglicanism as a halfway house to Rome.

Later, John Henry Newman gave this line of thought added impetus by his claim that the Church of England was committed to a *via media* between Rome and Protestantism. The Thirty-Nine Articles could be interpreted congruously with the Council of Trent. In his book *An Essay on the Development of Christian Doctrine* (1845), he dismissed Protestantism in general as being averse to history and the development of the church. Protestantism is not the Christianity of history, he maintained, for 'to be deep in history is to cease to be a Protestant'.[2]

---

1. See, *inter alia*, Roy Jenkins, *Churchill: A Biography* (New York: Farrar, Straus and Giroux, 2001), p. 819.

2. John Henry Newman, *An Essay on the Development of Christian Doctrine* (Notre Dame: University of Notre Dame Press, 1989), pp. 7–11.

Moreover, the Assembly has been given a bad name by the excesses of some of its followers. The dour face of much later Scottish Presbyterianism cast the Assembly – which provided its foundational documents – in a negative and alien light in the minds of the English. This was particularly so since Presbyterianism in England went into eclipse and its main base was north of the border. With the incursion of the Enlightenment, Westminster's appeal to the supreme authority of God in Holy Scripture was no longer flavour of the month. In an age of doctrinal lassitude, it was out of harmony with the prevailing tide of opinion.

Some of this opprobrium may be relieved by an examination of the Assembly's commitment to the communion of the saints. This is in many ways a forgotten chapter in the Westminster Confession of Faith, one that does not arouse the intellectual or logical excitement of other doctrinal features – whichever side a person may take – and one that lacks the potential for endless disputes for the argumentatively inclined.

The documents, letters and papers of the Westminster Assembly of divines (1643–52) indicate that, within the parameters set by Parliament for the reconstitution of the church in the three kingdoms, the unity and catholicity of the church was a prominent theme. The divines brought this to expression in chapter 26 of the Confession of Faith, in their exposition of the phrase in the Apostles' Creed on the communion of saints. In this they affirmed the unity of all who call on the name of the Lord Jesus.

Since the Assembly's comments are founded in the words of the ancient creed, we will start by reminding ourselves of the short but rather contentious debate that surrounded the creeds in its early days. The heat of controversy on this point is rather surprising since there is no real evidence outside this occasion that it was a matter that aroused significant differences.

The Debate on the Three Creeds

The first task assigned by Parliament to the Westminster Assembly in July 1643 was to defend the doctrine of the Church of England from all false calumnies and aspersions. For this it was given the task of revising and updating the Thirty-Nine Articles of Religion. These were composed at a time when the Reformation had only just recovered from the short reign of Queen Mary (1553–58) and the martyrdoms associated with it. The Articles were a statement of faith, not a systematic doctrinal treatise. They stood within the stream of Augustinian Anglicanism to which the divines themselves belonged.[3] Article 8 of the Thirty-Nine Articles affirmed that the Apostles' Creed, the Nicene Creed and the Athanasian Creed 'ought thoroughly to be received and believed: for they may be proved by most certain warrants of holy Scripture'. Prolonged and heated debate occurred over this article.

3. Robert Letham, *The Westminster Assembly: Reading Its Theology in Historical Context* (Phillipsburg, NJ: Presbyterian & Reformed, 2009), pp. 47–83.

The Assembly was to give clear primacy to Scripture as the Word of God (WCF 1:6), as the supreme and only rule of faith and practice. In view of this, the edicts of church synods were never to be made the rule of faith and practice but only to be used as a help (WCF 31:4). All claims to spiritual experience and all human traditions – including the past and present teaching of the church – were to be tested and adjudicated on the basis of the voice of the Holy Spirit speaking in Scripture. However, the Assembly did not reject tradition as such. It recognized its usefulness and that it was an authority; however, it was not the supreme authority. The Assembly's debates are replete with frequent citations of the fathers, medieval theologians, and even of Bellarmine, as authorities in support of biblical and theological arguments. All were united in this. However, the issues lay elsewhere.

Earlier, in session 3, on Wednesday 12 July 1643, in a debate on Article 3, on Christ's descent into hell, the question arose of whether the revised Articles should contain proofs from Scripture or be left as they were. The committee that presented its report to the body for debate and decision thought scriptural proof was unnecessary, but the Assembly voted that they be included, adopting the position that no sense could be made of the article without express support from Scripture.[4] This itself is surprising, since in its later, magisterial statement on the sense of Scripture in WCF 1:4, it insists that express textual support is not necessary for the whole counsel of God for His glory, our salvation, faith and life, for this is also contained in deductions from Scripture by good and necessary consequence. According to John Lightfoot, an Assembly member of Episcopal persuasion, the debate 'grew very earnest' over whether the article should be entirely expunged: an astonishing proposal, given the Assembly's task to *defend* the Articles. Those who favoured expunging were 'generally opposed'. Eventually, the following statement was approved: 'As Christ died for us, & was buried, so also it is to be beleved that he continued in the state of the dead & under the power & dominion of death untill his resurrection: which otherwaies hath bin expressed, he descended into hell.'[5] So despite unexpected opposition, the creedal clause was affirmed. Later, the report from the third committee said that it could not provide scriptural support for Article 8 on the creeds – this, although Thomas Rogers had popularized such a set of scriptural proofs sixty-five years before.[6]

The debate on this article took a week of tumultuous agitation and disagreement. It was argued that the phrase 'they ought thoroughly to be received' set them in equality with Scripture.[7] There were votes, revocations and re-votes. High confusion reigned. The main issue was the mandatory use of the creeds. The full settlement

---

4. Chad Van Dixhoorn, 'Reforming the Reformation: Theological Debate at the Westminster Assembly 1643–1652' (7 vols; doctoral dissertation, Cambridge University, 2004), vol. 1, pp. 215–16.

5. Lightfoot, MS Journal, fol. 19v; cited by Van Dixhoorn, 'Reforming the Reformation', vol. 1, p. 232.

6. Van Dixhoorn, 'Reforming the Reformation', vol. 1, p. 226.

7. Ibid., vol. 1, p. 233.

of Article 8 was put off until such time as the Assembly had finished revising all thirty-nine articles. This never happened as agreement to secure military help from the Scots against the King set aside the original mandate of Parliament and brought a new task to produce a confession and directories for worship and church government to unite the reformed church in the three kingdoms.

However, on 26 April 1647, when the Assembly eventually submitted to both Houses of Parliament its revisions of the Articles that it had considered before the mandate was changed, the article had only slight modifications. There was an alteration. 'The creedes that go under the name of ...' was inserted, due to concern that none of the three creeds were composed by the authors commonly ascribed to them. Additionally, the clause 'are throughly to be received & beleeved' replaced the article's statement that they 'ought ...' to be thoroughly received and believed, perhaps indicating that there was a wariness about making acceptance of the creeds mandatory.

Van Dixhoorn points out that in their published writings the Assembly men all use the creeds, cite them and support them. They never call for their removal or revision.[8] It is probable that the opposition encountered at this point may be an instance of group-think, where the dynamic of pressure from a minority of strong voices dominates discussion and carries a larger body with it, with many suspending their critical faculties and disregarding the consequences of their words and actions. It seems to be amazingly self-contradictory, for the Assembly was to spend several years painstakingly composing a confession of faith and two catechisms in order to provide a solid foundation for the Church of England.

Within the parameters of the doctrine of Scripture propounded later in the Confession of Faith and the Larger Catechism, objection to Article 8 on the creeds could theoretically have been raised if it were considered that the contents of the creeds were not in conformity with the whole counsel of God found in Scripture. However, to object to the article as such made no sense, since the basis for its assessment of the creeds was that 'they may be proved by most certain warrants of holy Scripture'. The article conformed to the Confession's later position: if the creeds were in harmony with Scripture, then they ought to be received and believed.

The Apostles' Creed and the Structure of the Assembly's Documents

Notwithstanding, the Assembly could not and did not write the Creed out of its documents. While the Assembly's catechisms do not follow the traditional catechetical structure of Apostles' Creed, Ten Commandments and Lord's Prayer, there is, nevertheless, evidence that this pattern was not entirely erased. The last section of the Confession treats, in order, the holy catholic church (chapter 25), the communion of saints (chapter 26), the forgiveness of sins, which is related in the New Testament and in the Nicene Creed to baptism (chapters 27–28) and, by

8. Ibid., vol. 1, pp. 265–8.

extension, the Lord's Supper (chapter 29), the resurrection of the dead and the life everlasting (chapters 32–33).

Westminster Confession of Faith, 26 on the Communion of the Saints: Text and Proof Texts

Bearing in mind its place in the overall structure of the Confession, the chapter comes immediately after the one on the church and before the sacraments, baptism, the Lord's Supper, church censures, and synods and councils. It is, therefore, integral to the Assembly's doctrine of the church. Moreover, it fits into the progressions of the Apostles' Creed – 'I believe in the holy catholic church, the communion of saints' – and the Nicene Creed – 'We believe in one holy, catholic, and apostolic church; one baptism for the remission of sins.'

The Larger Catechism, 63–90

The communion of saints is listed as one of the privileges of the visible church (LC, 63).

> The visible church hath the privilege of being under God's special care and government; of being protected and preserved in all ages, notwithstanding the opposition of all enemies; and of enjoying the communion of saints, the ordinary means of salvation, and offers of grace by Christ to all the members of it in the ministry of the gospel.

The invisible church, which is 'the whole number of the elect, that have been, that are, or shall be gathered into one under Christ the head' (LC, 64) 'enjoy union and communion with [Christ] in grace and glory' (LC, 65). This union and communion with Christ is then expressed in the various elements of the *ordo salutis* in both grace (LC, 66–81) and glory (LC, 82–90). These comprise effectual calling (LC, 67–8), justification (LC, 70–3), adoption (LC, 74), sanctification (LC, 75–9), assurance of salvation (LC, 80–1), and – in terms of union and communion with Christ in glory – resurrection and final vindication, particularly 'the immediate vision and fruition of God the Father, of our Lord Jesus Christ, and of the Holy Spirit, to all eternity' (LC, 82–90).

Hence, union with Christ embraces the entirety of salvation in this life and its full realization after the resurrection. It includes communion with Christ. In turn, the communion of the saints is an application of union and communion with Christ in grace and glory.

The Assembly's Debates on the Communion of the Saints

Very little was recorded on the debates on the communion of saints. The scribe, Adoniram Byfield, started his work by keeping relatively expansive records, but gradually flagged as time went by. It is reasonable to suppose that when he simply records that a debate occurred or a report was presented, without mentioning any of the details, that the matter was either of little interest to him or that it was uncontroversial, or both.

Thus in session 598, on Wednesday 4 March 1645, the Assembly debated the communion of the saints.[9] Sometime later, in session 742, on Tuesday 17 November 1646, and in the next two sessions on the Thursday and Friday of the same week, reports of the committee charged to bring proposals to the whole body were presented, recommitted, represented and debated,[10] without any details provided in the minutes. In session 816, on Friday 26 March 1647, the committee reported to the Assembly on the subject.[11] In the next session, on the following Monday, proof texts were approved.[12] That is all we know about the debates. If our reasoning is valid, it appears that the subject was not controversial.

The Theological Context of the Communion of the Saints

The Theological Basis of the Communion of the Saints is Union with Christ

We have already seen the priority of union with Christ in both the Confession 26:1 and the Larger Catechism, 63–90. The first section of the chapter in the Confession sums it up. Union with Christ the head of the church is the root of the communion of the saints.

> All saints, that are united to Jesus Christ their Head, by his Spirit, and by faith, have fellowship with him in his grace, sufferings, death, resurrection, and glory ...

The reach of the statement is comprehensive and anticipates the final clause of 26:2. All saints without exception participate in this communion. It is seen in a covenantal and churchly context, for it is union with Christ as their head. In this, His work as mediator of the covenant is in view (cf. WCF 8:1–8). He is the head who is joined to the members of the covenant. The idea that He is the head of the church – the sole head (WCF 25:1, 6) – is also present, following as it does in the wake of the previous chapter on the church. In short, this communion is not individualistic but corporate. This is so by definition; the *communion* of the saints, grounded in *union and communion* with Christ, cannot be a phenomenon of purely individual proportions. Additionally, Christ as head entails a body connected to

---

9. Chad Van Dixhoorn (ed.), *The Minutes and Papers of the Westminster Assembly 1643–1652* (5 vols; Oxford: Oxford University Press, 2012), vol. 3, pp. 763–5.

10. Ibid., vol. 4, pp. 336–9.

11. Ibid., vol. 4, p. 478.

12. Ibid.

Him. The communion of saints exists in the church and is to be found there, not in privatized seclusion.

Moreover, as it is governed by union with Christ, it involves sharing in Christ's own trajectory, in His sufferings, death, resurrection and glory. It is a thoroughly realistic matter. It embraces the impact of a world ravaged by sin and disorder. It is decidedly not a mystical experience divorced from the mire of a world marked by the effects of human sin and sorrow. This realization reflects the biblical teaching that we are called not only to believe in Christ but also to suffer with Him, that the path to glory cannot detour around the cross, just as His own life and ministry headed for the glory of the Father via Gethsemane and Calvary.

> And, being united to one another in love, they have communion in each other's gifts and graces, and are obliged to the performance of such duties, public and private, as do conduce to their mutual good, both in the inward and outward man.

The divines expand on the earlier theme. Flowing from union and communion with Christ is communion with one another in the church, as members of the body of which Christ is the head. So the saints are united to one another in love, reflecting on the horizontal level the relation into which they have been brought by Christ. It follows that the gifts and graces, given by the Spirit from Christ, are intended for the mutual good of the body of Christ. Any gifts Christ, the head, provides are intended not for individual aggrandizement or for private solace but for the common good and well-being of the church. They are not the possession of the individual person but a stewardship for the whole body. This places on the members an obligation. This is not the onerous demand of an oppressive lawgiver; it is the demand and obligation of love. Love promotes the interests of others. Gifts and graces are given by Christ to advance the good of others. This obligation is to love one another by using the abilities we have been given for precisely that end.

Takeshi Kodama argues that the Assembly had clear precursors in making union with Christ foundational to the doctrine of the church. One obvious candidate is James Ussher, whose Irish Articles (1615) are widely recognized as a main source for the Assembly. For Ussher, union with Christ was not only the foundation of soteriology but also of ecclesiology.[13] Kodama also identifies William Ames as influential. In his book, *The Marrow of Sacred Divinity*, Ames sees both the invisible and visible church as aspects of union with Christ. This, Kodama points out, was an innovation, since before Ames the visible church was derived from the invisible church. Now both are held to depend on union with Christ.[14] Kodama adds that if

---

13. Takeshi Kodama, 'The Unity and Catholicity of the Church: A Comparison of Calvin and the Westminster Assembly' (unpublished doctoral dissertation, University of Wales, Trinity Saint David, 2011), pp. 366–7, citing James Ussher, *A Body of Divinitie, or The Summe and Substance of Christian Religion* (London: Thomas Downes and George Badger, 1645), pp. 187–90.

14. Kodama, 'Unity and Catholicity', pp. 367–8.

union with Christ is the basis of the whole church, then the visible church can be seen as an aspect of the catholic church.[15] The divines shared this understanding, he concludes. Many of them held that the communion of the saints is a benefit of being members of the holy catholic church, which is founded in union with Christ. In particular, William Gouge, in *The Saints' Sacrifice* (1632), Richard Byfield, in *A Candle Lighted* (1627), Thomas Temple, in *Christ's Government* (1642), and John Jackson, in *The Key of Knowledge* (1640), clearly espoused this line of thought.[16] Kodama contrasts this with the later view of A. A. Hodge that the invisible church is at the heart of the Assembly's theology.[17]

Unity and Catholicity Relates to the Visible Church, WCF 26:2

The previous chapter of the Confession stated that the catholic church consists of all the elect (WCF 25:1). As was customary, the catholicity of the church was inseparably connected with its unity, for the whole number of the elect were seen there as gathered into one. The distinctive feature of the Westminster Assembly was to go beyond this to identify the catholic church with the visible church. As WCF 25:2 stated, 'The visible church, which is also catholic or universal under the gospel … consists of all those throughout the world that profess the true religion; and of their children: and is the kingdom of the Lord Jesus Christ, the house and family of God, out of which there is no ordinary possibility of salvation'.

Kodama points out that this development was something neither Calvin nor the earlier Reformed confessions were prepared to make.[18] Indeed, at the Assembly, the Independents opposed this identification of the visible church as catholic.[19] The Presbyterian majority at the Assembly evidently supported it, for Westminster states this identification 'explicitly and without any hesitation'.[20] Not that this was a black and white matter for the divines. They were well aware of the weaknesses, imperfections and sins of the church. The catholic church was 'sometimes more, sometimes less visible' (WCF 25:4). This followed from the obvious fact that all churches are affected by sin and that 'the purest churches under heaven are subject both to mixture and error' (WCF 25:5).

When the divines came to the communion of saints, they made sure that it was integrally related to the church's catholicity. WCF 26:2 spells out the details of what this communion entails and then proceeds to relate it clearly to its previous commitments. Communion finds expression on the horizontal, churchly level in three major forms.

15. Ibid., p. 368.

16. Ibid., p. 369.

17. Ibid., pp. 369–70.

18. Ibid., pp. 306–13.

19. In session 594 on Thursday morning, 26 February 1645: Van Dixhoorn (ed.), *Minutes and Papers*, vol. 3, p. 762.

20. Kodama, 'Unity and Catholicity', p. 308.

> Saints by profession are bound to maintain an holy fellowship and communion
> in the worship of God, and in performing such other spiritual services as tend
> to their mutual edification; as also in relieving each other in outward things,
> according to their several abilities and necessities.

Worship, spiritual services and outward relief according to ability – these are
the particular areas in which communion in the church is evident. The Shorter
Catechism (88) understands the means Christ uses to communicate the benefits
of redemption to be 'his ordinances, especially the Word, sacraments, and prayer'.
These ordinances are located in the church, and it is particularly here that the
first two elements are found: the worship of God and other spiritual services
for mutual edification. The following chapters on the sacraments expand on this
theme. The chapter on the Lord's Supper argues that what takes place is that
the faithful 'really and ... spiritually receive, and feed upon, Christ crucified ...
the body and blood of Christ being then ... really, but spiritually present'
(WCF 29:7).

We note the element of effort required to do this; this fellowship and
communion is to be maintained, and it is to be done as an obligation, something
that is a necessary element flowing from the union and communion with Christ
that underlies it. It requires vigilance and effort. At the back of such a comment is
Paul's exhortation to the Ephesians to be diligent in maintaining the unity of the
Spirit (Eph. 4.3).

The third element, the relief of outward needs, relates to diaconal ministry. This
was regarded by the apostles as a *sine qua non* for the church (Gal. 2.10; 6.9–10;
Jas. 1.26–27; 2.14–26). The office of deacon was soon turned into a stepping stone
towards the priesthood but it was revived in its biblical form by Calvin.[21] It finds
expression in various classic Presbyterian systems of government such as the
Second Book of Discipline (1581) of the Church of Scotland, and The Form of
Presbyterial Church-Government (1647) of the Westminster Assembly. Worship
and the relief of human need go together in Reformed thought and practice.

It is then that the connection with catholicity comes to the surface. These
activities, as expressions of the communion of the saints, and as outflows of union
with Christ, are to be lavishly and generously deployed.

> Which communion, as God offereth opportunity, is to be extended unto all
> those who, in every place, call upon the name of the Lord Jesus.

This communion is to be as extensive as Christ has established union with
Himself. This is a communion in the worship of God, in mutually beneficial
spiritual exercises, in the relief of tangible need. Union with Christ by the Holy

---

21. Jeannine Olson, *Calvin and Social Welfare: Deacons and the Bourse Française*
(Selinsgrove, PA: Susquehanna University Press, 1989); Elsie Anne McKee, *John Calvin on
the Diaconate and Liturgical Almsgiving* (Geneva: Librairie Droz, 1984).

Spirit through faith, and the unity of the catholic church are co-extensive. Within the boundaries of the church, and the profession of faith in Christ, sectarianism of all kinds is outlawed.

Some Caveats are Necessary So As to Avoid Misunderstanding WCF 26:3

The Assembly was keen to avoid possible misunderstandings. There were two such dangers that occurred to it. In the first place, union and communion with Christ does not mean that we are partakers of Christ's deity, or equal to Christ.

> This communion which the saints have with Christ, doth not make them in any wise partakers of the substance of his Godhead: or to be equal with Christ in any respect: either of which is impious and blasphemous.

This may reflect back on Calvin's battle against Andreas Osiander (1496–1552). Osiander held that justification entails the impartation of the divine righteousness of Christ, involves the indwelling of Christ's deity, so that we become righteous ourselves. He held that union with Christ was a union of essence, or being. Calvin had opposed him on the grounds, *inter alia*, that union with Christ is effected by the Holy Spirit through faith and is not a union of essence; rather, since Christ is mediator according to both natures, we participate by the Spirit in Christ's humanity, and so justification is by the imputation of Christ's righteousness as our mediator.[22] The divines think along similar lines in accordance with the tradition. There is a clear and unchallengeable distinction.

Second, the communion of the saints does not abolish the rights of private property. It does not mean that the goods of the saints are all available for common use.

> Nor doth their communion one with another, as saints, take away, or infringe the title or propriety which each man hath in his goods and possessions.

There had been a range of sects down the years that had taught or, to some extent, practised communal living. The Levellers were to spring into prominence within a couple of years of the Confession's completion, in around 1649, whereas the debates on this chapter occurred in March 1645 and the following November, the proof texts being finalized in March 1647. It is possible that this sentence may refer to the earliest Levellers, before the movement got its name, for they had been agitating for some time although there is no conclusive evidence that they wanted to abolish private property. The term had already been used in 1607 for protesters

---

22. John Calvin, *Institutes*, 3.11.5–12; see also Mark Garcia, *Life in Christ: Union with Christ and Twofold Grace in Calvin's Theology* (Milton Keynes: Paternoster, 2008), pp. 199–218, 223–9, 239–52; Julie Canlis, *Calvin's Ladder: A Spiritual Theology of Ascent and Ascension* (Grand Rapids: Eerdmans, 2010), pp. 139–46.

against enclosures, on the ground that they were trying to level fences that enclosed the land obtained by the landowners.[23] During the previous decades a series of popular disturbances had arisen in various parts of the country, economically driven in protest at enclosures and unemployment.[24]

In both these cases the Assembly opposes any idea that the union and communion in view leads to a blurring of the distinctions between those who are united; between Christ and the saints on the one hand, or between the saints themselves on the other. Behind this is the principle enshrined in the Definition of Chalcedon that the person of Christ and the human nature assumed are without confusion and without change, a prominent feature in Reformed Christology against the Lutherans, and a paradigm that applies to a range of theological relationships. Hence, the union the church has with Christ, together with the communion experienced reciprocally by its members, while indissoluble, preserves the distinctions.

The Communion of Saints in the Assembly's practice

Relations with Other Churches

I have written elsewhere of the extensive correspondence that took place between the Assembly and continental churches. The latter took a great interest in the Assembly's proceedings, expressing both admiration and concern as the situation arose.[25] Closer to home, the Scottish commissioners, who came to the Assembly upon the agreement with Parliament expressed in the Solemn League and Covenant, played a role far beyond their numbers. They were not members of the Assembly and did not vote on any matters that came before it. Their names are not recorded on the list of official members. They were present to advise, encourage and warn. In consequence, there was frequent correspondence between the Assembly and the Church of Scotland.[26]

Support for Needy Ministers and Others

On 20 October 1643 the Assembly petitioned the Committee for Plundered Ministers about the needs of ministers who had been imprisoned by the royalists

23. Whitney R. D. Jones, *The Tree of Commonwealth 1450-1793* (Madison, NJ: Fairleigh Dickinson University Press, 2000), pp. 133, 164.

24. Christopher Hill, *The Century of Revolution 1603-1714* (New York: W. W. Norton, 1961), pp. 27-8.

25. Letham, *Westminster Assembly*, pp. 84-98; Van Dixhoorn (ed.), *Minutes and Papers*, vol. 2, pp. 576, 581, 593, 681; vol. 3, pp. 38, 52, 132, 139, 158, 166, 170, 211, 314, 473, 512, 557, 611; vol. 4, pp. 564-5; vol. 5, pp. 12-16, 73, 179.

26. Van Dixhoorn (ed.), *Minutes and Papers*, vol. 5, pp. 17-21, 70-2, 160-4, 192, 202, 223, 297, 334-5, 342-3.

and about Assembly members without ministerial livings.[27] The following year another petition was sent to the committee on behalf of Cornelius Burgess. While the original manuscript is missing, the matter was of some delicacy and a strong commendation of Burgess's character was included.[28]

Kodama has found that sermons of the divines included a request to Parliament in 1644 by Richard Vines to erect workhouses for the poor, while in the following year Herbert Palmer urged the House of Commons to implement works of charity and mercy.[29] Earlier, in 1641, Stephen Marshall urged believers to relieve the needs of the poor. William Spurstowe himself founded six almshouses in Hackney.[30]

Citation of the Fathers, Medieval Theologians, and Roman Catholic Representatives

The Assembly's debates were replete with references to the theological riches of the church's tradition. While biblical exegesis formed the bread and butter of the discussions, the jam and honey added to it was frequently flavoured by the Fathers, medieval theologians and a host from the Reformation and the years following. This was a group of very learned ministers, at home with the biblical languages, Latin and the writings of church history.

A good test case is Robert Bellarmine (1542–1621), the leading Roman Catholic theologian and apologist of the late sixteenth and early seventeenth centuries, a greatly learned and remarkably fair-minded man. The divines cite him, sometimes as an authority and on other occasions as an opponent, but always with great courtesy and respect. On Thursday 7 September 1643, in session 48, in a debate on the imputation of the active obedience of Christ in justification, Thomas Gataker cited Junius against Bellarmine.[31] On the following Wednesday, in session 54, William Twisse, the prolocutor, referred to Bellarmine in a non-polemical manner.[32]

On Friday 1 December, in session 106, Samuel Rutherford, in a debate on the ruling elder, refers to Bellarmine among others in the Roman church who argued that the word of God was perfect but that a range of matters in the church were to be settled in accordance with prudence, a view with which he was in broad agreement.[33] On Monday 11 December, in session 112, in a debate on the

27. Ibid., vol. 5, p. 26.
28. Ibid., vol. 5, p. 73.
29. Kodama, 'Unity and Catholicity', p. 265.
30. Ibid., p. 266.
31. Van Dixhoorn (ed.), *Minutes and Papers*, vol. 2, p. 60.
32. Ibid., vol. 2, p. 119.
33. Ibid., vol. 2, p. 400.

Old Testament background to the New Testament eldership, George Gillespie referred to Bellarmine, disagreeing with him, but regarding him as a serious contributor to the question.[34] Later, on Wednesday 2 October 1644, in session 295, Gillespie cited William Ames, in a debate on synods and Matthew 18, as arguing against Bellarmine that the church is a *res publica* sufficient to itself.[35] Thomas Stapleton (1535–98), a leading English Roman Catholic polemicist, was also treated in a similar way. In session 84, on Monday 30 October 1643, the Assembly debated the extraordinary office of apostle and grappled with his arguments in some detail.[36] On the Friday of the same week, in session 88, reference was made to William Whitaker's debate with Stapleton.[37]

The Task of the Assembly Impelled It to this End

Kodama lists a range of works by Assembly divines stressing the unity of the church.[38] From this, the Assembly was prepared to make compromises within the bounds of acceptable doctrine. While making clear doctrinal pronouncements, the Assembly was conciliatory in its attitudes towards those who disagreed on matters within these boundaries. I have written elsewhere of how the differences with the Lutherans on the sacraments were handled in a careful and measured way. Extensive attempts were made to permit the Independents to present their arguments for church government. While the divines were opposed to the theology of Moyse Amyraut, and clearly declared against it, there were, nevertheless, a not inconsiderable number who were also hypothetical universalists. They, among whom Edmund Calamy was perhaps the most prominent, were not drummed out of the Assembly after the extensive and detailed disputes on the extent of saving grace but continued to exercise a prominent part in subsequent debates on a variety of matters.[39]

The Assembly's purpose, of course, was not to split hairs on this or that, nor was it to produce definitive verdicts on all matters before it. Rather, it was charged with compiling a confession of faith and a catechism, together with a directory for worship and a system of church government that would unite the church in the three kingdoms (England, Scotland and Ireland) and bring it into closer conformity with the Reformed churches on the continent. Its composition transcended the details of church government, composed as it was of Episcopalians and Independents as well as Presbyterians, while the latter held their views for differing reasons

34. Ibid., vol. 2, p. 433.
35. Ibid., vol. 3, p. 365.
36. Ibid., vol. 2, pp. 234–5.
37. Ibid., vol. 2, p. 273.
38. Kodama, 'Unity and Catholicity', pp. 280–3.
39. Letham, *Westminster Assembly*, pp. 111–19.

and with differing degrees of conviction. While opposing the Roman church, the Assembly took a measured position. Its differences with Lutheranism came to expression on the sacraments but were presented in a gentle manner. While Arminianism was unacceptable, some members were hypothetical universalists but were able to contribute to debate without rancour. Antinomianism was trenchantly opposed; its exponents were seen as a political threat as much as a theological one.[40] The Assembly's correspondence demonstrates a realization of unity across national boundaries; its debates evince its strong valuation of the great tradition of the church.

Some Contemporary Implications of the Assembly's Doctrine

The Assembly's commitment to the communion of the saints is not, of course, peculiar to itself but follows the classic belief of the church expressed in the Apostles' Creed and, behind it, in the Bible. This commitment should impel the church towards clarity and strong conviction on doctrine, together with generosity of spirit to those within the bounds of true doctrine who 'call upon the name of the Lord Jesus'.

Inevitably, as erroneous teachings appear, a tension emerges between the unity and catholicity of the church on the one hand and its apostolicity and holiness on the other. I have explored this question elsewhere.[41] A stress on the latter at the expense of the former leads to sectarianism, contrary to the clearly expressed will of Jesus in John 17, and to Paul in Ephesians 2 and Galatians 3. Stress on the former – unity and catholicity – at the expense of the latter is the hallmark of an ecumenism that lacks the doctrinal backbone to survive. Sacrifice the apostolic doctrine and the foundations have been removed. Abandon catholicity and unity and sectarianism results. The doctrine of the communion of the saints is a bulwark against both dangers.

Few, if any, could accuse the Westminster Assembly of falling into the former trap. However, both by precept and practice, it recognized the need to express the unity of the body of Christ as well as the solid foundations of Christian doctrine. It may not have succeeded. Few, if any, have done so. But it made strenuous efforts to secure agreement, conciliation and concord, recognizing the bonds that hold together the church, 'which communion, as God offereth opportunity, is to be extended to all those who, in every place, call upon the name of the Lord Jesus'.

---

40. On this see Kodama, 'Unity and Catholicity', pp. 334–42.

41. Robert Letham, 'Catholicity Global and Historical: Constantinople, Westminster, and the Church in the Twenty-First Century', *WTJ* 72 (2010), pp. 43–57.

Bibliography

Calvin, John, *Institutes of the Christian Religion* (ed. John T. McNeill; trans. Ford Lewis Battles; 2 vols; Philadelphia: Westminster Press, 1960).

Canlis, Julie, *Calvin's Ladder: A Spiritual Theology of Ascent and Ascension* (Grand Rapids: Eerdmans, 2010).

Garcia, Mark, *Life in Christ: Union with Christ and Twofold Grace in Calvin's Theology* (Milton Keynes: Paternoster, 2008).

Hill, Christopher, *The Century of Revolution 1603–1714* (New York: W. W. Norton, 1961).

Jenkins, Roy, *Churchill: A Biography* (New York: Farrar, Straus and Giroux, 2001).

Jones, Whitney R. D., *The Tree of Commonwealth 1450–1793* (Madison, NJ: Fairleigh Dickinson University Press, 2000).

Kodama, Takeshi, 'The Unity and Catholicity of the Church: A Comparison of Calvin and the Westminster Assembly' (unpublished doctoral dissertation, University of Wales, Trinity Saint David, 2011).

Letham, Robert, 'Catholicity Global and Historical: Constantinople, Westminster, and the Church in the Twenty-First Century', *WTJ* 72 (2010), pp. 43–57.

Letham, Robert, *The Westminster Assembly: Reading Its Theology in Historical Context* (Phillipsburg, NJ: Presbyterian & Reformed, 2009).

McKee, Elsie Anne, *John Calvin on the Diaconate and Liturgical Almsgiving* (Geneva: Librairie Droz, 1984).

Newman, John Henry, *An Essay on the Development of Christian Doctrine* (Notre Dame: University of Notre Dame Press, 1989).

Olson, Jeannine, *Calvin and Social Welfare: Deacons and the Bourse Française* (Selinsgrove, PA: Susquehanna University Press, 1989).

Van Dixhoorn, Chad, 'Reforming the Reformation: Theological Debate at the Westminster Assembly 1643–1652' (7 vols; doctoral dissertation, Cambridge University, 2004).

Van Dixhoorn, Chad (ed.), *The Minutes and Papers of the Westminster Assembly 1643–1652* (5 vols; Oxford: Oxford University Press, 2012).

Chapter 10

THE BOUNDLESS AND BLESSED GOD: THE LEGACY OF AMANDUS POLANUS IN THE THEOLOGY OF GEORGE SWINNOCK

J. Stephen Yuille

Richard Baxter asks, 'What books, especially of theology, should one choose, who for want of money or time can read but few?' He answers his own question by describing 'the smallest library that is tolerable', in which he lists the works of 'affectionate practical English writers', including George Swinnock.[1]

Very little is known of Swinnock. He was born at Maidstone, Kent, in 1627. When speaking of his cousin, he remarks, 'I had the happiness some time to be brought up with him in his father's … family.'[2] Whatever the circumstances surrounding this stay, Swinnock describes it in a positive light as he recalls that his uncle's home 'had holiness to the Lord written upon it.'[3] He remained in this 'school of religion' until departing for Emmanuel College, Cambridge, at sixteen years of age. He received his bachelor's degree from Cambridge and his master's degree from Oxford. In 1650, he resigned his fellowship at Balliol College, Oxford, to become vicar at St Mary's chapel in Rickmansworth, Hertfordshire. After eleven years, he moved to St Nicholas's chapel in Great Kimble, Buckinghamshire. Upon his ejection for nonconformity in 1662, Swinnock entered the household of Richard Hampden to minister as family chaplain. With the easing of political

Author's note: Dr Tony Lane supervised my PhD thesis at London School of Theology, which was later published as *Puritan Spirituality: The Fear of God in the Affective Theology of George Swinnock* (Studies in Christian History and Thought; Milton Keynes: Paternoster, 2007). I am extremely grateful for the contribution Dr Lane made to my academic research, and I count it a great privilege to contribute a chapter to this festschrift composed in his honour.

1. Richard Baxter, *The Practical Works of Richard Baxter* (4 vols; London: George Virtue, 1846; repr., Morgan: Soli Deo Gloria, 2000), vol. 1, p. 731.

2. George Swinnock, *The Works of George Swinnock* (5 vols; Edinburgh: James Nichol, 1868; repr., London: Banner of Truth, 1992), vol. 3, p. 409. Hereafter, *Works*.

3. Ibid., vol. 3, p. 409.

restrictions in 1672, he returned to his home of Maidstone to become pastor. He occupied this position for less than a year, dying at the age of forty-six.[4]

According to Edmund Calamy, Swinnock 'was a man of good abilities, and a serious, warm, practical, and useful preacher'.[5] Thomas Manton describes Swinnock as 'a name well known to most serious Christians by his former savoury and useful works, published for the good of the church'.[6] These 'savoury' works include: *The Christian Man's Calling*; *The Door of Salvation Opened by the Key of Regeneration*; *The Fading of the Flesh*; *The Gods Are Men*; *Men Are Gods*; *Heaven and Hell Epitomised*; *The Pastor's Farewell*; *The Sinner's Last Sentence*; *The Life and Death of Mr. Thomas Wilson*; and *The Incomparableness of God*.[7]

The subject of this chapter is the last book listed above: *The Incomparableness of God*.[8] Swinnock includes the following statement on its title page: 'True knowledge of God is a power by which we not only understand God to exist, but we also grasp what it concerns us to know regarding him, so that we might worship him properly'.[9] This statement is of interest for three reasons. The first is its *intellectual emphasis*; it mentions the 'true knowledge of God' and 'what it concerns us to know regarding him'. The second is its *experimental emphasis*;[10] it highlights the relationship between knowing God truly and worshipping God 'properly'. The third is its *historical background*; it is actually a citation from Amandus Polanus.[11] Interestingly, in this treatise (Swinnock's most thorough treatment of Theology Proper), the margins are bare. This stands in marked contrast to his other works, in which the margins reveal his frequent use of moralists, historians, philosophers and theologians. The lack of marginal notes makes his inclusion of a citation from Polanus on the title page all the more noteworthy.

---

4. For a brief account of Swinnock's life and ministry, see *Works*, vol. 5, pp. ix–xiv. There is no available funeral sermon or collection of letters, and there are scant references in the writings of his contemporaries.

5. Edmund Calamy, *The Nonconformist's Memorial* (2 vols; London, 1802), vol. 1, pp. 303–4.

6. Thomas Manton, 'To the Reader', in Swinnock, *Works*, vol. 5, p. 267.

7. *Works* includes all of these treatises except *The Life and Death of Mr. Thomas Wilson, M. A.* (London, 1672).

8. The full title is as follows: *A Treatise of the Incomparableness of God in his being, attributes, works, and words: opened and applied*. It was first published in London, 1672, and is found in *Works*, vol. 4, pp. 373–508. An updated edition is also available: George Swinnock, *The Blessed and Boundless God* (ed. J. Stephen Yuille; Puritan Treasures for Today; Grand Rapids: Reformation Heritage Books, 2014).

9. The words are in Latin: 'Vera cognitio Dei, est virtus per quam non modo concipimus esse aliquem Deum, sed etiam tenemus quod de eo scire nostra interest, ut eum recte colamus'. This statement is found on the cover of the original edition; it is not included in *Works*.

10. The Latin verb *experior* means to know by experience. Experimental (or experiential) theology, therefore, is that which aims to apply divine truth to the whole range of personal experience.

11. Swinnock provides the following reference: Polan. Syntag. Theolog. lib. 9. cap. 7.

These three points of interest shape the crux of this chapter, the goal of which is to consider Polanus's legacy in the formulation of Swinnock's theology. Many people have the mistaken impression that Reformed theology begins and ends with John Calvin.[12] As Tony Lane remarks, 'We can be misled into thinking of Calvin as the sole father of Reformed theology and into assessing all subsequent theologians in terms of fidelity to, decline from, or improvement on his position.'[13] In reality, Reformed theology extends well beyond the confines of Calvin's *Institutes* and commentaries. This is exemplified in Swinnock's use of Polanus.

Amandus Polanus von Polansdorf (1561–1610) was born in Opava, Silesia (modern-day Czech Republic).[14] Having completed his schooling in the liberal arts, he proceeded in 1577 to Wroclaw, Silesia (modern-day Poland), where he studied for six years. He furthered his education at Tubingen, Germany, before departing in 1583 for Basel, Switzerland, where he studied divinity. Having completed his studies, he tutored in several cities including Geneva and Heidelberg. In 1590, he returned to Basel to complete the Doctor of Divinity. Six years later, he was appointed Professor of Divinity, responsible for interpreting the Old Testament. He served in this capacity for fourteen years. He also served as rector from 1600 to 1609. According to Samuel Clark, Polanus was a man of 'true piety and solid learning'.[15] The year before his death in 1610, he published *Syntagma Theologiae Christianae* (*A System of Christian Theology*) – one of the most influential theological works of the early seventeenth century.[16]

---

12. Without question, Swinnock has great respect for 'judicious Calvin' (*Works*, vol. 3, p. 203), but Calvin is only one figure in the tradition from which he draws. In *The Incomparableness of God*, Swinnock consults commentaries by Calvin and Henry Ainsworth in his exposition of Ps. 89.6-7 (*Works*, vol. 4, pp. 381–5). He again appeals to Calvin's commentaries in his exposition of 1 Corinthians 1.25 (*Works*, vol. 4, p. 408). In his discussion of God's being and attributes, Swinnock makes reference to two Reformed scholars in addition to Polanus: Franciscus Junius (1545–1602) and Girolamo Zanchi (1516–90) (*Works*, vol. 4, pp. 387, 396, 402).

13. Anthony N. S. Lane, 'The Quest for the Historical Calvin', *Evangelical Quarterly* 55 (1983), pp. 95–113 (97).

14. The details in this paragraph are found in Samuel Clark, *The Marrow of Ecclesiastical History* (London, 1654), pp. 891–2; and Thomas Fuller, *Abel Redevivus: or, The Dead Yet Speaking. The Lives and Deaths of the Modern Divines* (London, 1651), pp. 499–500. For more on Polanus's academic career and literary works, see Ernst Staehelin, *Amandus Polanus von Polansdorf* (Basel: Verlag von Helbing & Lichtenhaln, 1955).

15. Clark, *Marrow*, p. 892.

16. *Syntagma Theologiae Christianae* consists of Volume 1 (Books 1–5) and Volume 2 (Books 6–10). For Volume 1, I consult the Hanover edition, 1610 (Typis Wechelianis, apud Claudium Marnium, & haerdes Johannis Aubrii). For Volume 2 (Tomus Secundus), I consult the Hanover edition, 1609 (also Marnius and Aubrius). In this chapter, I also make reference to Polanus's *The Substance of Christian Religion* (London, 1595). This is the English translation of *Partitiones Theologiae* (Basel, 1590). For a list of Polanus's works, see 'The Post-Reformation Digital Library' at www.prdl.org.

In *Syntagma*, Polanus classifies theology according to two parts: 'faith' ('de rebus credendis') and 'good works' ('de rebus faciendis').[17] He employs this division because he believes it reflects Scripture's twofold emphasis on instruction and exhortation.[18] This division provides the overarching structure for Polanus's *Syntagma*. In Books 1–7, he expounds 'faith' – what we are to believe. He begins by exploring the principles of sound theology and by establishing Scripture as central to all theological inquiry.[19] He then proceeds to discuss God's essence and

17. *Syntagma*, 2.1, col. 833. Polanus employs the same approach in *The Substance of Christian Religion*. It too is divided into two parts. The first concerns 'faith': 'What we must believe to salvation' (p. 1). The second concerns 'good works': 'What works are to be done by the faithful, that so men may perform thankfulness due to God, for the deliverance from sin and eternal death' (p. 179). From this basic division, Polanus breaks down every topic into subdivisions, demonstrating his predilection for Peter Ramus's *Ars Logica*. Ramus (1515–72), a convert from Roman Catholicism, proposed a method to simplify the orderly presentation of all academic subjects – a single logic for both dialectic and rhetoric. The task of the logician was to classify concepts, in order to make them understandable and memorable. This was accomplished through method – the orderly presentation of a subject. For more on this, see Robert Letham, 'Amandus Polanus: A Neglected Theologian?', *Sixteenth Century Journal* 21 (1990), pp. 463–76.

18. For an analysis of Polanus's theological method, see Max E. Deal, 'The Meaning and Method of Systematic Theology in Amandus Polanus' (unpublished doctoral dissertation, University of Edinburgh, 1980). For a study of Polanus's use of the Patristic authors, see Byung Soo Han, '*Symphonia Catholica*: The Relation of Reformed Orthodox Theology and the Church Fathers in Amandus Polanus (1561–1610)' (unpublished doctoral dissertation, Calvin Theological Seminary, 2013).

19. Polanus studied under Theodore Beza at Basel. This is noteworthy in terms of the discussion surrounding the extent to which Reformed theology succumbed to a revived scholasticism through the influence of Beza. See R. T. Kendall, *Calvin and English Calvinism to 1649* (Oxford: Oxford University Press, 1979); and Basil Hall, 'Calvin Against the Calvinists', in *John Calvin: A Collection of Distinguished Essays* (ed. G. E. Duffield; Grand Rapids: Eerdmans, 1966), pp. 19–37. Brian Armstrong argues that there are two very different intellectual traditions operative in the seventeenth century: scholasticism and humanism. The latter is consistent with the teaching of Calvin whereas the former – although known as Calvinism – departs from Calvin. See *Calvinism and the Amyraut Heresy: Protestant Scholasticism and Humanism in Seventeenth-Century France* (Madison: University of Wisconsin Press, 1969). Armstrong points to Amyraut as standing against the tide of scholasticism by faithfully articulating Calvin's humanistic emphasis, whereas he points to Beza as the one most responsible for the propagation of scholasticism within Protestantism (*Calvinism and the Amyraut Heresy*, p. 38). Richard Muller challenges this view in *Christ and the Decree: Christology and Predestination in Reformed Theology from Calvin to Perkins* (Durham, NC: Labyrinth Press, 1986). Also see Muller, *Post-Reformation Reformed Dogmatics: The Rise and Development of Reformed Orthodoxy, ca. 1520 to ca. 1725* (4 vols; Grand Rapids: Baker Academic, 2003).

attributes. This discussion provides the framework for his analysis of God's works, towards the end of which he considers Christ's person, offices and benefits,[20] the covenant of grace, the communion of saints, the sacraments and the last things. He brings his exposition of 'faith' to a conclusion by looking at the doctrine of the church. In Books 8–10, Polanus turns his attention to 'good works' – how we are to live. He explains the nature of worship, unfolds the difference between true and false religion and considers various topics such as marriage, divorce and the function of the civil magistrate.

Although Swinnock's terminology is different, his methodology is the same. In *The Incomparableness of God*, he emphasizes the essential relationship between what we are to believe ('faith') and how we are to live ('good works').[21] His chosen text is Psalm 89.6–7, 'For who in the heaven can be compared unto the LORD? Who among the sons of the mighty can be likened unto the LORD?' From the psalmist's assertion that no one in heaven or earth is like God, Swinnock derives his principal doctrine – namely, God is incomparable. In chapters 2–17, he focuses on the 'explication of this doctrine'.[22] He 'opens' it by demonstrating God's incomparableness in his being, attributes, works and words. In chapters 18–26, he focuses on the 'application of this great and weighty truth'.[23] He 'applies' it by demonstrating how God's incomparableness informs, counsels and comforts us.

In addition to employing the same basic structure as found in Polanus's *Syntagma*, Swinnock derives his central thesis from Polanus. As already mentioned, he includes an extract from *Syntagma* on the title page of *The Incomparableness of God*: 'True knowledge of God is a power by which we not only understand God to exist, but we also grasp what it concerns us to know regarding him, so that we might worship him properly.'[24] This statement encapsulates Swinnock's goal in writing. First, he emphasizes 'what it concerns us to know regarding [God]', stating that 'the incomparable excellency of the *boundless blessed* God is the subject of this treatise'.[25] Second, he emphasizes the fact that the 'knowledge of God' is a 'power', explaining that 'our awe of, love to, and trust in the divine Majesty, are founded in the right knowledge of him'.[26] Third, he emphasizes the connection between knowing God truly and worshipping God 'properly', declaring that 'he only lives above this present evil world, and all the riches and honours and pleasures thereof, who can look beyond it to the infinite God'.[27] These emphases

---

20. For a discussion of Polanus's Christology, see Muller, *Christ and the Decree*, pp. 129–73.

21. Swinnock's *The Incomparableness of God* is not nearly as exhaustive as Polanus's *Syntagma*; however, he does expound on many of the missing elements in other treatises.

22. Swinnock, *Works*, vol. 4, p. 386.

23. Ibid., vol. 4, p. 456.

24. Polanus, *Syntagma*, 9.7, col. 3811.

25. Swinnock, *Works*, vol. 4, p. 376, italics mine.

26. Ibid., vol. 4, p. 377.

27. Ibid.

are not original to Swinnock, but echo (to varying degrees) Polanus's *Syntagma*. We review each in turn.

The Boundless and Blessed God

'God is most perfect', declares Polanus.[28] He is one, simple, indivisible essence;[29] moreover, his essence is one simple act (infinite and immutable) by which he lives, understands, wills, loves, etc.[30] This conviction shapes Polanus's understanding of God's attributes. Because God is 'perfect being', it is impossible to distinguish anything within God's essence. His attributes, therefore, are not 'parts' of His essence, but are 'essential properties' of His total and complete essence. In other words, His essence and attributes are one and the same.[31]

Having laid this foundation, Polanus distinguishes between first and second order attributes. First order attributes are those that belong to God alone. They are incommunicable, in that He does not share them with His creatures.[32] They include His simplicity – He is not divided or compounded;[33] His infinity – He is above time and space;[34] His eternity – He is without succession of time;[35] His immensity – He fills all places, and is incapable of division or extension;[36] and His immutability – He does not change.[37] Second order attributes are those that are found in God essentially, and in us derivatively.[38] They are communicable, in that He does share them with His creatures.[39] Polanus expounds God's power, wisdom, love, patience and faithfulness – to name but a few.

28. 'Deus est summe perfectus. Summe perfectum non potest nisi unum existere' (Polanus, *Syntagma*, 2.5, col. 872). Polanus derives his insights concerning God's 'perfect being' from his consideration of God's names (*Syntagma*, 2.5–6, cols 865–901).

29. The content of this paragraph is found in Polanus, *Syntagma*, 2.7, cols 901–5. Here, Polanus provides eleven axioms for understanding God's essential properties.

30. 'Quicquid Deus est aut in sese agit, uno & eodem actu, qui est ipsius essentia, id est aut in sese agit: ideo uno & eodem actu simplex, infinitus, immutabilis est, uno & eodem actu vivit, intelligit, vult, amat, &c'.

31. 'Proprietates Dei non sunt partes essentiae divinae, sed quae libet proprietas essentialis est ipsamet Dei essentia tota & integra: ita ut essentia Dei & essentialis Dei proprietas non sint aliud & aliud, sed unum & idem'.

32. Polanus, *Syntagma*, 2.7, col. 905.

33. Ibid., 2.8, cols 905–14.

34. Ibid., 2.10, cols 924–7.

35. Ibid., 2.11, cols 928–33.

36. Ibid., 2.12, cols 933–65.

37. Ibid., 2.13, cols 965–82.

38. Ibid., 2.14, col. 983: 'Ita in Deo sunt essentialiter; in creaturis accidentaliter'.

39. Ibid., 2.14, col. 983. Polanus expounds these in 2.15–31.

Polanus's concept of 'perfect being' is the principal article in his theological system. It not only shapes his understanding of God's attributes, but also shapes his understanding of God's works (because God is 'perfect being', He is the first cause and ultimate end of all His works),[40] and God's decrees (because God is 'perfect being', He determines all things as the first cause).[41]

In *The Incomparableness of God*, Swinnock expresses the same theocentric commitment as Polanus. 'God is a perfect being', declares Swinnock. 'A being is absolutely perfect', he explains, 'when nothing can be added to it, or taken from it, when it is incapable of the least accession or diminution'.[42] Reminiscent of Polanus, Swinnock affirms that God is 'from himself' – His own first cause; 'for himself' – His own last end; and 'by himself' – completely independent.[43] In addition, God is infinite, eternal, universal, unchangeable and incomprehensible.[44] Swinnock adds, 'God is a most pure, simple, unmixed, indivisible essence; he is incapable of the least composition, and therefore of the least division. He is one most pure, one without all parts, members, accidents, and qualities'.[45] We consist of parts: body and soul. Our body consists of parts: skin, blood, arms, legs, bones, ligaments, tendons, organs, etc. Our soul consists of parts: understanding, will, memory and conscience. These, in turn, bear qualities such as intelligence, wisdom and emotions. But God is a simple being, incapable of the least division.

As in the case of Polanus, Swinnock's concept of 'perfect being' shapes his entire theological system. This is evident in his discussion of God's attributes. He quotes Polanus as follows: 'The attributes of God which are ascribed to him are spoken of in the sacred Scriptures, not so much to explain his essence and nature as to declare to us, in some manner according to our capacity, that which can be learned by us regarding him'.[46] In other words, the 'perfections in the divine nature' are called 'attributes' because they are attributed to God for our sakes 'that we might the better understand him'.[47] Like Polanus, Swinnock believes God's essence and attributes are inseparable. His attributes can no more be separated from Him than

---

40. Ibid., 4.1, cols 1513–17.

41. Ibid., 4.6, cols 1528–59.

42. Swinnock, *Works*, vol. 4, p. 391. Like Polanus, Swinnock's understanding of God's 'perfect being' arises from his consideration of God's name (pp. 386–7).

43. Ibid., vol. 4, pp. 388–9.

44. Ibid., vol. 4, pp. 388–402.

45. Ibid., vol. 4, p. 397.

46. Ibid., vol. 4, p. 402. 'Attributa Dei dicuntur quae Deo adscribuntur in Scripturis Sanctis, non tam ad essentiam naturamque Dei explicandam, quam ad declarandum nobis aliquo modo pro nostro captu illud quod de ipso a nobis cognosci potest.' Swinnock provides the following reference: Polan. Syntag. lib. 2. cap. 6. See Polanus, *Syntagma*, 2.6, col. 879. In the same context, Swinnock quotes Zanchi: 'They are called attributes, because God has attributed them to himself for our sake' ('Vocantur attributa, quia ea sibi attribuit Deus nostra causa'). He provides the following reference: Zanch. De Attribut., lib. 2, cap. 12.

47. Swinnock, *Works*, vol. 4, p. 402.

He can be separated from Himself.[48] God is not merely wise; He is wisdom. He is not merely powerful; He is power. He is not merely good; He is goodness. He is not merely holy; He is holiness. He is not merely just; He is justice.

While they are distinguished in their objects and effects, God's attributes are all one in Him – His justice is His mercy and His mercy is His justice; His wisdom is His power and His power is His wisdom; His knowledge is His patience and His patience is His knowledge; His wrath is His goodness and His goodness is His wrath; and so on. These attributes are 'boundless', affirms Swinnock, 'because they are [God's] being, himself'.[49]

Because God is 'perfect being', His works are incomparable. Swinnock affirms that God is incomparable in the 'manner' of His working.[50] For starters, He works 'irresistibly'. He does whatever He wills. All the combined power and wisdom of humans and angels cannot hinder Him. Second, God works 'arbitrarily'. That is to say, He works according to His pleasure. He is not responsible to anyone for any of His actions. He has absolute ownership over all His works and, therefore, governs them as He pleases. Third, God works 'effortlessly'. He works at all times without growing weary. He does the greatest things with the same ease that He does the least things. Fourth, God works 'independently'. He works entirely by His own power – without the least help from anyone. God did not make the creatures because He needed them, but because it was His pleasure to do so; therefore, He uses them because He chooses to use them.

Because God is 'perfect being', His words are also incomparable. Swinnock stresses that God is incomparable in the 'manner' and 'matter' of His speaking.[51] He speaks authoritatively – as one who has the right and power to command and as one who expects to be obeyed. God is also incomparable in the 'effect' of His speaking.[52] His words are operative as well as declarative of His pleasure; that is to say, they possess both power and virtue.

According to Swinnock, this God is 'blessed' precisely because He is 'boundless'. This too is reminiscent of Polanus. 'God alone is truly blessed', says he.[53] Moreover, 'God is his own blessedness.'[54] Polanus's reasoning is simple. If God is 'perfect being', then He is sufficient and satisfied in Himself. That being the case, He is the source of all good. If He is the chief good, then He is the only source of our blessedness; that is to say, we find our greatest good in communion with Him.[55] Swinnock embraces this paradigm. In many respects, it is the *sine qua non* of his experimental

---

48. Ibid., vol. 4, pp. 422–3.

49. Ibid., vol. 4, p. 424.

50. Ibid., vol. 4, pp. 435–41.

51. Ibid., vol. 4, pp. 445–9.

52. Ibid., vol. 4, p. 452.

53. Polanus, *Syntagma*, 2.17, col. 996: 'Deus solus est vere beatus'.

54. Ibid., 2.17, col. 996: 'Deus est ipse sua beatitudo'.

55. Ibid., 2.17, col. 997: 'Deus etiam dicitur beatitudo nostra: quia est objectum cujus fruitione beati sumus, quia est autor & conservator beatitudinis, & quia in ipso sumus, in quo fruimur ipso'.

theology.[56] 'If God be an incomparable God', then we are 'incomparably blessed' when we take Him for our God.[57] First, we are 'incomparably blessed' because this incomparable God is ours.[58] God is boundless; therefore, He cannot give us anything greater than Himself. Second, we are 'incomparably blessed' because this incomparable God's 'excellencies' are ours.[59] His boundless power is ours to protect us, His boundless wisdom to direct us, His boundless mercy to assist us, His boundless grace to pardon us, His boundless love to delight us, and His boundless joy to satisfy us. Third, we are 'incomparably blessed' because this incomparable God's 'excellencies' are ours forever.[60] God's incomparable eternity is ours, and so long as He is God, He will be our God.

For Swinnock, God is the greatest good that ever was, ever will be, and ever can be.[61] He is more than heaven and earth. He is the King of Kings, the Lord of Lords, the God of Gods, the blessed and glorious Potentate, the first Cause, the original Being, the self-sufficient, the all-sufficient, the absolutely perfect God. He is the high and lofty One who inhabits eternity – to Whom a thousand years are but a moment. He is boundless in His being, omnipotent in His power, unsearchable in His wisdom, inconceivable in His grace, and infinite in all His perfections. He made all things out of nothing. He supports all things and influences all things. He is all things, and He is infinitely more than all things. He is such a necessary

---

56. Elsewhere, Swinnock makes the point that people have 'a propensity towards that in which they place their felicity' (*Works*, vol. 4, p. 2). This means they move towards that which makes them happy and away from that which makes them unhappy. For Swinnock, this is part of the image of God in humanity (*Works*, vol. 3, pp. 405, 415; vol. 4, pp. 2, 12, 28). Similarly, Polanus writes, 'Perfect blessedness is that other part of the image of God, by which a natural creature, through an excellent joy, taking pleasure in God alone, doth enjoy perfect felicity' (*Substance*, p. 20). The framework for this teleological view of the image of God is found in Aristotle, who writes, 'There is some end (τέλος) of the things we do, which we desire for its own sake.' This 'end' is 'the chief good' (happiness), which is 'always desirable in itself and never for the sake of something else'. On this point, see *Nicomachean Ethics* (ed. W. D. Ross; The Works of Aristotle, vol. 9; Oxford: Oxford University Press, 1963), 1.2, 4, 7, 13. For Aristotle, the conclusion is primarily ethical; that is, the happy man is the virtuous man – virtue being the mean between two extremes. While embracing Aristotle's framework, Polanus rejects his view of the virtuous man. For Polanus, our 'chief end' is the blessed God. Swinnock agrees.

57. Swinnock, *Works*, vol. 4, p. 505.

58. Ibid., vol. 4, p. 506.

59. Ibid., vol. 4, pp. 507–8.

60. Ibid., vol. 4, p. 508. Elsewhere, Swinnock comments, 'Thy happiness dependeth wholly upon thy taking of the blessed God for thine utmost end and chiefest good' (p. 22). This means we experience happiness when we 'know' God who is 'the sweetest love, the richest mercy, the surest friend, the chiefest good, the greatest beauty, the highest honour, and fullest happiness' (p. 28).

61. The content of this paragraph is adapted from Swinnock, *Works*, vol. 4, pp. 493–4.

good that we are undone without Him. He is so plentiful a good that we can be perfectly happy in Him. This God is the well of salvation, the Lord of life, the God of all comfort – a hive of sweetness, paradise of pleasure, and heaven of joy. He is the richest grace, dearest love, surest friend, highest honour, greatest beauty and fullest joy. He is a universal good – not one good, but all good. He is riches, honours, pleasures, friends, family, health, life, earth, heaven, and infinitely more. He is an eternal good – a good that will stand by us and abide with us when all other good things fail.

The Knowledge of God: 'Faith'

The means by which this 'boundless' God (summum ens) becomes the 'blessed' God (summum bonum) in our experience is knowledge. For Polanus, 'The communication of theology to the rational creature has two ends: the first and greatest is the glory of God, which is the highest good; the second and subordinate is the blessedness of the rational creature.'[62] He adds, 'There are two parts to blessedness: freedom from every evil and the possession of every truly good thing, which the rational creature possesses in God. These truly good things consist of seeing God, conformity to God, sufficiency in God, and knowledge of his eternal goodness.'[63] For Polanus, we must first see God before we can desire or obey Him. That is to say, we must apprehend his 'eternal goodness' before we can move towards Him. This knowledge of God begins in the mind and terminates in the will whereby the boundless God becomes the blessed God.

Swinnock is in full agreement, declaring, 'Rich must be the delight which the most large and noble faculty of man, his understanding, shall receive, in its intimate acquaintance with, and clear and full apprehension of, the highest truth.'[64] This 'highest truth' is God. With the 'intellectual eye' we apprehend him – 'the first

---

62. Polanus, *Syntagma*, 'Synopsis Libri I', col. 1: 'Theologiae cum creaturis rationalibus communicatae fines sunt duo: primarius & summus est glorificatio Dei tanqua[m] summi boni: secundarius & subordinatus est beatitudo creaturarum rationalium'. Polanus develops this in *Syntagma*, 1.5, cols 15–52.

63. Ibid., 'Synopsis Libri I', col. 1: 'Partes Beatitudinis sunt duae: libertas a malis omnibus, & possessio verorum bonorum omnium, quibus in Deo creaturae rationales potiuntur: Cujus modi sunt: visio Dei, conformitas cum Deo, sufficientia in Deo & certa scientia aeternae suae felicitatis'. Polanus develops this in *Syntagma*, 1.6, cols 52–62.

64. Swinnock, *Works*, vol. 4, p. 381. As Richard Muller explains, the terms 'intellectualism' and 'voluntarism' refer to the two faculties of soul (intellect and will), and to the question of the priority of the one over the other. On this point, see '*Fides* and *Cognitio* in Relation to the Problem of Intellect and Will in the Theology of John Calvin', *Calvin Theological Journal* 25 (1990), pp. 207–24 (211). Intellectualism identifies the mind as the causal faculty in the soul's approval of good, whereas voluntarism identifies the will (inclination and choice). Swinnock ascribes temporal priority to the understanding. Prior to the fall, it was governed

cause, the being of beings, the original of all things'.[65] This is no mere intellectual knowledge, but experimental knowledge, which affects the heart with love for God, fear of God, and hatred for whatever is contrary to Him.[66] In other words, it is a knowledge that begins in the head, affects the heart, and regulates all of life.[67]

Swinnock identifies three marks of such knowledge.[68] First, it is 'sanctifying'.[69] It renders sin abominable and the world contemptible; it also renders God honourable, meaning the more we know Him, the more we admire Him. Second, this knowledge of God is 'satisfying'. God is a spiritual good, and suitable to the soul's nature; He is a universal good, and answerable to the soul's needs; and He is an eternal good, and equal to the soul's duration. Third, this knowledge of God is 'saving'. God does not require us to satisfy His justice, fulfil His law, or merit His favour. He has done all this for us through His Son. All He requires is that we accept Him as our God in His Son.

Given this conviction, Swinnock places tremendous emphasis on the pursuit of knowledge.[70] Without it, the soul is a 'dungeon of darkness and blackness' – full of

by the knowledge of God, and it was the vehicle by which God communicated to the soul. The affections were inclined to this knowledge, meaning the soul willed action according to its understanding and affections. However, this priority was lost when Adam disobeyed. According to Swinnock, the understanding is now darkened. For this reason, it must be illuminated. Swinnock remarks, 'It is observable, that in the covenant of grace the mind is still spoken of to be renewed before the heart (Heb. 10.8-9; Jer. 31.33). For it is by the understanding that grace slips down into the affections' (*Works*, vol. 5, pp. 201-2). Again, 'There must be a daybreak of light in the understanding, before there can be a heartbreak of sorrow in the affections' (*Works*, vol. 3, p. 334). When this occurs, the affections are stirred to hate what they formerly loved (sin) and love what they formerly hated (God) (*Works*, vol. 5, pp. 31-2).

65. Swinnock, *Works*, vol. 4, pp. 375-6.

66. Ibid., vol. 4, p. 377.

67. Ibid., vol. 4, p. 482. Elsewhere, Swinnock writes, 'The spring of this knowledge may be in the head, but it slideth down into the heart, breaketh out into the life, and so floweth along in the channel of grace and holiness, till at last it lose itself in the ocean of glory' (vol. 1, p. 373).

68. Ibid., vol. 4, pp. 482-7.

69. Elsewhere, Swinnock writes, 'Oh what a work, a gracious sanctifying work, doth the knowledge of God make in the soul! It makes the understanding to esteem him above all, the will to choose him before all, the affections to desire him, to delight in him, more than all; the whole man to seek him, to serve him, to honour and praise him beyond all in heaven and earth' (Ibid., vol. 3, p. 155).

70. Ibid., vol. 4, p. 480. Throughout his works, Swinnock exhorts his readers to mind 'solemn and set meditation', which he believes is 'the womb of [...] actions' (vol. 2, pp. 424, 471). He defines it as 'a serious applying the mind to some sacred subject, till the affections be warmed and quickened, and the resolution heightened and strengthened thereby, against what is evil, and for that which is good' (vol. 2, p. 425). For more on Swinnock's use of

confusion.[71] Elsewhere, he writes, 'They who know the infiniteness and immensity of [God's] being, cannot but [...] esteem all things as nothing to him', 'they who know the power of God cannot but fear him, and stand in awe of his presence', 'they who know the eternity of God, will choose him before temporal vanities', 'they who know the wisdom of God will submit to his providences, and acquiesce in all his dispensations', 'they who know the faithfulness of God will credit his word, and make him the object of their hope and faith', 'they who know the mercy, and love, and goodness of God, will love, and admire, and trust, and praise him', 'they who know the holiness of God will sanctify him in their approaches to him, and walk humbly and watchfully with him', and 'they who know the anger of God will stand in awe, and not sin'.[72] Swinnock exhorts, 'Reader, be persuaded, therefore, to study this knowledge of God; think no labour too much for it; pray, and read, and hear, and confer, and mourn that thou mayest know God.'[73]

The Worship of God: 'Good Works'

This knowledge of God is not an end in itself, but a means to an end: 'so that we might worship him properly'. For Polanus, theology's fundamental purpose is ultimately doxological.[74] It is designed to cultivate good works, which are performed from faith and for God's glory.[75] Polanus divides these good works into two categories: 'worship' and 'virtue'. The worship of God, in turn, consists of 'inward' and 'outward'. In Book 9 of *Syntagma*, Polanus expounds those works related to the 'inward' worship of God; namely, faith, hope, love, patience and humility.[76]

---

meditation, see J. Stephen Yuille, 'Conversing with God's Word: Scripture Meditation in the piety of George Swinnock', *Journal of Spiritual Formation & Soul Care* 5 (2012), pp. 35–55. The goal of meditation is to apply Scripture successively to the faculties of understanding, affections and will. According to Peter Toon, meditation opens a channel between the mind, heart and will – 'what the mind receives enters the heart and goes into action via the will'. See *From Mind to Heart: Christian Meditation Today* (Grand Rapids: Baker Books, 1987), p. 18. In terms of the affections specifically, he states, 'Meditation was seen as a divinely appointed way of stimulating or raising the affections toward the glory of God' (p. 94).

71. Swinnock, *Works*, vol. 4, p. 481.

72. Ibid., vol. 3, pp. 154–5.

73. Ibid., vol. 3, p. 158.

74. Polanus, *Syntagma*, 2.1, col. 836: 'Omnium autem practicarum disciplinarum finis est non sola cognitio, sed operatio: ita etiam theologiae finis non est nuda & ociosa speculatio, seu contemplatio, sed praxis, sed operatio ad quam homo est a Deo conditus, ad quam a Christo redemtus, ad quam a Spiritu Sancto sanctificatur, nempe glorificatio Dei & beatitudo hominis sempiterna; illa quidem ut finis summus, principalis, ultimus; haec vero ut finis subordinatus, secundarius, subalternus'.

75. Ibid., 2.1, cols 833–5. Also see Polanus, *Substance*, p. 179.

76. Polanus, *Syntagma*, 9.6–13, cols 3727–899.

His point is that the knowledge of God leads to the right ordering of these 'works', which in turn regulate all of life – worship.

Like Polanus, Swinnock's theology is couched in worship. 'If God be an incomparable God', says he, 'then incomparable service and worship is due to him'.[77] For starters, the incomparable God calls for 'incomparable awe and reverence'.[78] There is an infinite distance between God and us; therefore there ought to be (if it were possible) infinite reverence. The incomparable God also calls for 'incomparable humility and lowliness of spirit'.[79] We never come to a right knowledge of ourselves until we come to a right knowledge of God – what an excellent Majesty He is. Upon seeing the incomparable God, we loathe (rather than admire) ourselves.

The incomparable God also calls for 'incomparable love'.[80] For Swinnock, love is the cream of our affections. Its object is goodness; therefore, the greater the good, the greater our love. Since God is the greatest good, He deserves our greatest love. Desire and delight are the two acts of love, distinguished only by the absence or presence of the object.[81] When the object of our love is absent, our soul desires it. When the object of our love is present, our soul delights in it. The former is the soul's motion, whereas the latter is the soul's rest. The incomparable God deserves our incomparable desire; we must desire Him above all (Ps. 73.25). The incomparable God also deserves our incomparable delight; we must be ravished in the enjoyment of Him (Cant. 2.4).

Furthermore, the incomparable God calls for 'incomparable trust'.[82] The more powerful and faithful a person is, the more we trust him. God is incomparable in power and faithfulness; therefore, He merits our greatest love and firmest faith. Finally, the incomparable God calls for 'incomparable obedience in the whole course of our lives'.[83] God is incomparable in purity and majesty; therefore we walk carefully, obeying at all times and in all things. Our obedience ('good works') must be incomparable because partial obedience is unsuitable to such a great God.

Conclusion

Swinnock's *The Incomparableness of God* is not an exact replica of Polanus's *Syntagma*, but it does demonstrate a commitment to the same principal message:

77. Swinnock, *Works*, vol. 4, p. 471.

78. Ibid., vol. 4, p. 472.

79. Ibid., vol. 4, p. 473.

80. Ibid., vol. 4, p. 474.

81. Ibid., vol. 4, p. 475. Swinnock's view of the affections is rooted in Augustine. See *The City of God* (ed. P. Schaff; Nicene and Post-Nicene Fathers, Series I, vol. 2; repr. Peabody: Hendrickson Publishers, 2004), 14.5–9.

82. Swinnock, *Works*, vol. 4, p. 475.

83. Ibid., vol. 4, p. 476.

'True knowledge of God is a power by which we not only understand God to exist, but we also grasp what it concerns us to know regarding him, so that we might worship him properly.'

Swinnock shares Polanus's *intellectual emphasis*. He stresses the 'true knowledge of God' and 'what it concerns us to know regarding him'. This is no surprise given his conviction that the mind is the 'supreme faculty of the soul'.[84] 'Though the motions of the understanding and will are in some respect circular', writes Swinnock, 'yet the understanding is the first mover and the leading faculty.'[85] In making this assertion, he is not suggesting that the will necessarily follows the dictates of the mind, for he does not view the mind as the efficient cause of the will's choice. Rather, in referring to the mind as the 'supreme faculty of the soul', he means that first, the will ought to follow the mind; second, the will cannot choose what is unknown to the mind; and, third, the knowledge of God always begins in the mind.[86] Swinnock's commitment to the temporal priority of the mind is important for his approach to theology. In sum, he places tremendous importance on cognitive understanding because he views it as 'the eye of the soul, to direct it in its motions' and as 'the light of the soul, set up by God himself to guide it in its actions'.[87]

Swinnock also shares Polanus's *experimental emphasis*. He stresses the relationship between knowing God truly and worshipping God 'properly'. Swinnock is a consummate theologian – steeped in Scripture, proficient in the arts and philosophies, and familiar with a wide spectrum of theological writers. But equally important is the fact that he is an *affective* theologian. He views theology neither as a mere intellectual or theoretical exercise nor as a mere academic pursuit, but he sees it as the means by which we grow in acquaintance with God and consequently in godliness.[88] In his estimation, the goal of theology is to engage

---

84. Ibid., vol. 5, p. 420.

85. Ibid., vol. 4, p. 376.

86. J. I. Packer explains this emphasis among the Puritans in general: 'Man was made to know good with his mind, to desire it, once he has come to know it, with his affections, and to cleave to it, once he has felt its attraction, with his will; the good in this case being God, his truth and his law. God accordingly moves us, not by direct action on the affections or will, but by addressing our mind with his word, and bringing to bear on us the force of truth'. On this point, see *A Quest for Godliness: The Puritan Vision of the Christian Life* (Wheaton: Crossway Books, 1990), p. 195.

87. Swinnock, *Works*, vol. 4, p. 481.

88. For Calvin, theology 'is not apprehended by the understanding and memory alone ..., but it is received only when it possesses the whole soul, and finds a seat and resting place in the inmost affection of the heart'. On this point, see *Institutes of the Christian Religion* (ed. John T. McNeill; trans. Ford Lewis Battles; The Library of Christian Classics, 20–21; Philadelphia: Westminster Press, 1960), 3.6.4. Swinnock would agree wholeheartedly. As Martyn Lloyd-Jones notes, 'There is nothing that [the Puritans] more deplored than a mere academic, intellectual, theoretical view of the truth' (*The Puritans: Their Origins and Successors* [Edinburgh: Banner of Truth, 2002], p. 55). David Sceats

the mind with the ultimate purpose of embracing the heart's innermost affections so that we worship God. 'The more the blessed God is known,' says Swinnock, 'the more he is prized, desired, and obeyed.'[89]

Bibliography

Aristotle, *Nicomachean Ethics* (ed. W. D. Ross; The Works of Aristotle, 9; Oxford: Oxford University Press, 1963).

Armstrong, Brian, *Calvinism and the Amyraut Heresy: Protestant Scholasticism and Humanism in Seventeenth-Century France* (Madison: University of Wisconsin Press, 1969).

Augustine, *The City of God* (ed. P. Schaff; Nicene and Post-Nicene Fathers, Series I, 2; Peabody: Hendrickson Publishers, 2004).

Baxter, Richard, *The Practical Works of Richard Baxter* (4 vols; London: George Virtue, 1846; repr., Morgan: Soli Deo Gloria, 2000).

Calamy, Edmund, *The Nonconformist's Memorial* (2 vols; London, 1802).

Calvin, John, *Institutes of the Christian Religion* (ed. J. T. McNeill; trans. Ford Lewis Battles; The Library of Christian Classics, vols 20–21; Philadelphia: Westminster Press, 1960).

Clark, Samuel, *The Marrow of Ecclesiastical History* (London, 1654).

Deal, M. E., 'The Meaning and Method of Systematic Theology in Amandus Polanus' (unpublished doctoral dissertation, University of Edinburgh, 1980).

Fuller, Thomas, *Abel Redevivus: or, The Dead Yet Speaking. The Lives and Deaths of the Modern Divines* (London, 1651).

Hall, Basil, 'Calvin Against the Calvinists', in *John Calvin: A Collection of Distinguished Essays* (ed. G. E. Duffield; Grand Rapids: Eerdmans, 1966), pp. 19–37.

Han, B. S., '*Symphonia Catholica*: The Relation of Reformed Orthodox Theology and the Church Fathers in Amandus Polanus (1561–1610)' (unpublished doctoral dissertation, Calvin Theological Seminary, 2013).

Kendall, R. T., *Calvin and English Calvinism to 1649* (Oxford: Oxford University Press, 1979).

Lane, A. N. S., 'The Quest for the Historical Calvin', *Evangelical Quarterly* 55 (1983), pp. 95–113.

Letham, Robert, 'Amandus Polanus: A Neglected Theologian?', *Sixteenth Century Journal* 21 (1990), pp. 463–76.

Lloyd-Jones, M., *The Puritans: Their Origins and Successors* (Edinburgh: Banner of Truth, 2002).

Muller, Richard, *Christ and the Decree: Christology and Predestination in Reformed Theology from Calvin to Perkins* (Durham, NC: Labyrinth Press, 1986).

concurs: 'Puritans would hardly have acknowledged the notion of "pure theology" and would have been distinctly uncomfortable with the idea that theology might have been studied as an academic discipline without reference to its situational application' (*The Experience of Grace: Aspects of the Faith and Spirituality of the Puritans*, [Grove Spirituality Series, 62; Cambridge: Grove, 1997], p. 12).

89. Swinnock, *Works*, vol. 4, p. 377.

Muller, Richard, '*Fides* and *Cognitio* in Relation to the Problem of Intellect and Will in the Theology of John Calvin', *Calvin Theological Journal* 25 (1990), pp. 207–24.

Muller, Richard, *Post-Reformation Reformed Dogmatics: The Rise and Development of Reformed Orthodoxy, ca. 1520 to ca. 1725* (4 vols; Grand Rapids: Baker Academic, 2003).

Packer, J. I., *A Quest for Godliness: The Puritan Vision of the Christian Life* (Wheaton: Crossway Books, 1990).

Polanus, Amandus, *Syntagmatis Theologiae Christianae* (2 vols; Hanover, 1609).

Polanus, Amandus, *Syntagma Theologiae Christianae* (2 vols; Hanover, 1610).

Polanus, Amandus, *The Substance of Christian Religion* (London, 1595).

Sceats, D., *The Experience of Grace: Aspects of the Faith and Spirituality of the Puritans* (Grove Spirituality Series, 62; Cambridge: Grove, 1997).

Staehelin, E., *Amandus Polanus von Polansdorf* (Basel: Verlag von Helbing & Lichtenhaln, 1955).

Swinnock, George, *The Blessed and Boundless God* (ed. J. Stephen Yuille; Puritan Treasures for Today; Grand Rapids: Reformation Heritage Books, 2014).

Swinnock, George, *The Works of George Swinnock* (5 vols; Edinburgh: James Nichol, 1868; repr., London: Banner of Truth, 1992).

Toon, Peter, *From Mind to Heart: Christian Meditation Today* (Grand Rapids: Baker Books, 1987).

Yuille, J. Stephen, 'Conversing with God's Word: Scripture Meditation in the piety of George Swinnock', *Journal of Spiritual Formation & Soul Care* 5 (2012), pp. 35–55.

Chapter 11

FRANCIS TURRETIN AND JONATHAN EDWARDS ON CONTINGENCY AND NECESSITY[1]

Paul Helm

In trying to form an estimate of Jonathan Edwards's anthropology in the light of that of his Reformed forebears, the issue of contingency and necessity is important. As we shall see later, Edwards sets out his views of both in *The Freedom of the Will*. The views of Reformed Orthodox (RO) such as the Genevan theologian Francis Turretin (1623–87), whom Edwards read and had a high regard for, on contingency and necessity are somewhat more diffuse, requiring a certain amount of cutting and pasting. In this chapter I try to piece them together, and to reflect on their consequences for Edwards's relations with the RO more generally. For with whatever voice they speak, the RO share a common outlook. On the arrival of Edwards, is there a parting of the ways or an orderly development?[2]

The difficulty of answering that question is due to the different conceptual outlooks of the parties: on the one hand, the language of indifference and rational spontaneity, and on the other, that of determinism and indeterminism. But there is some overlap in some of their vocabulary. Each had things to say about contingency and necessity. Whether this use of the same vocabulary also indicates conceptual identities is what is to be investigated here. I hope that the findings will be of some interest and help in estimating matters of theological continuity and development in a situation where the underlying conceptuality of an issue undergoes change.

The question of the position of Jonathan Edwards in the Reformed tradition and Turretin's view of contingency is part of a wider debate about the contingency and the freedom of indifference in the anthropology of the RO. In *Reformed Thought on Freedom*, Professor Willem van Asselt and his colleagues argue that, in contrast to

1. Thanks to Oliver Crisp and Richard Muller for their comments on an earlier draft.

2. For the claim that there is significant divergence, see Richard A. Muller, 'Jonathan Edwards and the Absence of Free Choice: A Parting of Ways in the Reformed Tradition', *Journal of Jonathan Edwards Studies* 1/1 (2011), pp. 3–22, and the response of Paul Helm, 'Jonathan Edwards and the Parting of the Ways?', *Journal of Jonathan Edwards Studies* 4/1 (2014), pp. 42–60.

the presumption that the RO espoused some form of compatibilism, the evidence points the other way, that the RO adopted the doctrine of contingency, and, indeed, that of synchronic contingency derived ultimately from Duns Scotus.[3]

If true, this would have been a surprising position to have been taken, as the freedom of synchronic contingency was characteristic of the position of the Jesuits, who appealed to it in defence of the liberty of indifference against what has been called the compatibilism[4] of the Augustinians of the Church of Rome. Not surprisingly perhaps, the recent claims of van Asselt and his colleagues, that the outlook of RO theologians, including Turretin, were not compatibilistic, has been challenged.[5] However, the present discussion does not enter further into this wider question. Our question is, does what Turretin has to say about contingency strengthen or weaken the claim that he himself espoused a version of the liberty of indifference? For evidence of his views on contingency, I shall focus exclusively on his work *The Institutes of Elenctic Theology*.[6]

Turretin on Contingency

Turretin uses the terms 'contingent' and 'contingency' in a variety of contexts, but there is no one place where the term is comprehensively defined and comparisons made between different uses of the term, and only one place in which one use of the term is contrasted with another. In what follows, I will consider this discussion and two others, to do with contingency and providence and contingency and the divine decree, respectively. Besides these, there are several other references to contingency, some of which I shall mention in footnotes. His treatment of contingency is very different from that of necessity, where in one place no less than six different uses of necessity are differentiated.[7] The other interesting general feature of his discussions is that where the freedom of the will is discussed, the terms 'indifference' and 'spontaneity' and 'rational necessity' are routinely used, but 'contingent' rarely if ever.

---

3. Willem J. van Asselt, J. Martin Bac, and Roelf T. te Velde (eds), *Reformed Thought on Freedom: The Concept of Free Choice in Early Modern Reformed Theology* (Grand Rapids, MI: Baker, 2010). It should be said, however, that the contributors to *Reformed Thought on Freedom* distinguish between Reformed and Jesuit approaches to contingency.

4. See the 'Introduction' by Alfred J. Freddoso to his translation of Part IV of Luis de Molina's *Concordia* (Ithaca: Cornell University Press, 1988).

5. See, for example, Paul Helm, '*Reformed Thought on Freedom*: Some Further Thoughts', *Journal of Reformed Theology* 4 (2010), pp. 185–207, and '"Structural Indifference" and Compatibilism in Reformed Orthodoxy', *Journal of Reformed Theology* 5 (2011), pp. 184–205.

6. Francis Turretin, *Institutes of Elenctic Theology* (ed. James T. Dennison; trans. G. M. Giger; 3 vols; Phillipsburg, NJ: P & R Publishing, 1992-7).

7. Turretin, *Institutes*, vol. 1, pp. 661–2.

So we begin with the one place where Turretin distinguishes between two senses of contingent, which happens to be his first discussion of contingency. He is discussing the question of whether God can know future contingents and is arguing *contra* the Socinians who denied any such knowledge to God. This leads Turretin, as part of his argument against them, to distinguish two senses of 'contingent'.

> On the state of the question observe (1) that a thing may be contingent in two ways – either with respect to the first cause (inasmuch as it can be produced or not produced by God, and so all creatures are contingent with respect to God because he might not have created any had he so willed); or with respect to second causes (which can produce or not produce their effect and are thus distinguished from necessary causes).[8]

Turretin is concerned here with preserving a proper place for what the *Westminster Confession of Faith* referred to as the 'contingency of second causes'[9] and seems to be saying that there are at least two ways in which a 'thing' can be contingent. Human beings and (say) insects are contingent beings because their existence depends upon God, the first cause. He may not have created them. If God may not have created insects and there are insects, then they are contingent. If there are human beings and insects, then it is only with respect to the will of God that they may be said to be necessary. Both the insects and the human beings are necessary in the sense that the RO called 'hypothetical necessity', necessary only in virtue of the prior 'hypothesis' that God had willed their existence.

The second way in which something can be contingent is in virtue of a secondary cause having the power to either produce an effect or not. So in his view insects do not possess such a power, but human beings do, possessed as they are of reason and will. So now the contrast Turretin wishes to draw is between a contingent effect and a necessary effect. For instance, insects act and react by instinct; likewise, a flame does not have a choice as to whether or not it will produce heat. Applying a thumbscrew produces pain in the victim; it cannot produce pleasurable feelings, anymore than a sheep can choose to eat ham and eggs. The occurrence of all such events are necessary, not contingent, even though the insects, and fire and a thumbscrew and sheep, considered as classes of thing, exist contingently, by God's decree. They are all, insofar as they produce causal effects, secondary causes.

All events are capable of having consequences that are not foreseen by human beings. All sorts of agents are capable of producing effects that, as far as their human bystanders are concerned, are not intended. They are unintended consequences, which usually are unforeseen. A tree may fall over unexpectedly, and a wave may be a freak wave, an insect may suddenly sting, and so on; and Joe may surprisingly decide to wear his new tie this morning. Each change, including human actions it

---

8. Ibid., p. 208.
9. *Westminster Confession of Faith*, III.1.

may seem, are capable of bringing about changes that surprise everyone, including the agent himself.

But are there contingent things whose powers and the effects they produce are contingent in a second sense? Turretin says that the Reformed theologians aver that there are such actions. No one doubts that God can know that the occurrence of such physically necessary events will or will not take place. But what of contingent events in the second sense, the actions of human beings, that possess reason and will? Scripture teaches that God nevertheless has infallible knowledge of contingent effects, effects that 'have a free cause'.[10]

So far, so straightforward, or so it may seem. Within the contingent world order, certain classes of events are necessary, certain kinds of other events are contingent, 'free'. But to make things a little more complex for the interpreter, Turretin also employs a different expression to cover this second sense of contingency, or at least provides some more explanation of what he has in mind. He asserts that future contingent things are not absolute and in every respect indeterminate. He goes on to explain that if they are indeterminate with respect to the second cause and also in themselves, then they are not indeterminate as to the first cause 'which decreed their futurition'. If, he explains, their truth is indeterminate with respect to us – we being incapable of seeing in which direction the free second cause is going to incline itself – it is not indeterminate with respect to God 'to whom all future things appear as present'.[11] So God's decree, besides being that to which the existence of human beings as a class is due, is a knowing decree, which reaches towards all future events, including human actions. In respect of the divine decreer, therefore, to whom the future appears as present, God knows each of them from an eternal standpoint. But we, the human agents, and the creaturely knowers of human actions, 'cannot see in which direction the free second cause is about to incline itself'.[12]

That is, while God who decrees a future creaturely free action thereby knows it, we (who cannot (usually) know for sure the direction in which the free second cause is about to incline itself) do not know, *for it is contingent.* I have added the italicized words of explanation, for that is what Turretin is implying. He says a few paragraphs later:

> There remains always this distinction between necessary and contingent things. The former have an intrinsic necessity because they arise from necessary proximate causes and are such in themselves, while the contingent, although they have an extrinsic necessity by reason of the event, [here Turretin is referring to the fact that contingent events are nonetheless decreed by God and foreknown by him] yet in their nature take place by contingent causes.[13]

10. Turretin, *Institutes*, vol. 1, pp. 208–9.
11. Ibid., p. 211.
12. Ibid.
13. Ibid.

In the case of those things that possess both understanding and will, powers to make contingent choices, they take place in such a manner that we the observers cannot see in what direction the cause of the action is about to incline itself. By his use of these expressions, does Turretin think that this ignorance is a feature of a person's lack of knowledge of *others'* actions only, or may it include his lack of knowledge of *his own* actions? Surely he must be referring to both. We are frequently unable to tell for sure how people are going to make up their minds, and are similarly unsure about how we are going to make up our own minds. Until we do so, the decision as to what to do may go either way, to choose A or not-A, or to choose A or B. And anyway our knowledge is not like God's, infallible, but is more like an educated guess. Not until we have finally and irrevocably made up our minds can we ourselves be said to know what we have decided to do. Necessarily (Only if Jones has finally and irrevocably made his mind up to do A can he know for sure that he is going to do A.).

So maybe the following represents the position: Turretin holds that an agent is frequently in the condition of not knowing the outcome of his own and others' deliberations. So long as action is being performed as a result of past deliberations, there is no problem. But with the prospect of new choices, there are new indeterminacies until these choices have been made, minds are not irrevocably made up, and the choices made may surprise us, even if they are our own choices. These activities are contingent in Turretin's second sense. So as I understand things, Turretin is here explaining further a phrase he uses in his earlier discussion of contingency: 'Their truth is indeterminate with respect to us (who cannot see in which direction the free second cause is about to incline itself).'[14] The epistemic contingency we are referring to here (i.e. a contingency that arises in connection with a choice because the mind has not been made up and so the choice has not been finally made) is an intrinsic feature of someone who is freely making up his or her mind (i.e. whose action is not the result of coaction or of brute necessity, like horses eating hay). It is not so much another kind of contingency as a feature of the second kind of contingency until the mind reaches a condition of having made a fixed choice. All this is from his discussion of the divine foreknowledge of human free acts.

The second substantial discussion of contingency arises out of Turretin's treatment of the decrees of God, in connection with the following question and answer: *Does the decree necessitate future things? We affirm.*[15] This follows the lines of the earlier discussion; it is an expansion of the meaning and the consequence of hypothetical necessity. Turretin's point is that the divine decree does not take away contingency with respect to second causes 'because the same decree which predetermined also determined the mode of futurition, so that the things having necessary causes should happen necessarily and those having contingent causes, contingently'.[16] The basic idea is that the divine decree does not smother or collapse

---

14. Ibid.
15. Ibid., p. 319.
16. Ibid., p. 321, also pp. 217, 218.

or override the distinction between necessary causes and contingent causes, but respects these, and preserves them. So, while all things that are decreed are necessitated by the decree, and so are hypothetically necessary, 'taken according to themselves'[17] they retain their distinctive character. In this connection, Turretin cites Aquinas: 'Every effect in necessity and contingency follows the proximate cause and not the first.'[18] So the liberty and spontaneity of actions possessing these properties is not compromised. This is 'extrinsic and hypothetical' necessity, extrinsic because it secures the happening of an action or event, but only through the outworking of its own nature, freely and contingently in the case of a thing that has such properties or powers, necessary in other cases.[19]

A third discussion arises in Turretin's treatment of providence in the Sixth Topic, the Third Question in which he asks whether *all things*, both small things and large, contingent things as well as free, and natural things as well as necessary fall under divine providence. He answers in the affirmative.[20]

> Scripture in many places asserts that contingent and fortuitous events fall under providence. Nothing is more contingent than the killing of a man contrary to his own intention, and yet this is ascribed to God, who is said to deliver him into the hand of the slayer. (Ex. 21:22, 23; Deut. 19:4f). Nothing is more casual and fortuitous than lots, and yet their falling out is referred to God himself. ... Nothing was more contingent than the selling of Joseph and his incarceration and exaltation, yet Joseph himself testifies that these were all ordered by the providence of God. (Gen. 45.8)[21]

And further, as far as free acts are concerned, 'whose mode of action is contingent',

> For that infallibility of the event from the hypothesis does not take away their contingency from the condition of second causes and from their mode of acting (in which there is always an intrinsic faculty and indifference to the opposite). So it was necessary for Joseph to be sold by his brethren and to go down to Egypt because it had been so determined by God for the preservation of Jacob's family. Yet it was contingent with respect to the brothers of Joseph who might either have killed him or not have sold him.[22]

So Joseph's brothers had a choice whether to sell him or to kill him. Before they made up their minds, they did not know which it would be, and so they did not

---

17. Ibid., p. 321.

18. The citation given by the English translator is *De Praescientia et Predestinatione, Opera Omnia: Opuscula Varia* (Rome, 1889), 32:92.

19. Turretin, *Institutes*, vol. 1, p. 321.

20. Ibid., p. 497.

21. Ibid., p. 499.

22. Ibid., p. 500.

know what exactly they were going to do.[23] (Had they been coerced into making a choice, the matter would have been significantly different.) So the outcome was contingent, not in the sense of being fortuitous, but in that it involved the settling of indecision. Here Turretin underlines what he had previously discussed, and what we have been trying to understand. All events are capable of producing unintended consequences. A lot – the tossing of a coin, the turning of a card, the choice of a straw – may be a necessary event, fixed through shuffling or tossing, and yet have surprising and significant consequences. For example, it may turn out that after the shuffle, the top four cards are a sequence of a 1, a 2, a 3 and a 4 of Spades. And free acts may also have unintended and unforeseen consequences, which adds to their contingency. It is the free acts that Turretin is here interested in, and the part that settling an indecision plays in the genesis of an action. In the next paragraph he writes, 'Therefore, nothing in the nature of things can be granted as so fortuitous and casual as not to be governed by the providence of God and so not happening necessarily and infallibly with respect to the divine decree.'[24]

By 'more contingent'[25] Turretin refers to an action whose performance depends upon the outcome of other contingent actions and so is doubly or multiply contingent. For example, the dilemma of Joseph's brothers as to what to do with him was intensified and ultimately solved by the sudden, unexpected appearing of the Ishmaelite caravan on its way to Egypt (Gen. 37.29). Turretin uses the phrases 'contingent and fortuitous' (*contingentia et fortuita*)[26] and 'fortuitous and casual' (*fortuita et casualia*)[27] to refer to an event that is unexpected and yet may have an explanation, such as the woodcutter's chopping of wood, which is a contingent act, but when the axe-head suddenly flies off, this is additionally 'fortuitous', the result of a natural necessity that is unanticipated.

It seems that in the case of free actions there are two factors for us to bear in mind. 'Man is always free in acting and many effects are contingent.'[28] Here the focus is not on the free action itself, but in its effects, the outcomes of the action. Not all effects, but many, including those that are unknown until the very need for a decision arises and the decision is made. Turretin's interest in the outcomes of a free action suggests the following question: if mere ignorance of the outcome of a future choice is contingency to some degree, maybe such an as yet undecided choice itself is contingent in this sense, for a person does not know the outcome of his own action until he has made up his mind to act in a certain way. And maybe this is the chief thing to note about those effects that are free, that many of them

23. The story of Joseph and his brothers seems to have been a favourite of Turretin's. References to it occur in six places in the *Institutes*: vol. 1, pp. 493, 499, 515, 522, 537; vol. 2, p. 538.

24. Turretin, *Institutes*, vol. 1, p. 499.

25. Ibid.

26. Ibid.

27. Ibid., p. 320.

28. Ibid., p. 512.

may be presently undecided and when the choice is made, it may be unanticipated by the agent, and may be surprising to him. 'With the indefinite and free, however, they also determine themselves by the proper judgment of reason and the free disposition of the will.'[29] It is interesting to compare Turretin's approach to that of his predecessor, John Calvin.

In his treatment of providence in his *Institutes* he has this to say:

> I say then, that though all things are ordered by the counsel and certain arrangement of God, to us, however they are fortuitous – not because we imagine that fortune rules the world and mankind, and turns all things upside down at random ... but as the order, method, end and necessity of events are, for the most part, hidden in the counsel of God, though it is certain that they are produced by the will of God, they have the appearance of being fortuitous, such being the form under which they present themselves to us, whether considered in their own nature, or estimated according to our knowledge and judgment. ... The same thing holds in the case of future contingencies. All future events being uncertain to us, seem in suspense as if ready to take either direction.[30]

The choice is open, there is no reason evident to the agent that prevents him from choosing A and not B. Which choice has God decreed? Calvin says that which in the event is chosen.

> Since providence does not concur with the human will, either by coaction (compelling the unwilling will) or by determining it physically (as a brute and blind thing without judgment), but rationally (by turning the will in a manner suitable to itself), that it may determine itself as the proximate cause of its own actions by the proper judgment of reason and the spontaneous election of the will so that it does no violence to our will but rather kindly cherisheth it. ... For whoever does spontaneously what he wills from a judgment of reason and a full consent of will cannot help doing that freely even if he does it necessarily (from whatever source that necessity flows, whether from the very existence of the thing [because whatever is, when it is, is necessarily] or from the object efficaciously moving the mind and the will or from a first cause decreeing and concurring).[31]

So it seems to me that if we note the scholastic distinction between primary and secondary causation, what should interest us is not the first but the second level of causation. With regard to the products of secondary causes, Turretin holds that

29. Ibid., p. 513.

30. John Calvin, *Institutes of the Christian Religion* (1559) (trans. William Beveridge; Peabody, MA: Hendrickson, 2008), I.16.9 (pp. 120–1). See also John Calvin, *Concerning the Eternal Predestination of God* (1552) (trans. J. K. S. Reid; London: James Clarke, 1961), pp. 170–1.

31. Turretin, *Institutes*, vol. 1, p. 513.

they are all contingent in that God could in his wisdom have decreed otherwise. 'All creatures are contingent with respect to God because he might not have created any if he had so willed.'[32] This is made clear from Turretin's remarks on hypothetical necessity and the working of the decree. In the case of secondary causes, some of them are contingent or involve contingencies; they are 'contingent and fortuitous', not expected and so not foreseen. Others, though their outcome is decreed, are contingent in that they are yet undecided by an agent; such actions when they are decided may give rise to unforeseen consequences, and so we might say (though as far as I can see, Turretin does not say) that they are doubly contingent.

Turretin on Necessity

So far we have looked at Turretin's treatment of contingency in various contexts, and noted that Turretin has a place for contingent choices, and unexpected and fortuitous events, calling each class 'contingent', without offering a principled distinction between these classes, perhaps because, as we have seen, they overlap.

There is one other way of getting at what Turretin means by contingency, and that is by considering his views on necessity, and forming an estimate of those senses of necessity that in his view are consistent with contingency, and those that are at odds with contingency. This comparison is not made with the endeavour of gaining an explanation of what Turretin means by human freedom, but to discern where contingency and freedom coincide in their application, and what this may show us. As I mentioned at the beginning, Turretin has more to say about kinds of necessity than he has about contingency. The Tenth Topic of his *Institutes* is entitled 'The Free Will of Man in a State of Sin'.[33] In it he distinguishes no less than six senses of necessity. Or rather he 'distributes' it in 'six heads', as a consequence of which these six senses arise.[34] These are as follows:

1. The necessity of action arising from an external agent. 'He who is compelled, contributing nothing' is necessary in this sense. In the case of someone who carries a wounded man to safety, the wounded man getting from A to B is necessitated by his being compelled.
2. The 'physical and brute necessity occurring in inanimates and brutes who act from a blind impulse of nature or a brute instinct and appetite ...' Here Turretin instances the act of burning, or of a horse eating straw or grass.
3. The necessity of the creature's dependence on God. This is the hypothetical necessity arising from God's infallible knowledge or eternal decree.

32. Ibid., p. 208.
33. Ibid., pp. 659–60.
34. Ibid., pp. 661–2.

4. Rational necessity – the determination of one thing by a judgement of the practical intellect.
5. Moral necessity or slavery arising from good or bad habits. 'Hence it happens that the will (free in itself) is so determined either to good or to evil that it cannot but act well or badly.'
6. The necessity of the existence of the thing or of the event, in virtue of which, when a thing is, it cannot but be. That is, necessarily, if a thing is sitting, it is sitting.

Of these six, Turretin holds that only two senses are incompatible with free action, namely (1) and (2). 'For the things done from a physical necessity by natural agents determined to one thing by nature and without reason, cannot be done freely i.e. with the previous light of reason, And the things done by force and compulsion cannot be done voluntarily.'[35] 'That which maintains a determination to one thing by a physical necessity or a necessity of coaction, takes away liberty and contingency.'[36] The former takes away free choice, the latter willingness.

The other four are consistent with free will.[37] So free will does not exclude dependence on God, nor rational necessity.[38]

Interesting though the question of the nature of free will is, our sole concern here is with necessity's modal opposite, contingency. To try to bracket the specific issue of free will from this discussion, I shall refer to one sort of contingency, the sort that brings uncertainty about what a person will do to an end, as *contingent choice*. Turretin implicitly makes this distinction by using the phrases 'contingent and free' and 'contingent and fortuitous'. Something that is contingent and free involves a contingent choice, which is one 'which can or not produce their effect and are thus distinguished from necessary causes.'[39] Something that is contingent (hypothetically necessary) and fortuitous may or may not have a contingent cause.

Is it possible to transpose these remarks about freedom into remarks about contingency? To attempt this, we must turn elsewhere than to this discussion of free will in the Tenth Topic. Where are we to go and what do we find? We find that the four senses of necessity that are consistent with free will must also be consistent with a sense of contingency that is a case of making up one's as yet unmade up mind, though Turretin does not say as much.

We have already seen that in Turretin's view, contingency is consistent with hypothetical necessity, the dependence of all things on the decree or the foreknowledge of God.[40] And also that, at first glance, paradoxically, rational necessity is consistent with contingent choice. For rational necessity is simply the

35. Ibid., p. 662.
36. Ibid., p. 321.
37. Ibid., p. 662.
38. Ibid., p. 663.
39. Ibid., p. 208.
40. Ibid., pp. 208–9.

working of the practical reason, and the choice that must follow this, a contingent choice of some kind.[41]

So what of the remaining two, the slavery of good or bad habits, and the necessity of tautologies expressed as inferences? The tautologies are easily dealt with. Being purely formal in character, being of the form N(If A, then A), they apply universally. 'Fourth, as to necessity of the event. For although whatever is, when it is, is necessarily (so that it can no more but be); still not the less freely or contingently is it said to be done as depending upon free or contingent causes. The certainty and truth of the existence of a thing cannot change its essence.'[42]

But the remaining case of the six, slavery of good or bad habits, may seem trickier. Necessities arising from such enslaved choices are consistent with contingent choice because a person may still be able to make the choice for bad thing A or bad thing B, or for good thing A or good thing B. 'Although the sinner is so enslaved by evil that he cannot but sin, still he does not cease to sin most freely and with the highest liberty.'[43] That is, slavery to sin is, nevertheless, consistent with the making of contingent choices.

What we may conclude from this brief survey is that wherever Turretin says there is freedom, there is contingency in the sense of an outcome of a decision that is unknown to the person deciding until he has made up his mind, a contingency of choice. But we cannot conclude that wherever there is contingency, there is human freedom, since 'contingency' can refer to an unforeseen, fortuitous consequence of a necessary event, such as the falling of the branch of a tree, or the sudden appearance of a meteor.

Jonathan Edwards on Contingency

Between Turretin and Jonathan Edwards there is a considerable change in the philosophical climate, the intervention of the philosophical influence of John Locke on Edwards, along with other philosophical influences on him, and his disenchantment with scholastic ways of doing things. This is despite the admiration he had for the scholastic theologians Petrus Van Maastricht and Francis Turretin, and despite the evidence that he did not himself entirely shake off the influence of scholasticism. Though he favoured a more unitary view of the self at the expense of the faculty psychology of the RO, he continued to talk about faculties. And volitions, acts of will, play an important part in his view of the self. So it is not true that Edwards totally repudiated scholasticism, but his style of argumentation was very different from theirs, more direct and 'up front'.[44]

41. Ibid., p. 663.

42. Ibid., p. 664.

43. Ibid., p. 663.

44. For an instance of Edwards's estimate of scholasticism, see *Freedom of the Will* (ed. Paul Ramsey; New Haven: Yale University Press, 1957), p. 424.

In Section 3 of Part I of his *Enquiry into the Modern Prevailing Notions of that Freedom of the Will which is supposed to be essential to Moral Agency, Vertue and Vice, Reward and Punishment, Praise and Blame* (1754), Edwards discusses and defines contingency as follows:

> Anything is said to be contingent, or to come to pass by chance or accident, in the original meaning of such words. When its connection with its causes or antecedents, according to the established course of things, is not discerned; and so is what we have no means of the foresight of. And especially is anything said to be contingent or accidental with regards to us, when anything comes to pass that we are concerned in, as occasions or subjects, without our foreknowledge, and beside our design or scope.[45]

The style follows that of the work in general, defining terms in everyday language, and eschewing the technical terminology of scholastically inclined theologians such as Turretin. In this he follows John Locke. Nevertheless, it is clear that Edwards thinks along Turretin's lines, in so far as he distinguishes between 'the established course of things', the occurrences of physical nature and so on (what Turretin calls physical necessity), and those matters that are contingent of accidental 'and especially is anything said to be contingent or accidental with regard to us, when anything comes to pass that we are concerned with, as occasion or subjects, without our foreknowledge, and beside our design and scope'.[46] So there is physical nature and there are those matters that are contingent 'with respect to us … as subjects'. So that if a person, as the subject, decides to do A and not B, and this is not a case that apart from the decision he has made, he already has foreknowledge of, the decision is a case of contingency. Edwards does not use the expression 'contingent choice' partly because, as part of his dismantling of scholastic concepts, he rarely, if ever, talks of secondary causes or of God as the 'primary cause'.

Edwards on Necessity

As we have seen, according to Turretin, different kinds of events, necessary and contingent, are governed by God's decree, which embraces all things and at the same time consistently preserves the way in which they behave.[47] His decree renders its objects hypothetically necessary, necessary on the hypothesis of the decree, rooted in his conception of divine freedom. For example, some are rationally necessary, some are morally necessary, some are necessary because they are coerced or the outcome of brute instinct, some are contingent. In decreeing certain outcomes, God preserves the natures of the various sorts of things He has created.

45. Edwards, *Freedom of the Will*, p. 155.
46. Ibid.
47. Ibid., p. 257.

This is what Edwards says about necessity:

> Philosophical necessity is really nothing else than the full and fixed connection between the things signified by the subject and predicate of a proposition, which affirms something to be true. When there is such a connection, then the thing affirmed in the proposition is necessary, in a philosophical sense. ... When the subject and predicate of the proposition, which affirms the existence of anything, either substance, quality, act or circumstance, have a full and certain connection, then the existence or being of that thing is said to be necessary in a metaphysical sense. And in this sense I use the word 'necessity,' in the following discourse, when I endeavor to prove that necessity is not inconsistent with liberty.[48]

The divine decreeing secures cases of such connectedness. And, in parallel with Turretin, according to Edwards there are different ways in which subject and predicate can have such a full and perfect connection. They may be connected in and of themselves. To deny this would be 'the sum of all contradictions'. Similarly God's infinity is necessary, and that two and two should be four.[49] Second, if an event is past, and is now 'fixed and decided', 'tis become impossible that it should be otherwise than true, that such a thing has been'.[50] Like Turretin, Edwards distinguishes between events that take place through constraint and coaction and through unconstrained or uncoerced volitions, and actions that are physically necessary.[51]

Yet, there is a radical difference between the two of them on the question of the necessity of the decree. This is brought out in their respective attitudes to the scholastic distinction between the necessity of the consequence and the necessity of the consequent.

The distinction can be expressed in the following way:

a. Whatever state of affairs is decreed by God, it is true that the state of affairs must be.

This is a *de re* proposition, since necessity is ascribed to a thing, a *res*.
Now contrast (a) with

b. The proposition 'whatever God decrees is the case' is necessarily true.

For Turretin, (b) is the way to understand the divine decrees, for according to him the decree imparts a hypothetical necessity, the necessity of the consequence.

---

48. Ibid., p. 152.

49. Ibid., p. 153.

50. Ibid. Such necessity is of special interest to Edwards because it secures the necessity of what God foreknew, or eternally knew. See *Freedom of the Will*, Part II, Section 12, pp. 264–5.

51. Edwards, *Freedom of the Will*, p. 269.

Many, such as Francis Turretin and Anthony Kenny,[52] think that the distinction is well drawn, and is of general application. But Edwards demurs. This is because he thinks not only that it is necessary that God decrees, but that it is necessary that God foreknows what He foreknows. And if everything that exists does so necessarily, then whatever God knows is the case is necessarily true, though not because God's knowing causes it to be true. So, rather confusingly perhaps, Edwards uses the expression 'Necessity of connection and consequence'.[53]

In a system that is necessitarian in Edwards's sense,[54] in which both the decree itself and what is decreed are necessary, there is no use for the distinction between the necessity of the consequence, or *de re* necessity, and the necessity of the consequent, or *de dicto* necessity. Or rather, this is a distinction without a difference. And so there is no use for Turretin's hypothetical necessity.[55]

So it seems that a significant difference between the RO, as represented by Turretin, and Edwards, insofar as there is a difference, lies not at the secondary level. Turretin affirms, but Edwards denies, that God has an alternative with what he may decree. For Edwards, there is no divine freedom in the sense that there is an alternative state of affairs that God could have had a good reason for choosing.[56] So there is no hypothetical necessity, no events that are necessary *only* in virtue of the divine decree. This is certainly an important difference from the RO such as Turretin, who has an important place for hypothetical necessity. What Edwards calls 'the necessity of consequence' is the connection between necessary *things*,

52. Anthony Kenny, 'Divine Foreknowledge and Human Freedom', in Anthony Kenny (ed.), *Aquinas: A Collection of Critical Essays* (London: Macmillan, 1969), pp. 255–70.

53. Edwards, *Freedom of the Will*, p. 262. It may be that this scheme is what Arthur Prior referred to as Edwards's '"metaphysical *logic*" with which we may still grapple profitably'. A. N. Prior, *Papers on Time and Tense* (Oxford: Clarendon Press, 1968), p. 59.

54. Edwards is not alone. Martin Luther, as a consequence of holding that 'it is fundamentally necessary and wholesome for Christians to know that God foreknows nothing contingently, but that he foresees, purposes and does all things according to His own immutable, eternal and infallible will', holds that the distinction between the necessity of the consequent and the necessity of the consequence is an 'absurd formula'. Martin Luther, *The Bondage of the Will* (1525) (trans. J. I. Packer and O. R. Johnston; London: James Clarke, 1957), pp. 80–3.

55. This suggests that one reason why Edwards turned away from scholastic theology was the view that its terms of art obscure rather than clarify what for him were the clear lines of Christian metaphysics, lines that could be expounded using terms derived from how we ordinarily speak rather than terms of art devised in the ivory tower. Hence the attraction to him of Locke's philosophy.

56. For Edwards's discussion of the nature of divine action, see *Freedom of the Will*, Part IV, S.1, 'God's Moral Excellency Necessary, yet Virtuous and Praiseworthy'; S.7, 'Concerning the Necessity of the Divine Will'; and S.8, 'Some Further Objections against the Moral Necessity of God's Volitions, Considered'.

and their consequences, not decrees and their logical consequences.[57] He has no place for a necessity that arises merely on the hypothesis of God's alternate decree or of God's foreknowledge.

Each holds that the divine decree covers necessary and contingent occurrences. An example of the first is the movement of the heavenly bodies; of the second, Joseph's treatment at the hands of his brothers. Joseph's brothers did not know what would happen until they had made a decision to sell him to the Ishmaelites, and similarly as with every subject of human indecision, until it is resolved by a choice. And each asserts that as a consequence of something being contingent in this sense, in the sense of awaiting our decision, what the RO referred to as a 'judgment', the agents cannot have foreknowledge or foresight of what they will decide, they can know only when the decision has been irrevocably made.

This indicates that Edwards most certainly had a different doctrine of God from the RO, but it is not clear that such a difference, important though it is for making an overall estimate of the degree to which Edwards modified the theology of his RO and Puritan forbears, necessarily affects his view of what the RO referred to as human contingency.

It may be thought that the recognition of this distinction indicates the recognition by the users of the distinction of the presence of acts of the liberty of contingency/indifference, and its denial, the ruling out of such acts. But this would be a mistake. Edwards indicates by the absence of the use of this distinction, and his use of the 'necessity of the consequence' in a different sense, that he is committed to the denial of divine contingent choice. It is from Edwards's denial of *divine freedom* in this sense that the distinction means that the consequence – consequent distinction has no application in his theology.

What has been Attempted and What Left Untouched

We have been examining the views of Francis Turretin and Jonathan Edwards on contingency and necessity, and have seen that the most salient differences between them is over the doctrine of God, over the nature of divine freedom. As far as their anthropology is concerned, the crucial term for the question of what contingency has to do with free will is that, for Turretin, a 'contingent cause' is correlated with freedom, as it is in Edwards. Whether this leads to a difference in their views of free will is here left uninvestigated, as is whether for Turretin an action is free in virtue of it being a contingent cause of a further kind, such as possessing indifference in another question. There is a good deal of circumstantial evidence in the case of Turretin that a contingent cause includes a conditional cause, of the necessary consequence of the 'last judgment' of the practical intellect, hence a case of what he calls rational necessity. The matter is not easy to adjudicate because when Turretin discusses free will at length, in the Tenth Topic of the *Institutes*,[58] the terminology

---

57. Edwards, *Freedom of the Will*, p. 155, See also pp. 257, 270.
58. Turretin, *Institutes*, vol. 1, p. 639.

is that of indifference, rational necessity and rational spontaneity. Contingency is strangely absent. But to open up this question here would be to go beyond what I have tried to show are Turretin's and Edwards's views about contingency and necessity.

Bibliography

Asselt, Willem J. van, J. Martin Bac, and Roelf T. te Velde (eds), *Reformed Thought on Freedom: The Concept of Free Choice in Early Modern Reformed Theology* (Grand Rapids, MI: Baker, 2010).

Calvin, John, *Concerning the Eternal Predestination of God* (trans. J. K. S. Reid; London: James Clarke, 1961).

Calvin, John, *Institutes of the Christian Religion* (trans. William Beveridge; Peabody, MA: Hendrickson, 2008).

Edwards, Jonathan, *Freedom of the Will* (ed. Paul Ramsey; New Haven: Yale University Press, 1957).

Freddoso, Alfred J., 'Introduction', in Luis de Molina (ed.), *On Divine Foreknowledge: Pt. IV of the Concordia* (trans. Alfred J. Freddoso; Ithaca: Cornell University Press, 1988).

Helm, Paul, 'Jonathan Edwards and the Parting of the Ways?', *Journal of Jonathan Edwards Studies* 4/1 (2014), pp. 42–60.

Helm, Paul, '*Reformed Thought on Freedom*: Some Further Thoughts', *Journal of Reformed Theology* 4 (2010), pp. 185–207.

Helm, Paul, '"Structural Indifference" and Compatibilism in Reformed Orthodoxy', *Journal of Reformed Theology* 5 (2011), pp. 184–205.

Kenny, Anthony, 'Divine Foreknowledge and Human Freedom', in Anthony Kenny (ed.), *Aquinas: A Collection of Critical Essays* (London: Macmillan, 1969), pp. 255–70.

Luther, Martin, *The Bondage of the Will* (trans. J. I. Packer and O. R. Johnston; London: James Clarke, 1957).

Muller, Richard A., 'Jonathan Edwards and the Absence of Free Choice: A Parting of Ways in the Reformed Tradition', *Journal of Jonathan Edwards Studies* 1/1 (2011), pp. 3–22.

Prior, A. N., *Papers on Time and Tense* (Oxford: Clarendon Press, 1968).

Turretin, Francis, *Institutes of Elenctic Theology* (ed. James T. Dennison; trans. G. M. Giger; 3 vols; Phillipsburg, NJ: P & R Publishing, 1992–7).

Chapter 12

'PSEUDO-MACARIUS', FLETCHER-AND-WESLEY, AND LUKE ON PENTECOST

Max Turner

In an uninformed moment, writing for a Grove booklet published as *Baptism in the Holy Spirit*, I incorrectly stated that we could probably trace that *noun* phrase and concept to John Fletcher, John Wesley's designated successor.[1] Luke-Acts takes up the promise that the messiah will 'baptize you in Holy Spirit and fire' (Lk. 3.16 and //s) and slightly reinterprets it in Acts 1.5. But Luke does not use the noun phrase '*baptism* in Holy Spirit' (nor does any other NT writer), which might suggest a distinct, even initiatory experience, rather than a part or the whole of an ongoing broad Isaianic new-exodus process I consider Luke addresses. So I suspect a disjunctive move between the more verbal hope that John the Baptist expressed (and which I think Luke took up) that the messiah would 'baptize in the Holy Spirit' and the later more concrete usage in the noun phrase 'baptism in the Holy Spirit'.[2] Fletcher, with Wesley's strong approval, made such a move, and it motivated the whole search for an experience of a higher empowerment that dynamically affected the enormous American summer camp movements seeking such an experience, and eventually leading to Pentecostal versions of that search.[3]

But where did they get the idea that there was such a distinct post-conversion 'baptism in the Spirit'? The simplest answer is that Fletcher and Wesley took it, or at least developed it, from a fourth-century writing known as Pseudo-Macarius. The evidence for that influence is clear, as Laurence Wood's careful study of early Methodism demonstrates.[4]

---

1. In Max Turner, *Baptism in the Holy Spirit* (Cambridge: Grove Books, 2000), p. 4.

2. For the argument in outline, see, ibid., pp. 7–19; and for some consideration of the ambiguities of the phrase 'baptism in Holy Spirit', see pp. 18–19.

3. See Donald W. Dayton, *Theological Roots of Pentecostalism* (Peabody: Hendrickson, 1987), chs 2–4, for a brief overview.

4. Laurence W. Wood, *The Meaning of Pentecost in Early Methodism: Rediscovering John Fletcher as John Wesley's Vindicator and Designated Successor* (Lanham: Scarecrow Press, 2002), esp. pp. 24, 68, 131–2 and 346–51.

This chapter will first briefly introduce 'pseudo-Macarius' on the subject; second, reflect on Fletcher-and-Wesley's development of the Pentecost gift; and then, third, offer what a Lucan scholar might reasonably make of it all.

Part 1 'Pseudo-Macarius' and Its Contribution

We do not know with assurance who wrote the *Fifty Homilies* attributed to St Macarius of Egypt, other than it was most probably *not* that figure.[5] The *Fifty Homilies* were written by an anonymous figure who wrote in fine Syrian Greek and from that culture (*not* Egypt's), in the same period, the latter half of the fourth century. He, too, was a charismatic desert ascetic monk and spiritual advisor, and one apparently in contact with the Cappadocian Fathers, especially Gregory of Nyssa.[6] I will refer henceforth to the writer simply as Macarius (dropping the slightly misleading and prejudicial qualifier 'pseudo-'), as the homilies make no *pseudonymous* pretence to Macarian identity or claims, and/but we have no other name as candidate, except, just perhaps, Symeon of Mesopotamia.[7]

The *Fifty Homilies* are just one of several textual collections of homilies attributed to Macarius, but they are the most generally accepted,[8] and, significantly for our purposes, the collection known, and popularized by, Wesley. They are essentially multiform guidance for what their author regards as full and authentic spiritual life.

Macarius is probably the first person to make a noun phrase out of John the Baptist's verbal promise, *and to use it in a significant new way*. We see this move at the linguistic level most concretely in Homily 47.1, where he states, 'With them was a baptism sanctifying the flesh, but with us there is *a baptism* of the Holy Spirit and fire. For John preached this: "He shall baptize you in the Holy Spirit and fire" (Mt. 3:11)'.[9] That merely linguistic point could be considered trivial, but on inspection it quickly proves not to be so. Macarius clearly taught that such baptism was a second *quite distinct* post-baptismal experience that transformed the believer from agonistic struggle with sin to Christian 'perfection' (read 'full maturity'). For Macarius, it is a fiery baptism of the love of God (and of neighbour) that leads to

---

5. That saintly priest, lived in Egypt, was a hermit monk in the Scetis desert, and was known for his charismatic deeds and gifted counsel. He died in 391 AD and wrote little.

6. For all questions of Introduction, and secondary literature, the most accessible competent guide is George A. Maloney (ed. and trans.), *Pseudo-Macarius: The Fifty Spiritual Homilies and the Great Letter* (New York: Paulist Press, 1992). It is his sensitive translation that will be used, in what follows.

7. Maloney, *Pseudo-Macarius*, pp. 7–10. Macarius is the Latin form of the Greek *Makarios*, which simply meant Bléssed, and was understandably a common enough name in Christian circles.

8. For the complicated textual tradition, see ibid., pp. 4–6.

9. Ibid., p. 232. But he elsewhere uses the same language: cf. pp. 172, 220, 233, etc.

such fellowship with the Spirit that makes authentic life ('divinisation') a delight, potentially, and considerably, free from sin, and abounding in transfiguring grace and light: this is what it *means* to be fully born again as children of God (1 Jn 3.9).[10] And that is *not* a minor point, or aside, in the *Homilies*: it is a major thrust. In that respect, he is not merely a forerunner of Wesley and Fletcher: Maloney is right that 'Macarius is one of the first witnesses of what modern Christians would call "Baptism in the Holy Spirit"', uplifting, often rhapsodic, but, in his case, never truly triumphalist.[11] For Macarius, it was a state to be constantly renewed by self-surrendering prayer rather than a one-off event.[12]

The *Homilies* are remarkable for their analysis of the thoroughly *experiential* interior life of the Spirit. For Macarius (as for the NT),[13] the action of the Spirit was often 'immediately' perceived (not merely deduced by arguments): the Spirit brought a profoundly felt, warm, affective life. Macarius sets all this in a Semitic, essentially monistic, understanding of the relation of human anthropology to this creation, and to the eschaton, and reflects Pauline understanding of the relation of the Spirit to this body and that of the resurrection.[14] But he also knows the fight of flesh and Spirit in Romans 7–8 and Galatians 5–6. In a fourth-century period, when interest in the Spirit had tended to become eclipsed by a focus on Christology, the *Homilies* were a stark recall to the importance of the Spirit in the *life of the heart before, in, and with, God*. It could be argued that the Macarian homilies are among the best (most heart-warming, challenging and deeply reflective) post-canonical writings on the Spirit before the age of the Puritans. Alluding to Wesley's diary entry for 30 July 1736 ('I read Macarius and sang'), Kallistos Ware, from a rather different

---

10. 'When your soul has fellowship with the Spirit and the heavenly soul enters into your soul, then you are a perfect man in God and an heir and son' (Homily 32.6; ibid., p. 199). Cf. 'For the soul that is deemed to be judged worthy to participate in the light of the Holy Spirit by becoming his throne and habitation, and is covered with the beauty of ineffable glory of the Spirit, becomes all light, all face, all eye. There is no part of the soul that is not full of the spiritual eyes of light' (Homily 1.2; *Pseudo-Macarius*, p. 36).

11. Ibid., p. 19. Cf. most uncompromisingly, Homily 8.5: 'I have not yet seen any perfect Christian or one perfectly free'.

12. Ibid.

13. On the nature of the NT *experience* of the Spirit, see *inter alia*, J. D. G. Dunn, *Jesus and the Spirit: A Study of the Religious and Charismatic Experience of Jesus and the First Christians as Reflected in the New Testament* (London: SCM, 1975); Max Turner, *The Holy Spirit and Spiritual Gifts: Then and Now* (Carlisle: Paternoster, rev. edn, 1999), and for more recent studies, see in idem, 'Spiritual Gifts and Spiritual Formation in 1 Corinthians and Ephesians', *JPT* 22 (2013), pp. 187–205.

14. Macarius speaks frequently of the resurrection as our true hope and glorious light. In Homily 5.7 he makes a direct appeal to Romans 8.11 and 2 Corinthians 4–5; and in Homily 47.15 he comes close to 1 Corinthians 15.45 when he speaks of it as a becoming spirit enfleshed. See also Homilies 30–33, 47.15, and Maloney, *Pseudo-Macarius*, p. 26.

Christian spirituality, concludes his preface to Maloney's *Pseudo-Macarius* with the words, 'Like Wesley, let us also read Macarius and sing.'[15] I do not dissent.

That, of course, raises an obvious question: why was this spiritually challenging and discerning early set of writings ignored (in the West)?[16] The answer seems twofold: First, at point of origin, the writings were deemed too close to the Messalanian 'heresy' (read 'excessive interest in charismata, rather than focus on the transforming love of God').[17] Second, written in Greek, they circulated in the east and only late came to the Roman west. But, even before Wesley, they came to be revered in Protestant pietistic circles, beginning with Johann Arndt (1555–1621), and Wesley probably first came across the works in Thomas Haywood's 1721 translation into English.[18] This observation leads us to Fletcher and Wesley.

Part 2 Fletcher and Wesley on Baptism in the Spirit

Anthony Thiselton's usually authoritative *The Holy Spirit* gives a disappointingly bland and rather misleading portrait. For him, any interest Wesley had in 'baptism in the Spirit', and 'perfectionism', was marginal and inconsequential to Methodism.[19] Had he read Wood's *The Meaning of Pentecost in Early Methodism*, I suspect Thiselton would have written rather differently. Wood's monograph is an exemplary piece of senior research and is based on a much wider range of Fletcher's and Wesley's writings than Thiselton was able to consider,[20] including copious correspondence to and from Fletcher, in the oft-ignored later period of Wesley's ministry (1770–91). The evidence is that Fletcher developed a comprehensive doctrine of 'baptism in the Holy Spirit' (or Pentecost gift of the Spirit, or fullness of the Spirit); that he did so in continuous dialogue with Wesley; that they both thought it cardinal, not marginal; and that this legacy was hushed by later Methodist historians who did not favour the teaching. That, at least, is the provocative (but to my mind convincing) case Wood makes.[21]

15. Maloney, *Pseudo-Macarius*, p. xvii.

16. More surprising still is the apparent lack of awareness by Pentecostals, who are not unknown for their trawling of historical writing to find pre-Pentecostal allies!

17. Ibid., pp. 8–9 on Macarius and this controversy.

18. For the history of influence, see ibid., pp. 20–4.

19. Anthony C. Thiselton, *The Holy Spirit – In Biblical Teaching Through the Centuries and Today* (London: SPCK, 2013), pp. 282–6.

20. Thiselton relies largely on Wesley's edited *Sermons* and his *Journal*, and significantly his 1736 Sermon 141 ('On the Holy Spirit'). That is very early Wesley (coincidentally, the very year he later 'sang', on reading pseudo-Macarius), preceding his watershed Aldersgate Street experience (1738), and long before his major association with Fletcher from 1770 onwards.

21. I am grateful to Larry Wood, not merely for the gift of his monograph, but for his hospitality and long enjoyable conversations, when I was Scholar in Residence at Asbury Theological Seminary, in the first Semester of 2002–03.

While Fletcher and Wesley earlier had some misunderstandings, these were resolved, and Wesley visited the vicar of Madeley on 26–29 July 1771. Thereafter their strong and affectionate relationship was cemented and constantly renewed until Fletcher's untimely death in 1785. Wesley saw Fletcher as the very best, most systematic, theological expositor of his thought, and by January 1773 had written to him entreating him to become his right-hand man, and designated *sole* successor, and so to carry the Methodist movement forward. Wesley edited and published Fletcher's work in partnership with him, and he began a biography of Fletcher in 1786, very soon after the latter's death.[22]

They were both vitally concerned with a form of Christian life that was not merely nominal, but vibrantly experiential,[23] and, like Macarius, they crystallized that in terms of a concept of Christian 'maturity/perfection', understood as a quite separate 'degree' of spiritual life, dependent on a 'receiving of the Spirit'.

Wesley used the metaphor of 'babes', 'young men' and 'fathers' (drawn largely from 1 Jn 2.12–14) to make the distinctions he was seeking to elucidate. In terms of experience of the Spirit, he considered converts (and nominal Christians) to be 'babes' who have 'some' experience of the 'Spirit of adoption', while 'young men' were those *progressing* in spiritual life, encountering, and often prevailing in, the agonistic struggle of flesh-and-Spirit, but the desirable state was full maturity/ Christian perfection of 'entire sanctification' encountered by the 'fathers' in a distinct 'giving/reception' of the Spirit.

Fletcher preferred the model of 'dispensations', which he did not take simply as hard and fast epochs, but as adumbrating stages of development. Accordingly, God's people *even after* Pentecost, might live (1) with minimal experience of the Spirit, like (OT) pious Jews, or (2) like believers in the period of John the Baptist and Jesus, or (3) like those truly belonging in the post-Pentecost epoch of the Spirit. Fletcher, predictably, preferred the language of 'baptism in the Holy Spirit' to mark entry into stage (3), based on Macarius, whom he had clearly read, and to whom he actually appeals.[24] Fletcher regularly uses *this* term to mark the all-important transition to Wesley's 'entire sanctification'/'Christian perfection'. After all, the former was the language of Acts 1.5–8 looking forward to the Pentecost

---

22. For detail, see Wood, *Pentecost*, esp. chs 3–6.

23. Wesley argued, 'It cannot be … that a man should be filled with this peace and joy and love by the inspiration of the Holy Spirit without perceiving it as clearly as he does the light of the sun. … And I will still believe none is a true Christian till he experiences it.' See Wood, ibid., p. 123 for the full quote and reference.

24. It is a tribute to the influence of Macarius on both Wesley and Fletcher, that Wesley made his own translation and abridgement of the *Homilies*, and gave them prominence at the opening of his *Christian Library*. It is from this that Fletcher makes his appeal that 'if Macarius … so clear[ly] preached the baptism and dispensation of the Holy Spirit' then Wesley and he could not be charged with novelty: see ibid., p. 68, cf. pp. 24, 67–8, 73, and esp. 131–2 (for Fletcher's appeal to Macarius's Homilies 8 and 15, as he read them in Wesley's *Christian Library*).

event. Wesley himself only used the term 'baptism in Holy Spirit' twice in his published works, preferring instead a variety of synonyms such as: 'the gift of the Spirit', 'the love of God poured out in the heart', 'filled with the Spirit', 'sealed with the Spirit', 'the kingdom within' and others.[25] But their differing language does not mark anything much more than literary-aesthetic choices. Both argued the view that while all believers experienced a degree of the Spirit's activity, many (most?) remained as 'babes' or 'carnal' Christians, or even 'half-' or 'almost' Christians. While most Methodist preachers equated being 'born of water and the Spirit' (Jn 3.5) with Reformation 'salvation/justification by faith', Wesley and Fletcher often equated 'salvation by faith' with 'full salvation' (read 'perfection'/'entire sanctification'),[26] and distinguished baptism of water quite sharply from baptism with Holy Spirit. While Wesley prevaricated somewhat when he referred to some believers as 'partly born' and others as those who were 'fully born of the Spirit',[27] Fletcher reserved language of 'new birth' or 'born of the Spirit' for reception of the Pentecost outpouring of the Spirit, and so equates the former expressions with being baptized with Holy Spirit and entirely sanctified in love, while trying all along to show (with a degree of plausibility) that this is what Wesley really meant.[28]

We need to be absolutely clear: Fletcher and Wesley were almost entirely at one. Fletcher was writing and Wesley was lovingly editing almost every line he wrote. They were strongly united in their belief that a cardinal 'immediate' experience of Spirit-baptism was the key to real, authentic, Christian life: a life so drenched with the love of God that it was 'abundant' to others, and largely without known sin – 'entire sanctification' and 'Christian perfection' as one.

Fletcher and Wesley both used Luke-Acts to ground, or at least promote, their view. They both found in Acts 2, 8, 9 and 19 specific evidence for the concept that 'the gift of the Spirit' was consequent to initial saving belief,[29] and that this could regularly be granted through the post-baptismal laying on of hands, while not necessarily being dependent on that rite. Dr Wood has given us a comprehensive and penetrating analysis of Fletcher and Wesley on their interpretation of Pentecost, and has ventured, in nuanced fashion, an important argument therefrom that we should reconsider a rite of Confirmation to embody and impart that second empowering gift of higher authentic life.[30]

But would Luke support such a project? Was it his view that 'Spirit-baptism' (though he did not use that term) might accomplish such an end?

---

25. For the range, and references, see ibid., p. 121 and notes.
26. Wood, ibid., pp. 9, 88; Dayton, *Roots*, pp. 44–8.
27. Wood, *Pentecost*, p. 128.
28. Ibid., pp. 127–32.
29. Ibid., pp. 88–9.
30. Ibid., chs 15 and 16.

Part 3 Being Baptized in the Spirit in Luke:
Was it about Sanctifying Empowering?

We shall first look at how Pentecostal scholars have shifted somewhat from their Wesleyan heritage,[31] and taken 'Baptism in the Spirit' in a different direction (§1), then (§2) examine the issues at stake between Pentecostal scholars and those Lucanists who see a stronger relationship between the Spirit and transformation in Luke-Acts.

§1 Pentecostal Reinterpretation of 'Baptism in Holy Spirit'

In facing the question, 'Was baptism with Holy Spirit about sanctifying empowering?', ironically some of the strongest demurrals come from Pentecostal churches; but they have come from two quite different interpretative strategies.

The *first* Pentecostal interpretative set of moves, embraced probably by the majority of Pentecostal teachers, provides a synthesis of Pauline and Lucan teaching. According to that merging of horizons, all believers after Jesus's ascension receive what Paul calls the 'Spirit of Christ' (Rom. 8.9-11) at conversion, experienced richly as the regenerating, transforming and sanctifying eschatological power of the Spirit enabling fruitful communion with the risen Lord, and new-covenant 'life' (in contrast to the 'death' of living under the Law/Flesh; Gal. 5-6; 2 Cor. 3; Rom. 6-8, etc.). And all this is simply *assumed* by Luke without specific mention. It perhaps corresponds to the paschal gift of the Spirit in John 20.22 (though Luke shows no sign of knowing of such). By contrast, the 'baptism in the Holy Spirit', and what Luke means by 'receiving/being filled with' the Spirit, or the Spirit 'poured out' on disciples, is a *theologically separate* gift and usually *subsequent* to conversion (so, allegedly, Acts 2, 8, 9 and 19). This more characteristically Lucan 'coming of the Spirit' on people is purely profoundly charismatic empowering of revelation, wisdom, different types of inspired speech and miraculous powers, *all primarily to enable the proclamation of the gospel to outsiders.* A 'two-stage pneumatology' of Luke-Acts of this kind is defended by such scholars as H. D. Hunter, H. M. Ervin, J. R. Williams and F. L. Arrington.[32] Fletcher and Wesley would have agreed in principle on a synthesis of Lucan and Pauline theology, if not with the account of Luke's view.

---

31. For the gradual shifts, see Dayton, *Roots*, pp. 48-113.

32. H. D. Hunter, *Spirit-Baptism: A Pentecostal Alternative* (Lanham: University Press of America, 1983); H. M. Ervin, *Spirit-Baptism: A Biblical Investigation* (Peabody: Hendrickson, 1987); J. R. Williams, *Renewal Theology* (3 vols; Grand Rapids: Zondervan, 1990), esp. vol. 2; F. L. Arrington, *The Acts of the Apostles* (Peabody: Hendrickson, 1988). Arrington's view is clearest in his discussion of Acts 19.1-6, where he states 'the disciples at Ephesus were believers in Christ and were indwelt by the Holy Spirit, but they had not received the fullness of the Spirit. Paul asked them not about the regenerating work of the

A *second* line of interpretation, adopted by the great majority of those Pentecostals who are *Lucan* specialists, including R. Stronstad, J. Shelton, R. P. Menzies, J. M. Penney and Y. Cho,[33] insists that Luke only knows *one* gift of the Spirit, not two. Luke did *not* know (or perhaps did not *understand*, or did not *accept*?) Paul's soteriological 'Spirit of Christ', which was the apostle's own distinct new contribution. For these scholars, Luke only knew the older Jewish understanding of the Spirit as the 'Spirit of prophecy' promised in Joel 2, with which the ascended Lord 'baptized' the disciples at Pentecost, almost exclusively as an empowering for the prophetic mission to preach the good news, and so 'separable' and 'subsequent' to conversional reception of 'salvation'.[34]

I have to agree with the Lucan Pentecostal scholars that the 'two-stage pneumatology' of those from Hunter to Arrington is simply an argument from silence. Luke only knows of *one* 'reception' of the Spirit by believers (Acts 2.39; 10.47; 11.15; 15.8), and, in the case of Jesus's disciples, this is at least co-referential with being 'baptized with the Spirit' (1.5), 'filled with the Spirit' (2.4), and Joel's promised gift of the Spirit of prophecy being 'poured out' on them (2.17, 18, 33) and 'falling upon them' (11.15). The same collection of phrases ('fall upon' [10.44], 'poured out on' [10.45]') is equated with Cornelius's household's 'reception' of the gift of the Spirit (10.47) and their being 'baptized' with Holy Spirit (11.16), and 'given' the 'Spirit' (15.8). The Samaritan incident is particularly significant:

> It equates the Spirit's 'falling upon' the Samaritans (8.16) with their 'receiving' or 'being given' the Spirit (8.15, 17, 18, 19). … Luke's editorial explanation in 8.16 virtually precludes the view that he thinks the Samaritans have already earlier

Spirit that is realized at the time of belief but about their post-belief reception of the Spirit', which Arrington then describes as charismatic endowment equipping the disciples to proclaim the gospel (*Acts*, p. 193). My friend and colleague William Atkinson has brought a subtle defence of something like this position, attempting to hoist me with my own petard. Space does not allow the full reply his case deserves: see William P. Atkinson, *Baptism in the Spirit: Luke-Acts and the Dunn Debate* (Eugene: Pickwick, 2011).

33. R. Stronstad, *The Charismatic Theology of Saint Luke* (Peabody: Hendrickson, 1984); idem, *The Prophethood of All Believers: A Study in Luke's Charismatic Theology* (Sheffield: SAP, 1999); James B. Shelton, *Mighty in Word and Deed: The Role of the Holy Spirit in Luke-Acts* (Peabody: Hendrickson, 1991); Robert P. Menzies, *The Development of Early Christian Pneumatology With Special Reference to Luke-Acts* (Sheffield: SAP, 1991); idem, *Empowered for Witness: The Spirit in Luke-Acts* (Sheffield: SAP, 1994); John Michael Penney, *The Missionary Emphasis of Lukan Pneumatology* (Sheffield: SAP, 1997); and Youngmo Cho, *Spirit and Kingdom in the Writings of Luke and Paul* (Milton Keynes: Paternoster, 2005). Of these, Shelton's work does allow for at least some soteriological significance of reception of the Spirit: see *Power*, p. 70.

34. For a more detailed discussion of the 'two-' and 'one-stage' Pentecostal views, see my 'Interpreting the Samaritans of Acts 8: The Waterloo of Pentecostal Soteriology and Pneumatology?', *PNEUMA* 23/2 (2001), pp. 265–86, esp. pp. 266–8.

received a gift of the Spirit which brought salvation and life. In 8.15 we read that Peter and John prayed for the Samaritans 'that they might *receive* the Spirit' and in 8.16 he explains 'for the Spirit had not yet fallen upon any of them, but they had only been baptised in the name of the Lord Jesus'. Then in 8.17 he goes back to the language of receiving the Spirit. He tells us that when the apostles laid hands on them, the Samaritans '*received* the Holy Spirit'.[35]

Luke thus appears to know of only one giving of the Spirit to any disciple. But this raises an urgent question (or set of questions): If the Spirit is simply the 'Spirit of prophecy' given exclusively as a charismatic *donum superadditum* (read 'second blessing', i.e. one logically subsequent to the gift of 'the life of salvation') to guide and empower Christian mission, *then by precisely what divine power and presence does God bring to the believer the primary gift of inner cleansing of heart, new covenant life, ethical transformation, and growth and depth in saving fellowship with God and with the people of God?* Or, to put it in terms first raised by Schweizer, if 'Luke adopts the typically Jewish idea that the Spirit is the Spirit of Prophecy', and if this 'prevents him from attributing to πνεῦμα [Spirit] ... strongly ethical effects like the common life of the primitive community', and if he consequently does not attribute salvation to the Spirit (rather the Spirit is given to those already converted and baptised), then *by precisely what other power or agent of the Lord are salvation and the vibrant life of the community achieved?*[36] Fletcher and Wesley might turn in their graves at tidings of such a dismissal of their cherished understanding of baptism with Holy Spirit.

In contrast to these Pentecostal readings, Dunn and I, in line with most Lucan scholars, argue that Luke knows of only one gift of the Spirit, but this for him is no mere 'second blessing': Luke's very *concept* of 'salvation' (we argue) consisted in the dynamic *experience* of God's transforming and empowering reign (read 'kingdom of God'). I argue additionally that it is precisely the Spirit *as 'the Spirit of prophecy'*, that is central to both these aspects of salvation in Luke-Acts,[37] and that the same is true, with different language and emphases, in Paul and John.[38] For the three, the Spirit poured out from the Father, by the ascended Lord, comes to us as what Paul calls the 'Spirit of Christ' (Rom. 8.9; cf. Gal. 4.6, Phil. 1.19), and the comparable 'Spirit of Jesus' of Acts 16.7. So what some of us call 'the Spirit of prophecy' is more importantly the proto-trinitarian self-revealing, joy granting, *presence* of the Father-and-Son (to put it in slightly more Johannine language), *which alone maintains the central and transforming communion with Christ*, and life 'in Christ', which enables the ascended Jesus to continue the work he began

---

35. Turner, 'Interpreting the Samaritans', p. 267.

36. For Schweizer's quotations here, and their complicated relationship to *TWNT*, vol. 6, p. 407, and the well-known mistranslation in *TDNT*, vol. 6, p. 409, see my *Power from on High: The Spirit in Israel's Restoration and Witness in Luke-Acts* (Sheffield: SAP, 1996), pp. 60, 59–62, and the rest of the chapter for the place and influence of Schweizer's contribution.

37. The major emphasis of my *Power from on High*.

38. The main thesis of my *Holy Spirit and Spiritual Gifts* (henceforth *HSSG*).

to do (so Acts 1.1) through his disciples.[39] And that 'continuation', I have argued, involves an *intensification* of their experience of the salvation/kingdom of God, which the disciples merely *began* to enjoy in ministry of Jesus.[40] We need to give further consideration to the extent to which Luke shared this christological understanding of the Spirit below (§4).

§2 Issues at Stake in Opposing Views of 'the Spirit and Salvation in Luke-Acts'

In 2004, I set out some principal issues at stake on the topic between Dunn and myself, on the one side, and Pentecostal one-stage-pneumatology interpreters, especially Bob Menzies, on the other.[41] Since then, a Korean Pentecostal scholar, Youngmo Cho, has published his Aberdeen (2002) doctoral thesis, under the slightly revised title *Spirit and Kingdom in the Writings of Luke and Paul* (2005). It very much follows in Menzies's footsteps, so I shall merely briefly summarize what was said in the 2004 article, avoiding repetition where possible, but extending the discussion where Cho has further contribution. I pointed to four main areas of difference/disagreement on the topic.[42]

1. Issues of Disagreement over What is Meant by 'Salvation'[43] Menzies and Stronstad work with a definition of 'salvation' (reflecting Methodist/Arminian roots of their Pentecostalism) according to which salvation in essence means justification and cleansing (read 'Luke's "forgiveness of sins"'), and incorporation (=baptism) into

39. See my '"Trinitarian" Pneumatology in the New Testament?–Towards an Explanation of the Worship of Jesus', *Asbury Theological Journal* 58/1 (2003), pp. 167–86. This is the published form of a plenary paper first offered at BNTS in 2000.

40. *Power*, esp. chs 13–14; idem, 'Interpreting', pp. 268–86.

41. Max Turner, 'The Spirit and Salvation in Luke-Acts', in Graham N. Stanton, Bruce W. Longenecker, and Stephen C. Barton (eds), *The Holy Spirit and Christian Origins: Essays in Honor of James D. G. Dunn* (Grand Rapids: Eerdmans, 2004), pp. 103–16. I was, of course, fully aware that there were many other views in the arena (for which see the history of scholarship in *Power*, pp. 20–79), but this was, after all, a Festschrift for James Dunn, and so focused on his dialogue partners. For Dunn's most thorough response to Pentecostal scholars, see James D. G. Dunn, 'Baptism in the Spirit: A Response to Pentecostal Scholarship on Luke-Acts', *JPT* 3 (1993), pp. 3–27. This is reprinted in James D. G. Dunn, *The Christ and the Spirit, Vol. 2: Pneumatology* (Edinburgh: T&T Clark, 1998), pp. 222–42.

42. One of my research students at LST has published a thorough critical review of Cho's work: see Carsten T. Lotz, 'A Critical Evaluation of Youngmo Cho: *Spirit and Kingdom in the Writings of Luke and Paul: An Attempt to Reconcile These Concepts*', *EvQ* 82/2 (2010), pp. 124–41. I am very grateful to Dr Cho for accomplishing the monumental task of translating my *Power* into Korean! I can only lament that his own monograph accidentally misrepresents me as often as it does, and so introduces a measure of confusion into the ongoing dialogue.

43. See Turner, 'Spirit and Salvation', pp. 106–9.

the church with its eschatological hope.[44] It is then no wonder they doubt Luke believes the gift of the Spirit is necessary for the life of 'salvation' – for such, Menzies considers, the only spiritual wisdom required falls within ordinary unaided human capacities.[45] The gift of the Spirit (for Menzies and Cho), brings, instead, what they call 'extraordinary' wisdom and other charismata, and is granted only to, and only needed by, those *already* saved.[46]

One may imagine the ghosts of Fletcher and Wesley rising up in indignation to oppose such a restriction on the meaning of 'salvation'. May their spirits rest in peace!: the broad community of Lucan scholars would totally disagree with the restriction, and many of us would voice surprise that neither Menzies nor Cho searches for a *Lucan* understanding of 'salvation' as a starting point – nor even as a significant reference point.[47]

Nearly all recent Lucan scholarship regards Luke's soteriology as something close to a mirror image of his presentation of the Kingdom of God; that is, as God's dynamic liberating and transforming rule.[48] Most have also seen a strong and *explanatory* correlation between this and Luke's portrait of the Spirit's activity: it is the *Spirit* working through Jesus, and then through the Church, which is the transforming power of the kingdom of God.[49] Part of the originality of Cho's thesis

44. Cf. W. W. Menzies, and R. P. Menzies, *Spirit and Power: Foundations of Pentecostal Experience* (Grand Rapids: Zondervan, 2000), p. 89; Stronstad, *Prophethood*, p. 121. Though Cho uses the word 'salvation' very regularly, unfortunately he does not specify what he means by it. To clarify, W. W. Menzies was Bob's father, himself the author of an official history of the Assemblies of God.

45. Menzies and Menzies, ibid., pp. 91–4.

46. Lotz rightly criticizes this for the vague terminology and false antithesis that is implied: see 'Evaluation', pp. 132–6.

47. After all, there are plenty of good guides on offer. To give just three key anchors, see I. H. Marshall, *Luke: Historian and Theologian* (Exeter: Paternoster, 1970 [Marshall was at Aberdeen, where both Menzies and Cho studied]); F. Bovon, *Luke the Theologian: Fifty-five Years of Research (1950–2005)* (Waco: Baylor University Press, 2006), of which they will have known in slightly earlier editions, and Darrell L. Bock, *A Theology of Luke and Acts* (Biblical Theology of the New Testament, 2; Grand Rapids: Zondervan, 2012).

48. Most recently, Twelftree sums up his chapter on 'Salvation and the Church' with the words '*For Luke, salvation is the realization of the powerful presence of God in present as well as future experience*' (author's italics), see Graham H. Twelftree, *People of the Spirit: Exploring Luke's View of the Church* (London and Grand Rapids: SPCK and Baker Academic, 2009), p. 51. Compare also Bock, *Theology*, esp. chs 6, 8, 10 and 11.

49. So, in pioneering fashion, J. D. G. Dunn, 'Spirit and Kingdom', *ExpTim* 82 (1970–1), pp. 36–40; reprinted in *Christ and the Spirit, Vol. 2*, pp. 133–41. Cho (*Spirit*, ch. 4) argues that Luke does *not* see matters in the same way as Paul: for Luke, the Spirit is not a dynamic equivalent of the kingdom. The Spirit is *not* the power that actually brings people the blessings of the kingdom (in which case I ask, 'then what is?'), rather the Spirit merely inspires the *proclamation about* the kingdom and its blessings (and it is human faith that acquires these). See Lotz, 'Evaluation', pp. 128–9.

is that he brings out that relationship between Spirit and kingdom in Paul: for him, Paul effectively switches Jesus's kingdom language for Spirit language, at least in contexts of realized eschatology, and so makes the Spirit soteriologically necessary to 'life in the kingdom'.[50] But in this, he thinks, Paul was an innovator; for Cho, Luke trod a separate path: 'The Spirit should [rather] be seen as the divine agent that lies behind the *proclamation* of the kingdom of God.'[51] I suspect few would disagree with the positive assertion just quoted, but most would regard it as a false antithesis. What was required for salvation in Luke was not just more inspired preaching – the great truths of which might be acquired and enjoyed by 'unaided human capacities'. What was needed was at very least an impact on the human heart *through* the Spirit on the speaker (cf. e.g., Acts 16.14).

An increasing number of scholars are recognizing that Luke's hopes for the kingdom of God/salvation take the particular shape of 'a christocentric version of Isaianic New Exodus hopes for Israel's restoration'.[52] The bright New Exodus expectations of Luke 1–4 seem to lie dashed at the foot of the cross, but are resurrected by Acts 1–2, partially realized in the quasi 'paradisal' community in Acts 2–8, and seen as, in essence, fulfilled by James's words in Acts 15:16–17, according to which the promises of Davidic restoration are sufficiently complete so that the gospel is henceforth open to 'the rest of men' (15.17; i.e. Gentiles). The Isaianic hope that Israel will be restored from its spiritual doldrums to become a 'light to the nations' (Isa. 49.6, cf. Acts 1.8, 13.47) is here.[53] And it is no coincidence that all this is because the Pentecost Spirit has been poured out to baptize believers with Holy Spirit. Indeed, all this is what I earlier spoke of as an 'intensification' of God's in-breaking reign in the period of the church. Neither Menzies nor Cho have reacted with the dynamic of these Isaianic New Exodus hopes, which point in another direction from theirs, which leads to the next question.

2. The Spirit at the Literary Centre of Luke-Acts[54] The literary 'centre' of Luke's two works is provided by the highly redactional transitional passages in Luke

---

50. Cho, *Spirit*, ch. 3.

51. Ibid., p. 195, my italics.

52. Turner, 'Spirit and Salvation', p. 107. The view was first published by Mark L. Strauss, *The Davidic Messiah in Luke-Acts: The Promise and Its Fulfillment in Lukan Christology* (Sheffield: SAP, 1995), and I developed it extensively in *Power* (and define it over against other kinds of 'New Exodus' interpretations in an excursus on pp. 244–9). The picture has been taken further by David W. Pao, *Acts and the Isaianic New Exodus* (Tübingen: Mohr/Siebeck, 2000), and related more directly to the Spirit's work in Matthias Wenk, *Community-Forming Power: The Socio-Ethical Role of the Spirit in Luke-Acts* (Sheffield: SAP, 2000). Wright gave a similar shape to his quest for Jesus: N. T. Wright, *Jesus and the Victory of God* (London: SPCK, 1996).

53. Turner, *Power*, *passim* (esp. ch. 13).

54. Turner, ibid., pp. 109–11.

24.44–52 and Acts 1.1–11. Here the Baptist's promise that the messiah will 'baptize in Holy Spirit' (Acts 1.5) is taken up, modified and interpreted *within* Luke's Isaianic framework, conjoined with reference to Isaiah 32.15 (Lk. 24.49; Acts 1.8), which is about the Spirit being poured out 'from on high' like water on the 'desert' (which metaphor describes Israel's sad state), and thereby lushly transforming her (as even more clearly in the parallel in Isa. 44.3–4). It is just possible that Luke restricted that vision to mean that God provided the church *as* lots of Spirit-inspired proclaimers, and that their message was accepted by purely human understanding, and that *that* understanding alone was sufficient to transform Israel. But such a novel interpretation is hardly inviting, and would not be found anywhere in the Judaism of Luke's day. When Judaism thought about the Spirit given to all for Israel's restoration, they thought of Ezekiel 36, as did Paul (1 Thess. 4.8; 2 Cor. 3.3), and that meant the gift of the Spirit was also about God-enabled *inner* transformation. Which moves us on… .

3. Issues of Disagreement Concerning the 'Spirit of prophecy' in the Judaism of Luke's Time[55] I have argued at some length that in many Jewish texts the 'Spirit of prophecy' affords such revelation and wisdom as to be a *transformative* power, giving a vibrant new quality of higher relational-spiritual life, to the one endowed, and indirectly to those he impacts. And that while Judaism regarded that largely as the benefit of messianic or other eschatological figures – and the basis of their redoubtable righteousness and intimate life with God – Luke partly *democratizes* the gift for the people of God in the eschatological age. Cho has completely misunderstood me when he takes my references to the Spirit's 'life-giving' wisdom to mean anything so minimal as 'sufficient wisdom to live within the covenant that gives life'.[56] I clearly meant the charismatic wisdom and revelation that brings a sparkling eschatological level of 'life' more like what Macarius, Fletcher and Wesley would recognize as approaching 'baptism with the Holy Spirit', and which Jews in Luke's time were coming to think of as available to God's people in the eschatological age. That thinking was on the margins of what most Jews would think of as activities of the Spirit of prophecy, *but it was there*, even before Paul, most clearly at Qumran, just one day's journey on the major highway from Jerusalem to Galilee. Here they read the Spirit of prophecy to provide the intimate knowledge of God, through the Spirit's presence in wisdom and revelation, that would fulfil Ezekiel's promise of restorative transformation – and it was certainly not just here, at Qumran.[57]

---

55. Ibid., pp. 111–13.

56. See Lotz, 'Evaluation', pp. 132–5 for a critique of Cho's misunderstanding. Cho may be dependent on Menzies and Menzies, *Spirit*, pp. 91–3, which makes the same mistake and develops a similar false antithesis.

57. See briefly *HSSG*, pp. 15–23. But the connection between the 'Spirit of prophecy' and religious-ethical transformation was much more widely held in Luke's time (see *Power*, ch. 5). I need to reject two other key misrepresentations by Cho. I did *not* claim that 'one of

4. Differences concerning the intended Beneficiaries of the Spirit of Prophecy[58] Menzies makes two extraordinary claims:

> The Spirit comes upon the disciples to equip them for their prophetic vocation (i.e. for their role as 'witnesses'). The disciples receive the Spirit ... not ... as the essential bond by which they (each individual) are linked to God; indeed, *not primarily for themselves*. Rather, as the driving force behind their witness to Christ, *the disciples receive the Spirit for others*.[59]

Again:

> The Spirit ... is not given principally for the benefit of the recipient; rather, it is directed towards others.[60]

Strange though it seems, and as hard as I have tried to find substantial counter-evidence, Menzies really does appear to *deny* that the Spirit is significantly and directly involved in the individual's own spiritual life: for him reception of the Spirit is *not* necessary as the source of the believer's 'cleansing righteousness, intimate fellowship with and knowledge of God', and certainly *not* 'the essential bond by which they (each individual) are linked to God'.[61] I can readily agree that Luke's *emphasis* is on the Spirit's mission through the believer to others – *everyone* affirms *that*. It is the third of the five points I listed as the consensus of Lucan scholarship, namely: 'For Luke the Spirit is largely the "Spirit of prophecy"; in Acts especially as an "empowering for mission"'. The fourth is 'correspondingly Luke shows relatively little interest in the Spirit as the power of spiritual, ethical and religious renewal of the individual'.[62] Anyone trying to prove these is simply running in at an open

---

the main features of the Spirit in this [inter-testamental Jewish] literature is a "life-giving function" as a soteriological agent' (contra Cho, *Spirit*, p. 14 and following). I said it was occasional, marginal, but, nevertheless, significant. Nor did I rest any significant part of my argument anachronistically on the Midrash of Psalm 14.6 or *Deut. R.* 6.14 (as claimed by Cho, *Spirit*, p. 40), far less was their interpretation of Ezekiel 36 something on which my 'interpretation mainly depends' (so ibid., p. 48). What I actually said was that 'the evidence of these two midrashim ... is late' and that 'we cannot depend on such a view having been in circulation in the New Testament period' (*Power*, p. 131). And I made no reference to these texts in my summarizing conclusion (pp. 136–7).

58. Cf. my 'Spirit and Salvation', pp. 114–15.

59. *Development*, p. 207 (my italics).

60. This quotation simply modifies the claim that the Spirit in Luke-Acts is 'exclusively' empowering for mission to recognize some community-orientated dimension of the Spirit's work. See *Spirit*, pp. 88–92, and further assertions along similar lines.

61. *Spirit*, p. 89.

62. Turner, 'Spirit and Salvation', p. 105. For a fuller 'commentary' see my 'The "Spirit of Prophecy" as the Power of Israel's Restoration and Witness', in I. Howard Marshall and

door. But when Menzies and Cho attempt to shrink '*relatively little* interest' to '*no* interest', do they not attempt to defend a bridge too far, and create an unexpected and problematic vacuum? If not the Spirit of prophecy, what is it then that brings to the believer the 'intimate fellowship with and knowledge of God' of which Menzies speaks? Surely the most obvious candidate would be something like the Spirit of prophecy experienced as, for example, 'a spirit of wisdom and understanding, a spirit of counsel and might, a spirit of knowledge and the fear of the Lord' such as is found in Scripture in Isaiah 11.1–2 and developed in the messianic portraits of inter-testamental Judaism (for example *1 En.* 49.2–3; 62.1–2 [here the Spirit is actually called the 'Spirit of righteousness'!]; *Pss. Sol.* 17.37; 18.7; 1QSb 5.25; 4Q215 iv.4; 4QpIsa[a] 7–10 iii.15–29; 4QMess ar (=4Q536) 3 i.4–11; *T. Levi* 18.7–8, etc.). This is what Judaism understood as the source of the *messiah's own* redoubtable righteousness and filial intimacy with God, not merely his empowering for mission, or simply his *Amtscharisma*. Why would not the same apply to the messianic community, with the Spirit poured out at Pentecost on the people of God as the 'Spirit of Jesus' (Acts 16.7)? Macarius, Fletcher and Wesley, not to mention Paul and John, would have recognized that logic.

If the Spirit of prophecy is *not* the 'organ of communication' between God and his people, if believers are *not* linked individually in communion with God and Christ by the Spirit of prophecy, *then by exactly what are they so?* And *what* is the divine source and power of their evident transformation? Regular Pentecostal testimony to 'baptism in the Holy Spirit' is certainly to its transformatory power, not merely to its enabling for mission.

§3 'He will baptize in Holy Spirit and Fire' (Lk. 3.16, Acts 1.5, and 11.16)

Space allows only this peremptory summary. Luke's John the Baptist probably thought he had sifted Israel, with his dividing water baptism, and that the Messiah's job was now to cleanse the threshing floor, burn the chaff and gather the wheat into the eschatological granary (Lk. 3.17).[63] The Baptist would be expected to have understood this as accomplished *by the powerful and transforming action of a strongly Spirit-anointed messianic figure*: no Jew could quite imagine the scenario of Acts 2, with a messiah pouring out God's *very own* Spirit. The Spirit-anointed messiah, on earth, *in Israel*, was the key to the promised Isaianic New Exodus restoration of Israel. And the Baptist could not have thought of the messianic baptism with Spirit-and-fire as some 'second blessing' given to the *already* saved, as modern Pentecostal interpreters might be tempted to think. His message was about Israel's restoration/salvation itself, and how it comes: his baptismal metaphor is a picture of that. Anything less would be (to reverse the usual metaphor) to make a molehill out of a mountain!

David Peterson (eds), *Witness to the Gospel: The Theology of Acts* (Grand Rapids: Eerdmans, 1998), pp. 327–48, esp. pp. 328–33.

63. See *Power*, ch. 7, for my arguments.

Luke did not think the Baptist he portrays fully understood the issues. For Luke, Jesus continued the 'sifting of Israel', albeit in deeper kind, and after His death and vindication, and as now 'Lord of all' (Acts 10.36, cf. 2.36), He poured out a much deeper 'baptism in the Spirit' than hitherto even fleetingly imagined – one of virtually trinitarian import – as His power and presence to restore and transform Israel.[64] The Spirit is not just empowering for proclamation *about* the salvation of Israel and her witness to the nations, He is the *transforming* empowering for Israel's mission. In that, Macarius, Fletcher and Wesley would find some justification of their emphases.

§4 Luke and Paul on the Spirit: Radically Different or Fellow Workers?
Some Ill-disciplined Questions

If what I have argued above has any cogency, Luke is closer to Paul (and to John) than Menzies or Cho think. If I am wrong, and they right, other significant questions arise about the shape of their respective teachings, and how the differences came about. I offer the following observations in no particular logical order.

What do we know of the relationship between Paul and 'Luke'? As we have seen, Menzies and Cho tend to defend the striking difference between the pneumatology of Luke and Paul by arguing that Luke holds an older, more Jewish, understanding of the 'Spirit of prophecy' than does Paul. Lotz observes the irony that in this they make the dazzling variety of Jewish writing – spread over at least three centuries, and vast distances, physically, conceptually and ideologically – more unified and consistent than the writings of first-century Christian movements, by authors who knew each other.[65]

But how *well* they know each other's teaching becomes a vital question. Traditionally, Luke was regarded as the fellow worker of Paul mentioned in Colossians 4.14, 2 Timothy 4.11 and Philemon 24, and *with him* in Rome. Menzies admits this as a possibility, but notes Luke may not have seen or read the letters Paul wrote there.[66] But Philemon refers to Luke as a 'fellow-worker' who sends his greetings, and a fellow worker would be someone who was Paul's trusted aid and representative, and would be expected to understand his teaching and be able to

---

64. The supporting arguments are there in *Power*, chs 7, 9 and 10, and '"Trinitarian" Pneumatology'. Both Menzies and Cho are wrong to say I distort Luke by my portrait of John's own understanding of his relationship to the promised baptizing in the Holy Spirit (cf. Cho, *Spirit*, pp. 117–23). I specifically say that portrait is *not* Luke's own understanding of how things were to come about. Cho, following Menzies at this point, has overlooked the important final §4 of my chapter on the Baptist in Lucan perspective: see *Power*, pp. 186–7.

65. Lotz, 'Evaluation' pp. 131–2. I suspect a Procrustean bed to be in service, with the marginalization and/or reinterpretation of Jewish voices like Qumran, *Testament of the Twelve Patriarchs*, *Joseph and Aseneth*, Philo, etc.

66. Menzies and Menzies, *Spirit*, p. 61, n. 37.

explain it to congregations. And significant letters were not written in a corner, but in semi-public events, with the contents openly discussed by interested parties.[67] In that scenario, Luke would probably have heard on several occasions – as the drafts were revised – the total contents of the three Lycus valley letters (Colossians, Philemon and Laodiceans (=Ephesians?)).[68] It is possible, however, that the writer of Acts was *not* the Luke mentioned, and that would change the nature of the relationship.

Whoever the author was, he seems to have travelled with Paul in those parts of Acts known as the 'we' sections, where the narrator speaks in the first person plural, as one present: Acts 16.10–17 (arriving at Philippi and the conversion of Lydia); 20.5–15 (the Troas to Miletus stretch); 21.1–18 (onwards to Jerusalem) and 27.1–28.16 (the epic ship voyage from prison in Caesarea to house arrest in Rome, which itself slightly supports the Lucan hypothesis above). The pattern does not suggest the author of Acts was a happenstance traveller, but a purposeful supporter of Paul. And we should not assume he dropped out of the picture whenever the 'we' passages turn to 'they' passages; it is very possible, for example, he was with Paul at times during his two-year imprisonment in Caesarea, and in Rome. How long would it be before Paul's pneumatology became a topic of discussion for Luke, who in anyone's hypothesis had an interest in the subject? It would probably have arisen at the baptism of Lydia in Acts 16.15, as we know Paul made a strong connection between conversional faith and Spirit-reception (Gal. 3.3 etc.). But if Luke actually became a recognized fellow worker, he would certainly have been brought back to the subject many times. There are no knock-down arguments here, but it would be very unwise to *assume* that the author of Acts was casual and ill-informed on a subject so close to his heart. Of course, Luke misses all the Pauline emphasis on the 'interiority of the Spirit' – what the Spirit does for the internal life of the recipient – but then, he is not writing spiritual counsel. His engagement is with activity in public view, the expansion of Christianity, not the existential experience of the believer.

Having raised the question of the believer's experience of Spirit, we need provisionally to explore a related question. It is clear from Paul's letters that the Spirit was a matter of what I have termed 'immediate (and often emotional) experiences' such as 'the love of God poured out in our hearts' (Rom. 5.5); receiving the gospel 'with joy of the Holy Spirit' (1 Thess. 1.6); 'crying out' 'Abba, Father' by the Spirit (Gal. 4.6), etc. I rather assume Luke knew of these experiences, not merely from what he saw happen in the Pauline communities, but from what he saw in his own; or were they radically different? Equally, I rather assume he knew of the sort of charismata discussed in 1 Corinthians 12–14 for the building up of the church, and even including the private use of tongues for worship, whether

---

67. E. Randolph Richards, *Paul and First-Century Letter Writing: Secretaries, Composition and Collection* (Downer's Grove: IVP, 2004).

68. I argue that equation: see my 'Ephesians, Letter to', in K. D. Sakenfeld (ed.), *New Interpreter's Dictionary of the Bible* (5 vols; Nashville: Abingdon, 2007), vol. 2, pp. 269–76.

in Pauline circles or others. Did he not regard these as obviously activities of the *same* Spirit of prophecy that empowered mission in the churches he knew? It was a feature of the churches he describes, not least in the 'we' passages of Acts, that the Spirit of prophecy gave dreams, charismatic wisdom, revelations and other types of direction/leading. But did he and his circles not experience a similar 'leading' in their general life of discipleship and formation under Christ, as Romans 8 and Galatians 5–6 suggest? If they did, and if Luke himself did, could he have considered such to come from a *different* source or power of God than the 'Spirit of prophecy' he allegedly believed given 'exclusively' for mission? I have put this rather trivially, but I think the important question is clear: Why would Luke think the Spirit of prophecy was just about 'mission', and how would he otherwise explain parallel charismatic phenomena that surfaced in contexts *not* essentially connected with deliberate outreach?

And then one last question. Given that in the Pauline communities there was a life-devotion *to*, and open worship *of* Christ, that would have seemed idolatrous unless offered as to the one Lord God of Israel,[69] and given that this was seen by Paul as inspired and fuelled by the Spirit experienced as the self-revealing, utterly transforming 'Spirit of Christ', did Luke's churches evince a similar pattern of Christ-devotion? I think they did. Then would Luke, or would he not, see that as driven by the Spirit of prophecy experienced as the empowering presence of Christ, the Spirit of Jesus, or was Jesus an absentee messiah? I have argued the former to be true,[70] and in this chapter I have suggested that Luke could not easily have avoided attributing these things to the Spirit (of prophecy). But then he has crossed the same Rubicon as did Paul – for this devotion is the heart of 'salvation' – and, so, the Spirit has for him become 'soteriologically necessary'.

Conclusion

Macarius, Fletcher and Wesley, raised the question of whether a post-conversion 'baptism with Holy Spirit' brought a thorough and liberating transformation that made for fully authentic Christian life: entire sanctification. We have looked at the question through the eyes of Lucan scholarship of two different kinds: (a) a Pentecostal one, which denies that the gift of Spirit is about ethical transformation, asserting instead that it is about empowerment for mission, and (b) one offered by Dunn and others that sees the Spirit in Luke as the transforming power of Israel's salvation and Isaianic witness as a 'light to the nations' (Isa. 49.6; Acts 1.8; 13.47). I have argued for the latter, which means I think Fletcher and Wesley were making a significant contribution.

---

69. The thesis of Chris Tilling's, *Paul's Divine Christology* (WUNT II, 323; Tübingen: Mohr Siebeck, 2012).

70. *Power*, chs 13–14.

Their contribution has been muted by unsympathetic voices from the later Methodist tradition, but Fletcher and Wesley actually articulated a fiery vision that Christian life should be strongly 'experienced', utterly 'sanctifying', and that the gateway to that was a distinct 'reception' of the Spirit. Their vision fuelled the vast 'holiness' and 'empowerment' movements of the nineteenth and early twentieth centuries, from Keswick 'Holiness' to Azusa Street's 'Pentecostalism'. With Macarius, Fletcher and Wesley sought to face down all kinds of merely 'nominal' Christianity of their day. And the challenge they faced is one that remains.

But we need to add that they were not mere pragmatists. Their elucidation of 'baptism in Holy Spirit' continues to dominate our twenty-first-century academic discussions, whether by approbation or denial, as the constant flow of NT monographs and articles on the view of the Spirit in Luke-Acts demonstrates. Macarius, Fletcher and Wesley have made us think hard about the shape of Christian life, and think hard, too, about the relationship between the NT vision of Christian 'life-with Christ' in the Spirit (supremely visible in the Pauline letters) and that of our congregations today.

I have to differ from Macarius, Fletcher and Wesley only in recognizing that for Luke as well as Paul, baptism in the Spirit is essential to what they regard as the *essence* of Christian being, not a merely post-conversional ideal.

Tony Lane has been responsible for getting me interested in Christian writings from a little later than the New Testament: I hope this chapter does not make him regret that influence.

Bibliography

Arrington, F. L., *The Acts of the Apostles* (Peabody: Hendrickson, 1988).

Atkinson, William P., *Baptism in the Spirit: Luke-Acts and the Dunn Debate* (Eugene: Pickwick, 2011).

Bock, Darrell L., *A Theology of Luke and Acts* (Biblical Theology of the New Testament, 2; Grand Rapids: Zondervan, 2012).

Bovon, F., *Luke the Theologian: Fifty-five Years of Research (1950–2005)* (Waco: Baylor University Press, 2006).

Cho, Youngmo, *Spirit and Kingdom in the Writings of Luke and Paul* (Milton Keynes: Paternoster, 2005).

Dayton, Donald W., *Theological Roots of Pentecostalism* (Peabody: Hendrickson, 1987).

Dunn, James D. G., 'Baptism in the Spirit: A Response to Pentecostal Scholarship on Luke-Acts', *JPT* 3 (1993), pp. 3–27.

Dunn, James D. G., *The Christ and the Spirit, Vol. 2: Pneumatology* (Edinburgh: T&T Clark, 1998).

Dunn, James D. G., *Jesus and the Spirit: A Study of the Religious and Charismatic Experience of Jesus and the First Christians as Reflected in the New Testament* (London: SCM, 1975).

Dunn, James D. G., 'Spirit and Kingdom', *ExpTim* 82 (1970–71), pp. 36–40.

Ervin, H. M., *Spirit-Baptism: A Biblical Investigation* (Peabody: Hendrickson, 1987).

Hunter, H. D., *Spirit-Baptism: A Pentecostal Alternative* (Lanham: University Press of America, 1983).

Lotz, Carsten T., 'A Critical Evaluation of Youngmo Cho: *Spirit and Kingdom in the Writings of Luke and Paul: An Attempt to Reconcile These Concepts*', *EvQ* 82/2 (2010), pp. 124–41.

Maloney, George A. (ed. and trans.), *Pseudo-Macarius: The Fifty Spiritual Homilies and the Great Letter* (New York: Paulist Press, 1992).

Marshall, I. H., *Luke: Historian and Theologian* (Exeter: Paternoster, 1970).

Menzies, Robert P., *The Development of Early Christian Pneumatology With Special Reference to Luke-Acts* (Sheffield: SAP, 1991).

Menzies, Robert P., *Empowered for Witness: The Spirit in Luke-Acts* (Sheffield: SAP, 1994).

Menzies, W. W., and R. P. Menzies, *Spirit and Power: Foundations of Pentecostal Experience* (Grand Rapids: Zondervan, 2000).

Pao, David W., *Acts and the Isaianic New Exodus* (Tübingen: Mohr/Siebeck, 2000).

Penney, John Michael, *The Missionary Emphasis of Lukan Pneumatology* (Sheffield: SAP, 1997).

Richards, E. Randolph, *Paul and First-Century Letter Writing: Secretaries, Composition and Collection* (Downer's Grove: IVP, 2004).

Shelton, James B., *Mighty in Word and Deed: The Role of the Holy Spirit in Luke-Acts* (Peabody: Hendrickson, 1991).

Strauss, Mark L., *The Davidic Messiah in Luke-Acts: The Promise and Its Fulfillment in Lukan Christology* (Sheffield: SAP, 1995).

Stronstad, R., *The Charismatic Theology of Saint Luke* (Peabody: Hendrickson, 1984).

Stronstad, R., *The Prophethood of All Believers: A Study in Luke's Charismatic Theology* (Sheffield: SAP, 1999).

Thiselton, Anthony C., *The Holy Spirit – In Biblical Teaching Through the Centuries and Today* (London: SPCK, 2013).

Tilling, Chris, *Paul's Divine Christology* (WUNT II, 323; Tübingen: Mohr Siebeck, 2012).

Turner, Max, *Baptism in the Holy Spirit* (Cambridge: Grove Books, 2000).

Turner, Max, 'Ephesians, Letter to', in K. D. Sakenfeld (ed.), *New Interpreter's Dictionary of the Bible* (5 vols; Nashville: Abingdon, 2007), vol. 2, pp. 269–76.

Turner, Max, *The Holy Spirit and Spiritual Gifts: Then and Now* (Carlisle: Paternoster, rev. edn, 1999).

Turner, Max, 'Interpreting the Samaritans of Acts 8: The Waterloo of Pentecostal Soteriology and Pneumatology?', *PNEUMA* 23/2 (2001), pp. 265–86.

Turner, Max, *Power from on High: The Spirit in Israel's Restoration and Witness in Luke-Acts* (Sheffield: SAP, 1996).

Turner, Max, 'The "Spirit of Prophecy" as the Power of Israel's Restoration and Witness', in I. Howard Marshall and David Peterson (eds), *Witness to the Gospel: The Theology of Acts* (Grand Rapids: Eerdmans, 1998), pp. 327–48.

Turner, Max, 'The Spirit and Salvation in Luke-Acts', in Graham N. Stanton, Bruce W. Longenecker, and Stephen C. Barton (eds), *The Holy Spirit and Christian Origins: Essays in Honor of James D. G. Dunn* (Grand Rapids: Eerdmans, 2004), pp. 103–16.

Turner, Max, 'Spiritual Gifts and Spiritual Formation in 1 Corinthians and Ephesians', *JPT* 22 (2013), pp. 187–205.

Turner, Max, '"Trinitarian" Pneumatology in the New Testament?–Towards an Explanation of the Worship of Jesus', *Asbury Theological Journal* 58/1 (2003), pp. 167–86.

Twelftree, Graham H., *People of the Spirit: Exploring Luke's View of the Church* (London and Grand Rapids: SPCK and Baker Academic, 2009).

Wenk, Matthias, *Community-Forming Power: The Socio-Ethical Role of the Spirit in Luke-Acts* (Sheffield: SAP, 2000).

Williams, J. R., *Renewal Theology* (3 vols; Grand Rapids: Zondervan, 1990).

Wood, Laurence W., *The Meaning of Pentecost in Early Methodism: Rediscovering John Fletcher as John Wesley's Vindicator and Designated Successor* (Lanham: Scarecrow Press, 2002).

Wright, N. T., *Jesus and the Victory of God* (London: SPCK, 1996).

Chapter 13

SOREN KIERKEGAARD AS A READER OF MARTIN LUTHER

Randall C. Zachman

This chapter examines the ways in which Soren Kierkegaard read Martin Luther, particularly from 1846 until his death in 1855, which covers the periods both of Kierkegaard's 'second authorship' (1847–51) and his subsequent attack on the established Church in Denmark (1854–55).[1] Most of Kierkegaard's engagement with Luther takes place via reflections on Luther's Church and House Postil in his journals and papers, whereas only a few of his reflections on Luther appear in the works published in his lifetime, especially towards the close of his second authorship in 1851.[2] Both Kierkegaard and his fellow Lutherans in Denmark view Luther as the decisive frame of reference, or 'point de vue', for the state of

1. For a recent study of Kierkegaard's reading of Luther's sermons, see David L. Coe, 'Kierkegaard's Forking for Extracts from Extracts of Luther's Sermons: Reviewing Kierkegaard's Laud and Lance of Luther', *Kierkegaard Studies: Yearbook* (2011), pp. 3–18. For an examination of Kierkegaard's view of himself as a possible successor to Martin Luther, see David Yoon-Jung Kim and Joel D. S. Rasmussen, 'Martin Luther: Reform, Secularization, and the Question of His "True Successor"', in Jon Stewart (ed.), *Kierkegaard and the Renaissance and Modern Traditions – Theology* (Burlington, VT: Ashgate, 2009), pp. 184–207.

2. Kierkegaard used a Danish edition entitled *En christelig Postille, sammendragen af Dr. Morten Luthers Kirke- og Huuspostiller efter Benjamin Lindners tyske Samling udgiven I ny dansk Oversættelse af Jørgen Thisted* (2 vols; Copenhagen: Wahlske Boghandling 1828). The title translates as 'A Christian Book of Postils, The Summary of Dr Martin Luther's Church and House Postils after Benjamin Lindner's German Collection Released in New Danish Translation by Jørgen Thisted'. Coe points out that Kierkegaard is reading a Danish edition of Lindner's German edition of the Leipzig German edition of the Church and House Postil. Lindner deletes much material from each postil, and creates an amalgamation of passages written at different times on each passage, and Thisted (unlike Lindner) does not note that these changes have been made. 'Thus, while Kierkegaard believes he is reading from one complete Luther sermon each sitting with *Thisted*, he is actually reading from

Christianity in their day.[3] As we shall see, Kierkegaard's impressions of Luther are quite complex.[4] On the one hand, Kierkegaard always thinks that Luther is closer to genuine Christianity than are Bishop Mynster and Hans Lassen Martensen. On the other hand, Kierkegaard thinks that Luther establishes the trajectory that leads directly to the Christendom represented by Mynster and Martensen. One of Kierkegaard's constant refrains is that 'Luther is no dialectician', meaning that Luther tends to emphasize one side of an issue, which blinds him to the importance of the other side that must always be kept in view. This leads to an instability in Luther's position that allows subsequent generations of Lutherans to take Luther in vain, and even to take the grace of God in vain, based on statements that Luther actually made. Kierkegaard acknowledges that Luther is a necessary corrective to the abuses of the Roman Church of his day, but because Luther is no dialectician, his position should never have been made normative. Kierkegaard attempts to avoid taking Luther in vain by reading his words in the context of his life, especially his twenty years of fear and trembling and spiritual trial. He attempts to avoid taking the grace of God in vain by always remembering the life of Christ and the duty to become a disciple, along with the death of Christ, which took place for the forgiveness of our sins.

Luther's Sermons in Kierkegaard's Copenhagen

Kierkegaard was acquainted with Luther's theology in a broad sense due to his preparation for his master's degree in theology (which was really much closer to our own PhD in theology). However, Kierkegaard did not read Luther intensively or thoroughly until 1846–47. In 1847, Kierkegaard writes in his journal, 'I have never really read anything by Luther. But now I open up his sermons.'[5] He decided to

---

an abridged amalgamation of more than one sermon via *Lindner*' (Coe, 'Kierkegaard's Forking', p. 7). Unlike Coe, I am not sure that this really changes anything with regard to the way Kierkegaard reads Luther.

3. Soren Kierkegaard, *Soren Kierkegaard's Journals and Papers* (ed. and trans. Howard V. and Edna H. Hong; 7 vols; Bloomington, University of Indiana Press, 1967–78), vol. 3, p. 81, para. 2516 (henceforth *JP*). Courtesy of Indiana University Press. All rights reserved.

4. Although Jamie Ferriera recognizes the complexity of Kierkegaard's engagement with Luther, she assumes that Kierkegaard fundamentally agrees with Luther about grace, and that Kierkegaard agrees with Luther unless he explicitly says otherwise. Neither of these assumptions will guide my reading of Kierkegaard's reading of Luther, both because Kierkegaard makes personal criticisms of Luther in his journals that he never publishes, and because he always maintains a critical distance from Luther even when he appears to be endorsing a position that Luther takes. See M. Jamie Ferriera, *Love's Grateful Striving: A Commentary on Kierkegaard's 'Works of Love'* (Oxford: Oxford University Press, 2001), pp. 19–20, 253.

5. *JP*, vol. 3, p. 64, para. 2463.

approach Luther by means of his Church and House Postil, as these came closest to the religious writings Kierkegaard was composing during this time. He appears to have created a schedule for reading Luther's sermons patterned on the schedule for reading Mynster's sermons first practised by his father, and then observed by Kierkegaard throughout his adult life. Thus in 1848 he will note, 'Today I have read Luther's sermon according to plan.'[6] Two years later he will observe the remarkable coincidence between the events of his life and 'the Luther sermon I read according to plan.'[7]

The creation of the plan to read Luther's sermons the way he read Mynster's sermons was hardly accidental. It is clear that Kierkegaard was hoping to find in Luther a supporting voice to strengthen his own impression of Christianity over against the secularized version of Christianity represented by Mynster and the established Church in Denmark. Kierkegaard clearly thought that Luther challenged him more deeply than did the preaching of Mynster and the other pastors of his day.

> What a relief for the person who hears and reads the contemporary pastors and almost has to say to himself, 'I understand from you what I am to do – simply take it easy, because I have already become too perfect' – what a relief to read Luther. There is a man who can really stay by a person and preach him farther out instead of backwards.[8]

For this reason, Kierkegaard enthusiastically notes in his journal, 'O Luther, still the master of us all.'[9] Kierkegaard imagines planning to preach a sermon by Luther to a congregation without letting them know who wrote it, in order to see how outraged the pastors would be. 'It might sometime be appropriate to memorize one of Luther's sermons and deliver it without giving any hint of it – and then see how furious the clergy would become – and then say: This is a sermon by Luther, word for word.'[10] He was particularly interested in thinking about what would happen if Mynster were to read a sermon by Luther from the pulpit, for Kierkegaard thought that this would lead Mynster to admit that he had watered down Christianity. 'Some Sunday let Mynster, instead of preaching himself, take one of Luther's sermons, particularly one of the characteristic ones, and read it aloud – and the whole thing will sound like a satire on Mynster, unless he hurries and makes a little admission [*Indrømmelse*] concerning himself.'[11] Kierkegaard imagined the same situation for the theologian Hans Lassen Martensen, whose speculative theology Kierkegaard deeply opposed. 'Let Martensen be obliged to

6. *JP*, vol. 3, p. 64, para. 2465.

7. *JP*, vol. 6, p. 344, para. 6666.

8. *JP*, vol. 3, p. 64, para. 2464.

9. *JP*, vol. 3, p. 64, para. 2465.

10. *JP*, vol. 3, pp. 72–3, para. 2493.

11. *JP*, vol. 3, p. 88, para. 2530.

read one of Luther's sermons aloud, not to mention one in which Luther talks about speculation – and no one will need to write against Martensen.'[12]

Kierkegaard thought that such an exercise would lead Mynster and others to realize that Kierkegaard was not guilty of exaggerating the meaning of Christianity, for reading the sermons of Luther aloud would show that Luther exhibited the same exaggeration. 'Perhaps Luther's preaching, too, is excessive – so we have become Lutherans to a degree! Yes, one can easily eulogize Luther – but read Luther aloud!'[13] Kierkegaard considered the possibility of defending his own vision of Christianity by publishing selections from Luther's sermons that he had highlighted in his edition, to show how far the Church of his day had strayed from Luther. 'I could be tempted to take Luther's book of sermons and extract a great many sentences and ideas, all of which are marked in my copy, and publish them in order to show how far the preaching nowadays is from Christianity, so that it shall not be said that I am the one who hits upon exaggerations.'[14] One can therefore understand why Kierkegaard would praise Luther so highly in the first book of his second authorship, describing him as 'the greatest preacher of our Church and also its most orthodox person'.[15] This praise is repeated in his last work in the second authorship, where he describes Luther as 'the superb teacher of our Church'.[16]

Kierkegaard was especially taken with Luther's observation in his sermon on Stephen that preaching should properly take place on the street, and not in churches. 'Luther rightly says (in the sermon about Stephen) that there should be no preaching in the churches. It is an accommodation with a kind of idolatry. It is a concession to our weakness.'[17] Kierkegaard was convinced that the preaching of his day had become a theatrical performance, making the churches into another kind of theatre. 'Luther was absolutely right in saying that preaching really should not be done in churches but on the street. The whole modern concept of a pastor who preaches in a church is pure hallucination, really a poet-relationship.'[18] Again, Kierkegaard was convinced that this was especially true with the preaching of Bishop Mynster and his fondness for the 'quiet hour in holy places', which placed preaching far from the actuality of life:

> It would be impossible, yes, most impossible of all, for Mynster to preach in the public square. And yet preaching in churches has practically become paganism and theatricality, and Luther was very right in declaring that preaching should

12. *JP*, vol. 3, p. 605, para. 3515.

13. *JP*, vol. 3, p. 88, para. 2530.

14. *JP*, vol. 3, p. 81, para. 2516.

15. Soren Kierkegaard, *Upbuilding Discourses in Various Spirits* (ed. and trans. Howard V. and Edna H. Hong; Princeton: Princeton University Press, 1993), p. 270.

16. Soren Kierkegaard, *For Self-Examination and Judge for Yourself* (ed. and trans. Howard V. and Edna H. Hong; Princeton: Princeton University Press, 1990), p. 169.

17. *JP*, vol. 3, p. 78, para. 2510.

18. *JP*, vol. 1, p. 287, para. 653:18.

really not be done in churches. In paganism the theater was worship – in Christendom the churches have generally become the theater. How? In this way: it is pleasant, even enjoyable, to commune with the highest once a week by way of the imagination.[19]

Kierkegaard realized that he did not have the physical capacity to preach on the street himself, but at the end of his life he appealed to this idea of Luther's to explain why his last writings were published in newspapers.

> Still I did want to achieve an approximation of preaching in the streets or of placing Christianity, thinking about Christianity, right into the middle of life's actuality and in conflict with its variants, and to that end I decided to use this newspaper. It is a political paper, has completely different interests, concerns itself with a great variety of subjects – but not with Christianity. Having these little articles printed in this daily paper got them a hearing in a medium quite different from what they deal with; the result corresponds somewhat to listening to a sermon about Christianity on the street.[20]

At the same time, Kierkegaard points out the irony of Luther having said this in a church, without ever attempting to preach on the street himself. 'Luther declares in one of his sermons that preaching actually should not be done inside of churches. He says this in a sermon which as a matter of fact was delivered inside a church. So it was nothing more than talk; he did not carry it out in earnest. But certainly preaching should not be done inside of churches.'[21]

Luther on Person and Doctrine

Kierkegaard seems at times to be genuinely surprised to find Luther saying things in his sermons that Kierkegaard has been saying throughout his authorship. To begin, Kierkegaard finds Luther expressing his own understanding of truth as subjectivity. 'Wonderful! The category "for you" (subjectivity, inwardness) with which *Either/Or* concludes (only the truth that builds up [*opbygge*] is truth for you) is Luther's own. I have never really read anything by Luther. But now I open up his sermons – and right there in the Gospel for the First Sunday in Advent he says "for you", on this everything depends.'[22] Kierkegaard thought that Luther was his ally in fighting against a kind of objectivity of doctrine in which the individual is lost in the abstraction of the Church in history, and thereby avoids the possibility of offence brought about by relating to God and Christ directly as an individual. 'But

19. *JP*, vol. 6, p. 6, para. 6150.
20. *JP*, vol. 6, p. 562, para. 6957.
21. Ibid.
22. *JP*, vol. 3, p. 64, para. 2463.

if *everyone for himself* shall believe that he also belongs to Christ and that Christ has such a fervent love for him – then everything comes to a halt. Praise God for Luther! He is always a good help against the almost insanely inflated dogmatic and objective conceitedness which, by going further, abolishes Christianity.'[23]

However, even here Kierkegaard sees Luther veering in the direction of modern objective theology and preaching, by means of Luther's insistence that the Word of God is objectively true regardless of the person preaching it.

> Luther was no dialectician. In his sermon on the Epistle for the Sixth Sunday after Easter, he develops (something he develops elsewhere also) the theme that in relation to faith the concern should not be with persons but only with the word: Even if it were an apostle and he taught anything different from Holy Scripture, one ought not follow him. Well and good – but Luther should still have been a little more careful. Indeed, Christianity has obviously come into the world conversely so that the person is higher than the doctrine.[24]

For Kierkegaard, the essential sermon is not what the pastor says, but what his life expresses; and in that sense, all who consider themselves to be Christians are preaching every day of their lives (which is why Kierkegaard agrees with Luther that preaching should be done on the street). 'The essential sermon is one's own existence [*Existents*]. A person preaches with this every hour of the day and with power quite different from that of the most eloquent speaker in his most eloquent moment.'[25] For this reason, Kierkegaard thinks that Christianity should adopt the principle first elaborated by Pythagorus, that all instruction should follow a prolonged period of silence. 'Shut up, and let us see what your life expresses, for once let this be the speaker who says who you are.'[26] In comparison to Pythagorus, Luther's emphasis on the objectively true Word does not fare very well. 'If, for example, I compare Luther with Pythagoras from this point of view, the comparison is not to the advantage of Luther with his insistence that the important thing is that the doctrine be proclaimed unadulterated – that is, objectively.'[27]

The danger in Luther's position is not only that it would allow me to ignore the fact that my life expresses the opposite of what I preach, but it would also allow me to ignore what Luther's own life expressed. This is precisely the way that Luther gets taken in vain by his followers, according to Kierkegaard, and yet this dynamic is in large part caused by Luther's attention to doctrine above person. 'Here again we see how infinitely important it is in respect to the essentially Christian to take the proclaimer along. For they took Luther's doctrine about faith – but Luther's life,

23. *JP*, vol. 4, p. 351, para. 4549.
24. *JP*, vol. 3, p. 79, para. 2512.
25. *JP*, vol. 1, p. 460, para. 1056.
26. *JP*, vol. 3, p. 12, para. 2334.
27. Ibid.

that they forgot.'[28] Kierkegaard raises this issue in the last work he published in his second authorship, an authorship that had as one of its main purposes preventing taking Luther and his life in vain. 'I have wanted to prevent people in "Christendom" from existentially taking in vain Luther and the significance of Luther's life – I have wished, if possible, to contribute to preventing this.'[29] The key to understanding Luther is to remember that even though he spoke about justification and salvation by faith alone, his life expressed works. 'His life expressed works – let us never forget that – but he said: A person is saved by faith alone.'[30] Once Luther is dead, it becomes all too easy to remember what he said, and forget what his life expressed, especially since Luther told us to focus on the Word over and above the person. 'Excellent! This is something for us. Luther says, it depends on faith alone. He himself does not say that his life expresses works, and since he is now dead it is no longer an actuality. So we take his words, his doctrine – and we are free from all works – long live Luther!'[31] The irony is that whereas for most of us, our lives are far inferior to the language we use, for Luther the opposite was the case. 'Luther acted rightly, but his preaching is not always clear or in agreement with his life – a rare occurrence – his life is better than his preaching!'[32] Thus Kierkegaard imagines Luther coming back and asking the Lutherans in Copenhagen why he sees nothing being expressed in their lives, no witnessing to the truth, no persecution, no self-denial and self-renunciation. These are the things that faith should be expressing, and these are the sermons we should be preaching on the streets.

> And this, in turn, is essentially what it is to preach, because to preach is neither to describe faith in books nor as a speaker to describe in 'quiet hours' that which, as I have said in a sermon, should actually 'not be preached in churches but on the street', nor is it to be a speaker but a witness – in other words, faith, this restless thing, should be recognizable in his life.[33]

Luther's Sermons and the Experience of the Anguished Conscience

Along with works, Kierkegaard also keeps in mind that Luther's sermons must be read in light of the fear and trembling and spiritual trial that form the context of what he preached, and that give what he says its proper meaning. One of the first insights Kierkegaard takes from his deliberate reading of Luther's sermons is Luther's claim that the atonement can only be understood by the anguished

---

28. *JP*, vol. 2, p. 475, para. 2140.

29. Soren Kierkegaard, *The Point of View* (ed. and trans. Howard V. and Edna H. Hong; Princeton: Princeton University Press, 1998), p. 17.

30. *For Self-Examination*, p. 16.

31. Ibid.

32. *JP*, vol. 3, p. 78, para. 2509.

33. *For Self-Examination*, p. 19.

conscience. 'What Luther says is excellent, the one thing needful and the sole explanation – that this whole doctrine (of the Atonement and in the main all Christianity) must be traced back to the struggle of the anguished conscience. Remove the anguished conscience, and you may as well close the churches and turn them into dance halls. The anguished conscience understands Christianity.'[34] Kierkegaard was especially taken by the contrast between the understanding of the anguished conscience, and the understanding of indifferent speculation. The atonement is like food for a starving person, and cannot be understood if the need for the atonement is not deeply felt in the conscience, any more than food can be understood by a creature that does not need to eat. However, the hunger of a conscience anguished by sin is not a natural phenomenon as is hunger, and so sin must be brought to consciousness by revelation, which Luther also noted. 'It is therefore very consistent for Luther to teach that a person must be taught by a revelation concerning how deeply he lies in sin, that the anguished conscience is not a natural consequence like being hungry.'[35]

Kierkegaard also takes from Luther the insight that only the conscience anguished by sin can bring a person through the repulsive force of the possibility of offence to have faith in Christ. Kierkegaard links these ideas in *Works of Love*, published one year after he first reflects on this issue in his journal. 'Therefore, take away from the essentially Christian the possibility of offense, or take away from the forgiveness of sins the battle of the anguished conscience (to which, according to Luther's excellent explanation, this whole doctrine is to lead), and then close the churches, the sooner the better, or turn them into places of amusement that stand open all day!'[36] Kierkegaard returns to this idea in 'The Moral' at the end of Part I of *Practice in Christianity*: only the consciousness of sin can force one through the terrifying and appalling nature of the possibility of offence to have faith in Christ. 'And at that very same moment the essentially Christian transforms itself into and is sheer leniency, grace, love, mercy.'[37] Kierkegaard was able to understand his own experience of Christianity by means of Luther's explanation. The impression of Christianity he received from his father actually caused him to be offended by Christianity; but when his conscience was struck by the awareness of his sin, he broke through the possibility of offence to believe in Christ. 'The correlations are: if I were not personally conscious of being a sinner, I would have to be offended with Christianity. The consciousness of sin shuts my mouth so that in spite of the possibility of offense I choose to believe.'[38] It is also clear that Kierkegaard at this point agrees with Luther that once the anguished conscience breaks through the

34. *JP*, vol. 3, p. 63, para. 2461.

35. *JP*, vol. 3, p. 64, para. 2461.

36. Soren Kierkegaard, *Works of Love* (ed. and trans. Howard V. and Edna H. Hong; Princeton: Princeton University Press, 1995), p. 201.

37. Soren Kierkegaard, *Practice in Christianity* (ed. and trans. Howard V. and Edna H. Hong; Princeton: Princeton University Press, 1991), p. 67.

38. *JP*, vol. 6, p. 64, para. 6261.

possibility of offence by faith in Christ, it experiences genuine joy through the forgiveness of sin.

> Luther is right in saying in his sermon on the Gospel for Christmas Day that there is nothing else to say about Christ than that he is 'a great joy' – but, but 'for sin-crushed consciences' – otherwise not, otherwise he is taken in vain. The part about joy is promptly seized upon – the part about 'a sin-crushed conscience' meets with extreme resistance.[39]

Luther's preaching about Christian joy can only rightly be understood in the context of the battle of the conscience anguished by its sin: otherwise, one takes Luther's preaching about the joy of God's mercy in vain.

However, between the years 1853 and 1854, Kierkegaard begins to raise serious questions about the legitimacy of Luther's preaching of the joy that follows upon faith in Christ. To begin with, he doubts that anything like the anguished conscience can be found in the Christendom of his day. 'Luther says that this whole doctrine is to lead to the battle of the anguished conscience. Have you seen anyone among us whom you could imagine to have the Christian presuppositions? I have not seen one.'[40] The joy Luther experienced took place after a very long period of such anguish, the likes of which are very rarely seen.

> Let us see how things went with Luther! After about twenty years of fear and trembling and spiritual trial [Anfægtelse] so terrible that – note this well! – there is hardly one individual in a generation who experiences anything like it, his human nature reacted, to put it this way, and this fear and trembling was transfigured into the most blissful and happy confidence and joy – wonderful![41]

Kierkegaard highlights two problems created by Luther's exceptional experience. First of all, since it is impossible to universalize Luther's experience of a terrified conscience, as it is only seen in one person in any generation, it is very dangerous to apply the solution Luther discovered as though it were universally applicable.

> Luther's approach presupposes that men are suffering under fear and trembling and spiritual trials, therefore console, console them, reassure them, reassure them so that no such poor Christian man sits in mortal anxiety and doubts his salvation – O, I know what this means – therefore reassure them. O, dear Luther, where are these Christian men you speak of? And if such an individual is found ever so seldom, can and ought this be made the universal principle which we swindlers have made it by taking advantage of Luther?[42]

---

39. *JP*, vol. 6, p. 354, para. 6686.
40. *JP*, vol. 2, p. 174, para. 1486.
41. *JP*, vol. 3, p. 94, para. 2544.
42. Ibid.

Secondly, by turning the gospel into the consolation and reassurance of anguished consciences, Luther fundamentally alters Christianity. 'Thus Luther turns Christianity upside down. Christianity exists to soothe and reassure, Christ came to the world to soothe and reassure, it is added, anguished consciences. This is completely opposite to the New Testament.'[43] Again, the problem with Luther is that he universalized both his anguished conscience and his need for consolation, and thereby fundamentally distorted Christianity. 'But the tragedy about Luther is that a condition in Christendom at a particular time and place is transformed into the normative. Luther suffered exceedingly from an anguished conscience and needed a cure. Well and good, but must Christianity therefore be converted *in toto* to this, to soothing and reassuring anguished consciences?'[44] In his final years, Kierkegaard insists that there is no alleviation of the anguished conscience in this life, 'nothing but fear and trembling, intensified by being in this evil world which crucified love, intensified by trepidation over the accounting when the Lord and Master will come again and judge whether they have been faithful.'[45] Luther's teaching of consolation for the anguished conscience represents the alteration of Christianity away from the point of view of the physician – God – towards the point of view of the patient, who seeks the alleviation of his suffering: 'He has the patient's passion for expressing and describing his suffering and what he feels he needs to relieve it, but he does not have the physician's comprehensive view.'[46]

Luther on Christ as Gift and Example

Another theme that Kierkegaard takes from his reading of Luther's sermons is Luther's distinction between Christ as example and Christ as gift. 'Luther is entirely right in what he says in the preface to his sermons about the distinction between Christ as pattern [*Exempel*] and as gift.'[47] Kierkegaard places Luther in the context of a medieval piety that focused solely on Christ as prototype or example, and forgot that Christ is also the gift and the Atoner. As a consequence, the Middle Ages underestimated the difference between Christ and the rest of us, and, like Kierkegaard in his youth, thought it would be a fairly straightforward matter to pattern its life after the life of Christ.

> The medieval conception of Christ as the prototype, its beautiful zeal to resemble him – this is youthfulness which wants to get along right away. But the older one becomes, the deeper becomes the qualitative distinction between the ideal and the man who wants to resemble it. Therefore Luther actually fought against a too

43. *JP*, vol. 3, pp. 99–101, para. 2550.
44. Ibid.
45. Ibid.
46. Ibid.
47. *JP*, vol. 3, p .76, para. 2503.

zealous and too enthusiastic desire to make Christ only the prototype – and now it appears all the more that the prototype is also something else, is the Atoner whom we cannot resemble, who can only help us.[48]

Luther therefore represents the transition of Christianity from the naïve youthful view that imitation is easy and is all that is required, to the adult realization that Christ as Pattern is infinitely removed from us, and makes all our striving to conform our lives to His seem either like nothingness or a jest. 'Since the Middle Ages had gone farther and farther astray in accentuating the aspect of Christ as the prototype – Luther came along and accentuated the other side, that he is a gift and this gift is to be received in faith.'[49] As gift, Christ gives us the grace by which we can strive to resemble Him; and by His death, He gives us the assurance that it is not our striving that justifies and saves us, but rather our faith in His atonement. 'Therefore it is not simply a matter of Christ's being the prototype and that I simply ought to will to resemble him. In the first place I need His help in order to be able to resemble Him, and, secondly, insofar as he is the Savior and Reconciler of the race, I cannot in fact resemble him.'[50] To counter the overemphasis on Christ as Pattern, Luther placed an even greater emphasis on Christ as gift, Who cannot be imitated, but in Whom we are to have faith.[51]

Over against the Middle Ages, which wanted to begin and end with Christ as Prototype, Kierkegaard initially agrees with Luther that one must begin with faith in Christ as gift, and only then strive to conform to Christ as Prototype. 'The teaching about the prototype, then, can no longer plainly and simply occupy the first place. Faith comes first, Christ as the gift.'[52] This turn made by Luther represents the coming of age of Christianity, into its adult realization of the distance between Christ's ideality and the reality of our lives. 'The adult comprehends with infinite depth the distance between himself and the ideal – and now "faith" must first of all intervene as that in which he actually rests, the faith that fulfillment has been made, the faith that I am saved by faith alone. So far Luther is perfectly right and is a turning point in the development of religion.'[53]

Kierkegaard also initially agrees with Luther that beginning with Christ the Pattern results either in the presumption that one can conform to Christ, intensified by the erroneous teaching of merit in the Roman Church, or in the despair that results when one is reduced to nothingness in the striving. 'Luther is completely right in saying that if a man had to acquire his salvation by his own striving, it would end either in presumption or in despair, and therefore it is faith that saves.'[54]

48. *JP*, vol. 1, p. 325, para. 693.

49. *JP*, vol. 3, p. 69, para. 2481.

50. *JP*, vol. 1, p. 325, para. 693.

51. Ibid.

52. *JP*, vol. 2, p. 16, para. 1135.

53. Ibid.

54. *JP*, vol. 2, p. 19, para. 1139.

However, faith in Christ the gift should not eliminate striving to conform to Christ as Pattern, but should rather make such striving possible, since it addresses my anxiety that such striving is impossible.

> Faith should make striving possible, because the very fact that I am saved by faith and that nothing at all is demanded from me should in itself make it possible that I begin to strive, that I do not collapse under impossibility but am encouraged and refreshed, because it has been decided I am saved, I am God's child by virtue of faith.[55]

Faith also gives me a place of rest in my striving, and gives me the grace by which I might strive. 'Only in this way can a poor human being be kept in the struggle. In order to gain courage to strive, he must rest in the blessed assurance that everything is already decided, that he has conquered – in faith and by faith.'[56] Indeed, it is precisely the joy that faith brings to the anguished conscience, noted above, that should inspire our striving.

> Then comes the reassurance and the blessedness – and then it would not be impossible for a man to be so moved by all this love and feel so blessed that it becomes love's joy for him to die to the world. Does there not come a moment when a man says: There really is grace; and imitation, as Luther says so superbly, ought not plunge a man into despair or into blasphemy. If that moment comes, then, in spite of all its pain, imitation is a matter of love and as such is blessed.[57]

However, in his later years Kierkegaard began to have serious doubts about the legitimacy of beginning with faith in Christ as gift, in the assumption that striving to conform to Christ as example would follow of its own accord. He was aware all along that Luther's emphasis on Christ as Atoner meant that 'His being the prototype almost evaporated as something altogether too transcendent. This, however, must not be done.'[58] Kierkegaard therefore sought to reintroduce the importance of Christ as Prototype in order to address the previously noted issue of taking grace in vain by the lack of an anguished conscience. Kierkegaard became convinced that it is only our attempt to strive after the example of Christ that reveals to us our own sinfulness, and our own need for grace. 'It is "imitation" (to suffer for the doctrine and what belongs to it) which must be emphasized again; in this way the task relates itself dialectically to the point where Luther eased up.'[59] However, as he began to attend more directly to imitation, Kierkegaard noticed that the New Testament does not begin with faith, as Luther did, but rather begins with obeying the unconditional command of Christ. Only when one acts in

---

55. Ibid.
56. *JP*, vol. 2, p. 165, para. 1473.
57. *JP*, vol. 2, p. 348, para. 1903.
58. *JP*, vol. 1, p. 325, para. 693.
59. *JP*, vol. 2, p. 346, para. 1902.

such a decisive way – by selling all one's possessions, or by loving one's enemies, etc. – does one discover the need for Christ both as gift and as example.

> In the New Testament the matter is very simple. Christ says: Do according to what I say – and you shall know. Consequently, decisive action first of all. By acting your life will come into collision with all existence [*Tilværelsen*], and you will get something to think about besides doubt, and in a double sense you will need Christianity both as the prototype [*Forbilledet*] and as grace.[60]

Kierkegaard therefore argues that one should not begin with faith, for that is where Luther ended up; rather, one should begin with works, with venturing out in obedience to Christ the Prototype, for that is where Luther himself began.[61]

Kierkegaard also rejected Luther's claim, with which he had previously completely agreed, that beginning with striving leads either to presumption or despair.

> Luther understood the problem thus: No man can endure the anxiety [*Angst*] that his striving will decide his eternal salvation or eternal damnation. No, no, says Luther, this can only lead to despair or to blasphemy. And therefore (note this!), therefore it is not so (Luther apparently alters New Testament Christianity because otherwise mankind must despair). You are saved by grace; be reassured, you are saved by grace – and then you strive as well as you can.[62]

Kierkegaard objects to this claim of Luther's on the same ground he came to reject Luther's need for a consoled and assured conscience: it transforms Christianity by teaching it from the human point of view rather than from the divine perspective.

> My objection is this: Luther ought to have let it be known that he reduced Christianity. Furthermore, he ought to have made it be known that his argument: 'otherwise we must despair' – is actually arguing from the human side. But, strictly speaking, this argument is without foundation when the question is what the New Testament understands by Christianity; strictly speaking, the fact that Luther could argue thus shows that for him Christianity was not yet unconditionally sovereign, but that this sovereignty, too, has to yield under the assumption that 'otherwise a man must despair.'[63]

By beginning with the imitation of Christ as example, but without the false teaching of merit, Kierkegaard insists that he is beginning where Luther began,

60. *JP*, vol. 2, p. 347, para. 1902.
61. *JP*, vol. 3, p. 93, para. 2543.
62. *JP*, vol. 3, pp. 101–2, para. 2551.
63. Ibid.

and is thereby correctly presenting the dialectic of Christ as Pattern and Saviour. Only the one who has already ventured to imitate Christ can come to need Christ both as Gift and as Pattern; and only one who begins with striving will return to striving after coming to know Christ as gift.

> Help us all, each one of us, you who both will and can, you who are both the prototype and the Redeemer, and in turn both the Redeemer and the prototype, so that when the striving one droops under the prototype, crushed, almost despairing, the Redeemer raises him up again; but at the same moment you are again the prototype, so that he may be kept in the striving.[64]

Luther on the 'double danger' of Faith

Related to the issue of imitating Christ is the inevitability of persecution if one truly follows Christ. Again Kierkegaard initially completely endorses Luther's understanding of this issue in his sermons. 'In his sermon on the Gospel for the Second Sunday after Easter ("I am the good shepherd"), Luther very movingly develops the way the true Christian becomes unrecognizable, as it were, through all the persecution and mistreatment etc. he suffers – but Christ still knows him and recognizes him as his own.'[65] Kierkegaard especially likes the way Luther makes persecution one of the three identifying marks of the life of the Christian, for this again distinguishes Luther from the position of Bishop Mynster. 'Somewhere in his sermons Luther declares that three things belong to a Christian life: (1) faith, (2) works of love, (3) persecution for this faith and for these works of love. Take Mynster now. He has reduced faith oriented toward tension and inwardness. He has set legality in the place of works of love. And persecution he has completely abolished.'[66] Kierkegaard also endorses the way Luther makes the suffering of persecution into a mark of the Church. 'Luther was entirely correct in referring to the true Church as a despised little flock – the pope and all that are not the true Church.'[67] Kierkegaard cites this teaching of Luther in *Judge for Yourself*, written in 1852 but unpublished in his lifetime. 'It is this that the prototype expresses; it is also this, to mention a mere man, that Luther, the superb teacher of the Church, continually points out as belonging to true Christianity: to suffer for the doctrine, to do good and suffer for it, and that suffering in this world is inseparable from being a Christian in this world.'[68]

However, Kierkegaard is also critical of the way Luther expresses his understanding of this issue in his sermons. On the one hand, Luther is

---

64. *Judge for Yourself*, p. 147.
65. *JP*, vol. 2, p. 72, para. 2491.
66. *JP*, vol. 6, p. 337, para. 6653.
67. *JP*, vol. 4, p. 361, para. 4566.
68. *Judge for Yourself*, p. 169.

contradictory, for in one passage he teaches that God blesses those who are faithful, which Kierkegaard sees as being 'Jewish piety', while in another passage Luther will say that the true Christian must suffer in every way in this world. 'On this point, as with so many existential points, Luther contradicts himself when one puts his thoughts together.'[69] On the other hand, Kierkegaard accuses Luther of being 'undialectical' in his understanding of the suffering of the faithful, for Luther in his sermons ascribes such suffering not to God, but to the devil. 'It is the same with Luther's understanding of Christianity. He distributes: the good is credited to Christianity; all sufferings, spiritual trial, etc., come from the devil. Dialectically one must say: both the consolation and the suffering come with Christianity, for this is the dialectic of the absolute, and Christianity is the absolute.'[70] Ascribing the suffering of Christians to the devil preserves Luther's attempt to make Christianity comforting, by ascribing suffering not to Christianity or to God, but to the devil.

The same holds true for the way Luther explains spiritual trial as being caused by the devil. For Kierkegaard, spiritual trial is created by the relationship to Christ, when one ventures a decisive act for the sake of Christ, in obedience to Christ, and then immediately wonders if one went too far, and needs to repent for this decisive act.

> Luther says that as soon as Christ has come on board the storm immediately begins; this storm is spiritual trial, which Luther attributes to the devil. This, however, is more childish than true. No, it is spiritual trial because it seems to the person himself as if the relationship were stretched too tightly, as if he were venturing too boldly in literally involving himself personally with God and Christ.[71]

Over against Luther, Kierkegaard insists that spiritual trial is dialectical, and is a direct consequence of coming into a direct relationship with God and Christ.

For Kierkegaard, Christian faith always involves the double danger, first that one dares to do the right thing by imitating Christ in humility, self-denial and love, and then that one suffers precisely because one dares to imitate Christ. Luther does not always hold to this dialectic, because Luther does not rightly distinguish between 'Jewish piety' and Christianity.

> Luther's sermon on the Epistle for the Third Sunday in Trinity may be cited as an example of his incorrectness. In his first point about humility he says that both God and the world resist the proud but love the humble. In his next point he shows how the pious man must suffer, why he needs consolation. (Cast all your cares upon God.) Here Luther has in the first place obviously forgotten to define accurately the Christian collision. It simply is not true that the world

---

69. *JP*, vol. 3, pp. 88–9, para. 2531.

70. *JP*, vol. 1, p. 192, para. 486.

71. *JP*, vol. 4, pp. 262–3, para. 4372.

loves the humble person. The world ridicules the humble person. And essential Christianity continually means to do the good and for that very reason to suffer.[72]

Luther's failure to maintain the dialectic of the double danger of Christianity not only affects his preaching, but it is also manifested in his life. Up until 1521, Luther appeared to be heading on a course towards martyrdom, which for Kierkegaard would have shown the right understanding of the dialectic of the double danger: to preach genuine Christianity, and be killed for it. But Luther turned aside from martyrdom immediately after his appearance at Worms, and as a consequence both his teaching and his life introduced confusion into the Lutheran Church regarding the dialectic of the double danger.

> If one wants to cite Luther, it must be pointed out that Luther, after all, turned off into worldliness and really was victorious in a secular sense and consequently did not reach the point of running the last lap, something for which at the very end of his life he upbraided himself, wondering whether he should not have gone to Rome and been put to death instead of permitting himself to be a protégé of secularity. If he had done that, this final suffering would have come to him, also. But honest Luther, in spite of all his integrity, nevertheless perhaps became an occasion for the prodigious confusion which has confounded Protestantism: mistaking secular victory for godly victory.[73]

Luther's decision to avoid martyrdom, and to seek and even to obtain victory over the Pope in this life, has corrupted the movement coming from Luther, and it is this corruption that Kierkegaard sought to expose and eliminate.

> This change really came in with Luther. He was the Christian hero who blinked, certainly not because of lack of courage; no, but ensnared in the idea that it is godliness to be made happy in this life, faith in the unconditioned value of martyrdom vanished. He did not refuse the assistance of men – in his hour of death he repented of it.[74]

By 1854, Kierkegaard sees that the errors Luther makes in his preaching about persecution and suffering have their ultimate source in the distinction Luther makes between the law and the gospel. For Luther, the law terrifies, whereas the gospel consoles the terrified. This is completely undialectical for Kierkegaard. It is the gospel itself that both terrifies and consoles, or consoles and terrifies. 'There is a shameful abuse fostered by the division: the law terrifies – the gospel reassures. No, the gospel itself is and must be terrifying at first. If this had not been the case,

---

72. *JP*, vol. 3, p. 70, para. 2482.
73. *JP*, vol. 4, p. 422, para. 4699.
74. *JP*, vol. 4, p. 189, para. 4220.

why in the world did it go with Christ as it did when he said: Come to me – and they all went away, they fled from him.'[75] Kierkegaard sees Luther's distinction between the terror of the law and the consolation of the gospel as bringing 'Jewish piety' back into Christianity, by claiming that there is an alleviation of suffering and the anguished conscience in this life. For instance, Abraham is tried by being commanded to sacrifice Isaac, but then Isaac is restored to him. Job is tried by having everything taken away from him, but then everything is restored to him in this life. According to Kierkegaard, 'Every human existence in which the tension of life is resolved within this life is Judaism. Christianity is: this life, sheer suffering – eternity.'[76]

Thus Luther's distinction of the law from the gospel is a departure from the preaching of Christ.

> The way in which even Luther speaks of the law and gospel is still not the teaching of Christ. [*In margin*: Luther's sermon on the Gospel for the Third Sunday in Advent can be used as an example.] Luther separates the two: the law and the gospel. First the law and then the gospel, which is sheer leniency, etc. This way Christianity becomes an optimism anticipating that we are to have an easy life in this world. This means that Christianity becomes Judaism. The law corresponds, for example, to what being tempted and tried by God was in the Old Testament, but then comes the gospel, just as in the Old Testament the time of testing came to an end and everything became joy and jubilation.[77]

According to Kierkegaard, the distinction between the law and the gospel represents yet another attempt by Luther to teach Christianity from the human point of view, rather than from the divine perspective, as we saw previously with regard to the consolation of the anguished conscience.

> It does not help that we men get angry ten times over and say: No human being can endure that. This does not help. God is not impressed. The error in Luther's preaching is that it bears the mark of this consideration for us poor human beings, which shows that he does not hold Christianity at the level which is found in the New Testament, specifically in the gospel: the unconditioned. No, God is not impressed; he changes nothing. Yet believe that it is out of love that he wills what he wills.[78]

The love of God is the cause of the fear, trembling and spiritual trial of the Christian, so any attempt to alleviate that fear and anguish actually represents a departure from the love of God.

75. *JP*, vol. 4, p. 240, para. 4333.
76. *JP*, vol. 3, pp. 102–4, para. 2554.
77. Ibid.
78. Ibid.

Luther, Paul and Christ

Kierkegaard is aware, however, that the preaching of the apostle Paul lies behind Luther's distinction between the law and the gospel, as well as his claim that there is an alleviation of our suffering and anguish in this life. The problem is that Luther uses Paul to criticize Christ, and where the two disagree, Luther places Paul above Christ.

> But it is easy to see that Luther's preaching of Christianity changes Christianity's life-view and world view. He has one-sidedly appropriated 'the apostle' and goes so far – as he frequently does with this yardstick (turned the wrong way) – that he criticizes the gospels. If he does not find the apostle's teaching in the gospel he concludes *ergo* this is no gospel. Luther does not seem to see that the apostle has already relaxed in relation to the gospels.[79]

Luther's followers compound the problem, for they place Luther above Paul, and even use him to correct Paul. 'When we found the apostle to be more rigorous (which he is) than Luther, we concluded: Here the apostle is wrong, this is not pure gospel. In this way we have systematically, step by step, cheated – that is, attempted to cheat God out of the gospel by turning the whole relationship around.'[80]

According to Kierkegaard, Luther assesses the teaching both of Christ and of Paul in light of his own deep need for comfort and consolation in the midst of his anguished conscience, and in the process places his own needs and concerns above those of God. Luther's preaching therefore represents a revolution against the unconditioned love of God.

> The turn which Luther gave – namely, that Christianity must first and foremost *quiet* and *reassure* – is really the language of revolution, even though in the language of the greatest possible submission. The Christian demand presses to the utter extremity, and then the purely human reacts: We cannot; this is sheer death-agony – Christianity must first and foremost quiet and reassure. But this kind of talking cunningly attributes a quality of deference to the unconditioned. And as soon as the unconditioned acquires a deference or as soon as it is assumed that something is able to set itself in relationship with the unconditioned, that the unconditioned defers to it, the unconditioned is no longer the unconditioned. Fundamentally, Luther's view makes the decisive factor in Christianity whether or not men are able to be comfortably disposed by it, but then Christianity is not the unconditioned and God is only a relative majesty. The law for revolution is declared in Luther's view.[81]

---

79. Ibid.
80. Ibid.
81. *JP*, vol. 3, p. 104, para. 2555.

This means that Luther's followers did not misunderstand him when they placed him above the apostle Paul, and the apostle Paul above Christ, for as early as 1849 Kierkegaard sees that Luther had already done this himself.

> Luther's teaching is not only a return to original Christianity but a modification of the essentially Christian. He onesidedly draws Paul forward and uses the gospels less. He himself best disproves his conception of the Bible, he who throws out the epistle of James. Why? Because it does not belong to the canon? No, this he does not deny. But on dogmatic grounds. Therefore he himself has a point of departure superior to the Bible, which probably was his idea, too.[82]

Kierkegaard sees this position emerging directly in Luther's sermons, especially in the way he makes his distinction between the law and the gospel normative for the reading of Scripture.

> In his sermon on the Gospel for the First Sunday in Advent, right at the beginning, Luther states that every legitimate gospel proclaims first faith and then works, and every gospel in which this is the case is legitimate gospel. But what about appealing to Scripture as the only norm? Here Luther has himself made a norm by which he determines what is a legitimate gospel.[83]

Kierkegaard certainly knew how radical this criticism of Luther would be. He never published his claim that Luther placed himself above Christ and the Apostle, and only referred to the way Luther places Paul above Christ in one of the last of his publications, in the article called 'My Task' in *The Moment* Number 10, which was prepared for publication but not, in fact, published before his death. In a footnote about the apostle Paul, Kierkegaard says:

> It is of great importance, to Protestantism in particular, to correct the enormous confusion Luther caused by inverting the relation and actually criticizing Christ by means of Paul, the Master by means of the follower. I, on the contrary, have not criticized the apostle, as if I myself were something, I who am not even a Christian; what I have done is to hold Christ's proclamation alongside the apostle's.[84]

The task was therefore clear to Kierkegaard. If there were to be any hope of restoring Christianity to Christendom, we would have to walk in the opposite direction from that taken by the Lutheran tradition: from Mynster back to Luther, from Luther back to Paul, and from Paul back to James and Matthew.

---

82. *JP*, vol. 3, p. 77, para. 2507.
83. *JP*, vol. 3, p. 88, para. 2529.
84. Soren Kierkegaard, *'The Moment' and Late Writings* (ed. and trans. Howard V. and Edna H. Hong; Princeton: Princeton University Press, 1998), p. 341.

Such a movement would also restore forms of life in the Church that Luther had erroneously eliminated in his concern to attain a decisive victory over the Pope. In order to set forth the preaching of beginning with a decisive act of discipleship in imitation of Christ the Prototype, monasticism needs to be restored, for over against Luther, it stands in a dialectical relationship to Christian faith. '"The monastery" is an essential dialectical element in Christianity; therefore we need to have it out there like a buoy at sea in order to see where we are, even though I myself would not enter it. But if there really is true Christianity in every generation, there must also be individuals who have this need.'[85] Monastic life sets forth the 'gymnastics' of asceticism that is the necessary preparation for all Christians to become witnesses to the truth.[86] Similarly, the single, unmarried life needs to be restored, for it stands in dialectical tension with marriage and family, and 'in these times it might be beneficial for a person to refrain from marrying, expressly in order to declare that spirituality still has so much reality [*Realitet*] that it can be enough, more than enough, for a life'.[87] Finally, over against Luther's preaching of the priesthood of all believers, the office of the clergy needs to be restored, for it stands in dialectical relation to the laity.

> There should be a clergy as the middle term. The clergy should be rigorously Christian, should express the most strenuous demands of Christianity, at least approximately, for otherwise the whole thing is destroyed and everything becomes secularism through and through, which is the actual case. Draconian laws amount to nothing, and the magnificent sublimity that we are all priests – leads to the tragic nonsense we see before us. This clergy must be recruited from such persons who have been brought to break completely with the world, either by great sins or very severe misfortunes, and the like.[88]

All of these offices manifest forms of personal existence that have broken with the world, and therefore preach the need to do this to all Christians, in conformity to the summons represented by Christ's life. 'His teaching was really his life, his existence. If someone wanted to be his follower, his approach, as seen in the Gospel, was different from lecturing. To such a person he said something like this: Venture a decisive act; then we can begin.'[89]

---

85. *JP*, vol. 3, p. 210, para. 2750.
86. *JP*, vol. 3, p. 216, para. 2763.
87. *JP*, vol. 3, p. 128, para. 2599.
88. *JP*, vol. 3, p. 444, para. 3153.
89. *Judge for Yourself*, p. 191.

Bibliography

Coe, David L., 'Kierkegaard's Forking for Extracts from Extracts of Luther's Sermons: Reviewing Kierkegaard's Laud and Lance of Luther', *Kierkegaard Studies: Yearbook* (2011), pp. 3–18.

Ferriera, M. Jamie, *Love's Grateful Striving: A Commentary on Kierkegaard's 'Works of Love'* (Oxford: Oxford University Press, 2001).

Kierkegaard, Soren, *For Self-Examination and Judge for Yourself* (ed. and trans. Howard V. and Edna H. Hong; Princeton: Princeton University Press, 1990).

Kierkegaard, Soren, *'The Moment' and Late Writings* (ed. and trans. Howard V. and Edna H. Hong; Princeton: Princeton University Press, 1998).

Kierkegaard, Soren, *The Point of View* (ed. and trans. Howard V. and Edna H. Hong; Princeton: Princeton University Press, 1998).

Kierkegaard, Soren, *Practice in Christianity* (ed. and trans. Howard V. and Edna H. Hong; Princeton: Princeton University Press, 1991).

Kierkegaard, Soren, *Soren Kierkegaard's Journals and Papers* (ed. and trans. Howard V. and Edna H. Hong; 7 vols; Bloomington, University of Indiana Press, 1967–78).

Kierkegaard, Soren, *Upbuilding Discourses in Various Spirits* (ed. and trans. Howard V. and Edna H. Hong; Princeton: Princeton University Press, 1993).

Kierkegaard, Soren, *Works of Love* (ed. and trans. Howard V. and Edna H. Hong; Princeton: Princeton University Press, 1995).

Kim, David Yoon-Jung and Joel D. S. Rasmussen, 'Martin Luther: Reform, Secularization, and the Question of His "True Successor"', in Jon Stewart (ed.), *Kierkegaard and the Renaissance and Modern Traditions – Theology* (Burlington, VT: Ashgate, 2009), pp. 184–207.

Luther, Martin, *En christelig Postille, sammendragen af Dr. Morten Luthers Kirke- og Huuspostiller efter Benjamin Lindners tyske Samling udgiven I ny dansk Oversættelse af Jørgen Thisted* (2 vols; Copenhagen: Wahlske Boghandling 1828).

Chapter 14

LESSONS FOR AN EVANGELICAL SPIRITUALITY FROM BERNARD OF CLAIRVAUX AND THOMAS MERTON

Matthew Knell

On being asked to contribute to this Festschrift, there was no doubt about the central subject for my chapter – Bernard of Clairvaux, with whom I had engaged when studying under Tony.[1] There have been a number of elements that have shaped this chapter's application of Bernard's writing. One of Tony's significant contributions to Evangelical engagement with the medieval period was his book on Calvin's use of Bernard, which helped to promote engagement with the pre-Reformation period.[2] In seeking to follow in the footsteps of this work, this chapter will evaluate Bernard's influence on Thomas Merton, who has been important in the development of a new spirituality in the second half of the twentieth century, beginning in his Catholic context but becoming increasingly influential in other denominations of the Christian faith. In an engagement with Bernard, this approach has certain advantages: first, Merton interacts with a medieval spirituality from a modern perspective and can thus be used as a filter to help access Bernard's thought; second, Merton applies this to a modern context, giving a basis for more focused application: 'he did not merely repeat the teaching of the abbot of Clairvaux. He gave it a powerful new expression in the existential terminology of our times';[3] and third, Basil Pennington has provided the groundwork for a link between the two writers, which allows this chapter to concentrate on the impact of their spirituality for the Evangelical movement.[4]

1. See the chapter on 'William of St. Thierry and Bernard of Clairvaux', in M. Knell, *The Immanent Person of the Holy Spirit from Anselm to Lombard: Divine Communion in the Spirit* (Milton Keynes: Paternoster, 2009).

2. A. N. S. Lane, *Calvin and Bernard of Clairvaux* (Studies in Reformed Theology and History, New Series, 1; Princeton: Princeton Theological Seminary, 1996).

3. B. Pennington, 'Like Father, Like Son: Bernard of Clairvaux and Thomas Merton', in J. Sommerfeldt (ed.), *Bernardus Magister: Papers Presented at the Nonacentenary Celebration of the Birth of Saint Bernard of Clairvaux, Kalamazoo, Michigan* (Citeaux: Cistercian Publications, 1992), pp. 569–78 (572).

4. Ibid. This chapter will not seek to define 'Evangelical' too narrowly, given that the intention is to provide lessons in spirituality that can be applied as widely as possible.

In order to establish the link between the two men, this chapter will begin by analysing the effects of Bernard of Clairvaux on Thomas Merton and the latter's use of the former in his spiritual work. This will naturally build on Pennington's chapter, and will also clarify the range of influences on Merton's spirituality in order to locate precisely Bernard's contribution. This is necessary because the focus of this analysis will be on two particular areas, building on each other, that seem pertinent to Evangelicalism: the balance between contemplation and activism, and the role of charity (*caritas*) in a person's ministry. Each of these will not be sought primarily in Merton's explicit analysis of Bernard in works such as *The New Man*, but rather in the devotional material of the two writers.[5] The aim is to provide a challenge to the roots of Evangelical activism and another perspective from which to consider priorities in the Christian life.

Bernard of Clairvaux's Influence on Thomas Merton

While Stephen Harding was the founder of the Cistercian order, Bernard of Clairvaux was clearly the dominant early voice and the defining figure in Cistercian spirituality. Given Merton's ultimate vocation to join the Cistercians as a Trappist monk, it is unsurprising that he was so drawn to Bernard's works.[6] Thomas Merton certainly drew from a wide range of sources in his reflective works, but it is clear that the abbot of Clairvaux was a primary resource in key areas relative to this study.

Merton's devotion to Bernard is perhaps best expressed in his book, *The Last of the Fathers*, which provides the first English translation of the Papal Encyclical on Bernard of Clairvaux – the *Doctor Mellifluus* – a document that Merton states, 'should now receive a wide dissemination, for nothing could be more timely than its timeless appeal for a return to genuine Christian charity, nourished by a deep interior life, sustained by contemplation, and bearing fruit not so much in material works as in true love for other men'.[7] In this book, Merton provides a very personal account of Bernard and a commentary on the Encyclical, showing his admiration for the abbot's contemplative wisdom and willingness, from this basis, to engage with the world in a variety of spheres. This is a more reflective engagement with the Saint than his other analyses of Bernard such as those collected in the book, *Thomas Merton on St. Bernard*.[8]

---

5. T. Merton, *The New Man* (New York: Farrar, Strauss and Giroux, 1961).

6. For a detailed account of Merton's vocational struggles, see his autobiography: T. Merton, *The Seven Storey Mountain* (London: Sheldon Press, 1975). The full name of the Trappist order is 'The Order of Cistercians of Strict Observance'.

7. T. Merton, *The Last of the Fathers: Saint Bernard of Clairvaux and the Encyclical Letter, Doctor Mellifluus* (London: Hollis & Carter, 1954), p. 14.

8. J. Leclerq (ed.), *Thomas Merton on St. Bernard* (Kalamazoo: Cistercian Publications, 1980). Pennington provides a list of Merton's works on Bernard in his chapter 'Like Father, Like Son', pp. 577–8.

This chapter is not seeking to draw direct comparisons between the two men, but to draw out two key themes from their respective contemplative writings. As a result, the concentration will be on these themes, rather than Merton's commentary on Bernard. Pennington shows well in his analysis 'Like Father, Like Son' how a similar motivation led to similar results: 'Both were moved powerfully by grace to seek the fullness of the mystical life. Both wrote extensively on this search for God. ... Yet long before they reached these final syntheses, circumstances and the love of Christ urged them to expand their contemplative consciousness to embrace a wounded humanity with its many pressing needs.'[9] In light of this chapter's focus, this Christological centrality for both writers is important to note, given their fame as 'spiritual' writers and a certain wariness in Evangelical circles about such Catholic spirituality. Tony Lane has recently shown us the vital importance of Bernard's teaching on Christ and the cross in his overall work, and Merton likewise highlights this in passages such as the following from *The Monastic Journey*: 'If we are to live as Christians, as members of the incarnate word, we must remember that the life of our senses has also been elevated and sanctified by the grace of Christ. ... He [the monk] must rejoice in the fact that by his hidden union with Christ he enables all things to come closer to their last end.'[10] It is good to establish that both writers have this Christological basis for the Christian's identity since this theme will not be picked up on in the main analysis.

One final point that needs to be made in this section on the relationship between Merton and Bernard is that the latter was not the sole influence on the former (indeed, there is a solid case that he was not even the primary influence). Merton's reflective works show an incredibly broad range of sources that are used alongside his own experiences and context. Given the monastic focus of many of his books, it is unsurprising that St Benedict and his Rule are prominent, although one may have expected that the *Carta Caritatis* – Stephen Harding's Rule for the Cistercian order – would have been more prominent. The other major influence on Thomas Merton was the Spanish mystic St John of the Cross. Lawrence Cunningham writes in his biography of Merton of St John's role as 'mentor', stating, 'During his first years in the monastery Merton studied Saint John assiduously, an interest that he had developed long before he entered the monastery'.[11]

This link is vital to understand in the context of this chapter, since St John informed Merton on the same themes that are studied here, but along different lines. In his clearest work on the mystic, *The Ascent to Truth*, Merton works extensively with St John on the practices of contemplation and charity.[12] Merton makes clear

---

9. Pennington, 'Like Father, Like Son', pp. 570–1.

10. T. Merton, *The Monastic Journey* (London: Sheldon Press, 1977), p. 18. See also A. N. S. Lane, *Bernard of Clairvaux: Theologian of the Cross* (Collegeville, Minnesota: Liturgical Press, 2013).

11. L. Cunningham, *Thomas Merton & the Monastic Vision* (Grand Rapids: Eerdmans, 1999), p. 38.

12. T. Merton, *The Ascent to Truth* (London: Burns & Oates, 1976).

in the first chapter the distinction that needs to be recognized between Bernard and St John, writing about two trends in the Christian tradition, 'a theology of light and a theology of darkness'; St Bernard is mentioned as one of the four 'great theologians of light', while St John of the Cross is one of the three 'great theologians of darkness'.[13] A key element in this difference here is the greater passivity in St John's thought on union with God and the application of this to contemplation and charity, whereas the spirituality that will be analysed here from Bernard and Merton is more clearly active. Thomas Merton picks up on this briefly in dealing with St John, offering 'a word of warning' on the benefits of asceticism: 'I mean the active self-purification by which the soul, inspired and fortified by grace, takes itself in hand. ... My stress is on the word active'.[14] Therefore, in the use of Merton below, it has been important to focus on those texts that mirror the spirituality of St Bernard of Clairvaux on contemplation and charity, built up primarily in his *On Loving God* and the *Sermons on the Song of Songs*, rather than scouring Merton's work for any teaching on these themes.

The Relationship between Contemplation and Activism

We turn now to the first of the two elements of spirituality that will be brought out of Bernard and Merton's works, which will then be used to provide suggestions for the development of Evangelical spirituality. This issue concerns the balance in the Christian life between contemplation and action, a key aspect in Bernard's writing and life and one that is frequently picked up by Merton.

Since both men had taken their monastic vows, it is not surprising that contemplation is held in high regard in their work. Indeed, the Cistercians of Bernard's time were reacting against a perceived worldliness of the times, being 'the outcome of the same restless search for a simpler and more secluded form of ascetical life ... it began as a reaction against the corporate wealth, worldly involvements, and surfeited liturgical ritualism, of the Carolingian monastic tradition'.[15] Merton makes clear that it was this remoteness that was vital to Bernard's Cistercian vocation, 'a powerful current which carried him away from the liturgical splendors of Cluny'.[16] While he believed in the glorious God that the Cluniac revival had focused on, the God whom Bernard sought 'in poverty, silence, and solitude was the *Verbum Sponsus*, the God who manifests Himself not only to the whole world as its King and Judge, but to the humble and solitary soul as its Bridegroom, in the secrecy of prayer'.[17] However, in finding wisdom

---

13. Ibid., p. 20.

14. Ibid., p. 116.

15. C. H. Lawrence, *Medieval Monasticism: Forms of Religious Life in Western Europe in the Middle Ages* (London: Longman, 1984), p. 146.

16. Merton, *Last of the Fathers*, p. 25.

17. Ibid.

and union with God in this renunciation of society, Bernard was drawn back into active service: 'It was because he was at once so much a person, and so much a mystic, that Bernard was also essentially a man of the church.'[18]

Thomas Merton took a different route into an ascetic life, rather against his initial inclinations when faced with the extreme condition of the Trappist life: 'That's not for me! I'd never be able to stand it. It would kill me in a week.'[19] Merton knew a vocational pull to the monastic life, but preferred the greater activism of the Franciscans. Having been rejected by that order, he later went into retreat at a Trappist monastery where he was impressed by the way the monks 'had found Christ, and they knew the power and the sweetness and the depth and the infinity of His love.'[20] Like Bernard, Thomas Merton joined a more extreme order (the Cistercian Order of Strict Observance) seeking a greater purity of life in retreat than was common for the time; and like Bernard, Merton's experiences of God in this place led him to active involvement in the world.

There are two ways in which Merton discerns the relationship between contemplation and action in understanding Bernard's spirituality: first, there are the passages in Bernard's work that deal directly with this theme; and second, there is the reality in Bernard's life. The first will therefore form the basis for this section, with the second acting as a bridge to Merton's own thought.

There are two of Bernard's works that reference this balance between contemplation and action, with the former always taking priority but being outworked in the latter. The first that we will deal with is his sermon series on the Song of Songs, which contains more sporadic references. Sermons 49 and 50 are a pair exploring Song 2.4: 'He brought me into the cellar of wine, he set in order charity in me' (Douay-Rheims Translation).[21] Sermon 49 begins with an explication of the first half of this verse, focusing on the individual in the contemplative experience: 'You also, if you shall enter into the House of prayer in solitude and collectedness of spirit, if your mind be thoughtful and free of worldly cares, and if standing in the Presence of God before some altar, you shall touch, as it were, the portal of heaven with the hand of holy aspiration and longing.'[22] The goal of this contemplative experience is twofold: on the one hand, an 'ardent love of God … a rapture of devotion' in terms of one's affections; and in the realm of understanding, 'a blaze of discernment.'[23]

This second is vital for Bernard's next stage from the second half of the verse, which is the outworking of charity. One may be zealous for action, but without

18. Ibid., pp. 25–6.

19. Merton, *Seven Storey Mountain*, p. 264.

20. Ibid., p. 316.

21. I refer to this translation as the most helpful for seeing what Bernard sought to bring out of the text.

22. Bernard of Clairvaux, *Sermons on the Song of Songs* (trans. S. Eales; London: Paternoster, 1895), p. 298.

23. Ibid., p. 299.

this understanding derived from an experience of God, 'zeal is found to be always less useful and less effectual; and most often it is even very dangerous.'[24] Bernard highlights the importance of this second element by preaching a whole extra sermon on the second half of the verse rather than continuing on to the next passage. In sermon 50, he delineates charity from the flesh, from reason and from wisdom, with the last being the goal of the Christian as one's 'love for all other things whatsoever is regulated by his love for God.'[25] Action should thus result not from a simple desire within oneself, nor from an anthropocentric reasoning, but from a love of God and the knowledge that flows from this. Sermon 85 picks up on the same theme of contemplation and action, working again with the idea of a wisdom gained from devotion to God that 'purifies the understanding', creating a beauty in the person.[26] This inner beauty, then, being 'diffused abundantly throughout the heart … [necessarily] should become visible also without, and be not as a light hidden under a bushel, but rather as a lamp shining in a dark place, and which cannot be concealed. Thus casting the bright illumination of its rays upon the body, it makes the latter an image of the soul.'[27] The merits of contemplation are thus again leading a person to take action and to work out the changes of heart and mind in the whole person. Sermon 85 then completes a circle by showing how this brings a person back to the Word for a closer union.

The second work of Bernard's that deals with this theme, and here much more explicitly, is his *Five Books on Consideration*. These are addressed to Pope Eugenius III, a protégé of Bernard's and one who owed his seat on the Papal throne to the influence of the abbot of Clairvaux. The whole work could, given sufficient space, be reviewed in detail in light of our current consideration on the relationship between contemplation and action, as Bernard declares in his review at the beginning of book five: 'The former books, although they are entitled "On Consideration," nevertheless contain many things which pertain to action, for they teach or advise some things which must not only be considered but acted upon.'[28] Bernard's purpose in writing to Eugenius was to encourage the Pope to take due consideration before taking action. The busy nature of Papal life may have led Eugenius to 'rush headlong into these affairs when there is an urgent reason', and thus Bernard considers it necessary 'to have warned you not to give yourself completely or continually to activity and to lay aside something of yourself – your attention and your time – to consideration.'[29] It is worth quoting Bernard at length on the results of this contemplative step before action is taken:

24. Ibid.

25. Ibid., p. 307.

26. Ibid., p. 521.

27. Ibid., p. 523.

28. Bernard of Clairvaux, *Five Books on Consideration* (trans. J. Anderson and E. Keenan; Kalamazoo: Cistercian Publications, 1976), p. 139.

29. Ibid., p. 37.

Now, of primary importance is the fact that consideration purifies its source, that is, the mind. Notice also that it controls the emotions, guides actions, corrects excesses, improves behavior, confers dignity and order on life, and even imparts knowledge of divine and human affairs. It puts an end to confusion, closes gaps, gathers up what has been scattered, roots out secrets, hunts down truth, scrutinizes what seems to be true, and explores lies and deceit. It decides what is to be done and reviews what has been done in order to eliminate from the mind anything deficient or in need of correction. Consideration anticipates adversity when all is going well and when adversity comes, it stands firm. In this it displays both prudence and fortitude.[30]

Bernard of Clairvaux is renowned as a great spiritual and mystical thinker, yet there is a thread in his writings that shows the need for contemplation to be an avenue towards action. As Thomas Merton stated, for Bernard, the 'most complete of all vocations [is] the union of action and contemplation in the care of souls', and the 'very completeness and integration of the Cistercian life ... gave Bernard his own peculiar strength and universality'.[31]

In addition, Merton importantly shows that this concept of contemplation leading to action was not merely theoretical in Bernard's own life. Rather, despite an initial desire for solitary mysticism and an ascetic life, 'his very reputation as a mystic, an ascetic, a miracle worker, a saint made it impossible for him to avoid becoming a great churchman, a defender of authority, of law, of the papacy, a man of God in politics, a preacher of Crusades'.[32] Merton is clear in stating that the public Bernard was the result of an internally transformed Bernard: 'God worked in him, and worked such wonders that men knew it was God they had seen at work, not man. The grace of the God who had possession of this frail man burst into flame in the hearts of all who heard him speak.'[33]

The combination of these two themes of contemplation and action in Bernard's writings made such an impression on Thomas Merton that he devoted an entire study to the topic.[34] Merton shows the development that Bernard makes on the earlier monastic thought of Cassian in that, 'Contemplation is in itself the highest expression of the monastic and Christian lives, but it rests on action and tends to overflow in apostolic activity for souls.'[35] In looking at Bernard's view on the work that results, Merton shows that 'the zeal of apostolic souls, flowing from contemplative union with God, leads to an activity which is in a sense higher than and preferable to contemplation.'[36] The importance of these two intertwining

30. Ibid., p. 38.

31. Merton, *Last of the Fathers*, pp. 13–14.

32. Ibid., p. 25.

33. Ibid., p. 27.

34. Reproduced as 'Part One: Action and Contemplation in St. Bernard' in Leclerq, *Thomas Merton on Saint Bernard*.

35. Ibid., p. 34.

36. Ibid., p. 38.

themes is thus clearly important for Bernard and is highlighted by Merton in presenting the man and his teaching; we turn now to Merton's own application of spirituality in his reflective works.

It seems right to start in the monastic realm to which Merton was called and from which he was writing in examining his ideas. There may be a temptation still for Evangelicals to consider the monastic vocation as one that is purely passive, although one would hope that such is no longer the case. At the beginning of a section on 'Action and Contemplation' in *The Monastic Journey*, Merton does provide some clarity on the monastic life: 'The monk is important more for what he *is* than for what he *does*'.[37] There is to be a transformation of the person through the contemplative side of monastic life. However, Merton does not separate out monks in this, stating that the same is true for every Christian. The key is that other Christians are called to specific works, whereas monks are '*not called to any particular work*'.[38] This can lead to what Merton calls a 'false and misleading' comparison that assumes a purely passive lifestyle, whereas the application asserted is that 'the mere fact that he is not bound to any *specific* enterprise, any *particular* project, means that the monk is called to *all* the works of charity at once, in a fuller and more eminent sense'.[39] This happens first in the monastery, and then in the wider community, and thus activity is a key result of contemplation even in this setting. On another occasion, Merton wrote of a 'false psychology of contemplation', which held that contemplative prayer is purely passive and 'is incompatible with any interior or exterior activity'.[40]

Moving out into the world, Merton continues to demand that the two go together as the fulfilment of the command to love God and neighbour. So, working with the thought of Pope Gregory the Great, Merton states: 'Both necessarily must be combined in any earthly vocation. ... The only solution to the conflict between those two claims on our hearts is to achieve the balance that is required by our own individual vocation'.[41] The personal experience of God is thus not simply for the benefit of the individual, but must be worked out in acts of love: 'There is no true mysticism without charity and there is no charity without incorporation into the Mystical Body of Christ, for charity is the life of that Mystical Body'.[42]

Perhaps the most powerful expression of this theme in Merton's works is the chapter on 'Creative Silence' in his book *Love and Living*.[43] This brings the relationship between contemplation and action into the modern context, where this reflection requires the absence of the radio or background music, asking 'What

---

37. Merton, *Monastic Journey*, p. 44 (italics original).

38. Ibid.

39. Ibid.

40. T. Merton, *Bread in the Wilderness* (London: Burns & Oates, 1954), p. 9.

41. T. Merton, *The Climate of Monastic Prayer* (Shannon: Irish University Press, 1969), p. 73.

42. Merton, *Bread in the Wilderness*, p. 12.

43. T. Merton, *Love and Living* (London: Sheldon Press, 1979), pp. 38–45.

would prompt modern people to do such a thing?'[44] Against the overly active life of people today, including Christians, Merton states that it is 'very important, in our era of violence and unrest, to rediscover meditation, silent inner unitive prayer, and creative Christian silence'.[45] He shows the necessity of this in forming and transforming Christians in their inner identity in order to prepare them for God's work through them in their lives. Merton believes that much of our activity and words are used to disguise a brokenness within that needs to be dealt with for Christians to be productive. In support of this, he discusses Dietrich Bonhoeffer (whom he calls 'the apostle of a radical and "secular" Christianity'), who 'wisely saw that the real purpose of this period of relative silence was a deepening of prayer, a return to the roots of our being, in order that out of silence, prayer, and hope, we might once more receive from God new words and a new way of stating not *our* message but *His*'.[46] Thomas Merton thus recognizes this key theme in Bernard of Clairvaux, elicits it in Bernard's writings and life and appropriates it for his own message.

The Nature of Action in Caritas

Before applying these insights to an Evangelical spirituality, one other area covered by Bernard and Merton should be elucidated, that being the nature of the action to which the Christian is called. This is another key teaching of Bernard of Clairvaux that Thomas Merton adopts without great alteration but does translate somewhat into the modern context, and concerns the love that we learn from God and exhibit in our lives. The Latin word used is *caritas*, which is usually translated as 'charity', but has more the sense of affective love, particularly a love for others, than that word generally conveys today. For those who have read anything of Bernard, this is likely to be familiar as it comes from his most famous work, *On Loving God*.

Towards the end of this book, Bernard develops his four degrees of love that Christians pass through as they deepen their knowledge of and relationship with God. It is a progression through these stages that people undergo in their contemplative life that will then be worked out in their engagement with God and the world around them, while an overly active life hinders this transformation in a believer.

The basic thought stated at the outset of the book responds to the question why and how God should be loved, to which Bernard replies: 'My answer is that God himself is the reason why he is to be loved'.[47] It is this point that Bernard develops at the end of the work, seeing a maturation of the Christian from a 'fragile and

---

44. Ibid., p. 38.

45. Ibid., p. 39.

46. Ibid., pp. 44–5.

47. Bernard of Clairvaux, *On Loving God* (trans. R. Walton; Washington: Cistercian Publications, 1974), p. 93.

weak' nature to one restored in the image of the maker.[48] The first stage of this love is fundamentally selfish, loving one's self for one's own sake, with an overflow of this in a love for one's neighbour. At this level, it is unclear whether this love is truly redeemed, given that 'it is impossible to love in God unless one loves God', which we do not achieve until the second degree of love examined below.[49] Bernard does allow for the beginnings of a change here, stating that this man 'who is animal and carnal, and knows how to love only himself, yet starts loving God for his own benefit'.[50]

This is picked up in the second degree of love, in which people do love God if only for their own advantage. There is an awakening to a realization that people are not able to do all things in their own power, but are in some measure dependent on God, with the result that a person increasingly turns to God for help, support and strength. Here Bernard sees an acknowledgement of the grace of God at work, freeing people and enabling them to come to love God. This culminates in a selfless love, which signifies the attainment of the third degree of love, when God is loved for God's sake. The transition to this stage results from an increasing experience of God: 'Tasting God's sweetness entices us more to pure love than does the urgency of our own needs'.[51] This leads to a love that is free and chaste, to one who 'will not have trouble in fulfilling the commandment to love his neighbor. ... He loves with justice and freely embraces the just commandment'.[52]

The fourth and final degree of love in Bernard's work is the love of self for the sake of God. Here we see a completed circle from contemplation through action and back to contemplation as this is seen as a foretaste of the love that will ultimately be known beyond this life: 'I would say that man is blessed and holy to whom it is given to experience something of this sort, so rare in life, even if it be but once and for the space of a moment ... to reduce yourself to nothing is not a human sentiment but a divine experience.'[53] The language that Bernard is using here is unfamiliar to Evangelicals, but the experience that he is describing is an ecstatic union of the self with God, a momentary knowledge of one's intimate life in Christ in which Christ is all that one perceives. In this degree, a person's 'strength is established in the power of God'.[54] Something of this circular nature of action and contemplation is seen in Merton's work: 'Even when we come to live a contemplative life, the love of others and openness to others remain, as in the active life, the condition for a living and fruitful inner life of thought and love.'[55]

48. Ibid., p. 115.

49. Ibid., p. 117.

50. Ibid.

51. Ibid., p. 118. The encyclical previously mentioned that was published on Bernard of Clairvaux confirmed him with the title, 'Doctor Mellifluus', or 'The Doctor whose teaching is as sweet as honey' (from Merton, *Last of the Fathers*, p. 11).

52. Bernard, *On Loving God*, p. 118.

53. Ibid., p. 119.

54. Ibid., p. 121.

55. Merton, *Climate of Monastic Prayer*, p. 56.

Merton picks up on this teaching of Bernard's at length in his book, *Bread in the Wilderness*, holding that this charity, this *caritas* love, is the only thing that can transform us and deliver us from human limitations. This selfless love of God results from a vision and knowledge of God that realizes the truth that, 'unless we are selfish enough to desire to become perfectly unselfish, we have not charity'.[56] The focus of the Christian's life at this point is fully on God, loving Him for His own sake, with the result that the highest good for self is achieved through 'sacrificing myself for love of Him'.[57] This is fundamentally an active love for others, since 'it is only in Him that we can really love them: and that in thus loving them we are also loving Him'.[58]

The degrees of love taught by Bernard and picked up by Merton demonstrate the work that contemplation achieves in the life of the believer with resulting effects in their love for God and neighbour. They show the merit of serious reflection in the presence of God as the basis for any activity in service of God, whether this takes place within the monastic setting or in the wider society. It is now time to propose how these insights may be applied to a modern Evangelical spirituality.

Application of Bernard and Merton's Thought to an Evangelical Spirituality

This is not the time or place to deal with all of the issues and nuances that might relate to a definition of Evangelical spirituality, hence the 'an' in the subtitle for this section. A standard work and helpful resource for a basic understanding of Evangelicalism is David Bebbington's history, which outlines four primary characteristics: Conversionism, Activism, Biblicism and Crucicentrism.[59] The noticeable aspect of these in the context of this work is the active element throughout and the lack of any necessity for contemplation. The resulting spirituality is a reflection of this, not only in a Protestant work ethic, but also in an anthropocentric approach to scripture, belief and prayer in the use of reason and experience. Evangelicalism thus shows its roots in Enlightenment rationalism with a nod to the developing humanist epistemology.

This is where an application of Bernard and Merton's thought can provide a challenge to the constant activity that is often associated with Evangelicalism in a call not only to contemplation, but also to the focus and goal of this in a transformed love of God for His own sake. Without this practice of the presence of God, it is difficult to ensure that the love being practised by the church is the *caritas*

---

56. Merton, *Bread in the Wilderness*, p. 98.

57. Ibid.

58. Ibid.

59. D. Bebbington, *Evangelicalism in Modern Britain: A History from the 1730s to the 1930s* (London: Unwin Hyman, 1989).

that Bernard urges us to, rather than the first or second degrees of love that have fundamentally selfish aspects. Ironically, the concept of monastic contemplation that many Evangelicals seem to hold is one that is entirely passive and self-centred, ignorant of (or at least ignoring) the concerns of society.[60] As this study of Bernard's writings has shown, the reality is precisely the opposite in a desire for loss of self in love of God and service of others.

The call of Bernard and Merton is to the primary importance of contemplation in the Christian life in order to realize one's identity in Christ. Only once this transformation has taken place and self has made way for love of God for God's sake is our activity solely motivated by a desire for His glory. Merton speaks of the need to develop a 'prayer of the heart [which] must penetrate every aspect and every activity of Christian existence'.[61] This is an inner meditative prayer that is not necessarily a personal, in the sense of individual, reflection, since Merton holds to its exercise within the context of the divine liturgy. However, he does state that, 'it cannot flourish where an activist spirit seeks to evade the deep inner demands and challenges of the Christian life in personal confrontation with God'.[62] Evangelicalism does not 'seek to evade' engagement with God, but its activism can prevent this foundational and transformational element of spirituality.

An important element in perceiving the worth of this contemplation is that this is not the end in itself. Rather, the goal of contemplation, and for Bernard and Merton the inevitable consequence of this reflection, is a more selfless, active love of God and neighbour. Thomas Merton writes, 'According to Saint Bernard of Clairvaux it is the comparatively weak soul that arrives at contemplation but does not overflow with a love that must communicate what it knows of God to other men.'[63] He goes on to list a number of great mystics who together agree that 'the peak of the mystical life is a marriage of the soul with God which gives the saints a miraculous power, a smooth and tireless energy in working for God and for souls, which bears fruits in the sanctity of thousands and changes the course of religious and even secular history'.[64] Contemplation is thus not a route away from activity, but the true preparation that all Christians should learn to practise in order to better follow the commandments to 'love God the Lord your God with all your heart and with all your soul and with all your strength and with all your mind; and, love your neighbour as yourself' (Lk. 10.27).

---

60. This is certainly the case in classes I teach, where much effort is often required to work through such preconceptions.

61. Merton, *Climate of Monastic Prayer*, pp. 146–7.

62. Ibid., p. 147.

63. Merton, *Seven Storey Mountain*, p. 415.

64. Ibid.

Conclusion

This chapter has sought to show how Thomas Merton appropriated the teachings of Bernard of Clairvaux on the relationship between contemplation and action and the nature of *caritas* love, and developed these in a more modern context both within the monastic scene and, more broadly, in the Christian life. Both writers showed in their lives and writings that the contemplative role is not simply an end in itself, but overflows into action and service for the church and society. The goal of this reflection is a changed heart and mind so that one seeks to avoid selfish motivations in order to love God for His own sake, with new foundations both in knowledge of oneself and in the actions that result.

From this study, a challenge was laid down to incorporate more of a contemplative aspect into Evangelical spirituality, which has traditionally had a much greater focus on activism. Given the purpose of contemplation in the writing of Bernard of Clairvaux and Thomas Merton, this should not lead to passivity, but to a greater love for God and neighbour that avoids some of the dangers of self-centredness that may result from a purely active approach.

Bibliography

Bebbington, D., *Evangelicalism in Modern Britain: A History from the 1730s to the 1930s* (London: Unwin Hyman, 1989).

Bernard of Clairvaux, *Five Books on Consideration* (trans. J. Anderson and E. Keenan; Kalamazoo: Cistercian Publications, 1976).

Bernard of Clairvaux, *On Loving God* (trans. R. Walton; Washington: Cistercian Publications, 1974).

Bernard of Clairvaux, *Sermons on the Song of Songs* (trans. S. Eales; London: Paternoster, 1895).

Bredero, A., *Bernard of Clairvaux: Between Cult and History* (Edinburgh: T&T Clark, 1996).

Cunningham, L., *Thomas Merton & the Monastic Vision* (Grand Rapids: Eerdmans, 1999).

Knell, M., *The Immanent Person of the Holy Spirit from Anselm to Lombard: Divine Communion in the Spirit* (Milton Keynes: Paternoster, 2009).

Lane, A. N. S., *Bernard of Clairvaux: Theologian of the Cross* (Collegeville, Minnesota: Liturgical Press, 2013).

Lane, A. N. S., *Calvin and Bernard of Clairvaux* (Studies in Reformed Theology and History, New Series, 1; Princeton: Princeton Theological Seminary, 1996).

Lawrence, C. H., *Medieval Monasticism: Forms of Religious Life in Western Europe in the Middle Ages* (London: Longman, 1984).

Leclerq, J., *Bernard of Clairvaux and the Cistercian Spirit* (Kalamazoo: Cistercian Publications, 1976).

Leclerq, J. (ed.), *Thomas Merton on St. Bernard* (Kalamazoo: Cistercian Publications, 1980).

Merton, T., *The Ascent to Truth* (London: Burns & Oates, 1976).

Merton, T., *Bread in the Wilderness* (London: Burns & Oates, 1954).

Merton, T., *The Climate of Monastic Prayer* (Shannon: Irish University Press, 1969).

Merton, T., *The Last of the Fathers: Saint Bernard of Clairvaux and the Encyclical Letter, Doctor Mellifluus* (London: Hollis & Carter, 1954).

Merton, T., *The Living Bread* (London: Burns & Oates, 1956).

Merton, T., *Love and Living* (London: Sheldon Press, 1979).

Merton, T., *The Monastic Journey* (London: Sheldon Press, 1977).

Merton, T., *The New Man* (New York: Farrar, Strauss and Giroux, 1961).

Merton, T., *The Seven Storey Mountain* (London: Sheldon Press, 1975).

Pennington, B., 'Like Father, Like Son: Bernard of Clairvaux and Thomas Merton', in J. Sommerfeldt (ed.), *Bernardus Magister: Papers Presented at the Nonacentenary Celebration of the Birth of Saint Bernard of Clairvaux, Kalamazoo, Michigan* (Citeaux: Cistercian Publications, 1992), pp. 569–78 (572).

Pennington, B., *A Retreat With Thomas Merton* (New York: Amity House, 1988).

Pennington, B. (ed.), *Saint Bernard of Clairvaux: Studies Commemorating the Eighth Centenary of his Canonization* (Kalamazoo: Cistercian Publications, 1977).

Sommerfeldt, J. (ed.), *Bernardus Magister: Papers Presented at the Nonacentenary Celebration of the Birth of Saint Bernard of Clairvaux, Kalamazoo, Michigan* (Citeaux: Cistercian Publications, 1992).

SELECT BIBLIOGRAPHY OF ANTHONY N. S. LANE

Books

The LION Concise Book of Christian Thought (Oxford: LION, 1984; further editions 1992, 1996, 2002; since replaced by *A Concise History of Christian Thought*).

Calvin and Bernard of Clairvaux (Studies in Reformed Theology and History, New Series, 1; Princeton: Princeton Theological Seminary, 1996).

John Calvin: Student of the Church Fathers (Edinburgh: T & T Clark; Grand Rapids: Baker, 1999).

Justification by Faith in Catholic-Protestant Dialogue: An Evangelical Assessment (London: T & T Clark, 2002).

The Lion Christian Classics Collection (Oxford: Lion, 2004).

A Concise History of Christian Thought (London: T & T Clark; Grand Rapids: Baker, 2006).

Baptism: Three Views (ed. D. F. Wright; Downers Grove: IVP, 2009; one of the three contributors).

A Reader's Guide to Calvin's Institutes (Grand Rapids: Baker, 2009).

Bernard of Clairvaux: Theologian of the Cross (Cistercian Publications, 2013).

Exploring Christian Doctrine (London: SPCK, 2013; Downers Grove: IVP, 2014).

Editions

(with Hilary Osborne) John Calvin, *The Institutes of Christian Religion* (London: Hodder & Stoughton, 1986; Grand Rapids: Baker, 1987).

John Calvin, *The Bondage and Liberation of the Will: A Defense of the Orthodox Doctrine of Human Choice against Pighius* (trans. G. I. Davies; Texts and Studies in Reformation and Post-Reformation Thought; Grand Rapids: Baker; Carlisle: Paternoster, 1996).

John Calvin, *Defensio sanae et orthodoxae doctrinae de servitute et liberatione humani arbitrii* (Ioannis Calvini Opera Omnia denuo recognita, IV/III; Geneva: Droz, 2008).

Edited Books

(with Antony Billington and Max Turner) *Mission and Meaning. Essays Presented to Peter Cotterell* (Carlisle: Paternoster, 1995).

The Unseen World. Christian Reflections on Angels, Demons and the Heavenly Realm (Carlisle: Paternoster; Grand Rapids: Baker, 1996).

Interpreting the Bible. Historical and Theological Studies in Honour of David F. Wright (Leicester: Apollos, 1997)

(with David F. Wright and Jon Balserak) *Calvinus Evangelii Propugnator; Calvin Champion of the Gospel: Papers Presented at the International Congress on Calvin Research Seoul, 1998* (Grand Rapids: Calvin Studies Society, 2006).

Articles and Essays

'Scripture, Tradition and Church: An Historical Survey', *Vox Evangelica* 9 (1975), pp. 37–55.
'Calvin's Sources of St Bernard', *ARG* 67 (1976), pp. 253–83.
'The Rationale and Significance of the Virgin Birth', *Vox Evangelica* 10 (1977), pp. 48–64.
  [Revised and abridged in D. F. Wright (ed.), *Chosen by God. Mary in Evangelical Perspective* (London: Marshall Pickering, 1989), pp. 93–119]
'The Fundamentalism Debate: A Survey of Reviews of James Barr's *Fundamentalism*', *Evangelical Review of Theology* 3 (1979), pp. 11–26.
'Did Calvin Believe in Freewill?', *Vox Evangelica* 12 (1981), pp. 72–90.
'Christology Beyond Chalcedon', in H. H. Rowdon (ed.), *Christ the Lord* (Leicester: IVP, 1982), pp. 257–81.
'John Calvin: The Witness of the Holy Spirit', in *Faith and Ferment* (Westminster Conference, 1982), pp. 1–17. [Reprinted in R. C. Gamble (ed.), *Articles on Calvin and Calvinism* (14 vols; New York and London: Garland, 1992), vol. 9, pp. 107–23]
'The Quest for the Historical Calvin', *EvQ* 55 (1983), pp. 95–113.
'B. B. Warfield on the Humanity of Scripture', *Vox Evangelica* 16 (1986), pp. 77–94.
'Conversion: A Comparison of Calvin and Spener', *Themelios* 13 (1987), pp. 19–21.
'Guide to Calvin Literature', *Vox Evangelica* 17 (1987), pp. 35–47.
'Evangelicalism and Roman Catholicism', *EvQ* 61 (1989), pp. 351–64.
'Early Printed Patristic Anthologies to 1566: A Progress Report', in E. A. Livingstone (ed.), *Studia Patristica* 18/4 (Kalamazoo: Cistercian Publications; Leuven: Peeters, 1990), pp. 365–70.
'Bernard of Clairvaux: A Forerunner of John Calvin?', in J. R. Sommerfeldt (ed.), *Bernardus Magister* (Kalamazoo: Cistercian Publications, 1992), pp. 533–45.
'Kenya's Turbulent Bishop', *Evangelical Review of Theology* 16 (1992), pp. 66–81.
'Justification in Sixteenth-Century Patristic Anthologies', in L. Grane, A. Schindler and M. Wriedt (eds), *Auctoritas Patrum. Contributions on the Reception of the Church Fathers in the 15th and 16th Century* (Veröffentlichungen des InstitutsfürEuropäische Geschichte Mainz. Im Auftrag der Abteilung Religionsgeschichte (hrsg. R. Decot), Beiheft, 37; Mainz: Philipp von Zabern, 1993), pp. 69–95.
'Saint Bernard et Calvin', in J. Leclercq, R. Genton and A. N. S. Lane, *Saint Bernard de Clairvaux* (Écublens: Église et Liturgie, 1994), pp. 25–38.
'Sola scriptura? Making Sense of a Post-Reformation Slogan', in P. E. Satterthwaite and D. F. Wright (eds), *A Pathway into the Holy Scripture* (Grand Rapids: Eerdmans, 1994), pp. 297–327.
'Ten Theses on Justification and Sanctification', in A. Billington, A. N. S. Lane and Max Turner (eds), *Mission and Meaning. Essays Presented to Peter Cotterell* (Carlisle: Paternoster, 1995), pp. 191–216.
'Bondage and Liberation in Calvin's Treatise against Pighius', in J. H. Leith and R. A. Johnson (eds), *Calvin Studies IX* (Davidson, NC: Davidson College and Davidson College Presbyterian Church, n.d.), pp. 16–45.
'Albert Pighius's Controversial Work on Original Sin', *Reformation & Renaissance Review* 4 (2000), pp. 29–61. [cf. 'Erratum', in *Reformation & Renaissance Review* 3 (2001), p. 215]
'The Council of Nicea: Purposes and Themes', (2000). Available online: http://www.debate.org.uk/debate-topics/theological/council_nicaea/.
'When did Albert Pighius Die?', *Nederlands Archief voor Kerkgeschiedenis* 80 (2000), pp. 327–42.

'Cyril's *Twelve Anathemas*: An Exercise in Theological Moderation', in M. Elliott and
J. L. McPake (eds), *The Only Hope: Jesus Yesterday Today Forever* (Fearn: Christian
Focus Publications/Mentor, 2001), pp. 39–58. [Earlier Romanian version: 'Cele
douasprezece anatematisme ale lui Chiril: un exercitiu de moderatie teologica', in
A. N. S. Lane, D. Bulzan, S. Rogobete and J. R. W. Stott, *Erezie si Logos. Contributii
romano-britanice la o teologie a postmodernitatii* (Bucharest: Anastasia, 1996),
pp. 9–41]
'The Wrath of God as an Aspect of the Love of God', in K. Vanhoozer (ed.), *Nothing
Greater, Nothing Better: Theological Essays on the Love of God* (Grand Rapids:
Eerdmans, 2001), pp. 138–67.
'Presenting the Challenge: Christ and Culture', in London Bible College Staff, *Christian
Life and Today's World: Not Conformed but Transformed* (Bletchley: Scripture Union,
2002), pp. 29–46.
'Tertullianus Totus Noster? Calvin's Use of Tertullian', *Reformation & Renaissance Review*
4/1 (2002), pp. 9–34.
'Calvin and Article 5 of the Regensburg Colloquy', in H. J. Selderhuis (ed.), *Calvinus
Praeceptor Ecclesiae* (Geneva: Droz, 2004), pp. 233–63.
'Cardinal Contarini and Article 5 of the Regensburg Colloquy (1541)', in O. Meuffels and
J. Bründl (eds), *Grenzgänge der Theologie* (Münster: Lit Verlag, 2004), pp. 163–90.
'Did the Apostolic Church Baptise Babies? A Seismological Approach', *TynBul* 55/1
(May 2004), pp. 109–30.
'Twofold Righteousness: A Key to the Doctrine of Justification? Reflections on Article 5 of
the Regensburg Colloquy (1541)', in M. A. Husbands and D. J. Trier (eds), *Justification:
What's at Stake in the Current Debates* (Downers Grove and Leicester: IVP, 2004),
pp. 205–24.
'Justification by Faith', in K. J. Vanhoozer, C. G. Bartholomew, D. J. Trier, and N. T. Wright
(eds), *Dictionary for Theological Interpretation of the Bible* (Grand Rapids: Baker, 2005),
pp. 416–19.
'Tradition', in K. J. Vanhoozer, C. G. Bartholomew, D. J. Trier and N. T. Wright (eds),
Dictionary for Theological Interpretation of the Bible (Grand Rapids: Baker, 2005),
pp. 809–12.
'Baptism in the Thought of David Wright', in *EvQ* 78 (2006), pp. 137–50.
'Calvin', in V. H. Drecoll (ed.), *Augustin-Handbuch* (Tübingen: Mohr Siebeck, 2006),
pp. 622–7.
'Justification by Faith in Sixteenth-Century Patristic Anthologies: The Claims that
were Made', in G. Frank, T. Leinkauf and M. Wriedt (eds), *Die Patristik in der
frühen Neuzeit. Die Relektüre der Kirchenväter in den Wissenschaften des 15. bis 18.
Jahrhunderts* (Stuttgart-Bad Cannstadt: Frommann-Holzboog, 2006), pp. 169–89.
'Lust: The Human Person as Affected by Sin', *EvQ* 78 (2006), pp. 21–35.
'The Role of Scripture in Calvin's Doctrine of Justification', in C. Raynal (ed.), *John Calvin
and the Interpretation of Scripture: Calvin Studies 10 & 11* (Grand Rapids: Calvin
Studies Society, 2006), pp. 368–84.
'A Tale of Two Imperial Cities: Justification at Regensburg (1541) and Trent (1546–1547)',
in B. L. McCormack (ed.), *Justification in Perspective: Historical Developments and
Contemporary Challenges* (Grand Rapids: Baker; Edinburgh: Rutherford House, 2006),
pp. 119–45.
'Was Calvin a Crypto-Zwinglian?', in M. Holt (ed.), *Adaptations of Calvinism in
Reformation Europe: Essays in Honour of Brian G. Armstrong* (Aldershot: Ashgate,
2007), pp. 21–41.

'Baptism in Water', in W. A. Dyrness and V.-M. Kärkkäinen (eds), *Global Dictionary of Theology* (Downers Grove and Nottingham: Inter-Varsity Press, 2008), pp. 97–101.

'Bernard of Clairvaux: Theologian of the Cross', in D. Tidball, D. Hilborn and J. Thacker (eds), *The Atonement Debate* (Grand Rapids: Zondervan, 2008), pp. 249–66.

'Anthropology', in H. J. Selderhuis (ed.), *Calvin Handbook* (Grand Rapids: Eerdmans, 2009), pp. 275–88. [Also in Dutch and German editions].

'Irenaeus on the Fall and Original Sin', in R. J. Berry and T. A. Noble (eds), *Darwin, Creation and the Fall* (Nottingham: Apollos, 2009), pp. 130–48.

'Anthropology: Calvin between Luther and Erasmus', in H. J. Selderhuis (ed.), *Calvin – Saint or Sinner?* (Tübingen: Mohr Siebeck, 2010), pp. 185–205.

'Calvin', in S. Westerholm (ed.), *The Blackwell Companion to Paul* (Oxford: Wiley-Blackwell, 2010), pp. 391–405.

'Calvin's Attitude towards Catholicity', in H. J. Selderhuis (ed.), *Calvinus Clarissimus Theologus* (Göttingen: Vandenhoeck & Ruprecht, 2012), pp. 206–27.

'Calvin's Doctrine of Assurance Revisited', in D. W. Hall (ed.), *Tributes to John Calvin: A Celebration of his Quincentenary* (Phillipsburg, NJ: P&R, 2010), pp. 270–313.

'Calvin's Way of Doing Theology: Exploring the *Institutes*', in J. R. Beeke and G. J. Williams (eds), *Calvin: Theologian and Reformer* (Grand Rapids: Reformation Heritage Books; London: Evangelical Press, 2010), pp. 39–61.

'John Calvin: Catholic Theologian', *Ecclesiology* 6 (2010), pp. 290–314.

'Calvin as a Commentator on Paul', in B. Boudou and A.-P. Pouey-Mounou (eds), *Calvin et l'humanisme. Actes du symposium d'Amiens et Lille III (25–26 novembre 2009)*(Cahiers d'Humanisme et Renaissance, 99; Geneva: Droz, 2012), pp. 73–92.

'Cyril of Alexandria and the Incarnation', in I. H. Marshall, V. Rabens and C. Bennema (eds), *The Spirit and Christ in the New Testament and Christian Theology* (Grand Rapids: Eerdmans, 2012), pp. 285–302.

'Is the Truth Out There? Creatures, Cosmos and New Creation', *EvQ* 84 (2012), pp. 291–306 and 85 (2013), pp. 3–18.

'Anthologies (Patristic)', in Karla Pollmann et al. (eds), *Oxford Guide to the Historical Reception of Augustine* (3 vols; Oxford: OUP, 2013), vol. 2, pp. 536–40.

'Augustine and Calvin', in *T&T Clark Companion to Augustine and Modern Theology* (London: Bloomsbury T&T Clark, 2013), pp. 174–95.

'Calvin, John (1509-64)', in Karla Pollmann et al. (eds), *Oxford Guide to the Historical Reception of Augustine* (3 vols; Oxford: OUP, 2013), vol. 2, pp. 739–43.

'Pighius, Albert (c.1490–1542)', in Karla Pollmann et al. (eds), *Oxford Guide to the Historical Reception of Augustine* (3 vols; Oxford: OUP, 2013), vol. 3, pp. 1547–9.

'Calvin and Calvinists', in *Oxford Handbook to the Reception History of Christian Theology* (Oxford: OUP, forthcoming).

'Justification', in *Oxford Handbook of Ecumenical Studies* (Oxford: OUP, forthcoming).

'Roman Catholic Views of Biblical Authority from the Late 19th Century to the Present', in D. Carson (ed.), *But My Words Will Never Pass Away: The Enduring Authority of the Christian Scriptures* (Grand Rapids: Eerdmans, forthcoming).

This bibliography does not include versions of essays that have been superseded, for example, the original appearance of chapters of *John Calvin: Student of the Church Fathers*.

INDEX